RONSARD

The Renaissance Ballet

RONSARD

By

D. B. WYNDHAM LEWIS

LONDON
SHEED & WARD
1944

FIRST PUBLISHED 1944
BY SHEED AND WARD, LTD.
FROM 110/111 FLEET STREET
LONDON, E.C.4

SECOND IMPRESSION 1944

FOR
HILAIRE BELLOC
souvenir d' Avril

THIS BOOK IS PRODUCED
IN COMPLETE CONFORMITY
WITH THE WAR ECONOMY AGREEMENT

PRINTED IN GREAT BRITAIN
BY PURNELL AND SONS, LTD.
PAULTON (SOMERSET) AND LONDON

CONTENTS

ILLUSTRATIONS

INTRODUCTORY NOTE

EXCEPT FOR ONE MODEST PLUNGE INTO ORIGINAL RESEARCH, connected with his stay in England and leading to practically nothing, I have derived the " basic data " of Ronsard's glowing and amorous existence, in an age nearly as treacherous and bloody as our own, but far more beautiful, from five main sources. His verse supplies copious autobiographic detail, amplified by Du Perron's funeral oration and Claude Binet's biography (1586). His friend Brantôme's diverting gossip yields a little more, and a perpetually vivid background. The rich treasury of Ronsardiana accumulated by MM. Champion, Laumonier, De Nolhac, Jusserand, and others provides most of the remainder. Comment and interpretation are mine. The interlude on pp. 177–181, inspired by Eugenio d'Ors' colloquy with the shade of Goya in his admirable biography of that master, may be skipped by the serious-minded.

My transcriptions from Ronsard's works are based on Laumonier's critical eight-volume edition of the definitive text of 1584 and Blanchemain's edition of the *Sonets pour Hélène*, the only one available. I have once or twice, consulting nobody's judgment but my own, taken leave to restore certain words, or lines, from earlier editions whose fate at Ronsard's ruthless hand, in his rage for perfection, has often made *ronsardisants* blench and cry Ha. The prose translations, barbarous but necessary—in view of the fact that those living British poets I approached and begged humbly for assistance in spreading Ronsard's fame (and their own) declined with unanimous cordiality to stir a finger—are mine. Were it not a pagan rite I would heap expiatory roses at the master's pedestal, pouring wine and milk.

I have to thank the following :

The Duke of Hamilton and Brandon, for permission to use a photograph of one of the Mary Queen of Scots deathmasks in Holyrood Palace ;

The Keeper of the Printed Books, British Museum, for allowing me to examine the rare first edition of *Les Amours*, 1552, and the Trustees, for permission to reproduce from it two pages of music :

The Secretary of the Public Record Office, London, for assistance;

Father Joseph Geraerts, D.C.L., for clearing up some points in Canon Law;

Miss Dorothy Collins and Messrs. Methuen, for G. K. Chesterton's rendering of a Du Bellay sonnet;

The Hon. Maurice Baring and Messrs. Heinemann, for renderings of a Ronsard verse and a Desportes sonnet;

Miss Euphemia Ann Wolfe, Messrs. Eyre and Spottiswoode, and the Clarendon Press, Oxford, for eight sonnet translations and a passage from the Zaharoff Lecture (1934), by Humbert Wolfe;

Mr. Curtis Hidden Page and the Houghton Mifflin Company, Boston, for a translated ode;

Messrs. Macmillan, for permission to quote some passages from Pater's *Renaissance*;

Messrs. Longman, for three translations by Andrew Lang; and

The Librarian and Staff of the London Library, for tireless courtesy.

I should add that the body of the autograph-ode facing page 276, described by De Nolhac as being in Ronsard's handwriting, is stated by Champion to be in the hand of Ronsard's secretary, Amadis Jamyn. There is no controversy over the signature.

D.B.W.L.

Petrus Ronsardus iacet hic: si caetera nescis,
Nescis quid Phœbus, Musa, Minerua, Charis.

(Epitaph by Pontus de Tyard).

Ronsard lies here: and if a question follow,
Ye know not Muses, Graces, and Apollo.

I

BALLET-DIVERTISSEMENT

Immortal God! what a world I see dawning! Why am I not young again?

(ERASMUS TO BUDÉ, 1517.)

These people are a little jaded.

(PATER, The Renaissance.)

§1

WHETHER, AS ONE OF THE *FIGARO'S* LITERARY GENTLEMEN ASSERTED next day, the faintest breath of the ghost of a rose drifted across the petrol-flavoured summer sky, whether a spectral pluck of lute-strings mixed at one moment with the wild goose cry of the Parisian taxicab and the *ramage de la Ville* that June day in 1928 when the statue of Pierre de Ronsard was unveiled, belatedly,[1] before the Collège de France, I am now inclined, on ransacking memory, to doubt. Scent and sound alike were probably illusory : fluid emanations of the spoken word and the massed thoughts of all that turbulent youth of the Sorbonne which listened so intently. But I am quite certain that for once, on such an occasion, no tricksy verse of Yeats came darting into the mind to mock the oratorical fugue with a vision of bald academic heads bent under midnight lamps, owlishly editing and annotating lines

> That young men tossing on their beds
> Rhymed out in love's despair
> To flatter beauty's ignorant ear.

For this prince of poets M. de Nolhac and the company were celebrating, the Orpheus of the French Renaissance, the gracious scholar and humanist, darling of the Muses, cynosure of Europe and friend of Queens, the master-lutanist, " almoner of the King our Lord and First Poet of this Kingdom ", the unconquerable maorist, the singer Ronsard rhymed with passionate vitality

---

[1] The statue at Vendôme is half a century older at least.

elegance, and nobility in hot and comely youth, in gouty middle-age, and in the cold sweats of his dying bed.

Nor were most of the beauties he made immortal ignorant of this honour. Indeed, the latest and greatest of his loves, a dainty Platonist, a frigid young intellectual, what one would call nowadays in mellow mood a highbrowed prig, one of those girlish pedants who provoked the old Spanish cry to Heaven, " From a noisy mule and a girl who speaks Latin, Lord, deliver us "—

> *De una mula que haʒe hin,*
> *De una hija que habla latín,*
> *Libera nos, Domine!*

—Hélène de Surgères, in short, was so nervously aware of her fame and alarmed for her reputation that she greatly intensified the six years' suffering which her elderly, jealous, passionate, illustrious poet crystallised in that sequence which Mr. Humbert Wolfe ranks sonnet for sonnet with Shakespeare's. Suffering, a modern critic has observed with callous accuracy, is good for poets and improves their style. It was difficult to contemplate the Ronsard statue that day without feeling, as one feels about Lesbia and Mary Fitton and all the other women who have hurt and harassed divine poets, that in the Ideal State a monument would be erected to Ronsard's Hélène in white marble, alabaster, or ice, demonstrating Civilisation's gratitude for the successful torture of a phoenix.

Phoenix Pierre de Ronsard has certainly proved. After two centuries and more of eclipse his resurgent magic is such in France of late years that a scholarly group of *ronsardisants* has arisen to surround his name and works with infinite research, and not a little neo-Renaissance pedantry. Some ten years ago, when fragments of bone were found under the site of his tomb in the ruined priory church of St. Cosme-lez-Tours, the news was given front-page honour even by the popular metropolitan *presse à grand bataclan,* a Press as divorced from the Graces, normally, as our own. A course of lectures by Professor Gustave Cohen at the Sorbonne a little time before helped infuse into the fourth centenary celebrations of 1924 an element of enthusiastic youth not commonly associated with literary junketings. M. Herriot's new government paused in its anticlerical activities to issue a commemorative postage-stamp, in the frivolous Gallic manner. No one who visited the Ronsard Exhibition at the Bibliothèque Nationale in that year and admired the fastidious skill with which that sumptuous collection of contemporary portraits, books, manuscripts, marbles, tapestries, medals, engravings, prints and music had been brought together, could fail to realise that the twentieth century was at last fully avenging Ronsard and his school for the treatment of the seventeenth, eighteenth and half the nineteenth. Ronsard to-day is certainly among the *gratin*, as he himself predicted not only in youth, with that tranquil assurance which is part of his charm, but in his very last verses, like Horace himself, even while commending his soul to Christ :

> *C'est fait, j'ay devidé le cours de mes destins,*
> *J'ay vécu, j'ay rendu mon nom assez insigne ;*
> *Ma plume vole au Ciel pour estre quelque signe*
> *Loin des appâts mondains qui trompent les plus fins.*[1]

What poetic and philosophic incense was offered him at the unveiling I do not recollect, though François Jammes and Paul Valéry took part in the celebrations. The poets of France owe Ronsard an eternal debt—not the least of his debtors is Victor Hugo—for the mass of new rhythmic forms he invented and bequeathed them. It was this lord of the lyric who naturalised the Pindaric ode and forged the six-foot national heroic iambic line, the alexandrine,[2] into that weapon of flexible strength and suppleness, of majesty, emotion, and satire, which Corneille and Racine were afterwards to wield like a Toledo blade. I am well aware that the alexandrine, the *danseur noble* of French verse-rhythms, is something of a stumbling-block to the English ear (so eagerly responsive to lyrical forms), except when the voice of a Rachel or a Bernhardt or a Mounet-Sully or a Jacques Copeau turns it

---

[1] It is done, I have wound the skein of my destiny,
I have lived, I have made my name famous enough ;
My pen flies skyward, to become some constellation,
Far from the worldly lures which cheat the subtlest.

[2] For precisians : " The French metre has the peculiarity that it falls naturally into four anapæstic divisions."—FOWLER.

into organ-music. When Rachel first spoke the lines from Racine's *Phèdre* beginning "*Ariane ma soeur*", it is recorded that Alfred de Musset fainted in his box at the Comédic-Française. Whatever specimens of Ronsard's alexandrines may adorn these pages, I can promise that even if they do not affect the reader to this extent they will be devoid of that marble frigidity we islanders traditionally associate with them. Consider, for example, the ring and glow of a line like

Car l'Amour et la Mort n'est qu'une mesme chose,[1]

and that couplet from the Appeal to Théodore de Beza,

Ne presche plus en France une Evangile armée,
Un Christ empistollé, tout noircy de fumée,[2]

and that cry to Isabeau de Limeuil:

Je suis jaloux de moy, de mon coeur, de mes yeux,
De mes pas, de mon ombre, et mon ame est eprise
De frayeur, si quelqu'un avecque vous devise,[3]

(which Rostand may have read before writing the letter-scene in Act II of *Cyrano de Bergerac*); and again, that vision, in one of the sonnets of the Hélène cycle, of that other Helen pacing the walls of Troy:

Il ne faut s'esbahir, disoient ces bons vieillars,
Dessus le mur Troyen voyant passer Hélène,
Si pour telle beauté nous souffrons tant de peine:
Nostre mal ne vaut pas un seul de ses regars . . .[4]

[1] For Love and Death are but the selfsame thing.

[2] Preach no more in France an armed Gospel,
A Christ bristling with pistols, blackened with smoke.

[3] I am jealous of myself, of my heart, of my eyes,
Of my step, of my shadow, and my soul is filled
With terror if anyone speaks to you.

[4] Let us not wonder (said these good aged men,
Seeing Helen pass on the Trojan Wall)
That we suffer such dule for such beauty:
Our pain is of less worth than one single glance of hers.

4

And once more, from the Great Sonnet everyone knows, the one on which Ronsard's fame with the million most securely rests, the loveliest and serenest of all, the sonnet of candlelight, firelight, fame, and repose, XLII of Book II of the *Sonets pour Hélène :*

> *Quand vous sere; bien vieille, au soir, à la chandelle,*
> *Assise aupre; du feu, devidant et filant,*
> *Dire;, chantant mes vers, en vous esmerveillant,*
> *Ronsard me celebroit du temps que j'estois belle . . .*[1]

and finally, from one of those vast cosmic themes for which he pulls out his deepest stops, the *Hymne de la Mort :*

> *Sans craindre comme enfans la Nacelle infernalle,*
> *Le rocher d'Ixion, et les eaux de Tantalle,*
> *Et Charon, et le chien Cerbere à trois aboys,*
> *Desquels le sang de* CHRIST *t'affranchist en la Croix,*[2]

culminating in that hailing of Death with a line which, Hilaire Belloc says somewhere, is like a salute with a sword, and which Maurice Baring has compared to the call of a silver trumpet :

> *Je te salue, heureuse et profitable Mort.*[3]

Such lines, fresh-minted gold, stamped like Greek coins of the best period, show what Ronsard can do with the alexandrine ; the emotional range behind that disciplined clarity, the scrupulous French command of a technique whose mechanism has often been compared, in its delicate strength, to a watch-spring.

His ear, which so rarely betrays him—he has his aridities and tediums and organic waste like every other great creative poet, but very few real lapses—may be accounted for to some extent

---

[1] When you are very old, at evening, by candlelight,
Seated by the fire, winding and spinning,
You will say, singing my verse and marvelling :
" Ronsard glorified me in the days when I was fair ! "

[2] Without childish fears of the Infernal Boat,
And Ixion's rock, and the waters of Tantalus,
And Charon, and the Dog Cerberus with triple bark,
From whom the Blood of Christ freed thee on the Cross.

[3] I salute thee, happy and profitable Death !

5

by his knowledge of that music, stringed and vocal, with which the whole Renaissance echoes. The European gentleman handled the lute then as naturally as the rapier. Ronsard himself had numbers of his odes and sonnets set for a "consort of sweet breasts" by Janequin and Goudimel and the great Orlando de Lassus and composers all over Europe. Moreover, he early proclaimed it a major dogma that the Ode must be so constructed that it may be sung. When, like Horace, Ronsard addresses his lute, he means no metaphor but the actual stringed instrument which stood at every elbow and was fingered with varying skill by soldiers and queens, lovers and scholars, courtiers and vagabonds, the light-minded and the grave, the evil and the holy—is there not a charming pen-picture of Bishop Ken, Anglicanism's gentlest saint, strumming his lute in the windowseat at dawn, as he sings his morning hymn a century later? But something more than music and natural genius refined and sharpened Ronsard's ear for rhythm. He owed a great deal, I think, to that partial deafness which came to him in early youth and never left him. As blindness perfected and illuminated Milton's interior vision, so Ronsard, deprived of much of the birdsong and water-music and forest-murmurs of his beloved Vendômois and driven in on himself, could pace his fields and river-banks (as his lieutenant, the sweet melancholy Du Bellay, in some achievement as great a poet as he, though Du Bellay lacked his captain's sweep and vitality, reminded him in a charming tribute) listening to those unheard melodies which, the English poet said, are sweeter.

> . . . *méditant les doulx sons*
> *Dont tu sçais animer tes divines chansons.*[1]

Well does De Nolhac remark that Ronsard orchestrated French rhythms for a concert not yet ended, and well might a passing illusion of lutes—or was it the nightingale?—have mixed with an illusory waft of roses to deceive the senses of one listening to the oratory in the Rue des Écoles on June 23, 1928.

[1] . . . pondering those sweet sounds
With which thou knowest so well to make thy divine songs live.

6

§2

Roses, nightingales, and lutes.

They rank among the essential stage-properties lavishly exploited by the majority of impresarios presenting the Grand Renaissance Ballet-Divertissement, with its ever-fresh and enchanting scenario. Mankind bursting suddenly from the prison-tomb of medieval ignorance with a whoop. Mankind casting off the chains of mental and spiritual tyranny and leaping, amid a fanfare of silver trumpets and a glad chorus of hosannas, into the blinding blissful sunshine of freedom, while the Human Spirit, *prima ballerina assoluta*, performs a solemn jig of ecstasy, like Isadora Duncan prancing barefoot before the Parthenon. One finds this familiar theme in every leading Continental historian of the liberal-materialist culture, Michelet, Ranke, Taine ; and, of course, the Whigs who have so long monopolised the writing of folklore in Great Britain have presented it from Macaulay down. And not only the historians but the aesthetes, Matthew Arnold, Ruskin, John Addington Symonds, Wilde, and above all Walter Pater, who could write without fear or favour in his quiet Oxford rooms, circa 1872, of " the catholic side, the losing side, the forlorn hope" which succumbed to " the strenuous, the progressive, the serious movement " of the Renaissance. Pater undoubtedly thought, mentally marking him β-minus for insight, that Ronsard should have stressed this point more strongly.

Pater, that homely nuncio of the Graces, whose moustache ruined Max Beerbohm's first impressions of Oxford, whose doctrine of Art and continuous excitement and Life burning with a hard gem-like flame had such a deleterious effect on romantic Oxford youth, is blunter than some of his fellow-thinkers, who disguise with a vast parade of allusive congees and salamalecs, becks and courtesies, side-glancings and œillades, cadenzas and fioriture, the essential Whig grievance against the Middle Ages, the great modern growl; namely that medieval man, driven in blinkers by the Catholic Church (which will have nothing to do with the philosophies, ancient or modern, which minister so cosily to human self-idolatry) thought far too much about God and far too little of his own marvellous, imperial, jolly self. Numbers of the men of the Renaissance agreed on this and thought Millennium had come, with far better excuse than modern dons. Erasmus' cry to Budé, which I have quoted at the head of this chapter, is the cry of Wordsworth at the French Revolution. " Bliss was it in that dawn to be alive, but to be young was very Heaven "—a quaint enough cry it sounds to anyone who has ever lived under the Revolution's final flowering, the late Third Republic, that paradise of crooks. The deistic Rabelais makes Gargantua write to Pantagruel : " For this [medieval] time was darksome, obscured with clouds of Ignorance, and savouring the infelicity and calamity of the Goths, who had, wherever they set footing, destroyed good Literature ; which in my age hath by the divine goodnesse been restored unto its former light and dignity." The atheist Etienne Dolet concurs : " Now men have learned to know themselves, now their eyes are opened to the universal light." This sentiment has been ritually repeated ever since by a cloud of authorities who have also had no doubt about it whatsoever.

In A.D. 1943 the residuary legatees of the Renaissance and recipients of the final fruits of all its blessings do not seem quite so certain of their immense good luck. Mr. Belloc's Essential Fellow, the Complete Nordic Man evolved by this glorious re-birth of the sixteenth century,[1] has a bewildered, lost look in his noble eyes at the moment. A haunting sense of precious irretrievable things slipping from his grasp and of great unease is evident from his frequent complaints, in the Press and in literary works alike. The shout of " This is Human, this is Natural, this is Me! " the great slogan of the Renaissance, the Reformation, the French and Industrial Revolutions, and the nineteenth-century nationalist upheavals alike,[2] is not so confident as it used to be. One feels the Essential Fellow is shouting to keep his spirits up as the quicksands tremble ominously under him and the tide roars nearer. One feels his British incarnation is not so certain, as formerly, of the efficacy of the rules of cricket as a complete spiritual rule of life. An interesting change.

[1] " . . . who turned out to be in the Germanies an East Elbe Prussian, in England a well-to-do Englishman, but in the United States a citizen of the United States." (*Richelieu* : London, 1929.)
[2] Rosalind Murray, *The Good Pagan's Failure* ; London, 1938.

Nevertheless the Renaissance of the Whigs makes a delicious ballet, with Nature's music orchestrated by Rousseau, Hegel, and Comte, choreography and costumes by the celebrated contemporary masters Botticelli and Rabelais. Serene, proud and lovely as the Primavera, the Spirit of the New Age stands against the dawnlight amid the glowing Hesperidean fruits of the Sacred Grove. At her right hand a radiant band of nymphs, pregnant like herself with joy and Spring (as it might be those nuns freed from bondage by Luther's banditti on Holy Saturday, 1523) trip a dainty galliard on the flower-starred grass. At her left, Love's votaries are seen indulging—even so early in the morning—in the chase, like amorous butterflies, while rosy Eros flies above and blesses them. *Viva la gioia!* And when the Primavera has relaxed her final gracious pose, how swiftly, how smoothly the scene changes to the Abbey of Theleme, the master-picture (Rabelais *pinxit*) of Renaissance emancipation, the New Age's reply to a thousand years of monkish imbecility. It is worth while contemplating Theleme again for a moment or two. Few major illusions of man have been so beautifully conceived.

There they pace, in their rich elaborate costume, on verdant lawns by the silver Loire, those gracious laughing beauties and handsome bucks, watching the tennis-players, lingering by alabaster fountains, flirting in the labyrinth, strolling through pleached alleys and rich orchards, exchanging conversation of the most elegant and illuminate kind. Behind them soar the six noble lofty towers of the hexagonal, six-storied Abbey, roofed with fine new slate and lead, gay with " antick figures" and gutters painted in gold and azure, " a hundred times more sumptuous and magnificent than ever was Bonnivet, Chambourg, or Chantillie " ;[1] with its nine thousand suites of fair sunlit chambers, its winding porphyry and marble stairs, its Great Hall, with two grand main staircases sweeping in and up from river and lawns, " in such symmetrie and largenesse, that six men at armes . . . might together in a breast ride all up to the very top of all the Palace " ; its spacious galleries " from the Tower Anatole to the Mesembrine ", painted with ancient prowesses, histories, and descriptions of the world ; its " faire great libraries in Greek, Latine, Hebrew, French, Italian,

---

[1] *Pantagruel*, Bk. 1, LIII-LVIII. (Urquhart's tr.)

and Spanish, respectively distributed "; and its Great Gate
whereon were carved in " antick letters " verses forbidding entry
to

> Curst snakes, dissembled Varlots, seeming Sancts,
> Slipshod caffards, beggers pretending wants,
> Fat chuffcats, smell-feast knockers, doltish gulls,

—in fact the whole tribe of monks, lawyers, usurers, and all
" mangie, pockie folkes ", the ruck of the populace ; but welcoming
all noble ruffling sparks and highborn lovely ladies and (a palpable
afterthought) expounders of the Scriptures, whose duties would
seem light enough in a community whose first and only rule was
" *Fay ce que vouldras* ", " Do what thou wilt " : the great
Renaissance cry.

Like Nuffield College (Oxon) a modern foundation of which
Theleme seems in many ways a slightly more gorgeous precursor,
Rabelais' dream-abbey has no chapel, though in the oratory
attached to each suite at Theleme private Platonico-Deist devotions
are doubtless offered up daily. Devotions before their mirrors,
judging from that tedious chapter Rabelais takes to describe in
detail, like a rednosed Chanel, the costly splendour and variety of
the habits and jewels and fal-lals these new-style friars and nuns
wore throughout the year, must have occupied at least as much
of the community's morning and evening hours. Life goes sweetly
in this aristocratic Thebaid, where no cloud of jealousy or dissension
or even momentary demurring dims the sky.

If any of the Gallants or Ladies should say, Let us drink, they
would all drink; if any one of them said, Let us play, they all
played ; if one said, Let us go a-walking into the fields, they went
all ; if it were to go hawking or hunting (etc. etc.).

An enchanting picture of life graciously lived by natural virtue.
No country-house party, even of British Simonite Liberals, could
hang together a week on such terms. Rabelais' psychology, for
all that he had a medical degree and mixed with the rich, does not
seem very sound. It is just possible, also, that a rarefied atmosphere was not breathed exclusively even at Theleme. The addiction

of the Renaissance to rank obscenity is remarkable : the lofty-souled mystical Marguerite of Navarre is one example, as her *Heptameron* reveals. Much lower down the scale of refinement and sensibility come the epileptic Luther, with his filthy table-talk, and Rabelais himself, for whose schoolboy fondness for scatology, like his violence and certain other characteristics, Léon Daudet accounted by postulating overmuch devotion to the charming little red wines of Chinon and Bourgueil and the delicious white of Vouvray; which seems as good a partial solution as any. This dirt-obsession is part of the general holiday from Christianity many intellectuals and the nobility enjoyed at this period. It is not a mark of the Middle Ages.

Theleme, then, is the ideal human existence portrayed by a universally-acknowledged spokesman of the Renaissance, whose gigantic work is itself crammed with as much recondite learning as buffoonery; or so it seems. I plead guilty, after some twenty years' affectionate intimacy, to a lurking doubt about Rabelais' scholarship. It is respectable, but not, I think, quite so encyclopædic as that Fifth Avenue parade in *Gargantua* and *Pantagruel* suggests at first sight. Anybody can dash down such a sequence as ". . . described by Hippocrates, Plato, Plotin, Iamblicus, Sinesius, Aristotle, Xenophon, Galen, Plutarch, Artemidorus, Valdianus, Herophilus, G. Calaber, Theocritus, Pliny, Athenaeus, and others", after a vinous evening with the pedants. It is a ritual device, like Gibbon's trick with footnotes, used even to-day to inspire awe and terror among the innocent, and also to deceive. On close examination much of Rabelais' learned display turns out to consist of lists of authorities reeled off thus. One is apt to feel it just possible that the playful and truculent Doctor, who, of course, did not lack Latin or Greek, quoted more classic authors than he read, and perhaps carried a notebook to dinner-parties and tavern symposia. I have heard Shakespeare's acquaintance with law and seamanship and half a dozen other arts accounted for in much the same Autolycan way. God knows this may be the most odious of heresies.

Rabelais, notwithstanding, remains the Voice of the Renaissance and Theleme the paradise of dainty devices, the design for happiness, the mirror of emancipated, Epicurean, hedonist, humanist

delights on the highest possible plane, moving the *sympathiqu*
Swinburne three centuries later to such dithyrambs as :

> But the laughter that rings from her cloisters that know not a ba?
> So kindles delight in desire that the souls of us deem
> He erred not, the Seer who discerned on the seas as a star
> Theleme.

Well might the despised monks laugh as well, having then as
now a bond, a discipline, a formula for successful communal
living which, taking rough with smooth and allowing for all the
quirks and "anfractuosities" (Dr. Johnson) of human nature,
defies the centuries. This retort to Theleme did not occur to
Rabelais' most doughty opponent, the monk Puits-Herbault,
who preferred a slanging-match. He could have pointed, even in
that rackety age, to monasteries in every part of Christendom where life under the pure monastic rule testified to the success
of this formula. The monks of the London Charterhouse were
not the only ones at this time who lived such Christlike lives that
they had to be put to a savage death.

Time, which loves to flout Whigs, has of recent years been
steadily compelling honest historians to the conclusion that so
far from emancipating the human spirit in a great upsurge of spiritual
and mental freedom, the Renaissance emancipated nobody in
particular and even imposed fetters of its own. It did not restore any
kind of Latin letters, to begin with ; the Middle Ages were steeped
in them and Virgil was practically canonised. It did not dispel
centuries of mental sloth and ignorance ; the Middle Ages had
boiled with inquiry and debate. O the long noise of the Schools,
the clash of wits, the enormous Nominalist-Realist controversy,
for one, the quarrelsome comely clerk Pierre Abelard filling all
Christendom with his clamour, till St. Bernard argued him down!
The monumental laboratory-work of the *Summa* of Aquinas,
most modern of philosophers,[1] compared with which Plato's report-
age of Socrates in the *Phædo* sounds like the prattle of an elderly
don at a tea-party! Granted that towards the end of the fifteenth

---

[1] Is it necessary to remark that St. Thomas Aquinas, who dethroned Plato in favour of
Aristotle, postulated, e.g., the relativity of Time seven centuries before Einstein ?

entury this intellectual uproar had died down to a mumbling and
he Sorbonne, once the intellectual power-house of Europe, was half
sleep, it is absurd even then to represent the Renaissance as sud-
lenly rending a veil and revealing Greek thought for the first time
n its glory to a blinking world, a claim which would puzzle St.
Jerome's grammar-school children at Bethlehem, that passionate
Platonist St. Augustine, the master-Aristotelian St. Thomas, and
others of the ages of " darkness " equally. Moreover the Platonism
of the Renaissance often resembles the Platonism of Plato about as
much as those glass jewels studding the frayed and shabby vest-
ments of the last of the Imperial Palæologues resembled the blaze
of gems on the cloth-of-gold in which Justinian and Theodora
swept to Mass at the Basilica of the Holy Wisdom.[1]

What the Renaissance did, then, was hardly to enlighten a world
of gaping cannibals but to collate and publish those Greek texts,
free of Arab and Jewish embroidery, rescued from the Byzantine
libraries when the Turk stormed and sacked Constantinople in
April, 1453, and the last Cæsar-Pope of the Orient, Constantine XI
Palæologue, died like a soldier in his purple shoes before the Top-
Kapou, the Cannon Gate. It would be tempting to digress here
and meditate at length on a singular resemblance, recently pointed
out,[2] between the technique of Sultan Mahomet II and that of the
Third Reich: the preliminary infiltration of enemy agents within
the walls of the doomed metropolis ; the long, skilful exploitation of
Greek sectarianism and Greek hatred of the Latin world ; the
patiently-spun, enormous web of Balkan intrigue ; the final
employment by the Herrenvolk of a superb, ruthless, and apparently
invincible military machine. What Europe chiefly gained from
Mahound's crushing blow at Christendom (which Don John of
Austria was nobly to avenge, by God's grace, at Lepanto a hundred
years later) was the re-discovery of the Greek poets and dramatists
whom the Middle Ages had largely neglected—even Homer,
whom St. Jerome's schoolboys knew. Thus they returned to the
West, Euripides and Sophocles and their high Calvinistic company,

---

[1] " The Catholic Church was to begin with, Platonist; super-Platonist. The golden air
of Greece breathed by the earliest sacred commentators is saturated with Plato ; the
Fathers of the Church are more authentic neo-Platonists than the 'Neo-Neos' of the
Renaissance." (G. K. CHESTERTON.)
[2] H. V. Morton, *Middle East*; London, 1941.

Pindar and sweet Theocritus and mighty Homer, and with them
Anacreon and Sappho, the extent of whose contribution to broaden-
ing and enlightening the Western mind is best known, doubtless,
to a certain type of academic.

These delights, brought to Italy by refugee Greek scholars
and other fugitives, might turn out on examination to be authentic
classical texts or the tagrag and bobtail of Byzantine pedantry.
Impostors were not unknown, and in genuine cases, no doubt,
some shrewd bargains were driven by wily Ulysses; but the
literati made many a lucky dip. In an ode dedicated to Jean du
Thier, Henri III's erudite Councillor of State, Ronsard cites an
example. Two ragged Greeks, unable for some reason to find a
protector at the Court of France—the Italian market being presumably at saturation-point at this moment—arrive, begging their
bread and driven to the last extremity, at Du Thier's door and
exhibit their merchandise.

> . . . *c'estoit du vieux Pindare*
> *Un livret inconnu, et un livre nouveau*
> *Du gentil Simonide éveillé du tombeau.*[1]

They did not offer this trove to a bibliophile in vain. The
courtois, gentil, et débonnaire Du Thier sped them from his library
with a "round harmony of golden guineas" to jingle in their
purse.

It is easy to imagine the alleluias of such Western intellectuals
and dilettanti, on many of whom Christianity sat so lightly that
the religion of that far-off pagan world, sun-gilt, marble-white,
idealised as a Flaxman vision, seeped unconsciously into their
veins, so to speak, as they devoured the manuscript, and hypnotised them. Modern travellers who see for the first time the smiling
Cyclades rising at sunset from a level summer sea of violet and
lapis-lazuli, rosy with such ethereal loveliness that they shake the
heart, know the instant spell of the antique world and can under-

---

[1] . . . it was a little unknown book
By ancient Pindar, and a new one
By the gentle Simonides, risen from the tomb.

De Nolhac identifies these two Greeks tentatively with the brothers Palæocappa, later
employed in the Royal Library at Fontainebleau.

and dimly how a Renaissance scholar felt on first seizing a Greek
odex. Actual palpable enchantment of

> Illyrian woodlands, echoing falls
> Of water, sheets of summer glass,
> The long divine Peneïan pass,
> The vast Akrokeraunian walls,[1]

he lofty pure serenity of the virgin Parthenon (though Time has
given it by our day a lovelier patina of honey and cream), the
grave and gracious sweetness of the Koræ on the Acropolis, the
musical surges of the wine-dark Aegean, the reedy piping on thyme-
scented, crocus-starred uplands of the shepherds of Crotona in
a wash of everlasting blue, the veiled Mysteries of Eleusis, the
olive-bronze, glistening nakedness of the athletes of Olympia,
the songs and torches and cymbals of the procession to the Delian
Apollo—no wonder, with all these new visions rushing on the
mind, that the splendour of the Gothic and its august mystical
harmonies seemed, to long-sated eyes and restless spirits swayed
by pride, something belonging to a dead and barbarous past.
Homer's dullest catalogues were an incantation.

As if this intoxication were not enough, there was the immediate
sunny magic of Italy, where the Renaissance cultural treasury had
been piling up for Europe's benefit since the early fifteenth century.
Italy too had been rediscovered. The armies of Charles VIII,
Louis XIII, and François I had stormed over the Alps to find
beyond the snows an earthly paradise peopled by vivid, gracious
beings, passionate lovers of beauty—" *Che bellezza!* " is still
their perpetual cry—and surrounded by it in every possible form.
In our own vulgar age Italy's spell is inescapable. When Titian
and Della Robbia, Michaelangelo and Da Vinci walked her streets
her magnetism must have been stupefying even to foreigners
themselves familiar with " the carven work, the golden shrine ".
Ronsard's father, Loys de Ronsard, was one of those many cultivated soldiers who had fought in Italy and returned transfigured
and furiously italianate.

This fever—Stendhal is perhaps its most notable literary victim, for
Browning, over and above an inclination to patronise the native, is

---

[1] Tennyson.

always fingering the return-half of the Cook's ticket in his trousers
pocket—has expressed itself in many strange forms among lover
of Italy throughout the ages ; not the least strangely among those
islanders of whom the smiling, shrugging Italian proverb says
Inglese italianato, diavole incarnato. In our own day it has led a
travelled Anglican squire to dignify his villagers' doorways with
Italian Baroque statues of the saints, charming, arresting, utterly
incongruous, and endured by the Hampshire native with truly
feudal resignation. With Messire Loys de Ronsard it took the form,
common in his day and sometimes leading to financial ruin, of tearing down the feudal home of his ancestors in the Vendômois
and building on its site that modestly charming manor of
La Possonnière which stands restored—perhaps over-restored—
and inhabited to-day, showing clear Italian influences tempered
by French discretion and elegance. *Salve magna parens frugum!*
Soon the scholars of Italy, who had long since begun to travel
East and West on voyages of intellectual discovery, were received
everywhere, and Italy was drawing the best minds of Europe to
her in return, as the sun draws up water.

Spain had also had a major share in magicking humanity.
Spanish courage, tenacity, inspiration, pride, and piety had by
the time of Pierre de Ronsard's manhood burst asunder the frontiers
of the old world and planted Christian civilisation in the remote
Americas, with the Royal and Pontifical University of Mexico
among its first-fruits. The world seemed to be expanding like rings
in a pool when a stone is thrown, and new and surprising things
were happening constantly—for example, that Bull of Paul III
acknowledging and confirming the equal rights before God with
Spanish Grandees of the fantastic chocolate-coloured aborigines
of the Americas, and forbidding their exploitation.

Next to Italy, which began the Renaissance, Spain is its *primum
mobile*, and like Italy, Spain managed without the aid of Luther or
Calvin. Indeed, Spain's proudest contribution to the Renaissance
and chief of the *cosas de España* (I have read in some proud Spanish
book) is not the Americas, or the Indies, or Velasquez, or the
sweet fiery mystic St. John of the Cross, or Lope de Vega, or
Calderon, or Don John, victor of Lepanto, or St. Teresa, that
starry wonder—" a woman for Angelicall height of speculation,

for Masculine courage of performance more than a woman "[1] or even Cervantes, but the captain of those shock-troops but for whom the Counter-Reformation might not have been half so immediate, or so powerful : the hidalgo, the soldier Don Iñigo de Onez, Ignatius of Loyola. A true son of the Renaissance, this eighth Champion of Christendom ; did not he, too, find time to write poetry like every other Renaissance man, if the magnificent sonnet

> *No me mueve, mi Dios, para quererte,*
> *El cielo que me tienes prometido . . .*[2]

is justly attributed to him, as many Spanish critics decide ?

One perceives therefore that the Renaissance of what one might call (without offence) the Manchester School of History is not entirely a fantasy.

The extravagances of this school indeed moved the eminent Guglielmo Ferrero, whom nobody could accuse of " clerical " or " reactionary " sympathies, to ask recently whether the Renaissance was not essentially decadent. Undoubtedly the gravest charge the Christian world can bring against it is that it damaged and to some extent destroyed within the Church the *mystique* of the Middle Ages, that pure joyous spiritual dynamism, that high rapt ecstasy, that fusion with the Divine of which the stones of Chartres are so eloquent. " The sixteenth century ", says Léon Bloy, " was an equinox in which the Ideal, mocked and ravaged by the storms of Sensualism, crashed at length, roots in air." From this disaster, says Bloy, the Church has never recovered, nor does he weary of scourging the drab and lamentable mediocrity of the modern soul. Thus viewed, the Renaissance, quite apart from the Reformation, is a major tragedy in human history. But the dour and apocalyptic Bloy exaggerates. Not all post-medieval devotion expresses itself in terms of the *bondieuseries* of the Rue St. Sulpice. The Renaissance itself produced St. Teresa and St. John of the Cross, and even one Charles de Foucauld and one Gerard Manley Hopkins in our own age seem evidence that the *mystique* is not dead.

[1] Crashaw.
[2] " My God, I love thee ; not because I hope for heaven thereby "—the well-known hymn, attributed sometimes, with less reason, to St. Francis Xavier, another typical product of the Spanish Renaissance.

Heralding a decadence or otherwise, there was certainly a stirring, a quickening of the human spirit, a rushing wind over the West, a new inspiration, for good or evil. Discovery brought new dreams, learning took new roads ; and one must endeavour to remember always that it was almost exclusively the intellectuals and the aristocrats who enjoyed these excitements. The proletariat[1] derived no benefit from the Renaissance except, in certain parts of Europe, civil war, bloody misery, new hatreds, and the forcible deprivation, at the whim of their local lords, of their ancestral religion, by virtue of the Lutheran dogma *Cujus regio, ejus religio*, with its consequent thefts and depressions, economic and other. As for their masters, the well-known *marotte* or whimsy of the liberals, which is, or was, to link the Renaissance indissolubly with revolt against spiritual authority—as if minds enlarged by reading *Oedipus Rex* in the original swung inevitably and logically away from the foundational Faith of Western Christendom into scepticism or atheism, which is what your rogue Whig really means by " emancipation ", however dainty and oblique his approach— seems divorced from reality to some extent. Popes like Nicolas V and Leo X, who so enthusiastically launched Humanism and the Classical Revival, St. Thomas More, the Christian Renaissance in person, and a few thousand more of the contemporary intelligentsia all over Christendom do not fit very neatly into this pattern.

Plainly there was never any universal, deliberate, concerted break with the ethos of the Middle Ages, whatever trimmers like Erasmus and restless intellectuals like Rabelais, dazzled by appearances and sceptics in grain, may have desired, thought, and said.[2] Ronsard himself allows his Muse to toy once or twice with the " darkness-into-light " refrain. It was the fashion, and he was a poet. Poets are very apt to dismiss the rhymesters of the immediate past with royal scorn—" a gallimaufry and hodge-podge ", said Spenser—and Ronsard does so with all the aplomb of a poet of 1943, say Mr. Stephen

[1] I except, naturally, craftsmen in the luxury trades, printers, jewellers, bookbinders, goldsmiths, etc., who often rose to wealth and honour.

[2] Luther and Calvin in the religious sphere naturally excepted. But heresiarchs are no novelty in any age of the Church's long history, and on this occasion the restless Renaissance spirit, widespread spiritual laxity, and the rich opportunity for loot played magnificently into their hands.

Spender, dismissing the grocer Tennyson. I write "grocer" advisedly. It seems to be a ritual word down the ages. Du Bellay dismisses medieval verse-forms as *épisseries* in his *Deffence et Illustration de la Langue Françoyse*, which we shall encounter in due course, and I have seen the word "grocer", which is current French literary slang for "philistine", applied by a young gentleman, writing in one of those fierce little Anglo-American reviews of the advance-guard lately published in Paris, to G. K. Chesterton. In each succeeding age the children of the Muses dance vivaciously on the graves of the last generation. In Ronsard's case it is a demonstration which chimes quite sweetly with indebtedness to certain medievals to whom he was on his own evidence devoted, such as the Provençal *trouvères* and Jehan de Meung. But he certainly plays up to his age. Even a poet so near him as Clément Marot seems to Ronsard deliciously quaint. As for Villon, the supreme magician of tears and laughter, the mastersinger, father of the modern poetry of France, only as distant from Ronsard in time as, say, Matthew Arnold is from us, Ronsard declines to notice his existence. Nevertheless hubris does not go unpunished by the Creator of men and banana-skins. For Ronsard in his turn the Parcæ had decreed the inexorable glissade. *Enfin Malherbe vint*, shortly after Ronsard's death : and after Malherbe arose Boileau, shaking his great magistral periwig and bringing law and order into the luxuriant garden of French poetry, and the Pléïade and their master were banished as triflers to limbo till Sainte-Beuve rescued them, two hundred years later.

But even a romantic like Ronsard never assumes that he and his contemporaries are torchbearers and banner-wavers leading mankind on a triumphant route-march up the long hill of Progress. This discovery was made on behalf of the men of the Renaissance much later.

§3

Or se cante . . .

"Here they sing", runs a rubric at regular intervals through the old tale of Aucassin and Nicolette. At this point the story-teller broke off and the musicians, preluding a little on their rebecks and

citoles, sang a sweet and courteous *lai* or *canzon* to refresh him and
the company. This seems a proper moment to pause a while and
solace ourselves with one of the songs of Pierre de Ronsard. I
am moreover impatient for the pleasure of setting down in print
one of those love-lyrics—a famous one, to begin with, full of subtle
art, found in every anthology—which make Ronsard's page smell
like May. It is a vesperal or evening-song to Cassandre Salviati,
first of his great passions. It contains all the Ronsardian doctrine
of loving.

> *Mignonne, allons voir si la rose*
> *Qui ce matin avoit desclose*
> *Sa robe de pourpre au Soleil,*
> *A point perdu cette vesprée*
> *Les plis de sa robe pourprée*
> *Et son teint au vostre pareil.*
>
> *Las! voyez comme en peu d'espace,*
> *Mignonne, elle a dessus la place,*
> *Las! las! ses beautez laissé choir!*
> *O vrayment marastre Nature,*
> *Puis qu'une telle fleur ne dure*
> *Que du matin jusques au soir!*
>
> *Donc, si vous me croyez, mignonne,*
> *Tandis que vostre âge fleuronne*
> *En sa plus verte nouveauté,*
> *Cueillez, cueillez vostre jeunesse:*
> *Comme à ceste fleur, la vieillesse*
> *Fera ternir vostre beauté.*

Which Andrew Lang renders:

> See, Mignonne, hath not the Rose
> That this morning did unclose
>   Her purple mantle to the light,
> Lost, before the day be dead,
> The glory of her raiment red,
>   Her colour, bright as yours is bright?

Ah, Mignonne, in how few hours
The petals of her purple flowers
    All have faded, fallen, died;
Sad Nature, mother ruinous,
That seest thy fair child perish thus
    Twixt matin song and even-tide!

Hear me, my darling, speaking sooth,
Gather the fleet flower of your youth,
    Take ye your pleasure at the best;
Be merry ere your beauty flit
For length of days will tarnish it
    Like roses that were loveliest.

(Why Lang makes Nature " sad " and not " harsh " is his own secret.)

Many poets have dwelt admiringly on the technical mastery underlying Ronsard's seeming simplicity and ease in this piece: the beat of the syllables, the fall of the cadences, the skilful varying of the rhythms (perceptible more to a French than a foreign ear), and the " pure and careful choice of verb "[1] which glorifies the fourteenth line. It is a very lovely thing, and some have believed that if the mass of Ronsard's poetry were swept away and only this one ode remained, his fame as a lyrical poet would still stand. This seems excessive.

And here is a Spring song:

Dieu vous gard', messagers fidelles
Du Printemps, gentes Arondelles,
Huppes, Coqus, Roussignolets,
Tourtres, et vous oyseaux sauvages
Qui de cent sortes de ramages
Animez les bois verdelets.

Dieu vous gard', belles Paquerettes,
Belles Roses, belles fleurettes
De Mars, et vous boutons cognuz
Du sang d'Ajax et de Narcisse,
Et vous Thym, Anis et Melisse,
Vous soyez les tresbien venuz.

[1] Hilaire Belloc, *Avril*; London, 1904.

Dieu vous gard', troupe diaprée
Des Papillons, qui par la prée
Les douces herbes suçotez,
Et vous nouvel essaim d'Abeilles
Qui les fleurs jaunes et vermeilles
Indifferemment baisotez.

Cent mille fois je resalüe
Vostre belle et douce venüe.
O que j'ayme cette saison,
Et ce doux quaquet des rivages,
Au prix des vents et des orages
Qui m'enfermoient en la maison!

Translated by Mr. Curtis H. Page:

God guard you and greet you well,
  Messengers of Spring:
  Nightingale and cuckoo,
  Turtle-dove and hoopoe,
  Swallow swift, and all wild birds
  That with a hundred varied words
    Rouse and make to ring
Every greening glade and fell.

God guard you and greet you fain,
  Dainty flowerets, too:
  Daisies, lilies, roses,
  Poppies—and the posies
  Sprung where ancient heroes fell,
  Hyacinth and asphodel—
    Mint and thyme and rue:
All be welcome back again!

God guard you and greet you true,
  Butterflies and bees,
  In your motley dresses
  Wooing the sweet grasses
  Flitting free on rainbow-wing,
  Coaxing, kissing, cozening
    Flowers of all degrees,
Red or yellow, white or blue.

A thousand thousand times I greet
 Thy return again,
Sweet and beauteous season,
In sooth I love with reason
Better far thy sunny gleams
And thy gently prattling streams
 Than Winter's wind and rain,
That shut me close in my retreat!

A song in the true manner of the Medievals, and one I would willingly rank for quality with Charles d'Orléans' more famous *Le temps a laissié son manteau.*

§4

What an age of violent productive energy! (One thinks of Lope de Vega's 1,500 plays and Ronsard's fifty years of powerful rhyming—how he would have laughed at the complaint of a modern poet like A. E. Housman, after chiselling a few dainty trifles on cherrystones, that the " continuous excitement " had left him—and the 300,000 sonnets which, it is computed, Europe produced in the sixteenth century alone.) What a driving, insatiable frenzy to discover and to enjoy! The passion with which Ronsard flings himself on the classics in his youth, hunting the obscurest Greek poets down and draining them dry, is equalled only by the ardour with which he plunges into every kind of pleasure.

> *J'ay l'esprit tout ennuyé*
> *D'avoir trop estudié*
> *Les Phænomenes d'Arate,*[1]

he announces in an early verse, and he shouts to his servant to fetch him wine and fruit down to the riverside, for it is high summer and this epicure will not touch meat.

> *Achète des abricots,*
> *Des pompons, des artichauts,*
> *Des fraises et de la cresme . . .*[2]

[1] My mind is thoroughly weary
 Of too much study
 Of the *Phenomena* of Aratus.

[2] Buy apricots,
 Melons, artichokes,
 Strawberries, and cream.

23

"Who, Sir, is there in this town that knows anything of Clenardus but you and I?" Johnson asked Langton. Who reads himself dizzy nowadays over the dim Aratus, whose chief honour is to have lit the astronomical splendours of the Georgics?[1] Be sure that Ronsard, reclining on the river-bank under a shady beech, devours his apricots and strawberries and empties his flask of Anjou with the same zest, and that if some *accorte fille* comes laughing by, as seems often to happen, the kisses concluding the meal are of the quality Daphnis gave Chlöe after his course of private tuition by the expert Lycænium.

Enjoyment and discovery—these twin appetites drive the Renaissance men always. One could quote a thousand examples, drawn from every sphere of human activity. This scientific zeal it was, for example, which moved Topcliffe, Director of the English Inquisition under Queen Elizabeth, to rack the sweet poet Blessed Robert Southwell with great care thirteen separate times on his private rack, to find out exactly how many inches he could stretch a Jesuit; in our own day the forces of Progress and democracy have been seen to rest content with merely roasting Spanish monks in the ordinary manner. Neither in great things nor small are many of us devoured by this particular Renaissance fever to-day, being doped and spoonfed, nor is our paganism of the same rich vibrant quality. The paganism of the modern intelligentsia seems a poor, awkward, emasculate, ill-bred thing in comparison, nearer akin to Voodoo than the Eleusinian Mysteries; its most cherished pundits intellectually qualified, perhaps, to hold the horse of some Renaissance don, its most admired artists to design and decorate a wealthy Renaissance nobleman's jakes in a " functional " manner.

"These people are a little jaded", observes Pater accurately of certain great French lords temporarily exhausted by splendid and complicated debauchery. So our modern pagans are a little jaded, but rather with lack of blood than excess of it, and the deplorable lack of scholarship with which they pursue their dismal pleasures is notorious. Few leading pathics of to-day can cite Anacreon or Catullus in support of their vagaries, few saphists Sappho. Their only apologist with any tincture of letters seems

[1] He may possibly have been the poet quoted by St. Paul to the Athenians on Mars Hill: " For we are also his offspring."

to be André Gide, that curious example of Attic perversity grafted on a Calvinist stem. Otherwise the upheaved and staggering world of 1943 bears not a few resemblances, in a bewildered, grubby way, to the age of Ronsard. It has seen the Second German Reformation deriving with humdrum fidelity from the first, from the apotheosis of the God-State[1] down to the Great Justifiable Lie of which Luther was so proud. It sees the spiritual force which brought about the religious disruption of the sixteenth century itself disrupted, as logic requires, broken of its own volition into smaller and smaller conflicting fragments and no longer accorded respect by intellectuals or esteemed a world-power, while the spiritual force it was to have destroyed stands still vigorous, commanding the loyalties of every type of mind, armed point-device as ever for the age-long unending quarrel with Caesars of every calibre. And it sees to-day, as then, vanity and hubris and confusion swelling the pagan tide—but with a simple and significant difference, which the briefest consideration of the nature of Ronsard's paganism will swiftly bring to light.

§5

Schizophrenia, one of the most useful jargon or vogue-words of the present decade, especially to elderly gentlemen at issue with their country's police, is said to mean " split-mind ", the condition of Dr. Jekyll, or alternatively Mr. Hyde. It would seem roughly accurate, considering the case of Pierre de Ronsard, to employ this term, within reason, to describe a condition of mind which enables a young man who has been just tonsured as a clerk in Minor Orders[2] to offer his shorn locks in lyrical verse to Apollo, to pray to Apollo in verse for the recovery of a sick prince, to Lucina for a woman in childbed. It is schizophrenia, I take it, for a Christian clerk to think and write constantly as if he were living under and practising the religion of Old Greece, and, when he turns to his own living religion, to mingle it in the oddest way with the dead one, making his risen Redeemer, the Christian Hercules, tread down the Hydra and vanquish Cerberus, and

[1] " Perhaps the cornerstone of German Lutheranism."—Dr. Inge.
[2] Ronsard was never a priest. See *post*, pp. 72–3.

quaintly urging Christendom to keep the festivals of the saints
with neo-Hellenic junketings :

> *Ha! les Chrestiens devroient les Gentilz imiter,*
> *A couvrir de beaux lys et de roses leurs testes . . .*[1]

For thus they feasted, sang, and danced round the altars in the
Age of Gold, when the Greeks invented the Hymn and Callimachus sang to his lyre of Apollo and Latona's twins, the Baths
of Pallas, Ceres, and Jupiter. The Rev. Robert Herrick, our
English Ronsard, who himself on occasion brings the cymbals
and the thyrsus and the dancing rout very near the vestry door,
never goes so far as to suggest to Convocation what Ronsard
seems to be blandly suggesting to the Sacred Congregation of
Rites. But Ronsard can travel so far from the atmosphere of
Christianity as to be able to devise an anagrammatic conceit on
the name of Marie, his rustic love, in a sonnet beginning :

> *Marie, qui voudroit vostre nom retourner,*
> *Il trouveroit aimer . . .*[2]

as if unaware that this lovely name had other connotations. He
seems to have doffed his religion in adolescence and hung it away
like an old cloak, to remember it at intervals, between adventures
of the world and the flesh, and don it again with obvious sincerity ;
to defend the Catholic Faith vigorously against the enemy ;
to practise it, in the country, much as an indifferent English squire
supports the Establishment, on principle ; to return to the Sacraments in later years, and, on his dying bed, to declare his faith and
penitence in one of the noblest farewells ever spoken by man, and
to embrace the crucifix with the same devotion as Marguerite of
Navarre, like him a one-time voyager in dark regions and perilous
seas. Seeing that his paganism, bred of an overwhelming passion
for the classics, is apparently his ruling influence, how does one
reconcile it with his equally sincere if fitfully-exhibited Catholicism ?
He never rejected or denied his faith, as many did in his time ;

[1] Ah! Christians should imitate the Gentiles (Pagans)
Covering their heads with roses and fine lilies . . .

[2] Marie, he who would twist your name around
Would find *aimer* . . .

..or did he adopt what many modern thinkers would admire as the essentially broadminded compromise of his (and, before him, Rabelais') patron Odet de Coligny, Cardinal de Chastillon, brother of the Calvinist leader. The Cardinal, a graceful, moody agnostic, professed Calvinism towards 1560 and married a wife, without relinquishing one jot of privilege pertaining to his Cardinal's or Privy Councillor's rank and office, still less his Roman scarlet. But even Chastillon, I think, would have drawn the line at turning Mahommedan (the sardonic Spanish Ambassador at Elizabeth Tudor's court reported to Philip II, not without reason, that the entire English nobility were ready to do this at a nod from the Crown) or Buddhist, a whimsy not unknown in modern England. And Ronsard, with all his passion for the Ancients, would not have comprehended the appeal of that bovine Mithraist cultus of the Legions with which Kipling, whose only experience of Christianity was connected with ill-treatment in childhood by a Puritan sadist, solaced his declining years. Submerged deep under classicism and sensuality most of his life, Ronsard's Catholicism remained intact. His departures from it in practice are nothing new or strange. " Sir," said Dr. Johnson, whom one is compelled to quote constantly for his commonsense, to the Rev. Mr. M'Aulay, " are you so grossly ignorant of human nature as not to know that a man may be very sincere in good principles, without having good practice ? " Schizophrenia, in a word. No doubt the moral theologians have a more scientific one.

Sainte-Beuve, doyen of all critics, compiled a list of essential questions for literary biographers to ask themselves before beginning work on a subject. One of them is " What is his religion ? " ; and as it is plainly more important, when beginning to understand a man, to know what fundamentals he believes in than to know his taste in friends, food, women, ties, or sport, Sainte-Beuve reasonably makes this question No. 1, embarrassing as the topic is for decent Nordic Man. In Ronsard's case the answer is clear. He was a Catholic. He said so loudly more than once or twice in his verse, and, questioned by a cautious monk before he died, said so angrily. But until near the end his faith is, as we have perceived, rarely active ; and when it does emerge its manifestations seem mixed and identified to a large extent with the new nationalism, a passion for France, her traditions, her monarchy, her leadership, her beauty and her unity, to which religious unity is essential. Four hundred years later—I do not think this deduction is fantastic—Ronsard might have been an honoured leader of the Action Française with Léon Daudet and Maurras and Bainville and Maxime Réal del Sarte, seeing nothing incongruous in the exploitation of the Catholic religion for political ends by the agnostic Maurras (a kindred spirit, with his fine Provençal brain, immense classical culture, hard irony, and crystalline prose), and possibly turning on the Holy See, or at least its "advisers", with the same acrimony as the rest when the movement earned the inevitable interdict from Rome. Judging by the bitter verve with which he attacks some of those current abuses in the Church which were shaming millions of Catholics more devout than he, a twentieth-century Ronsard might have produced some pretty invective, quite unjustifiable, against the Nuncio in Paris and the alleged *proboches* of the Sacred College.

Ronsard's paganism is far more than a literary pose. He had read himself from an early age so completely into the skin of a Greek or a Roman of the Golden Age, so called, that he normally thought and reacted to life like an antique pagan. His idol Horace's *carpe diem* is the perpetual undersong of all Ronsard's love-poetry. He is obsessed, more than Horace was, with roses, their beauty and fragrance, their fleeting life, their swift, inevitable decay, their resemblance to the sweet flesh of women. The rose-symbol is what one might call (with a light shudder) Ronsard's amorous theme-song. But it is never the Rosa Mystica of the Litany, and one would never guess from the major part of his verse that the Sacrifice of Calvary had any connection with this Christian, who can never see his beloved forest of Gastine, his fields and valleys, without filling them instantly with all the tricksy folklore of Hellas.

> *Je n'avois pas douze ans qu'au profond des vallées,*
> *Dans les hautes forests des hommes reculées,*
> *Dans les antres secrets, de frayeur tout couverts,*
> *Sans avoir soin de rien je composois des vers ;*
> *Echo me respondoit, et les simples Dryades,*

Faunes, Satyres, Pans, Napées, Oréades,
Aegypans qui portoient des cornes sur le front,
Et qui ballant sautoient comme les chèvres font,
Et les Nymphes suivant les fantastiques Fées
Autour de moy dansoient à cottes agrafées.[1]

I admit to deriving pleasure, *salva Fide*, from the early Ronsardian
pedantry, which makes many more learned critics moan despite
themselves. Granted that Ronsard overdid it in his youth and that
a hundred other poets, good and bad, have worked this vein to
exhaustion, there is a fascination in his intense enjoyment of plundering the Classics and the ease and grace with which he does it, like
a man strolling for his pleasure through a vineyard, taking great
clusters of purple grapes with both hands. Without this whimsy,
from which masses of his verse are free, he would not be a poet of
the Renaissance and its greatest save Shakespeare. His genius
sometimes recalls to me the façade of the Charterhouse of Pavia,
that gorgeous example of Renaissance sculpture run mad, on which
nymphs, Pans, and satyrs mingle with angels, saints, and martyrs,
and Hercules strangling Antæus jostles the Mother of God and the
Infant Christ; or equally, Michaelangelo's " Doni " Madonna,
in which the master brings, as Pater says, the naked human form
and " the sleepy-looking fauns of a Dionysiac revel " into the
presence of the Immaculate.

The paganism of the modern intellectual can hardly be compared
with this. Lacking Ronsard's tremendous erudition, it also, almost
invariably, reveals—as is patent from the writings of its foremost
thinkers—a quite refreshing ignorance of the Christian religion
as well; ignorance not only of the religion of the majority of
Christians, but of the leading nationalist substitutes brought in by
the Reformation. Such a proud ignorance is a new phenomenon;
nor does it hamper criticism or even condemnation of the Christian

[1] I was not yet twelve when, in the depths of the valleys,
In the high forests, remote from man,
In secret caverns, filled with terror,
Careless of all else, I made up verses;
Echo replied to me, and the simple Dryads,
Fauns, Satyrs, Pans, Hamadryads, Oreads,
Aegipans with horned heads,
Gambolling and leaping like goats,
And Nymphs, following the fantastic Fays,
Danced round me in their clasped petticoats.

ethic. I trace its origins to the Pascalian Method. One meditates the magnificent thunder, the appalling irony, the annihilating onslaught of the *Lettres Provinciales*, and one wonders, with Lytton Strachey, how the unfortunate Escobar and his fellow-Jesuits ever survived. But if, unlike Strachey and most other admirers of the great Pascal, one is moved by eccentricity or idle curiosity to turn up the Jesuits' case—lo and look ye! It is most clear that the great Pascal prefers the grossest misrepresentation to the task of " informing himself", as Whistler would say.[1] Logicians may not approve the Pascalian Method, but it is extremely popular to-day in the most elevated intellectual circles. To the pagan Ronsard, who knew the Christian faith as intimately as the classics and could, when necessary, state and develop the Creed at length, this attitude would have seemed a weakness, I think.

He was naturally accused by his Calvinist antagonists, when the slanging-match began, of rank atheism, also of unnatural vice and venereal disease, the other two stock controversial charges of the period. All three charges he indignantly repudiated, and spoke simple truth. But it must be admitted that in the matter of atheism he had given his enemies a noble opportunity. The echoes of an undergraduate prank of 1553 pursued him all his life. During Carnival week in that year Ronsard and his holidaying " Brigade " of poets—what we should call nowadays the Ronsard Group— paraded a goat crowned with flowers through the village street of Arcueil, on the outskirts of Paris, in honour of Bacchus and of Etienne Jodelle's new play, chanting the jolly ritual invocation:

Iach, iach, Evoë!
Evoë, iach, iach!

A harmless gambol enough, ending in laughter and yet more wine. Ten years later the Calvinist pamphleteers are raising a great howl that the shaven priestling Messire de Ronsard, the man of sin, the syphilitic atheist, sacrificed a goat with blasphemous rites that day to Bacchus. Ronsard denied it in resounding alexandrines, calling them impudent liars and demonstrating at length that this

---

[1] " There is hardly a page of the *Provinciales* that does not incline a man of sense to feel friendly towards the Jesuits." (REMY DE GOURMONT.)

licence honeste was as innocent a frolic as an Oxford bump-supper. But the libel stuck, and may even have some connection with the Calvinist bullets which nearly ended the poet's life some years later, and the sacking of his house later still.

§6

Here is a nocturne made for Hélène de Surgères, opening so nobly on the lunar stillness of a winter's night and merging soon into a groan of dragging pain for one cold, remote, unattainable as the languid Moon herself.

> *Ces longues nuicts d'hyver, où la Lune ocieuse*
> *Tourne si lentement son char tout à l'entour,*
> *Où le coq si tardif nous annonce le jour,*
> *Où la nuict semble un an à l'ame soucieuse,*
> *Je fusse mort d'ennuy sans ta forme douteuse*
> *Qui vient par une feinte alleger mon amour*
> *Et, faisant toute nue entre mes bras sejour,*
> *Me pipe doucement d'une joye menteuse.*
> *Vraye, tu es farouche, et fiere en cruauté;*
> *De toy fausse on jouyst en toute privauté,*
> *Près de ton mort je dors, près de luy je repose,*
> *Rien ne m'est refusé. Le bon sommeil ainsi*
> *Abuse pour le faux mon amoureux souci.*
> *S'abuser en amour n'est pas mauvaise chose.*[1]

By "your dead" in the eleventh line Ronsard means young Captain Jacques de la Rivière of the Guards, killed in action a few years before. He had been betrothed to Hélène, who wore per-

---

[1] These long winter nights, when the languid Moon
Turns her chariot so slowly round and around,
When the sluggish cock announces day,
When night seems a year to the tormented soul,
I should die of weariness without your doubtful form
Which comes, feignedly, to alleviate my pain,
And nestling in my arms, all naked,
Sweetly cheats me with imagined joy.
In the flesh you are perverse, proud in your cruelty;
I enjoy your dream-shape in all privacy—
Close to your dead I sleep, close I rest,
Nothing is refused me. Thus does sweet sleep
Cheat my lovelorn care with falsity;
To deceive oneself in love is no bad thing.

petual mourning for him, a little ostentatiously; and Ronsard's jealousy was ever acute.

And here is a careless, rapid, daintily-swaying song to the hawthorn in blossom, subtly wrought, like all Ronsard's effortless lyrics, full of bird-music and spring.

> *Bel Aubépin fleurissant,*
> *Verdissant,*
> *Le long de ce beau rivage,*
> *Tu es vestu jusqu'au bas*
> *Des long bras*
> *D'une lambrunche sauvage.*
>
> *Deux camps de rouges fourmis*
> *Se sont mis*
> *En garnison sous ta souche;*
> *Dans les pertuis de ton tronc*
> *Tout du long*
> *Les avettes ont leur couche.*
>
> *Le chantre Rossignolet,*
> *Nouvelet,*
> *Courtisant sa bien-aimée,*
> *Pour ses amours alleger*
> *Vient loger*
> *Tous les ans en ta ramée;*
>
> *Sur ta cime il fait son ny*
> *Tout uny*
> *De mousse et de fine soye,*
> *Où ses petits esclorront,*
> *Qui seront*
> *De mes mains la douce proye.*
>
> *Or vy, gentil Aubépin,*
> *Vy sans fin,*
> *Vy sans que jamais tonnerre,*
> *Ou la coignée, ou les vents,*
> *Ou les temps*
> *Te puissent ruer par terre.*[1]

[1] Sweet blossomy Hawthorn, flowering along this charming riverside, thou art twined to thy feet with the long arms of a wild vine. Two camps of red ants have made garrison under thy roots; in the crevices of thy trunk, all the way down, bees have their resting place. Every year in thy branches the little songful nightingale, courting his beloved afresh, comes to stay; on thy crest he makes his nest, of moss and fine silk all together, where his little ones will hatch, to be the soft prizes of my hands. So, live, gentle hawthorn, live for ever; may no thunder, no axe, no winds, no seasons bring thee down to earth!

This exquisitely dainty little Verlaine-ish thing is inscribed "To Cupid" and dedicated to "the cruel Janne", one of his minor loves of whom nothing is known.

Le jour pousse la nuit,
Et la nuit sombre
Pousse le jour qui luit
D'une obscure ombre.

L'automne suit l'esté,
Et l'apre rage
Des vens n'a point été
Après l'orage.

Mais le mal nonobstant
D'amour dolente
Demeure en moi constant
Et ne s'alente.

Ce n'estoit pas nous, Dieu,
Qu'il falloit poindre,
Ta flèche en autre lieu
Se devait joindre.

Poursuis les paresseux
Et les amuse,
Mais non pas moi, ni ceux
Qu'aime la Muse.[1]

---

[1] Day drives on Night,
And sombre Night
Drives on Day, glimmering
In dim shadow.

Autumn follows Summer,
And the harsh fury
Of the winds lives no more
After storm.

But the enduring pain
Of aching love
Remains in me always
And never slackens.

It was not I, godling,
At whom you should have aimed!
Your barb should have sped
To some other mark;

Pursue the idle
And amuse them—
But not myself, nor those
Beloved by the Muse.

33

§7

La chair est triste, hélas! et j'ai lu tous les livres.
(MALLARMÉ, *Brise Marine*)

Calling youth with so many siren voices to the worship of Beauty, Nature, Humanity, Art, and kindred fetiches, and the plenary enjoyment of love and wine and song before the rose-wreaths wither and the wax-lights burn low and the singers depart, the Renaissance had no difficulty in overcoming the scruples of many less generous, high-blooded natures than Pierre de Ronsard's. No one rushed to the voluptuous banquet more eagerly than he; and it may be noted that he and his youthful fellow-revellers had little reason to complain of their mentors. Emulating the rhetor Gorgias and the peripatetician Cratippus, quite elderly gentlemen, greybeard scholars, bald dominies, wizened preceptors, princes of erudition with a European reputation, like Dorat, presided over the feast and junketed as heartily as their pupils, crowned with flowers, clashing the winecups, chanting Greek and Latin bacchanals to the lute, joining carefree youth in country romps and tavern suppers, and, on occasion, dandling Laïs and Chloë on tremulous knees with no "surly virtue", but great complacency. Since the great Porson of Cambridge, modern dons —at least at the elder Universities of England and America—do not trip and toddle after the Classical Spirit quite so conscientiously, they say.

Possibly it was the consciousness, in grey moments of isolated self-examination, of being governed by dogma as inexorably as any medieval which was partly responsible for this Renaissance addiction to what we call nowadays The Party Spirit. Many of these erudite playboys were slaves to their spiritual pride to a pathetic degree. An appalling deadweight of donnishness had descended on Europe.

Elbowing really fine neo-Latin poets like Scaliger, Dorat, Buchanan, the Calvinist Beza, Salmon Macrin, and a whole cloud of them in Italy, Pontano and Cardinal Bembo and Sannazaro and the others, who wrote Latin verse not like clever college-men but like the Romans themselves—like, for example, Mgr. Ronald

Knox and Dr. Inge in England to-day—was a horde of pedants turning out, with painful conscientiousness, unerringly flat imitations of the ancient masters and swamping the earth with dullness, like floods over Friesland. Moreover the perpetual effort, demanded of so many enthusiasts at this time, to measure everything in human experience by the Pagan yardstick, to refer every idea and emotion to an idealised, far-off, utterly perfect past, to ignore as much as possible the riches of their Christian heritage, to galvanise the dusty worshipful bones of Greece and Rome into life from the textbooks, must often have been as wearisome as being chained to a mummy. " *Barbe-grise, barbe-grise, tu m'as trahi!* " cried Ronsard's dashing friend the Sieur Du Guast, captain of the Guards, when his assassins got him between bed and wall (his valet was polishing his toenails at the time and he leaped for his sword a second too late—a very Renaissance situation). " Grey-beard, greybeard, you have betrayed me !" The cry might well be taken up by all who have been misled by what Rabelais calls the brabbling of the sophisters.

However, the rich took their Renaissance less heavily than the dons. One long luscious Capuan orgy *à l'antique*, this period seems to the observer at times. There is a well-known contemporary print by Théodore Bernard which expresses the essence of Renaissance frolicking with grimmer accuracy than many better works of art. It is an *orgie*—Bernard's word—of highborn dames and seigneurs seated at table before fine dishes in rich massy plate, drinking and laughing and flirting to the inevitable lutes. Through the tall windows of their hall one sees a hilly landscape of which arson, pillage, and wholesale massacre of the poor are the principal natural features.

In the pages of another of Ronsard's friends, the entertaining old Gascon scandalmonger Pierre de Bourdeille, Seigneur de Brantôme, Chorus to this age, the grand seigneurs and noble dames of Bernard's print pace past like a procession of the Deadly Sins, to the music of trumpets and cymbals. Yet it is not their extravagance which impresses one so much (there were even then, as any moral theologian will tell you, no new sins) as their insolence, their cynicism, their heartlessness. High hot blood and unbridled lusts and the Renaissance pagan ferment have driven medieval pity and charity away. The Renaissance cuckold is not only swift to draw the blade and merciless in vengeance, *bonne espée et ombrageux*, but he takes a sadist's delight in stamping on the victims and exposing their shame, and his own, to the whole world. In Italy he is more terrible than anywhere, flinging, like Gesualdo of Venusia, the naked dead body of the faithless wife with her paramour's out of the window for a public show, strangling her, like Sampietro d'Ornano, with a silken scarf and giving her elaborate obsequies, or forcing her to bed with her lover's corpse. In France he will, like René de Villequier, stab her suddenly to the heart after jesting with her, and appear at Court next day glowing with complacency, or he will beat and starve the wanton to death, or destroy her by slow poison. For these vengeances he will sometimes be punished by justice, but will often escape. Brantôme, in every other way a product of his age, severely reprehends this monstrous flight from pity, quoting Our Lord's words about the woman taken in adultery, quoting St. Augustine, reminding these noble tigers of the *fragilitez de nostre nature* and the Christian obligation to forgive.

For the long-nosed, sprightly, saturnine Brantôme, with whatever relish he gossips about the great, retailing the most scabrous stories with objective interest and sparing no high personage— he knows all about Elizabeth Tudor's intimate physical malformation, for instance, and reports the exact crude words in which one of Catherine de Médicis' ladies describes her Majesty's halitosis —and chucklingly adding now and again his own embroideries, is no immoralist. He may not be a pattern Christian, but when he pauses to make some serious reflection on the gambols of the rich, it is based on the Christian ethic. I think it is only due to him to remark on this, for too often he is classed, by booksellers and others, with the ordinary muckrakers of literature.

It was, then, a heartless time, which the Middle Ages never were, with all their faults ; a period apt to be careless of the soul and, perhaps, a little blatant in its worship of the body, which the Greeks also pushed to excess, the fastidious cannot help feeling. That lavish Renaissance exposure of women's breasts—the cult of *le beau tetin* is as prominent in the poetry of Ronsard's time as in Marot's, his predecessor's—cannot invariably have pleased a udicious eye. Virtuous Frenchwomen, women of fashion, and street-drabs alike flaunted these twin rosy charms with more nonchalance, even, than they will when Classicism breaks out like a rash again under the Revolution and the Directoire. Ronsard's Cassandre, a young matron, newly married, of impeccable virtue, allows her portrait to be engraved and to appear opposite Ronsard's in *Les Amours*, modestly parading a naked, ripe, and comely bosom indeed; the comments, if any, of her husband are not preserved. In those *blasons* or catalogues of feminine physical attractions which are the vogue in amatory verse at this time the *beau tetin* ranks as Exhibit A.

There is an interesting physio-psychological theory bearing on this issue, propounded over the dinner-table to Eugenio d'Ors by the eminent Spanish critic Octavio de Romeu. Discussing the principal Goya portraits of Maria del Pilar Teresa Cayetana, Duchess of Alba, most superbly wayward of noble eighteenth century dames, De Romeu was of opinion that the secret of the Duchess's spell, cast instantly over everyone with whom she came in contact (and notably over artists and children, who adored her) was the form, volume, and disposition of her beautiful bosom, which the Venus of Milo might envy. For eighteenth century Baroquism, suggested De Romeu smilingly, " carried the poor human animal in its urge for retrocession from a virile libido for the woman to a puerile libido for the nurse".[1] I am not competent, natural delicacy apart, to discuss this theory, which seems a matter for Harley Street; it may possibly throw light on the cruder Renaissance cultus of the mammillary tracts and its influence on the arts. I would merely repeat, passing on, that not every display of the unveiled *beau tetin* in Ronsard's time can have ravished the aesthetic eye.

Of the athletic masculinity which marched with this cultus I must write with discretion and care. I am aware that I am touching now on a religious matter very precious to Nordic Man. It was, Pater assures us, equally precious to the Greeks. " The worshipper was to recommend himself to the gods by becoming fleet and fair, white and red, like them "; and red the average British and American devotee certainly became before the present

[1] Eugenio d'Ors, *La Vie de Goya* (Fr. tr. Marcel Carayon) ; Paris, 1928.

world-war diverted his activities from golf. It is my good fortune
to be able confidently to recommend the eminent French poet who
is the subject of these pages to the attention of my fellow-Nordics.
Pierre de Ronsard believed vehemently in keeping fit. In youth
and manhood he practised regularly and with ardour every kind of
violent sport, fencing, riding, hunting, wrestling, jumping, swim-
ming, running, tennis, and the football of the period[1] ; had the
University of Paris held slightly more modern views on education
he would certainly have been a double or even a triple Blue. In
middle age we perceive him, stouter, less agile, perspiring but
indefatigable, still leaping diligently over his vaulting-horse
daily. It is not invariably that one can glow with honest rectitude
when bringing a Latin or Gallic foreigner to the attention of the
Anglo-Saxon public of both hemispheres. This one might almost
have been one of us.

Apart from that hardness of hearing we have already noted,
Pierre de Ronsard seems to have been, until gout and ague conquered him, a fine Nordic specimen ; tall and strong, says Claude
Binet, vigorous in body as in mind, well-proportioned, his features
noble, martial, alert, " truly French " ; his eyes handsome and
grave, his nose aquiline, his forehead high and serene, his conversation " easy and fascinating". His hair, chestnut and curling,
began to retreat before he was thirty ; his clerk's tonsure he kept
covered, one may well believe. He wore, as was the fashion, a
trimly-clipped beard. The bust at Blois (modelled in his fifties,
they say) shows a fine, courteous, humorous, dignified head. With
the collared, cassock-like doublet it might almost represent a
dignitary of the Congregation of the Oratory with a faint resemblance to Voltaire. High breeding and virility, generosity, charm,
transparent sincerity and frankness and the gayest humour Ronsard
amply reveals in his verse ; nor can sensuality, caprice, over-sus-
ceptibility, moodiness, and apparent arrogance conceal from us
that he was emphatically what the Greeks called " the well-graced
man ", a born leader, essentially lofty and refined in thought
and aspiration, displaying a character (I quote Jusserand) of which

[1] Binet reports a match on the Pré aux Clercs, the University sports ground, between a
team in white, captained by the Dauphin, afterwards Henri II, and a team in red under M.
de Longueville. Ronsard's play for the Dauphin's team won the game, as his Royal Highness
loudly proclaimed.

Pierre de Ronsard
(*from the portrait-bust at Blois*)

a mixture of *amabilité conciliante* and *autorité dominatrice* was the basis. *Nobilmente* might justly be his favourite musical direction, as it is Elgar's. His arrogance (which we may examine later) is moreover not offensive but enchanting. From the first he has no need of the admiration of his friends to be calmly aware of genius, though we find him at intervals in moods of black despair, like every artist;[1] simultaneously with the Chief of the Brigade's expressions of authority, nervous diffidence and even doubt of himself is frankly displayed in more than one ode to a friend. Ronsard was a creature of moods, and it is often difficult to judge whether natural modesty or natural assurance is the dominant. There is ample testimony that he never inflicted hauteur on his intimates or his protégés, with whom he was ever affectionate, generous, and unassuming. On the other hand, he brandishes his fame to the world like an oriflamme. He mentions his pre-eminence here and there throughout his works casually, as the most natural thing in the world, and he uses it constantly to cajole women, as lesser men use yachts and diamonds. " I am Ronsard," he says to the fair Genèvre after that dashing encounter on the banks of the Seine :

> *Je suis, dis-je, Ronsard, et cela te suffise ;*
> *Ce Ronsard que la France honore, chante et prise,*
> *Des Muses le mignon, et de qui les beaux vers*
> *Sont temoins de sa gloire en ce grand Univers.*[2]

" I am Ronsard—that is enough for you." Can one imagine any other poet in the world, except Byron, announcing himself thus to a new flame ?

Possessing this mystic seal, this princely assurance, Ronsard stooped to none of the mean or squalid vices, and certainly to none of the fashionable exotic sins derived via Italy from the Levant and the Orient. It is possible perhaps to exaggerate the prevalence of *moeurs spéciales* during the Renaissance. There are periods, as

---

[1] "My art torments me grievously," he says in an elegy to Jacques Grévin. Other depressions may be noted as these pages proceed.

[2] I am (I said) Ronsard, and that suffices you :
That Ronsard whom France honours, sings, and prizes,
Darling of the Muses, whose fine verses
Witness to his glory in this great universe.

Jules Romains has remarked of the Paris of the 1920's, when they seem—but it may be illusion—to flourish more than at others when the Corydons and Gitons and Barons de Charlus emerge from the shadows with coy aplomb, flaunting the livery of Sodom boldly and "meditating their privileged case". This has been noted equally of recent years in Anglo-Saxondom, among those advanced elements which attach an intellectual *cachet* to sexual perversion. In the first half of Henri III's reign pederasty was likewise chic, the hobby of a Court set, paraded with elaborate cynicism and mocked and scorned, then as now, by the populace and the world of normal men. Ronsard's attitude towards the Corydons is almost New England, save for his fluency, when opportunity occurs, in expressing contempt. Natural fastidiousness preserved him moreover from such crapulous orgies as Byron—now we have remembered that great poet—wallowed in at Venice, partly to shock the British bourgeoisie and partly, one suspects, because Byron enjoyed them. Ronsard's amours are devoid alike of venality and brutishness. A completely normal man, in fact, moving amid not a few of those strange monsters who lend the Renaissance tapestry a sinister air. Henri III, last of the five kings he served, is an obvious example.

Henri III is the actor-manager's dream of the French Renaissance personified, and I cannot imagine why Irving or Tree never played him (perhaps they did). Against that splendid background of palaces and gardens, terraces and pleasaunces, Fontainebleau and the Tuileries and the Louvre, with their brilliant crowd in fantastic jewelled costumes posturing and peacocking like figures in some strange elaborate masque, he seems to move more naturally in torchlight than sunlight; a sombre, brooding, ambiguous personality, with his bodyguard of curled and scented *mignons*. A fascinating enigma, Henri III : a complete immoralist, a debauchee, a mystic, whose devotion when walking barefoot in later years among the Penitents of Avignon or taking the road to beg Our Lady of Chartres for an heir to France, is undoubted ; an impotent voluptuary yawning among the women, frizzed, perfumed, jewelled, and sometimes dressed as they, and a courageous soldier who charged and routed the Calvinist lansquenets at Jarnac and Moncontour and swung a pretty blade at St. Jean d'Angély and La

Rochelle ; a keen lover of philosophic and ethical debate, to which he would listen absorbedly at assemblies of his Academy of learned wits ; a dabbler in elementary alchemy, witchcraft, and mechanics.[1] The sad black eyes in the long, Mephistophelian face look out from his portraits with, one is tempted to say, a kind of despair. It is easy to read mysteries into the pictured faces of the dead. Monna Lisa's smirk has inspired one of the English-speaking world's most celebrated set-pieces of literary pyrotechnic, which Yeats insisted was not prose but free verse, as though that made it any less tiresome. To say that Henri III looks " haunted " would be to fall into the same kind of romantic whimsy. But it can be said accurately, I think, that his and many other male portraits of the Renaissance show the same curious brooding look in the eyes, watchful, calculating, unfriendly, *mystérieuse et rusée*, like the expression of Des Esseintes' ancestor, above all mournful; the eyes of men who have exhausted every sensation and are sick of the toils of the flesh. This would also be merely Paterism if one did not know that many of them actually had drained every intoxicating pleasure and come long since to the *amari aliquid*, the inevitable dregs. As for the great French Renaissance ladies, M. Champion is probably right when he politely dismisses their portraits as *si peu plaisantes*. There seems to have been a different standard of feminine beauty then.

But the men are often handsome by any standard. The *mignons* of Henri III, who undoubtedly deserved the title " Prince de Sodome " hurled at him by Calvinists and Catholics alike, eye the spectator insolently from those fine pencil-portraits by the Clouets and others with an oddly modern air, due to some extent to their fashion of well-groomed brushed-back hair. These popinjay did not lack bravery, they were intensely arrogant and alway fighting, and they were now and then killed in duels or assassinated, to the joy of the populace. Henri, though he never gave his *mignons* peerages, like Macaulay's hero and Ulster's demi-god William of Orange, buried them with tears in marble tombs of opulent and

---

[1] Charges of sorcery were brought against him by the Catholic League, and though not clearly proved are not improbable. A detailed pamphlet of 1589 accuses Henri of satanism. According to the Rev. Montague Summers, the authority on witchcraft, there were flourishing secret societies of diabolists in France at this time, as in France and England in the 1920's.

unrestful design. Henri had a great deal of generous but rather
forbidding charm. Except that he lacked ruthlessness, he might
pass very well for one of those princes of Italy we think of
instinctively when we see the name of his favourite author
Machiavelli, though that dark angel is by no means responsible
for all the cynicism and evil of his age. Henri III does not figure
in that slightly over-luscious chapter of *Dorian Gray*, among those
horrific Renaissance lay-figures whom " Vice and Blood and
Weariness had made monstrous or mad ". But he too would
have made a fine peg for Wildean embroidery and stage-jewel
work.

Immense wickedness, immense beauty, immense learning, and—
it seems time it was mentioned—immense goodness. (Everything
about the Renaissance is over lifesize.) In this same violent dissolute
Europe walked at least eighty canonised saints, I believe, many
of them—such as St. Charles Borromeo, Archbishop of Milan,
and St. Thomas More—of equal stature with the tallest of the
pagans. Beyond the saints, the cloud of Christian humanists of
Europe managed to amass and display extreme erudition without
running horn-mad after false gods. Nicholas V and Colet of St.
Paul's are examples. Scholarship was no more the monopoly of the
sceptics and the infidels than attacks on Church abuses, before the
Council of Trent ended them, were the monopoly of Lutherans
and Calvinists. Nor did Olympus retain its hold on every devotee
of Apollo and Pan or every quondam worshipper of Plato. There
is a fanfare of a poem by Paul Claudel called *Magnificat*, beginning :

> *Soyez béni, mon Dieu, qui m'avez délivré des Idoles,*
> *Et qui faites que je n'adore que Vous seul et non*
>   *point Isis et Osiris,*
> *Ou la Justice, ou le Progrès, ou la Vérité, ou la*
>   *Divinité, ou l'Humanité, ou les Lois de la Nature,*
>   *ou l'Art, ou la Beauté . . .*[1]

And Claudel sings on, praising God for deliverance from all
the empty babblers and sophists, phrase-makers and word-mongers

---

[1] Be thou blessed, my God, who hast delivered me from the Idols,
  And ordainest that I worship Thee only, and not Isis and Osiris,
    Or Justice, or Progress, or Truth, or Divinity, or Humanity, or the Laws of Nature
  or Art, or Beauty . . .

id Brains Trusts, the puppets and phantoms and chimeras bombi-
ating *in vacuo*, the supermen and the philosophers, filled with
ind and that unclean spirit which haunts deserts and vacant
laces, who infest our modern world. In some such glad Magni-
cat very many men and women of the Renaissance may have
elebrated at last their return to sanity and home; Shakespeare among
hem, Pico della Mirandola, Marguerite of Navarre, perhaps even
Rabelais, for the shadowy available evidence of his end is equally
convincing either way. Many were healed thus of the Renaissance
frenzy; many others continued dancing like dervishes till they
dropped.

Perhaps that theatre-simile inspired by the Renaissance of the
Whigs may be aptly used again. I would compare the Renaissance
in France to one of those huge geometrical ballets, lasting an hour,
danced on great occasions at the Louvre. The dancers mingle and
change positions bewilderingly, their evolutions are kaleidoscopic,
intricate, and recondite, as in that dazzling ballet danced by sixteen
ladies of the French Court before the Polish ambassadors in
August 1573, of which Ronsard says:

> *Le ballet fut divin, qui se souloit reprendre,*
> *Se rompre, se refaire, et tour dessus retour*
> *Se mesler, s'escarter, se tourner à l'entour,*
> *Contre-imitant le cours de fleuve de Meandre . . .*[1]

or that " ball in the form of a Tilt or Tournament " at the Court
of La Quinte Essence, described at excessive length in the Fifth
Book of *Pantagruel*. But behind the phantasmagoria there is a
pattern and a solution ultimately resolved. France's national
pattern after years of upheaval and confusion was seen to be, as
it had always been, Catholic.

§8

I propose, before proceeding, to refresh myself and any still
undefeated reader of this book with a little more Ronsardian

[1] The ballet was divine as it repeated itself, broke off, re-formed, and, turning and
returning, mingled again, drew away, twined itself round, imitating the flow of the River
Mæander . . .

43

music than we have enjoyed hitherto, beginning with that well
known gay and tender aubade or dawn-song to Marie, *la petit*
Angevine, which is so like Herrick's Mayday aubade to Corinna
The resemblance between some of Ronsard's song and Herrick'
I have touched on already; but whereas the English clergyma
longed for London and hated the warty oafs of his Devonshir
exile, the French Court poet, a countryman born, was happies
among his fields.

Here then is the aubade to Marie, heroine of the Arcadian
idyll, fresh and harmless (she had a vigilant mother), of 1553.
The sweet slugabed was fifteen, her poet thirty.

> *Marie, levez vous, vous estes paresseuse,*
> *Ja la gaye alouette au ciel a fredonné,*
> *Et ja le rossignol doucement jargonné*
> *Dessus l'espine assis, sa complainte amoureuse.*
>
> *Sus debout, allons voir l'herbelette perleuse,*
> *Et vostre beau rosier de boutons couronné,*
> *Et vos oeillets mignons ausquels aviez donné*
> *Hier au soir de l'eau d'une main si songneuse.*
>
> *Harsoir en vous couchant vous jurastes vos yeux,*
> *D'estre plutost que moy ce matin esveillée;*
> *Mais le dormir de l'aube, aux filles gracieux,*
>
> *Vous tient d'un doux sommeil encor les yeux sillée.*
> *Ça ça que je les baise, et vostre beau tetin,*
> *Cent fois pour vous apprendre à vous lever matin.*[1]

[1] Marie, get up, lazy one!
Already the gay lark has quired to Heaven,
Already the nightingale has sweetly babbled,
Under the thorn, his lovelorn plaint.
Up, up! Let us go and see the pearly grass,
And your fine rosetree, crowned with buds,
And your dainty carnations, which last evening
You watered with such a careful hand.
Last night on going to bed you swore by your eyes
To be awake before me this morning;
But the dawn beauty-sleep, so kind to girls,
Holds you still, with sewn eyes, in sweet slumbers.

Observe the sportsman's word " sillée ", " seeled " (Shakespeare), or " sewn "; a falconer's operation.

For Marie's untimely death Ronsard wrote this nobly sad, sweet, Greek farewell, one of many, bringing a phial of tears, a vase of milk, and flowers to her maiden tomb :

Comme on void sur la branche au mois de May la rose
En sa belle jeunesse, en sa premiere fleur,
Rendre le ciel jaloux de sa vive couleur,
Quand l'aube de ses pleurs au poinct du jour l'arrose :

La grace dans sa feuille, et l'amour se repose,
Embasmant les jardins et les arbres d'odeur :
Mais battue ou de pluye, ou d'excessive ardeur,
Languissante elle meurt, feuille a feuille declose.

Ainsi en ta premiere et jeune nouveauté
Quand la terre et le ciel honoroient ta beauté,
La Parque t'a tuée, et cendre tu reposes.

Pour obseques reçoy mes larmes et mes pleurs,
Ce vase plein de laict, ce pannier plein de fleurs,
Afin que vif et mort ton corps ne soit que roses.[1]

There, there! Let me kiss them, and your pretty breasts,
A hundred times, to teach you to wake early.

[1] As we see the rose on the bough, in the month of May,
In its lovely youth, in its first flower,
Making Heaven jealous of its vivid colour,
When dawn wets it with tears at the opening of day,
Grace in its leaf, and love reclined there,
Scenting the gardens and trees with its fragrance,
Till, vanquished by rain or by excessive heat,
Languishing it dies, leaf by leaf unfolded :
So in the primal freshness of your morning,
As earth and heaven honoured your beauty,
The Fates have slain you, and you sleep in dust.
For obsequies receive my tears and weeping,
This vase of milk, this basketful of flowers,
So that your body, in death as in life, may be nothing but roses.
(This is perhaps the most untranslatable of all Ronsard's sonnets.)

Roseate melancholy tinges this sonnet to Cassandre likewise.

Je vous envoie un bouquet que ma main
Vient de trier de ces fleurs epanies :
Qui ne les eust à ce vespre cueillies,
Cheutes à terre elles fussent demain.

Cela vous soit un exemple certain
Que vos beautez, bien qu'elles sont fleuries,
En peu de temps cherront toutes flaitries,
Et, comme fleurs, periront tout soudain.

Le temps s'en va, le temps s'en va, ma Dame,
Las! le temps non, mais nous, nous en allons,
Et tost serons estendus sous la lame :

Et des amours desquelles nous parlons,
Quand serons morts, n'en sera plus nouvelle :
Pour ce, aymez-moy, ce pendant qu'estes belle.[1]

But he is not always obsessed with the rose-theme. This nocturne reveals a Ronsard in dashing gear, a Mercutio cocking his hat at the spheres :

Cache pour cette nuit ta corne, bonne Lune!
Ainsi Endymion soit toujours ton amy,
Ainsi soit-il toujours en ton sein endormy,
Ainsi nul enchanteur jamais ne t'importune.

[1] I send you here a wreath of blossoms blown,
And woven flowers at sunset gathered,
Another dawn had seen them ruined, and shed
Loose leaves upon the grass at random strown.
By this, their sure example, be it known
That all your beauties, now in perfect flower,
Shall fade as these, and wither in an hour,
Flowerlike, and brief of days, as the flower sown.

Ah, Time is flying, lady—Time is flying ;
Nay, 'tis not Time that flies, but we that go,
Who in short space shall be in churchyard lying,
And of our loving parley none shall know,
Nor any man consider what we were :
Be therefore kind, my Love, whiles thou art fair. (LANG.)

Ballet-Divertissement

Le jour m'est odieux, la nuit m'est opportune :
Je crains du jour l'aguet d'un voisin ennemy,
De nuit, plus courageux, je traverse parmy
Le camp des espions, remparé de la brune.

Tu sais, Lune, que peut l'amoureuse poison :
Le Dieu Pan, pour le prix d'une blanche toison,
Put bien flechir ton coeur. Et vous, Astres insignes,

Favorisez au feu qui me tient allumé,
Car, s'il vous en souvient, la plupart de vous, Signes,
N'a place dans le Ciel que pour avoir aimé![1]

And here is a drinking-song, inspired by Anacreon, from the
Livret de Folastries :

Du Grand Turc je n'ay soucy,
Ny de l'Empereur aussi :
L'or n'esclave point ma vie,
Aux Roys je ne porte envie:
J'ay soucy tant seulement
D'oindre mon poil d'oignement,
J'ay soucy qu'une couronne
De fleurs ma teste environne,
Le soin de ce jour me point,
Du demain, je n'en ay point,
Et qui sçauroit bien cognoistre
Si un lendemain doit estre?
Vulcan, fay moy d'un art gent
Un creux goblet d'argent,

[1] Hide for to-night your horn, good Moon!
So shall Endymion prove always your lover,
So shall he lie always on your bosom,
So shall no enchanter ever harm you.
The day I hate ; the night is my ally,
I dread by day the snare of some near foe,
By night, more bold, I tread athwart
The spies' camp, armoured by the dark.
You know, Moon, the power of Love's poison ;
The God Pan, at the price of a snowy fleece,
Was able to move your heart. And you, noble Stars,
Be kind to this fire which enflames me,
For, if you remember, Constellations, most of you
Are only in the skies because you loved!

Ronsard

> Et de toute ta puissance
>   Large creuse-luy la panse,
> Et ne fay non point autour
>   Des estoilles le retour,
> Ny la Charrette celeste,
>   Ny cet Orion moleste,
> Mais bien un vignoble verd,
>   Mais un cep riant, couvert
> D'une grappe toute pleine,
>   Avec Bacchus et Silène ![1]

The second half Ronsard later rewrote and expanded even more gaily :

> Vulcan! En faveur de moy
>   Je te pri, depesche toy
> De me tourner une tasse
>   Qui de profondeur surpasse
> Celle du vieillard Nestor :
>   Je ne veux qu'elle soit d'or
> Sans plus fay-la moy de chesne,
>   Ou de lhierre, ou de fresne,
> Et ne m'engrave dedans
>   Ces grand panaches pendans,

[1] For the Grand Turk I care nothing,
Nor for the Emperor either ;
Gold does not enslave my life,
I bear no envy to Kings ;
My one and only care
Is to anoint my hair with perfume,
My concern is that a crown
Of flowers surrounds my head ;
To-day's cares suffice me,
For to-morrow's I have no thought—
And who is able to foretell
Whether there be a to-morrow ?
Vulcan, make me with your fine art
A deep goblet of silver
And with all your skill
Hollow its belly large
But do not grave around it
A sequence of stars,
Nor the celestial Chariot,
Nor troublesome Orion,
But a flourishing vine,
A smiling vine, laden
With bursting bunches,
With Bacchus and Silenus!

Ballet-Divertissement

Plastrons, morions, ny armes,
  Qu'ay-je soucy des alarmes?
Des assauts ny des combats?
  Aussi ne m'y grave pas
Ny le soleil, ny la lune,
  Ny le jour, ny la nuict brune,
Ny les astres radieux,
  Eh, quel soin ay-je des cieux?
De leurs Ours, de leur Charrette?
  D'Orion, ou de Boëte?
Mais pein-moy, je te supply,
  D'une treille le reply,
Non encore vandangée,
  Pein une vigne chargée
De grappes et de raisins,
  Pein-y des fouleurs de vins
Pein-y Venus et Cassandre,
  Laisse de Bacchus espandre
Le lhierre tout autour,
  Pein-y la Grace et l'Amour,
Le nez et la rouge trogne
  D'un Silene, ou d'un yvrongne![1]

[1] Vulcan! in my favour,
  I pray thee, hasten
  To turn me a cup
  Surpassing in depth
  That of aged Nestor;
  I do not desire one of gold—
  Make me one forthwith of oak,
  Or of ivy, or of ash-wood,
  And do not grave for me inside
  Those great hanging plumes,
  Breastplates, helmets, or arms—
  What care I for war's alarms,
  Assaults, or combats?
  Likewise do not grave me
  Sun, or moon,
  Or day, or shady night,
  Or the radiant stars—
  What concern have I with the skies,
  With their Bears, their Chariots,
  Orion or Boötes?
  But design me, I pray thee,
  The twines of a vine-trellis
  Not yet harvested,
  Grave me a vine, laden
  With bunches of grapes,
  Design there the treaders of the press,
  And Venus and Cassandra,

§9

It seems to me suitable, since this poet was born under such fickle amorous star—or was he steadfastly pursuing Beauty, th *Insaisissable ?*—to divide his rich and vibrant life into seven period: or (*si j'ose m'exprimer ainsi*) Cupades ; each ruled by one of hi major loves. The first of these, since Pierre de Ronsard undoubtedl visualised Letters as a feminine figure, august, whiterobed, level browed, Greek, imperial, with those calm clear features whic we are apt, as Disraeli said, to describe in moments of despondenc as classic, is plainly Pallas Athene. To this divinity succeec Cassandre Salviati ; Marie Dupin ; Genèvre, whose surname i: not known ; the " cruel Sinope ", about whom nothing at all i: known, though Ronsard fell so violently in love with her as to babble of marriage ; Isabeau de Limeuil ; "Astrée", whose name was Françoise d'Estrées ; and, *finis amorum*, Hélène de Surgères.

My plan may not be so simple in practice as it seems. It must not be supposed that these goddesses each hold undisputed sway. Their reigns often overlap or run simultaneously. Athene, for example, has to share her sceptre with Cassandre, and Marie Dupin with Mary Stuart, Queen of Scots, with whom everybody was (and is) in love, who returned Ronsard's chivalrous worship with an admiration of which her gifts to him are not the only token. The other beloveds share his heart from time to time with a *grande dame* or two, often platonically admired, like Madeleine de l'Aubespine, and a small troop of Jannes, Macées, Marguerites, Madeleines, Roses, and other rustic unknowns to whom he presents, up and down his verses, a flower, a kiss, a compliment, a complaint ; for the illustrious Ronsard is not by any means the conquering hero. I judge his technique with women to be far from flawless. That haughty promise of immortality made more than one pretty mouth yawn, I think. That *Ronsardismus*, as German pedantry would call it, that lofty, erudite, masterful passion palled before long, doubtless, on many an artless and practical feminine nature.

Let the Ivy of Bacchus spread
All around,
Design there the Graces and Loves,
And the nose and the red jowl
Of a Silenus, or some drunkard!

We know from Ronsard's own complaints that little Marie Dupin grew tired of the worship of her exacting seigneur and was attracted by another, that the *grande dame* Isabeau de Limeuil was beckoned from him by Condé, Prince of Bourbon, that great lord, and that the bluestocking Hélène de Surgères at times preferred the simple prattle of *un mortel de plus fresche jeunesse,* as Ronsard bitterly reminds her. But we can be grateful to these ungrateful ones. An unhappy poet writes better verse than a happy one, with the single exception of Browning; which explains why the greatest poet of Browning's century is Baudelaire.

II

ATHENE

Thus grew this gratious Plant, in whose sweet shade
The Sunne himselfe oft wisht to sit, and made
The Morning Muses perch like Birds, and sing
Among his Branches.

(CRASHAW, Upon the Death of Mr. Herrys.)

§1

" MR. TENNYSON IS, AFTER ALL, TO BE A PEER," REMARKED THE
London *Observer* in a chilly leading article on December 16,
1883, " and the fact has gravely disconcerted and depressed many
worthy people. Perhaps, however, Mr. Tennyson is the best
judge of what will, in the long run, make for the reputation of his
name." In a more democratic age British Governments have
recognised and hallowed the last infirmity but one of noble
minds by selling titles for cash down to all comers, irrespective
of class or occupation. In the Renaissance, when such a rage of
vanity possessed the great of Europe that they must needs trace
their lineage from Charlemagne, or from the Caesars, or even
from Hector or Hercules, when the most ordinary country gentlemen claimed ancient royal forebears with more than Celtic aplomb,
it followed that the *novus homo* had either to discover or invent a
noble ancestor, ignoring the gibes of the satirists.[1] If less ambitious
you slipped the patrician " de " between your Christian and surname
almost imperceptibly, and carried on.

In a long ode to the humanist Pierre Paschal (who assumed the
" de " himself in this manner) Ronsard accordingly awards himself
a shadowy ancestor from Thrace, the country of Orpheus ; a
Marquis de Ronsard of wealth and power, whose eldest son came
to France and took distinguished service under Philippe VI.
Ronsard was supplying autobiographical matter for a glorified
Who's Who of the French intelligentsia which the untrustworthy

---

[1] Cf. Montaigne's raillery on this topic, *Essais*, I, 46.

aschal was supposed to be compiling, in choice Latin prose, and was not on oath. Whether the Marquis, possibly a Ronsard family legend, is a total myth is still disputed. His existence has been recently regarded as a possibility by the Rumanian historian, orga. Whatever may be ultimately established, the immediate forebears of Pierre de Ronsard were of what we should call nowadays small squirearchy or upper middle-class stock.[1] His family, for generations wardens of the Forest of Gastine and vassals of the Dukes of Vendôme, had raised themselves by his grandfather's time to the Royal service. His mother, Jeanne de Chaudrier, distantly related to the great La Trémoïlles, had eloped with, or been abducted by, a passionate gentleman from her grandmother's care in girlhood, had married another, and been left a widow at thirty-five. Evidently she was the "dominant", as Mendelians say, from whom the poet derived his richly ardent temperament, and certainly, judging by her tomb-effigy at Couture, some of his good looks. His father, Loys de Ronsard, we have already met : a soldier and a cultivated gentleman, who had fought in Italy and, as a *maître d'hôtel* to the Dauphin, accompanied the Royal children and their suite into their four-year Spanish exile (1526–30) after the disaster of Pavia.

Pierre de Ronsard, youngest of six, was born at the family manor of La Possonnière, near Couture-sur-Loir, twenty-five kilometres from Vendôme, on September 11, 1524. Never was infant launched more thoroughly into the spirit of his age. The gracious white house Loys de Ronsard had built on the slope above the village only some ten years before is an epitome of the Renaissance. That hexagonal central tower, those Ionic-pilastered mullioned windows with gnomic Latin mottoes on the lintels, that great sculptured chimney-piece in the hall, luxuriant with armorial bearings, lutes, viols, suns and stars, Roman helms, arms and armour and twisting foliage, the very device over the tower entrance-door, *Voluptati et Gratiis*—"to Pleasure and Beauty"—are eloquent. Christian and Pagan alternately the mottoes run, *Domine conserva me* jostling *Non fallunt Futura merentem*. Had Messire de Ronsard possessed Greek as well he would have decked his lintels equally lavishly, doubtless,

---

[1] An archæologist of the Maine, the Abbé Froger, revealed some years ago that during Louis XIV's great purge of the nobility in the 1660's, the Ronsard family made good their claim to be *gentilshommes* only after a lawsuit.

with those Homeric and Pindaric distichs with which Lazare d
Baïf's Paris house awed and baffled the passer-by.

Pondering these inscriptions, haunting the Forest of Gastine
on the left bank of the Loir stretching towards Tours—its spars
remains still overhang the manor—wandering in the fields and
along the little river (to be distinguished from the great Loire o.
the Châteaux), with its cavern-lined banks, relics of the Celts
the child Ronsard had begun to think in verse before the age o
twelve, he tells us. There is a flowery field, the Pré Bouju, where
his nurse accidentally dropped him, they say, on the way to
baptism at the parish church of SS. Gervase and Protase at Couture.
The legend, whether invented or repeated by Claude Binet, still
lingers in the countryside. It is not bold enough to claim further
that a flowering poplar sprang up immediately on the spot, as when
Virgil's mother bore him in the Mantuan meadows, but, says
charming André Bellessort, the symbolism is equally attractive.[1]
Both infant poets touched the natal earth whose choicest flowers
were to bloom again in their songs (their indignant yells the Muse
has kindly agreed to ignore), and the infant Ronsard, moreover,
was revived with a sprinkling of rosewater by a passing *damoyselle*.
One feels Binet himself is slightly dubious about this latter touch.

Loys de Ronsard was the typical foursquare Gaul, as his observations to his son some years later on the economic consequences
of the Muses' service amply show. He did not have the child
Pierre—two elder sons were alive, Claude, a soldier, and Charles,
a priest, and there was a daughter, Louise, who later married a
country gentleman—immediately stuffed with Plato and Euripides,
as so many unfortunate Renaissance children were stuffed, to the
detriment of their natural bonhomie (the later case of John Stuart
Mill is typical). After being tutored in elementary French and Latin,
most likely by his uncle Jean, Prior of Sougé-sur-Loir, who later
left him a considerable library, and also, perhaps, by his father's
friend and protégé the learned Jean Bouchet, Pierre was sent at
the age of barely ten to the Collège de Navarre in the University
of Paris.

A brusque change from the kindly influence of home, the College
of Navarre. This ancient foundation, whose site is now occupied

[1] *Virgile, son Oeuvre et son Temps. Paris,* 1920.

by the École Polytechnique, was celebrated for its Latinity, its Tory loyalism and atmosphere, and the severity of its discipline. It has one more title to fame for lovers of letters and crime. Seventy years before Ronsard was entered the Grand Beadle of the College of Navarre was still on the track of one of the greatest poets of all time, who, assisted by two other lights of the Parisian underworld and a lapsed Picard monk, had burgled the College of 500 gold crowns at Christmas, 1456. Resisting the temptation to dwell on this interesting adventure, which has been described at length elsewhere, from the official dossiers,[1] I pause merely to marvel again at Ronsard's elaborate avoidance, all his life, of any mention whatsoever of the existence, let alone the works, of the great Villon, his predecessor. The burglary must still have been a legend at the College of Navarre in his time. The servants at least would be familiar with it, and now some of the elder dons must surely have discussed it afresh at High Table, for in this very year 1533 Clément Marot published the first critical edition of Villon's *Testaments*, (the twenty-first since his death), with that memorable preface in which Marot says truly that the best of Villon's verse is of such excellence,

tant plain de bonne doctrine, & tellement painct de mille belles couleurs, que le Temps, qui tout efface, jusques icy ne l'a sceu effacer, & moins encor l'effacera, ores & d'icy en avant, que les bonnes escriptures françoyses sont & seront myeulx congneues & receuillies que jamais.[2]

I refuse with loud cries to believe that this, the literary event of the year,[3] would not give rise, in the buttery and Hall of Navarre alike, to a buzz of reminiscence, from the Regent de Vailly down to the scullions. No gossip is the equal of your academic gossip. One mild domestic scandal will serve a Senior Common-room for years, as is well known. The dons of Navarre may even have known—which we, alas, do not—whether Villon ended by the

[1] *François Villon, a Documented Survey*, by D. B. Wyndham Lewis. London, 1928.
[2] " . . . so full of good doctrine, so glowing with a thousand lovely colours, that Time, which effaces all, has till now been powerless to touch it; and will henceforth be still more powerless, as the fine literature of France is and will be more known and cherished than ever before."
[3] Rabelais' *Pantagruel* came out in the summer of the same year, at Lyons; but I doubt if this piece of anti-Sorbonnical buffoonery impressed serious academic circles.

rope, in exile, in prison, or in his bed. Be sure the name of that illustrious crook, just surrounded by Marot with fresh glory, was bandied round the students' tables, and that the boy Ronsard must have heard about the Villon burglary and enjoyed it. His silence in later years seems deliberate. The first poet of the new age will not know the medieval barbarian, and hardly deigns to recognise the Sieur Marot his editor, either.

Ronsard did not stay long at the Collège de Navarre. Two terms, during which he apparently got Virgil by heart, or nearly, were enough. He dismisses this early stage of his University career with a shrug:

> *Je mis tant seulement un demy-an à peine*
> *D'apprendre les leçons du regent de Vailly,*
> *Puis, sans rien profiter, du college sailly.*[1]

"Nothing profited" is not quite accurate. He had made the acquaintance of a very high-born fellow-student indeed, the boy Charles de Guise, afterwards the powerful Cardinal of Lorraine, a very valuable future " contact ", to adopt modern literary jargon, in that age of patronages.

The unimaginative Toryism of his pedagogues and the rough régime of Navarre possibly fretted the child Ronsard's sensitive and imperious spirit. Or perhaps he simply yearned boyishly for action. Dreamer or not, his ambition, like that of most spirited boys, was, he says, to be a soldier, like his father and his elder brother—*je voulois me braver au nombre des gens-d'armes*—and but for a fortunate accident he might soon have filled some hasty grave in Picardy or Flanders, as so many young men of promise have done down the ages.

> *Su tumba son de Flándes las campañas,*
> *Y su epitafio la sangrienta luna.*[2]

[1] I took only half a year, or hardly that,
To learn the lessons of the Regent de Vailly,
Then I left College, having nothing profited.

[2] His tomb is the plains of Flanders
And his epitaph the bloodshot moon.

(Quevedo, *Memoria Inmortal de Don Pedro Girón, Duque de Osuna.*)

In the meantime he could serve a useful apprenticeship to arms as a Court page, which may have been his parents' reason for removing him from college.

Messire Loys de Ronsard arranged the immediate future accordingly. A year later he orders Pierre to report to him at Avignon, where François I and his army are waiting to engage the Emperor Charles V's troops as they advance into Provence. Here Messire de Ronsard, still a *maître d'hôtel* in the Royal household and commandant of a troop of Swiss lansquenets, is able to attach Pierre as a page to the Dauphin François. Very soon afterwards the attractive, sport-loving young Dauphin, his father's idol, tosses off a goblet of iced water after a violent game of tennis on a hot day, takes a chill and pleurisy, and dies. Looking round, then as now, for the nearest foreigner, the police arrest the Dauphin's Italian wine-butler, Montecuculli, and execute him as a tool of the Emperor, on suspicion of poisoning. The autopsy does not seem to have justified this sentence, one of the ordinary occupational risks of Renaissance butlerhood.

The sequel for the twelve-year-old Pierre de Ronsard, the handsome, intelligent boy, was transference, still as a page, to the suite of Charles, Duke of Orleans, the King's third son. A little later the Court left Provence for Touraine, and Ronsard with it.

§2

Speaking after dinner, Scotsmen are apt to trace their country's bond with France, the Auld Alliance, as far back as Charlemagne. I fancy this is about as probable as those portraits of the ancient Scottish kings, stretching back to the dawn of Time, which hang in Holyrood, or the stain of Rizzio's blood in that same palace. But there is no doubt that by Ronsard's day the French and the Scots had for some time established a bond in hatred of the common enemy. There had been minor tiffs. Scots poverty, pride, and wildness occasionally raised French eyebrows. In Saint Joan's time the peasants of Touraine complained bitterly of the Scots men-at-arms attached to the Dauphin's army, describing these lantern-jawed allies as wineskins and sheepstealers. There is evidence on the other hand that the Scots passion for improving the light-minded flourished then as now; I think it is on one of the pillars of the chapel at Chenonceaux that a Renaissance Scotsman scratched with his knife, in Scots, that moral apophthegm which may be seen to-day. But on the whole the two nations got on very well, with a trifle of condescension, perhaps, on the French side. The persistence to-day of Lowland words in constant use like gigot, tassie, aumrie, ashet (*assiette*), and even haggis (possibly *hâchis*) reveals, no less than the variety and elegance of Scottish cakes— and, occasionally, castles—how strong French influence has been on Scotland over the centuries.

The Auld Alliance had been re-sealed, a century before Ronsard, by the marriage of Charles VII's son Louis, later Louis XI, to Margaret, daughter of James I of Scotland, that excellent poet. The marriage had not been a success. Poor little Margaret's swift unhappiness, decline, and death, neglected by her hard, suspicious young husband, surrounded by hostile eyes and malicious tongues, make one of the most pathetic stories in history. The Stuarts, then merely at the beginning of those long misfortunes which moved even Voltaire to sympathy, had shrugged this unfortunate affair off long before bright-eyed, stocky, agile, vigorous, darting, dashing, voluble little James V arrived in Paris in the summer of 1536—having wisely refused to meet Henry VIII at York, where Chesterton's Fat White Czar had hoped to kidnap him[1]—to survey the bride he had tentatively selected at long-distance: Marie de Bourbon, daughter of the Duc de Vendôme. Something of a connoisseur in women, James Stuart doubtless winced when he saw his homely choice, though Stuart good manners prevented his voicing disappointment as his Royal brother of England did in similar circumstances. He merely changed his mind at once and selected the Princess Madeleine.

From now until his wedding-day King James enjoys his Parisian holiday as visiting monarchs have ever done, dashing about the capital in disguise (a Haroun-al-Raschid-like addiction he had long indulged by night in Edinburgh, where he was known as the Gudeman of Ballinbreich), spending money freely for the honour of Scotland, pointed at by an interested populace, dogged every-

---

[1] For breaking with Henry, James received in 1537 that cap and sword of honour from Pope Paul III which are displayed to-day in the Scottish National Treasury at Edinburgh Castle.

where by spies of his enemy Archibald, the Red Douglas. His passion for adventure *incognito* is recorded to have got James Stuart into trouble only once. Flirting with a comely wench at Cramond Brig, near Queensferry, he was set upon by her betrothed and half a dozen villagers and defended himself stoutly; but the odds were great, and but for a peasant named Jock Howieson, who galloped up brandishing a flail and crying " Sax agens' ane ? I'm for the ane !" the little King might have taken a woundy thrashing. To this day the head of the Howieson-Crauford family, to whose founder James granted the lands of Braehead, exercises the right of presenting ewer, basin, and towel for the ablutions of every monarch who passes by Cramond Brig.

The solemn second re-sealing of the Auld Alliance after the royal wedding in Notre-Dame on New Year's Day, 1537, at which Cardinal du Bellay officiated, was impressive. Ronsard records it years later in one of those clear little pictures of his :

> . . . *ces deux grands Roys, l'un en robe françoyse,*
> *Et l'autre revestu d'une mante escossoise,*
> *Tous deux, la messe ouye et repeuʒ du sainct pain,*
> *Les yeux leveʒ au ciel et la main en la main,*
> *S'estoient confedereʒ ; les fleurs tomboient menues,*
> *La publicque allegresse erroit parmy les rues.*[1]

James Stuart spoke French fairly well, with a broad Scots brogue. His Gallic vivacity seems to have made him highly popular with the French Court and the citizens of Paris alike, and his sixteen-year-old bride, romantic, consumptive Madeleine, was madly in love with him. A jolly little man, with all the Stuart verve and charm, and a dry humour. He astonished the Court at his wedding-banquet by distributing to the officials what he called " products of Scotland "; brought in solemnly on covered dishes, they turned out to be gold pieces, says the chronicler Sir David Lindsay, who does not blench. James also richly tipped the band.

[1] . . . these two great Kings, one in a French gown,
And the other vested in a Scottish mantle,
Having both heard Mass and feasted on the Holy Bread,
Their eyes lifted to Heaven, hand clasped in hand,
Were now conjoined ; the flowers fell fine and fast,
And public joy roamed every street.

The page Ronsard naturally enjoyed his share of the festal merrymakings: jousts, masques, banquets, fireworks, horse-races and all the rest. A greater excitement was to follow. The boy learned from his master Orleans that he had been chosen to go to Scotland as page to Queen Madeleine. In May, 1537, he sailed from Havre de Grâce in the King of Scotland's ship, the *Great Lyon*, amid a joyous concert of hautboys, viols, flutes, and drums from the escorting fleet, and five days later landed at Leith.

It was still the Scotland whose mode of living Dr. Johnson was to describe as that of Hottentots, though for a little time yet the Doctor would have been spared those spasms of fury stirred in him by viewing some of the handiwork of Knox's wreckers. In their mountain fastnesses over the Highland Line the chieftains dispensed life and death, fought each other, meditated their descent from Alpin and Fingal to harp accompaniment, and stalked regally abroad with their " animating rabble ". Along the English Border, hardly less vivacious, some of those massy foursquare towers stand to-day to warm the imagination irresistibly with visions of their past : the non-combatant clansmen and their families and cattle pouring into the vast stone ground-floor chamber at the warning blast of the sentinel's horn ; the locking and barring of the great outer doors ; the chieftain's womenfolk peering over the countryside from the tall parlour above, with its Gothic altar-niche where the clan priest said Mass and De Profundis during a siege ; the paved exterior walk round the steep roof where the men-at-arms were placed, and whence the chief surveyed his oncoming neighbour and prepared for parley or fight. Life went more smoothly in the Lowlands, where the monks had less interruption in their civilising labours, but the capital itself was not especially favourable to recollection and repose. The prodigious tall gabled houses of Edinburgh springing up on either side of those narrow, dark twisting wynds and closes, nearly blocking out the sky with their leaning rooftops, the swarming traffic and jangling colours of the old city, before Calvinism stamped everything vivid out of it except the stinks, may have stunned young Pierre de Ronsard as they stunned David Balfour.

This strange Northern metropolis humped round its high rock,

alf fortress, half rabbit-warren, swept by icy winds and brooding
alf the year under heavy grey skies—" the windy and richt
npleasand Castell and royk of Edinburgh ", as Scotland's greatest
oet calls it, yearning for London, " gemme of all joy, jasper of
ocunditie "—must have impinged fantastically on an eye accustomed to Paris and Touraine. The Royal Palace of Holy Rood
nestling in its hollow resembled no palace Ronsard had yet seen,
with its small dark panelled rooms and mazy corridors, and its
heavy furtive air. Even under the electric light of to-day the
Holyrood Charles II restored is faintly " unco ", as the Scots say.
Like the Old Serail at Istanbul, the original palace must have
seemed still more designed for complots and cantrips. The town
houses in the Canongate and elsewhere of the nobility and the
wealthy bourgeoisie were civilised enough, and fine French wines
and fine French manners might often be found there ; but the
bleakness and the poverty surrounding them, and the wild, ragged,
rawboned Edinburgh mob, more uncouth in its grimness, less
volatile than the mob of Paris, menacing even in friendly mood,
must have surprised Ronsard as much as the mud-floored, smoke-
filled kraals beyond the city walls and—strange contrast—the
Continental air of beautiful St. Andrews and its academic enclosures,
like a little Mediterranean coast-town washed in silver-greys.

To us, with the great and good Sir Walter and that treasury
of ballads behind us, there is a bright turbulent magic about Old
Edinburgh, strongly communicated in such glimpses as

> When she gaed up the Tolbooth stairs
> The corks frae her heels did flee . . .
> When she cam to the Netherbow Port
> She laugh'd loud laughters three,

and in that galloping line about the Bonny Earl of Moray in his
steel and velvet " sounding through the toun ". In its rich full-
blooded bustle pre-Reformation Edinburgh somewhat resembled
other remote outposts of Christendom like Warsaw and Christiania.
Fine feathers jostled deerskins and rags in its streets ; scholars
fresh from Rome and the Sorbonne elbowed wolfish, Tartar-like
hillmen with high cheekbones and glaring eyes ; noblemen and

ladies stepped daintily over aromatic sewage-runnels into house
full of French tapestry and Italian silver, sniffing at oranges stuc
with spices. The Scottish scene had not notably charmed th
humanist and diplomat Æneas Sylvius Piccolomini, later Pius I
half a century before Ronsard. The aquiline highly-cultured Italia
nose is somewhat elevated, the shrewd Italian eye is unimpresse
by brown heath and shaggy wood, unawed by mountain and flood
To a youthful page fresh from the French Court Scotland ma
have seemed for a long time a goblin dream.

Ronsard published no Scottish diary and does not tell Pascha
how or where he spent his time. In the autumn of 1538 he returne
home on leave for, apparently, a few weeks, returning to Scotland
again in December and staying several months more with the Court
at Linlithgow. There is one faintly possible trace of his presence
in Scotland, a recently-found entry in the accounts of the Lord
Treasurer for July, 1538, recording a gift of twenty crowns to a
page, " one named Wandomoy ". Champion, Laumonier and
others assume this to be Ronsard, who signed himself habitually
" Pierre de Ronsard Vandomoys ", Pierre de Ronsard of Vendôme,[1]
a custom of the time ; but there may have been other pages from
his province in the Queen's suite. M. Champion's suggestion
that the Scottish national archives might throw a clearer light on
Ronsard's stay, if thoroughly ransacked, seems to me optimistic ;
an obscure young French page is not likely to figure greatly in the
records of the Scots Court. Delivering Ronsard's funeral oration
fifty years hence Messire du Perron will assert that the youth
" learned the Scots language " during this stay, and fed his passion
for poetry by daily reading Virgil and Horace and the French poets
with a Scots gentleman, a fine Latinist, " le seigneur Paul ", untrace-
able.[2] Certainly no lettered foreigner in Scotland need feel himself
wandering in the outer darkness at this period. The Benedictine
monasteries were not yet looted and razed and their libraries
burned and dispersed, the University of St. Andrews had not yet
begun to decay. Scots like Buchanan, one of the first scholars and
Latin poets of the age, as even Dr. Johnson acknowledged, Gavin

---

[1] Compare, in his own circle, " Joachim du Bellay Angevin" (of Anjou), " Bertrand Bergier Poictevin " (of Poitiers), and so forth.

[2] De Nolhac identifies him with Claudio Duchi, a Piedmontais.

Douglas, translator of Virgil into Scottish verse, Hector Boece
(Boethius) of Aberdeen University, and David, Bishop of Moray,
founder of the Scots College in Paris, had given their country a
respectable name in Europe; and persons of cultivation, clerics
apart, like the poet Alexander Scott and Lindsay, Lyon King of
Arms, were always about the Court in Ronsard's time.

I do not doubt that young Pierre got leave of absence occasionally and saw something of the countryside; he may have gazed
at the Trossachs and even uttered the same exclamation as other
visitors to the Trossachs; he may even have crossed the Highland
Line with an armed pleasure-party and seen Lomond and Leven
and Laggan flaming in apocalyptic sunsets, and the Cairngorms
towering bloom-purple against a colossal angry sky, and dark
Glencoe brooding over its bloody destiny, and the Isles, and
the heather in its autumn glory. They did not inspire him to verse
at any time. The cult of Nature in gloomy grandeur came in
with the Romantics three hundred years after him, and he probably
thought the Highlands, if he ever saw them, frightful. As for
the Scottish climate, it had recently earned itself a treasonable
notoriety. Frail, consumptive little Queen Madeleine, who had
been warned by her physicians not to marry or to travel (but the
fascination of the Stuart and his crown prevailed), had died, within
two months of her arrival, of the mists and rain of a Northern
summer, and low-lying Holyrood in its belts of fog, and that
famous east wind from the Firth of Forth which lashes Edinburgh
with barbed steel whips; and James, her husband, so distracted
that he would have fallen on his sword, had to begin marriage-
negotiations all over again, when the year of mourning was over,
with his brother of France. His second wife, Marie de Lorraine,
daughter of Claude de Guise, sister of the great Duke François,
not only survived the Scottish climate but was enchanted by it,
and indeed by everything she saw. If her ecstasies as reported
sound a trifle, perhaps, like those of a kindly *grande dame* peering
through lorgnettes at some new exotic arrivals at the Zoo, it is
probably my imagination.

From Ronsard's always acquiescent references to Scotland,
a few years later to be epitomised for him at the Court of France
in the lovely laughing grace of James' and Marie's daughter, it

is plain that the too-brief spring, the wayward summer, the grim
autumn and winter skies, the black " haar " scourging him as he
wandered by the Nor' Loch, down the Lang Dykes—now called
Princes Street and scourged likewise—or up and over wooded
Corstorphine Hill, or among the Figgate Whins, or among the
Pentlands, did not spoil his stay, if they did not inspire his Muse.
Nor did the bushy-eyebrowed, high-cheekboned, powerful face
of a stocky priest with a long dark beard and irritable eyes, whom
Ronsard may conceivably have encountered often along the Royal
Mile, or seen emerging from that house in the Canongate which is
now a showplace, leave any recorded distaste in his memory.
Edinburgh swarmed—though probably less than to-day—with
grim visages, and the features of John Knox were not yet of national
importance. The thirty-two-year-old priest of the diocese of St.
Andrews had still to declare formally, after the murder of his
Archbishop by vengeful reforming hands, for the new religion,
for which he had already been seen waving a two-hand sword in
the train of the Calvinist Wishart ; then to abjure his priesthood,
marry a wife, and seek fresh spiritual inspiration from the town of
Geneva and its Dictator, whose absolutism was to be demonstrated
to the world shortly before Knox's arrival by the burning (1553)
of Michael Servetus at a slow fire.

No type, had Knox and Ronsard ever met, could have been
more abhorred by the poet, who might have been drawing one
of Knox's followers from life years later when he made that acid
little etching of a typical black-cloaked *cafard,* or minister of
the armed and militant *secte Calvine* :

> *Il faut seulement avecques hardiesse*
> *Detester le Papat, parler contre la Messe,*
> *Estre sobre en propos, barbe longue, et le front*
> *De rides labouré, l'œil farouche et profond,*
> *Les cheveux mal peignez, un sourcy qui s'avale,*
> *Le maintien renfrongné, le visage tout pasle . . .*
> *Avoir d'un reistre long les espaules couvertes,*
> *Bref, estre bon brigand et ne jurer que "certes".*[1]

[1] It is only necessary to abuse the Papacy with effrontery and to rail against the Mass;
to be a precisian in language, long-bearded, with a wrinkled forehead, the eyes savage and
deep-set, the hair disordered, over lowering eyebrows; a scowling expression and a pallid
face . . . and the shoulders covered with a long ritter's cloak [a cloak worn by German
mercenaries] ; in short, to be a good brigand and to use no oath but " truly".

Knox himself may—who knows?—have glanced in passing at
the tall, handsome French youth in Court clothes and muttered a
commination against all finicking, feckless, foreign popinjays and
papists, this latter word being a knobbly little missile recently
launched from Geneva with great success. The youth was obviously
one of those " devoted from the womb to certain [eternal] death,
that His Name may be glorified in their destruction ".[1]

The page Ronsard went home to France on leave in December,
1538. He returned at the end of the month to Scotland in the suite
of the Seigneur de Lassigny by way of Flanders, hearing the
carillons showered in silver rain from those huge openwork bell-
towers over the rolling misty Flemish plains, visiting Valenciennes
at kermesse-time, delighting boyishly doubtless in the good gross
gaiety of the Flemish scene. His ship thence was wrecked in port
at Queensferry after driving before a three-day gale off the English
coast, he does not say where; all the baggage but no lives were
lost. The Scottish Court was at Linlithgow, and for the next few
months Ronsard stayed there. Then Lassigny, who was on a diplo-
matic mission, bearing letters to the King of Scots, had to return
to Paris and did so by way of England, and Ronsard went with
him.

His stay in England for the next few months is a blank, left as
such by previous editors, or filled in with vaguest conjecture.
Hoping to discover something of Lassigny's movements, in which
his page would normally accompany him, I have dragged the
Letters and Papers, Foreign and Domestic, 29-31 *Henry VIII*,
and other arcana and State papers, with disappointing results.
Lassigny, Groom of the Stables to François I, was not an accredited
ambassador but a special envoy, and although Castillon, French
Ambassador in London, mentions him frequently in dispatches,
he gives practically no information of his whereabouts. In the
summer of 1538 Lassigny had seen Henry VIII, who was apparently
meditating a French marriage, at Kingston, at Arundel or there-
abouts, in Chelsea, and in London. His mission in England was to
report a recent friendly meeting at Aigues-Mortes between Henry's
more brilliant and courageous rivals in the European chess-game,
the Emperor Charles V and François I, and Chapuys, the Emperor's

[1] Calvin, *Institutes*, III.

ambassador in London, reports that Henry greatly resented Lassigny's news. After Lassigny's return from Scotland with Ronsard the only mention of him is an entry in Thomas Cromwell's accounts, dated September 4, 1539, of a gift of £100 to " Lassegny " for his services. His mission was therefore at an end by that date; and he presumably returned to France shortly afterwards, taking Ronsard with him.

It is most probable that for the greater part of this return visit London and Chelsea were Lassigny's headquarters. Castillon, his ambassador, had a country house at Chelsea and gave good dinner-parties. I cannot discover M. Champion's authority for stating that Pierre de Ronsard " visited the principal cities of the kingdom ". The young page must certainly have accompanied his master into the Royal presence at Chelsea or Hampton, and indeed may frequently have gazed on the Supreme Head of the Church in England, then engaged in plundering and closing down the English shrines and monasteries and prosecuting a reign of terror with surprising energy for one so fat, so syphilitic, and so sunk in amours and cuckoldries. For the Gospel-light (as the most cruelly satiric line in English poetry puts it) had shone from Boleyn's eyes.

Melancholy reading, these State papers make ; a chronicle of English docility, of bestial tyranny and greed, of utter bewilderment, savage coercion, and noble resistance here and there ; the bulk of the 350 English Catholic martyrs is furnished by succeeding reigns.[1] Marillac, Castillon's successor, in a dispatch of 1540, reports " the bishops in irreconcilable division, and the people in doubt what to believe". *Maistre Cromwel*, Henry's lackey-in-chief, is supreme and relentless. Marillac mentions in the same dispatch that the Bishop of Chichester, just arrested suddenly for " treason ", will shortly face a fate " as horrible to tell as frightful to see ".

The resentful pig-eyes of Tudor majesty may or may not have rested a moment on a tall, comely boy in Lassigny's suite who is destined a few years hence to make such a figure in Europe that

[1] The total so far canonised or beatified is 316: Henry VIII, 50 ; Elizabeth 189 ; James I, Charles I and the Commonwealth, 52 ; Charles II (the Popish Plot), 25. To these martyrs, of whom 237 are clergy, must be added at least 44 more whose case is still being examined at Rome. " Political " cases, (e.g. Father Garnet of the Gunpowder Plot) are excluded.

Queen Elizabeth's ambassador in Paris will include in his dispatches bulletins concerning the health of the illustrious Ronsard, and his miserly Royal mistress will even send the poet a fine diamond. If Ronsard met any interesting or distinguished Englishmen, he does not mention any by name in his later reminiscences. He seems to have been impressed by Henry VIII's nobility:

> . . . . *ces grands milords,*
> *Accorts, beaux, et courtois, magnanimes et forts,*[1]

but more by the swans of silver Thames, and even more by those vast flocks of sheep against which many despairing voices were crying aloud at this time, hearing in those multitudinous baa-ings the death-cry of English agriculture. He made no English friends, apparently. No Englishman is mentioned in his verse, as I have said, nor does one figure in his myriad dedications. The noblest and merriest of all the English, having resigned the Chancellorship of England when Henry VIII created himself, in Stubbs's words, " the Pope, the whole Pope, and something more than the Pope," had already passed from Chelsea to martyrdom. It is mildly to be regretted that so little of Ronsard's youthful impressions of the Island Race, with whose barbarous language he was probably acquainted to some little extent, is preserved. The poetry of the *blonds nourrissons de la froide Angleterre*[2] may have seemed to this fifteen-year-old critic unworthy of notice —even the Italianate graces of Wyatt and Surrey—and their late Laureate Skelton, for all his humanist learning and Oxford laurels, a low and beastly fellow, fit only to belch doggerel in bowsing-kens.

§3

Pierre de Ronsard, back in France early in 1540, was posted to the Écuries, the vast stables of the Duke of Orleans in the present Place des Vosges, which were not a haunt of grooms but an academy where cadets of family learned the arts of war and horsemanship and practised athletics in the gymnasium. Here, having shown

[1] These tall lords, affable, comely, and courteous, magnanimous and strong.

[2] *Response aux Prédicans de Genève.*

himself an adept at fencing, riding, wrestling, vaulting, music
and dancing, Ronsard ends his apprenticeship and is dismissed
from Orleans' service, *mis hors de page*, still in his sixteenth year,
and a little later is chosen—thus Fortune, and his own undoubted
gifts and charm, continued to gild his way—to accompany the
diplomat Lazare de Baïf on a mission into Germany.

It was a difficult mission. The task of De Baïf, one of the most
cultured men in France, translator of Sophocles, correspondent of
Erasmus and Cardinal Bembo, a noted collector of books and
manuscripts, was to go to Hagenau, in Alsace, where an assembly of
divines was proceeding, and win over the German Lutheran
princes to the side of François I, at loggerheads with the Emperor
once more. Endless theological argument in Latin occupied the
assembly at Hagenau; endless heavy German eating and drinking
filled in the rest of the time. Wearied by Lutherans and Calvinists
alike, Ronsard was especially bored by the sulphurous German
wines, he later told Claude Binet, and even the privilege of gazing—
if M. Jusserand's supposition is right—on the features of Calvin
himself did not compensate. He was not bored long. De Baïf's
mission failed. The long-suffering Emperor managed temporarily
to buy the loyalty of his chief Lutheran vassals by allowing them
to hold the Church property they had grabbed, and to keep them
quiet during his next struggle with the French. By August, 1540,
Ronsard was at home again at La Possonnière, suffering from an
otitis, an inflammation of the ear of arthritic origin, which left
him partially deaf for the rest of his life. It is not known how this
happened. Fatigue and a chill caught while travelling might easily
have begun, and the marsh-mists of the Loir, and their fevers,
increased it; or excess of German food may have poisoned
the system of one who was ever fastidious at table. Perhaps, as
Jacques Velliard suggests,[1] the shipwreck incident may have had
some connection with it. The Calvinist cry of "pox", raised
years afterwards, can be dismissed, not only because Ronsard
himself hotly denied it, but because his intense lifelong energy,
mental and physical, rebuts such a charge, as anybody can perceive.
His half-deafness never became a burden, nor did it prevent his
enjoying conversation, debate, dinner-parties, and music, making

---

[1] In his funeral oration for Ronsard, 1586.

figure at Court, and pouring out vast quantities of love to women.
t afflicts his supersensitive pride so little that years later he can
make a graceful jest about it in a sonnet to, I think, Sinope. She
complains that it is unpleasing to have to raise the voice in love-
talk ; he reminds her that his imperfect ear is an excuse to approach
her red mouth and close it with kisses. To speculate whether his
disability, had it become total, would have turned him morose
and misanthropic and filled him with macabre visions like those
deaf Goya painted during his self-immurement in the Quinta
del Sordo,

> *. . . plein de choses inconnues,*
> *De foetus qu'on fait cuire au milieu des sabbats,*
> *De vieilles au miroir et d'enfants toutes nues,*
> *Pour tenter les démons ajustant leurs bas,*[1]

or whether it would have inspired him, like Beethoven, to more
celestial harmony, is probably what dons call " otiose ". Ronsard
being neither a violent, egocentric Aragonese nor a dreamy transcendental German but a Frenchman of the Vendômois, I fancy
anything like complete deafness would have brought him merely
a lucid, golden melancholy, like Du Bellay's.

Such as it was, this misfortune (if it can be so called in the light
of his subsequent fame), changed Ronsard's life. No longer was
a military career possible. We may imagine long, depressed
discussions with Messire de Ronsard at La Possonnière for the
rest of the summer, walking together in the fields or sitting
long, by candlelight, over the supper-table at night, with the
scent of flowers and hay drifting in at the open windows, the
meadows drowned in moonlight beyond, the forest rustling
gently behind the house. Messire de Ronsard, a practical Frenchman, inclined now for the Church, reminding his son, no
doubt, of his old college-acquaintance Charles de Guise, a rich
possible source of future benefices. Ronsard demurred, having
no vocation and already ensnared by the Sirens. The matter was
not settled and he continued for some time to drift at home, devouring Virgil and Horace, trying (and tearing up) verse experiments

---

[1] . . . full of visions unknown, of embryos cooked in the midst of sabbats, of hags at the
mirror, and young naked girls adjusting their stockings for the luring of demons. (Baudelaire,
Les Phares.)

in Latin and French, mooning and dreaming. This did no
please his father. In lines in which we can hear the very tones o
the paternal voice, kindly enough but slightly irritated, and stand
ing no nonsense, Ronsard smilingly recalls one telling-off out o
many. "You poor idiot!" says Messire Loys de Ronsard—on
can see the neat soldierly figure leaning upright against a richly-
carved chimney-piece after dinner, feet firmly planted, forefinger
wagging, bushy eyebrows and trim grey beard vibrating slightly
with unaccustomed eloquence :

> . . . *Pauvre sot, tu t'amuses*
> *A courtiзer en vain Apollon et les Muses!*[1]

You'll never be worth a penny, my lad, Messire de Ronsard assures
his youngest son. Poetry never filled an empty belly yet—look
at Homer! Try the law, says Messire de Ronsard, or medicine,
the moneyed art, *l'argenteuse science* (even then Harley Street knew
its business). There is one passage of sardonic humour which
pertains to some earlier scolding. "Best of all", says Messire de
Ronsard, "be a soldier."

> *Prends les armes au poing et va suivre la guerre,*
> *Et d'une belle playe en l'estomac ouvert*
> *Meurs dessus un rempart, de poudre tout couvert :*
> *Par si noble moyen souvent on devient riche,*
> *Car envers les soldats un bon Prince n'est chiche.*[2]

It would seem that Pierre de Ronsard has made up his mind
to serve the Muses nevertheless, and his father eventually becomes
resigned to some extent. At least, then, the *pauvre sot* can get
himself qualified to receive a benefice or two from some hypo-
thetical patron of letters. This opportunity arrives early in 1543,
when we find father and son attending the obsequies in Le Mans
Cathedral on March 3 of a distant relation, Guillaume du Bellay,

---

[1] You poor fool, it amuses you thus vainly to court Apollo and the Muses!
[2] Take arms in hand and go to the wars, and die, black with powder, on some rampart,
of a fine wound in your belly. One often becomes rich by this noble means ; a good prince
is never stingy to soldiers. (The playful force of " a fine wound " is enhanced if it is remembered that bullet-wounds at this time were often treated with boiling oil, until Ambroise
Paré reformed French military surgery.)

eigneur de Langey, brother of the Bishop and one of the patrons
of Dr. François Rabelais, who refers in the Fourth Book of *Pantagruel* to " the dreadful Prodigies that happen'd before the death of
the late Lord de Langey " ; which prodigies, however, the Doctor
does not relate.

Rabelais was at the funeral. It is permissible to imagine the
fascinated awe with which a lover of letters like nineteen-year-
old Pierre de Ronsard gazed across the nave at the celebrated and
disconcerting author, the George Bernard Shaw of his time (barring
a slight addiction to meat, women, wine, scholarship, and frivolity),
now in his fifties and, no doubt, bearing all the rubicund stigmata
of a lifelong *bon beuveur*. Precious little Ronsard heard that day,
I dare guess, of the sublime harmonies of Pontifical Mass for the
Dead, with living literary fame so near him. This seems to be his
only recorded glimpse of Rabelais. A story of his drinking wine
with the Doctor a few years later at Meudon, when Rabelais held
that cure for a time, clashes with the dates alleged, and I have
not traced it to its source.[1] Ronsard certainly does not mention
such a festa himself, and the merry squib called *Epitaphe de
François Rabelais*, published in 1554, the year after the great
man's death, is merely a *jeu d'esprit*, the learned say. It is not great
verse, but jolly. Some of it may be worth quoting.

> *Si d'un mort qui pourri repose*
> *Nature engendre quelque chose,*
> *Et si la generation*
> *Se faict de la corruption,*
> *Une vigne prendra naissance*
> *De l'estomac et de la panse*
> *Du bon Rabelais qui buvoit*
> *Tousjours ce pendant qu'il vivoit . . .*
> *Jamais le Soleil ne l'a vu*
> *Tant fust-il matin, qu'il n'eust bu,*
> *Et jamais au soir la Nuit noire*
> *Tant fust tard, ne l'a vu sans boire*
> *Car altéré sans nul séjour*
> *Ce galant buvoit nuit et jour. . . .*
> *Il chantoit la grande massue*

[1] It is quoted in a eulogy of Rabelais written in 1699 by a Dr. Jean Bernier, but is held
by competent critics to be fantasy, though it inspired Michelet to a typical piece of bravura.

Ronsard

Et la jument de Gargantua,
Le grand Panurge, et le pays
Des papimanes ebahis,
Leurs loix, leurs façons et demeures,
Et Frère Jean des Entoumeures ;
Et d'Episteme les combats ;
  Mais la Mort qui ne buvoit pas
Tira le beuveur de ce monde,
Et ores le faict boire de l'onde
Qui fuit trouble dans le giron
Du large fleuve d'Acheron.[1]

On the day after Guillaume du Bellay's funeral Ronsard knelt in the chapel of the episcopal palace and received the " simple " tonsure of Minor Orders at the hands of Mgr. René du Bellay, Bishop of Le Mans. This formality has been absurdly misconstrued ; deliberately by contemporary Calvinist pamphleteers (" Priest ! " they bawl. " Don't I wish I were ! " retorts Ronsard, " I could do with a bishopric ! ") and by one or two modern writers in ignorance. This tonsuring did not make Ronsard a priest. It was a widespread legal subterfuge, condemned by the Council of Trent soon afterwards, enabling a layman to acquire

[1] If from a body lying rotten-ripe
Nature engenders anything,
And if generation
Springs from corruption,
A vine will be born
From the belly and paunch
Of the good Rabelais, who drank
All the days of his life . . .
Never the Sun has seen him,
However early, unless he had drunk,
Never dark Night at eventide,
However late, has seen him not drinking,
For with a thirst without surcease
This gallant drank night and day . . .
He sang the great club
And the Mare of Gargantua,
The great Panurge, and the country
Of the astonished Papimanes,
Their laws, customs, and dwellings,
And Friar John of the Funnels,
And the combats of Epistemon . . .
But Death, which did not drink,
Drew the drinker from this world
And now makes him quaff of the wave
Which flows murkily into the bosom
Of the great river Acheron.

and enjoy the income of an ecclesiastical benefice—an offence under Canon Law. This device led naturally to scandals, denounced years later by Ronsard himself as bitterly as by any adherent of the Reform. He accuses the Crown especially of trafficking in benefices with the unworthy.

> *Il ne faut s'etonner, Chrestiens, si la nacelle*
> *Du bon pasteur Sainct Pierre en ce monde chancelle,*
> *Puisque les ignorans, les enfans de quinze ans,*
> *Je ne sçay quels muguets, je ne sçay quels plaisans,*
> *Ont les biens de l'Eglise, et que les benefices*
> *Se vendent par argent ainsy que les offices.*[1]

There is poetic licence here. Simony, the buying and selling of spiritual offices, such as Ronsard properly denounces, is one thing; what Canon lawyers call the "proximate occasion" of simony is another. Because a transaction involving a given benefice might become an occasion of simony, it did not follow that the transaction itself was allied to simony. This method of disposing of benefices must moreover be clearly distinguished from the more ancient, still-existent and respectable custom of lay-patronage. Even this is only tolerated by the Church, the whole tendency of Canon Law being to restrict and to suppress it as far as possible, "because", a learned doctor has explained, "of the easy transition from use to abuse to which human nature is so subject".

Ronsard's tonsure, with which every candidate for Holy Orders is invested as a preliminary, gave him no priestly privileges. It merely implied celibacy, the wearing of the ecclesiastical bonnet, and the performance of certain minor ritual duties. We therefore find Ronsard, when in possession some years later of an honorary canonry of Le Mans, seated in choir on feast-days, vested, like the cantors, in cassock, surplice, and cope, joining in the singing (rarely—he admits his voice was not beautiful), and censing the

---

[1] We need not wonder, Christians, that the Ship
Of the good shepherd St. Peter in this world staggers,
When ignorant men, children of fifteen,
All kinds of fops, all kinds of light-minded fellows,
Hold the goods of the Church, and benefices
Are sold for money, like [other] offices.

Bishop at the proper moment at High Mass. And when Ronsard comes home to die at St. Cosme-lez-Tours his monks will receive their honorary prior and give him the last rites, and he will be buried as one of themselves.

It is not solely the formality of the tonsure (Ronsard would have been more interested, belike, if the bishop had proceeded, robed like the pontiff in the *Carmen Seculare*, to vest him in the white toga and to offer the discarded *bulla* round his neck to the Lares, before sacrificing to Diana), which makes this visit to Le Mans memorable. Bishop René du Bellay had a highly-cultured secretary, one Jacques Peletier, who might be described as a *humaniste enragé* and a fanatic poetry-lover. His meeting with Ronsard should be marked with a white stone in any survey of the poet's life. Together the two walked and talked all that day. One sees them pacing to and fro in the bishop's garden, the newly-tonsured clerk and the cassocked secretary, deep in honeyed talk of letters ancient and modern, from Virgil to Marot, oblivious of time. Ronsard recited, perhaps a trifle nervously—though on second thoughts I doubt it ; he knew his own worth—some little things of his own. The critical appreciation of Peletier, his elder by a few years, who could not write verse but knew it when he heard it, fanned the young poet's flame and showed him his way. Peletier moreover gave him extremely sound advice. Ronsard was not to waste his talents on exercises in the classical languages, like so many thousand pedants ; he was to write in *French*, to make the French language as magnificent a vehicle as the ancients had done theirs. As to models, the principal ones suggested by Peletier were Petrarch, Bembo, Sannazaro—the Neapolitan pastoralist who had recently invented that pink-sugar Arcadia which bears so little resemblance to the grim Arcadia of the Greeks—and, of all people, Aretino ; queer choice for a bishop's secretary, typical of the age.

Dizzy with visions, Pierre de Ronsard returned home, to consecrate himself henceforth to the Muses and to offer his tonsured curls, in a mannered but not memorable little ode, to Phœbus Apollo.

> *Dieu Crespelu (qui autrefois,*
> *Banni du Ciel, parmi les bois*
> *D'Admete gardas les taureaus,*

Fait campaignon de pastoureaus)
Mes cheveus j'offre à tes autels . . .[1]

He made three other vows at the same time. The first was to
challenge the vogue of the neo-Latin poets and to make his mother-
tongue the instrument of a new poetry ; as he says :

. . . aymant certes mieux estre
En ma langue ou second, ou le tiers, ou premier,
Que d'estre sans honneur à Rome le dernier.[2]

and again, addressing his lute in Horatian strain :

Sus, maintenant, Luc doré . . .
Change ton stile et me sois
Sonnant un chant en françois.[3]

His second vow was to enrich his style by infusing into it some of
that legendary Greek colour, flame, sweetness and subtlety it still
lacked, and to learn Greek as soon as possible for this purpose.
His third vow was to edit, correct, and polish the verses, chiefly
French, he had already written, and which Jacques Peletier had
praised, and to publish the best of them in due course.

All these vows he kept. The learned have established that in
this year, 1543, Ronsard had a considerable mass of verse piling up
in his cabinet-drawers. Much of it he will publish for the first
time in 1550, a collection of Odes and other pieces. The learned
have carefully analysed this book, showing which lines, phrases,
and metaphors of the Odes are inspired by Pindar, by Homer, by
Callimachus, by Archilocus, by Menander, and so forth, and what
the other pieces owe for their imagery to Anacreon, Horace,
Propertius, Ovid, the neo-Latins, and others. I am not qualified
to hold forth on this topic, nor to show, as the learned have done,

[1] O curly-headed god (who formerly, banished from heaven, guarded the cattle of
Admetus among the woods, a companion of shepherds), I offer my locks on thy altars . . .

[2] . . . certainly preferring
To be second in my own tongue, or third, or first,
Than to be last at Rome, without honour.

[3] Up now, my golden Lute!
Change your style and follow me,
Singing a song in French.

75

how Ronsard took the Pindaric Ode, adapted and developed it preserving its panegyric essence, remodelled strophe, antistrophe and epode to suit himself, hit the gold and missed it equally, and finally abandoned and passed this form on for Victor Hugo to orchestrate. Those who relish such discussion are at liberty to file into the lecture-room (or to turn to the critical edition of M. Laumonier, whose tireless scholarship and Benedictine labours have left no line unaccounted for). Like the Idle Apprentice, I am content to lie outside and play pitch and toss till sermon is over.

§4

Or se cante . . .
Of Ronsard's very first poems none is more pleasing than the water-music of the Ode *A la Fontaine Bellerie*, clear and harmonious and cool as Horace's Bandusian Fount, which prompts it.

> *O Fontaine Bellerie*
> *Belle fontaine cherie*
> *De nos Nymphes quand ton eau*
> *Les cache au creux de ta source*
> *Fuyantes le Satyreau,*
> *Qui les pourchasse à la course*
> *Jusqu'au bord de ton ruisseau . . .*
> *L'Esté je dors ou repose*
> *Sus ton herbe, où je compose,*
> *Caché sous tes saules verts,*
> *Je ne sçay quoy. . . .*[1]

A familiar theme. The poet praises his fountain's shade and coolness, so grateful under the burning Dog-Star to shepherds and weary kine, and ends, almost in the words of Horace :

> *Iô, tu seras sans cesse*
> *Des fontaines la princesse,*
> *Moy celebrant le conduit*

[1] O Fountain of Bellerie, lovely fount, beloved of our nymphs when thy waters hide them, in the hollow of thy source, from the pursuing satyr, who chases them at a gallop to the borders of thy stream . . .
In summer I sleep or repose on thy grass, where hidden under thy green willows, I compose I know not what. . . .

Athene

> *Du rocher percé qui darde*
> *Avec un enroué bruit*
> *L'eau de ta source jazarde*
> *Qui trepillante se suit.*[1]

To Bertrand Bergier of Poitiers young Ronsard dedicates an de full of tranquil, even supercilious mastery and ease, lready basking in the smile of Melpomene and admitted to high, chosen company.

> *La mercerie que je porte,*
> *Bertrand, est bien d'une autre sorte*
> *Que celle que l'usurier vend*
> *Dedans ses boutiques avares,*
> *Ou celles des Indes barbares*
> *Qu'enflent l'orgueil du Levant.*

> *Ma doulce navire immortelle*
> *Ne se charge de drogue telle,*
> *Et telle de moy tu n'attends,*
> *Ou si tu l'attens, tu t'abuses :*
> *Je suis le trafiqueur de Muses*
> *Et de leurs biens, maistres du temps . . .*[2]

It is a long ode. Ronsard's immense vitality often makes him as prolix, in these early years, as Hugo. Whether this is a defect or not we may pleasurably discuss in due course.

I take this ode to " pitiless Joan ", *à Janne impitoyable*, to be among the earliest flowerings of his individual genius, inspired by Anacreon but no longer merely an echo. In it the rose-*motif* appears, I think, for the first time.

> *Jeune beauté, mais trop outrecuidée*
> *Des presens de Venus,*

---

[1] Io! Thou shalt be for ever princess of fountains, and I shall celebrate the conduit whence pours loudly from the pierced rock the babbling water of thy spring, flowing and leaping on.

[2] The merchandise I carry, Bertrand, is of a very different kind from that the usurer sells in his grasping booths, or that from the savage Indies which swells the pride of the Levant. My sweet immortal bark is not laden with such drugs, nor need you expect such from me— and if you do, you are deceived. I am the merchant of the Muses and of their gifts, which conquer Time. . . .

Ronsard

Quand tu verras ta peau toute ridée
  Et tes cheveux chenus,
Contre le Temps et contre toy rebelle
  Diras en te tançant :
Que ne pensoy-je, alors que j'estoy belle
  Ce que je vay pensant ?
Ou bien, pourquoy à mon desir pareille
  Ne suis-je maintenant ?
La beauté semble à la rose vermeille
  Qui meurt incontinent ;
Voilà les vers tragiques, et la plainte
  Qu'au ciel tu envoyras,
Incontinent que ta face dépainte
  Par le temps tu voirras.
Tu sçais combien ardemment je t'adore,
  Indocile à pitié,
Et tu me fuis, et tu ne veux encore
  Te joindre à ta moitié.
O de Paphos et de Cypre regente,
  Deësse aux noirs sourcis !
Plustost encor que le temps, sois vengente
  Mes desdaignez soucis ;
Et du brandon dont les coeurs tu enflames
  Des jumens tout autour,
Brusle-la moy, à fin que de ses flames
  Je me rie à mon tour.[1]

[1] Young beauty, too presumptuous
  Of Venus' gifts,
When you shall see your skin all wrinkles,
  Your hair turned hoary,
Rebelling against Time and yourself
  You will say, self-scolding :
" Why did I not think, when I was fair,
  The thoughts I think now ?
Or rather, why am I now not equal
  To my desires ?
Beauty seems like the blushing rose
  Which sudden dies ! "
Thus the tragic song, the plaint
  You will send to Heaven
As soon as you survey
  Your features, faded by age ;
You know how ardently I adore you.
  Wayward one, bereft of pity,
And you fly me, and you refuse still
  To mingle with your other half !
O Queen of Paphos and Cyprus,
  Black-eyebrowed goddess,

ke Anacreon, also he prattles.

> *Ma petite Colombelle,*
> *Ma petite toute belle,*
> *Mon petit oeil, baisez-moy,*
> *D'une bouche toute pleine*
> *D'amours, chassez-moy la peine*
> *De mon amoureux emoy* . . .[1]

Deeper and serener is his passion for his countryside, and of all ne first poems of his youth none rings more truly than the Ode a which he chooses his sepulchre once and for all on a little reen tree-shadowed island in his beloved home-river. Of the venty-seven stanzas these eight have the most solemn and eautiful cadences :

> *Antres, et vous fontaines*
> *De ces roches hautaines*
> *Devallans contre bas,*
> *D'un glissant pas,*
>
> *Et vous, forests et ondes,*
> *Par ces prez vagabondes*
> *Et vous rives et bois,*
> *Oiez ma voix.*
>
> *Quand le ciel et mon heure*
> *Jugeront que je meure*
> *Ravi du doux sejour*
> *Du commun jour,*
>
> *Je veil, j'enten, j'ordonne*
> *Qu'un sepulchre on me donne*
> *Non près des Roys levé*
> *Ni d'or gravé.*

Do thou, even more than Time, avenge
  My sighs, thus disdained,
And with that torch with which thou inflamest
  Everywhere the hearts of mares,
Inflame her for me, so that in my turn,
  I may laugh at her flame!

[1] My little tiny dove, my little very lovely one, little apple of my eye, kiss me, with lips charged with love, drive from me the pain of love's desire. . . .

Ronsard

Mais en ceste isle verte,
Ou la course entr' ouverte
Du Loir, autour coulant,
Est accolant,

Là où Braie s'amie,
D'une eau non endormie,
Murmure à l'environ
De son giron.

Je deffen qu'on ne rompe
Le marbre pour la pompe
De vouloir mon tumbeau
Bâtir plus beau,

Mais bien je veil qu'un arbre
M'ombrage au lieu d'un marbre,
Arbre qui soit couvert
Tousjours de vert.[1]

[1] Caverns, and you, fountains,
From the high rocks
Leaping below
With your sliding surge,

And you, forests, and you, waves,
Flowing through these meadows,
And you, banks and woods,
Hear my voice.

When Heaven and my hour
Decree that I must die,
Ravished from the sweet habitation
Of the common day,

I desire, I intend, I order
That my sepulchre be made
Not lifted high near kings,
Nor graved with gold,

But in this green islet,
Where the divided tide
Of Loir, flowing round,
Embraces it,

There, where Braye her beloved
With sleepless waters
Murmurs around
Her bosom.

I forbid them to quarry
Marble for pride,
Desiring to make my tomb
More comely,

It was not until 1924 that the Green Islet received, if not Ronsard's ~~to~~mb, at least a votive tablet *à l'antique*, affixed to its stoutest tree ~~by~~ the Ronsardians of Vendôme. The waters of the Loir and the ~~L~~aye wash round it as they did when Ronsard dreamed there, the ~~sil~~ence under the poplars is cool, green, and fragrant with the ~~sa~~me "thrilling-sweet and rotten, unforgettable, unforgotten" river-~~sm~~ells Rupert Brooke longed for in exile ; the reeds grow thick, the ~~r~~eeds and water-lilies float on the glassy tide, the birds still sing. ~~It~~ is a haunted and enchanted spot.

§5

And now Pallas Athene seizes her joyful prey *toute entière*, like ~~V~~enus in the play.

In the Paris house of Lazare de Baïf, diplomat, scholar, and con-~~n~~oisseur, in the Fossés Saint-Victor,[1] with its Greek inscriptions ~~f~~lowering on every lintel, there was a wrinkled, pale, meagre, vital ~~l~~ittle man of rustic-gentle birth from the Limousin, to whom the ~~l~~anguages of Greece and Rome were as his own. He was tutor to ~~D~~e Baïf's son Jean-Antoine ; his name, originally Disnamandy, he ~~h~~ad shortened to the more tractable Daurat, or Dorat. In the fine ~~p~~encil-profile till lately in the Hermitage Palace at Leningrad, ~~J~~ean Dorat looks what he was, one of the leading classical scholars ~~i~~n Europe. A noble head and nose ; sad, handsome, humorous ~~e~~yes in bearded, pensive features, worn and refined from rusticity by years of intense intellectual labour, with a kind of light behind them, as of candlelight shining through thin horn—Dorat's personality is extremely attractive. In 1544, the year of the death of Messire Loys de Ronsard, who left very little money, a second pupil came to him at the invitation of Lazare de Baïf ; a pupil worthy of such a master, the diplomat's late clever and attractive page, Pierre de Ronsard of Vendôme.

> But I firmly desire that a tree
> Shade me instead of marble,
> A tree that shall be always
> Vested in green.

[1] Now the Rue du Cardinal Lemoine. De Baïf's house was pulled down in the following century and a convent of English Augustinian nuns took its place. George Sand was educated here in the early nineteenth century. The convent in turn disappeared in the 1860's.

It is already clear, I trust, that Ronsard was thirsting wildly f
Greek. The Latin poets he had long since drained dry. The
were, he knew, headier draughts still in the newly-recovered win
skins of Hellas. It was his good fortune to sit now at the fe
of the most consummate Grecian in France, a master-philologi
to whom the most crabbed text presented no difficulties, a tru
lover of the thought enshrined in the words, an expositor with th
sacred fire, intoxicating his pupils with Hellenism. A little tim
after Ronsard's arrival Dorat read to him, *tout de go*, reeling it o
in French from the Greek, the *Prometheus* of Aeschylus. To Claud
Binet, his secretary and first biographer, Ronsard later recalle
that when Dorat laid the book smilingly down a cry burst from hi
young listener. " *Et quoy, mon maistre, m'avez-vous caché si lon*
temps ces richesses? " "Master! Why have you hidden thes
riches from me so long?"

This was merely a foretaste. In 1547, on the death of Lazare de
Baïf, Dorat accepted the mastership of the Collège de Coquere
in the Rue Chartière, and his pair of pupils swelled swiftly to a
hundred or more. Coqueret was one of the minor colleges of the
University of Paris, clustered then so thick and glorious on the
sacred hill of St. Geneviève. It had no famous *alumni* and its history
was dim. It was the foundation, in the early Middle Ages, of a
native of Montreuil-sur-Mer in Picardy, and—once again the
shadow of Villon flits over the scene—had been the scene, eighty
years before Ronsard's time, of those violent undergraduate
affrays with the Provost of Paris and his police centring round the
famous stone called the Pet-au-Diable, in which rioting Villon
played such a part. Nothing remained of this college in 1938,
when I last saw the site, but a piece of waste ground behind the
Lycée Louis-le-Grand and the remains of an ancient well, long
since condemned. It may have been since built over. This obscure
little foundation was destined to be the nursery of a *groupe de
ieunes* who would shortly revolutionise French poetry.

Here for the next five years Ronsard will soak himself to saturation-point in Greek letters. The discipline of the University, severe
by modern standards, probably presented few fresh problems to
a youth already broken to Court routine. In most of the colleges
the students rose all the year round at 4 a.m. and after prayers heard

ctures from five to ten, when a meal was served, varying in quality according to the status and wealth of the foundation. After this they read till one o'clock, when lectures were resumed and continued ll five. At six they supped, and the rest of the day, except for a ttle reading, was theirs. On holidays of obligation they attended lass and Vespers and spent the rest of the day in music and games. nvitations to dine or sup out of college were very sparingly pproved. Even this iron régime did not satisfy Pierre de Ronsard, of whom Binet records that having read till two or three in the morning, as was his habit, he would wake Antoine de Baïf, with whom he shared a room. De Baïf would then take the candle, Ronsard the bed. A hard, happy life.

Striving after one of those pictures in the mind without which it is impossible to see a man of the past " standing on his legs ", as Whistler said of Velasquez' hidalgos, I think of Ronsard and his companions at this time as seated on oaken benches in a smallish, darkish, high-beamed, panelled hall of no great architectural pretentions, with books, inkhorns, and paper before them. Cross-legged they listen, rapt, book in hand. Sunlight pouring through a high window throws a long dusty ray across the dais on which the master's high-backed chair is placed. The little man in sad-coloured hose and doublet, with a shabby black gown, is striding up and down, flourishing the text, pouring out in his musical voice (*voix sucrée*) a running commentary in Latin and French on a passage of Homer or a Pindaric ode, breaking now and again into fluent idiomatic Greek while running a hand through his rusty grey hair, pausing constantly to untwist some knotty passage with swift dexterity, to expatiate with gusto on some beauty of verb or epithet, to emend some corruption, to remove some obscurity, to reveal some mystical interpretation. For it appears, from the only lecture of Dorat's which has come down to us, that he indulged in allegorical exegesis, that darling hobby of the Middle Ages. The sixth-century Planciadus Fulgentius was one of the first to specialise in this. His study of the hidden meanings of Virgil, *De Continentia Virgiliana*, displays the *Æneid* as a parable of human life, with Wisdom, in the person of Æneas, triumphing over the Passions, represented by Dido, Turnus, and others. Similarly does Dorat incidentally expound Homer. Ulysses is the Searcher

after Wisdom, symbolised by Penelope; Ithaca is that happine
the hero attains only after a myriad tests and trials. It is surprisir
enough to find a champion of the New Learning addicted to th
antique caprice. Perhaps it may be taken as evidence that th
great Renaissance scholars did not despise medievalism so entirel
as we are told to believe.

One sees the faces of Dorat's pupils, hypnotised by this Niagar
of puissant scholarship. It is clear that they took copious note:
and that when lecture was over they wrote these up with care an
little escaped them. Few pedagogues have produced more brillian
classical scholars than Jean Dorat the Limousin, and he worke
them like galley-slaves.

Ronsard's frequent tributes to his master mingle admiratior
and gratitude with real affection. The little man must have been
very lovable. There are many pedagogues who can make the
classics fascinating. There are few who, after analysing, construing,
explaining, and commenting a few hundred lines of the *Iliad*
like an angel, can sing a good Latin or Greek drinking-song of
their own composition at a tavern supper, accompanying themselves on the lute, and perhaps dancing, like Socrates, before the
evening ends. Tremendous fun Ronsard and his companions of
the " Brigade ", the Ronsard Group, had in their Coqueret days,
in the best Latin Quarter tradition, which is no invention of
Mürger's. The Parisian *escholier* from the earliest ages down to
Francis Carco, at least, has always shown a fantastic verve at
playtime. A romp in the country in the July of 1549, less anti-
social than some of Villon's, is celebrated by Ronsard in an
enormously long and merry poem called *Le Folastrissime Voyage
d'Herceuil*, from which the shouts and laughter ring out as clear
as yesterday.

> *Io! J'entens la Brigade,*
> *J'oy l'aubade*
> *De nos compaings eniouez,*
> *Qui pour nous eveiller sonnent,*
> *Et entonnent*
> *Leurs chalumeaux enrouez.*[1]

[1] Io! I hear the Brigade! I hear the reveille of our jolly companions, hawking and
booming on their hoarse pipes to wake us.

Under the windows of Coqueret in the dawn stand the first arrivals, waking half the Quarter, no doubt, with their whoops and cries. And Ronsard shouts to the College porter :

> *Sus Abel! ouvre la porte,*
> *Et qu'on porte*
> *Devant ce trouppeau divin ·*
> *Maint flaccon, mainte gargouille,*
> *Mainte andouille,*
> *Esperon à picquer vin!* [1]

And so, very early, in the cool hush of the morning, they set out, Dorat their master with them, laden with lutes, bottles, bread, ham, pasties, the chitterlings aforesaid and other thirst-producing belly-furniture Rabelais is so fond of listing. A dozen or more, they gambol and sing ; even the melancholy Du Bellay is gay, and the clown of the party, Bertrand Bergier of Poitiers, is at the top of his form. One sees them trooping down the quiet Paris streets in the early sunlight, perhaps in that swaying *monôme* of which Sorbonne students are still so fond, or in straggling noisy bunches surrounding the beaming Dorat. When they get into the fields round Paris, along the banks of the little Bièvre (it was not far to go in those days) they whoop and run wild, chasing butterflies, rolling on the grass, wrestling and making horseplay, and very soon René d'Urvoy is impelled to take a running jump into the water.

> *Voyez Urvoy qui s'eslance*
> *Sur la pance*
> *Tout vestu dans le ruisseau,*
> *Et voyez comme il barbouille*
> *En grenouille*
> *Dessoubz les vagues de l'eau!* [2]

So they come to the village of Arcueil and halt near its Roman aqueduct, where they shortly spread the feast on the grass, near

---

[1] Up, Abel, open the door! Order up masses of flagons and garglers for the divine troop, and masses of chitterlings for a spur to drinking.

[2] Look at Urvoy diving on his belly into the stream, with all his clothes on ! Look at him splashing like a frog under the billows !

the spring where their wine is cooling, and fall to with an *aboyan* *appetit*. Soon the bottle circulates briskly, the talk and laughte grow louder. At length there is cheering as the golden Master o Coqueret, *Dauratus auratus*, rises to his feet, perhaps a trifl unsteadily, strums a few chords on his lute, and begins to chan in his dulcet voice a fine long neo-Horatian Ode composed on the journey, celebrating the Spring of Arcueil and its aqueduct, and (of course) deriving its origin from Hercules. M. de Nolhac has discovered and reprinted this song, which begins:

> *O fons Arculii sydere purior,*
> *Aestam marmoreo frigore qui domas . . .*[1]

Yet another gush from the Bandusian Fount, one perceives. It was difficult to see a spring anywhere in this age without immedi- ately invoking Horace III, 13. And so, after further invocations and odes in the classic tongues, and renewed merriment and attacks on the bottle, Ronsard and his band perceive that evening is stealing over the hills, and Hesperus has lit his lamp, and it is time to trail homewards.

> *Donque puis que la nuict sombre*
> *Pleine d'ombre,*
> *Vient les montaignes saisir,*
> *Retournons, troupe gentille,*
> *Dans la ville,*
> *Demysoulez de plaisir!*[2]

Such days do not too often occur. The Ronsard Group, like so many Parisian *groupes de jeunes* since them, have a mission and are in furious earnest about it. Like every other subsequent group their mission is to reform French literature, and unlike every other subsequent group they succeed gloriously. Like every other subsequent group, also, they issue a manifesto. In a later age they would launch a little review of violent aspect called *La Revue des*

---

[1] O Fount of Arcueil, purer than a star, vanquishing summer's heat with thy marble coldness. . . .

[2] And now, since sombre Night comes swooping full of shadow on the hills, let us return to town, charming troop, half-intoxicated with pleasure!

ept or *Le Portique de Coqueret*, or perhaps something more
esoteric, *Zénith*, or *Niké*, or simply " 7 ", and you would see them
nightly at their reserved table at the Closerie des Lilas, with Ronsard
thunderously laying down the law to his disciples, like Paul Fort,
the cynosure and envy of every adolescent eye in the Quarter.

We should glance a moment, before proceeding, at the six
other principal members, the élite of this group, soon to be called
the Pléïade.[1] Only one of them, Joachim du Bellay, Ronsard's
second cousin,[2] is a major poet, on more occasions than one
Ronsard's equal. For the rest, the rare French verse of Jean Dorat,
a fine Greek and Latin poet, is negligible. Remy Belleau, translator
of Anacreon and a minor Ronsard, wrote one fresh and lovely
poem which is memorable—the one beginning

> *Avril, l'honneur et des bois*
> *Et des mois:*
> *Avril, la douce esperance*
> *Des fruicts qui sous le coton*
> *Du bouton*
> *Nourissent leur jeune enfance . . .*[3]

—and few more. Antoine de Baïf is artificial. Etienne Jodelle's
imitations of Greek tragedy I find heavy going, though they were
rightly hailed in his time as a splendid new dramatic experiment.
Pontus de Tyard, skilled in Latin verse and mathematics, in French
verse extravagant and mannered, died Bishop of Châlons and a

[1] I cite the traditional Pléïade, familiar to all the world, but there is controversy over
this. M. Laumonier asserts with a wealth of evidence, in his notes on Binet's *Vie de Ronsard*
(pp. 219–225), that the position is as follows. The original " Brigade " consisted of some
fifteen of Dorat's pupils, ranged under Ronsard's banner after the publication of Du Bellay's
Deffence in 1549. In the following years this band attracted so many mediocrities and
hangers-on that Ronsard, in an elegy of 1553 addressed to the poet La Péruse, distinguishes
and names an élite—Du Bellay, Pontus de Tyard, De Baïf, Jodelle, Guillaume des Autels,
La Péruse and himself (the place of La Péruse, who died in the next year, was taken by Remy
Belleau). But it is not until 1563 that Ronsard uses the word " Pléïade ", rather tentatively,
to describe this inner circle, in the manner of the seven Greek poets of the Alexandrian
School. Moreover he did not popularise the name, which he uses only once ; the Calvinists
took it up in mockery in 1563 and spread it abroad.

I have thought it advisable to quote Laumonier's view, though it does not seriously upset
the traditionalists, who derive their Pléïade from Ménage in 1666. The only case for correction is Dorat's, who stood above and outside the group, as their spiritual father. Des Autels
and La Péruse are very minor lights in any case.

[2] Their maternal grandmothers were sisters, of the De Beaumont family.

[3] April, honour of the woods and the year ; April, sweet hope of fruits which nourish
their tender infancy under their woolly buds . . .

peer of France. They made an admirable *claque* for Ronsard ar
sincerely loved and admired him, as he did them, Du Bellay an
De Baïf particularly. The sombre Du Bellay, whom we may no
meet again in these pages, wrote at least three poems so super
that I propose to set them down here and now, as a salute, and
foil to his captain's work, and for the pleasure of transcribing them

Firstly, that sonnet from the *Antiquetez de Rome* of which th
music has been justly compared with " thunder in the hills far of
on summer afternoons ; the words roll and crest themselves and
follow rumbling to the end".[1]

> *Telle que dans son char la Berecynthienne,*
> > *Couronnée de tours, et joyeuse d'avoir*
> > *Enfanté tant de Dieux, telle se faisoit voir*
> *En ses jours plus heureux ceste ville ancienne:*
> *Ceste ville qui fust plus que la Phrygienne*
> > *Foisonnante en enfans, et de qui le pouvoir*
> > *Fust le pouvoir du Monde, et ne se peult revoir*
> *Pareille à sa grandeur, grandeur sinon la sienne.*
>
> > *Rome seul pouvoit à Rome ressembler,*
> > *Rome seule pouvoit Rome faire trembler:*
> *Aussi n'avoit permis l'ordonnance fatale,*
> > *Qu'autre pouvoir humain, tant fust audacieux,*
> *Se vantast d'égaler celle qui fust égale,*
> *Sa puissance à la Terre, et son courage aux Cieux.*

Nobly translated by Edmund Spenser :

> Such as the *Berecynthian* Goddesse bright
> In her swift charret with high turrets crownde,
> Proud that so manie Gods she brought to light :
> Such was this Citie in her good daies fownd,
> > This Citie, more than that great *Phrygian* mother
> Renown'd for fruite of famous progenie,
> Whose greatness by the greatness of none other
> But by her selfe her equall match could see :
> > *Rome* onely might to *Rome* compared bee,
> And onely *Rome* could make great *Rome* tremble ;

[1] Belloc, *Avril.*

Soe did the Gods by heavenly doome decree
That other earthlie power should not resemble
    Her that did match the whole Earths puissance
    And did her courage to the heavens aduance.

  Now comes that lovely gossamer thing made of the quin-
essence of summer scents and zephyrs and soft blue skies, the
Winnower's Hymn to the Winds, from the Latin of Andrea
Navagero the Venetian:

> *A vous troppe legere,*
>   *Qui d'aele passagere*
>   *Par le monde volez,*
>   *Et d'un sifflant murmure*
>   *L'ombrageuse verdure*
>   *Doulcement esbranlez,*
> *J'offre ces violettes,*
>   *Ces lis et ces fleurettes,*
>   *Et ces roses icy,*
>   *Ces vermeillettes roses,*
>   *Tout freschement escloses,*
>   *Et ces oeillez aussi.*
> *De vostre doulce haleine*
>   *Eventez ceste plaine,*
>   *Eventez ce sejour ;*
>   *Ce pendant que j'ahanne*
>   *A mon blé que je vanne*
>   *A la chaleur du jour.*

Rendered by Andrew Lang:

> To you, troop so fleet,
> That with winged wandering feet
>   Through the wide world pass,
> And with soft murmuring
> Toss the green shades of Spring
>   In woods and grass,
> Lily and violet
> I give, and blossoms wet,
>   Roses and dew,

This branch of blushing roses,
Whose fresh bud encloses
    Windflowers too.
Ah, winnow with sweet breath,
Winnow the holt and heath
    Round this retreat;
Where all the golden morn
We fan the gold o' the corn
    In the sun's heat.

Finally, the homesick Sonnet of Exile, written at Rome:

Heureux qui, comme Ulysse, a fait un beau voyage,
Ou comme cestuy là qui conquist la Toison,
Et puis est retourné, plein d'usage et raison,
Vivre entre ses parents le reste de son aage!
Quand revoiray-je, helas! de mon petit village
Fumer la cheminée: et en quelle saison
Revoiray-je le clos de ma pauvre maison,
Qui m'est une province, et beaucoup d'avantage?
Plus me plaist le sejour qu'ont basty mes ayeux,
Que des palais Romains le front audacieux;
Plus que le marbre dur me plaist l'ardoise fine,
Plus mon Loyre Gaulois que le Tybre Latin,
Plus mon petit Lyré que le mont Palatin,
Et plus que l'air marin la doulceur Angevine.

Which Gilbert Chesterton miraculously renders:

Happy, who like Ulysses or that lord
    Who raped the Fleece, returning full and sage,
With usage and the world's wide reason stored,
    With his own kin can wait the end of age.
When shall I see, when shall I see, God knows!
    My little village smoke; or pass the door,
The old dear door of that unhappy house
    That is to me a kingdom and much more?
Mightier to me the house my fathers made
    Than your audacious heads, O Halls of Rome!
More than immortal marbles undecayed
    The thin sad slates that cover up my home;

> More than your Tiber is my Loire to me,
>   Than Palatine my little Lyré there,
> And more than all the winds of all the sea
>   The quiet kindness of the Angevin air.

So Ronsard yielded to Du Bellay, whom he loved and admired, the duty of preparing on behalf of the Pléiade that blast on a silver trumpet called *La Deffence et Illustration de la Langue Françoyse* (1549), that 48-page manifesto which is so famous, though certain modern critics, Villay for one, have described it as hasty, superficial, and derivative, its inspiration being Italian. Pater, justly praising Du Bellay's prose, so "transparent, flexible, and chaste", puts the gist of the *Deffence* in one sentence :

"Du Bellay's object is to adjust the existing French culture to the rediscovered classical culture ; and in discussing this problem, and developing the theories of the Pléiade, he has lighted on many principles of permanent truth and applicability."

Briefly, the Ronsard Group is determined to ennoble the French tongue, at present a starveling plant, *pauvre plante et vergette*, to refresh and invigorate it and make it *parfaict en toute elegance et venusté de paroles*, perfect in all elegance and grace of words. For it is necessary, says Du Bellay, to refute the claim, made by some pedants, that the only vehicles of gracious and scientific thought are the dead classical languages. "Those who speak in this way," says Du Bellay, shrugging, "put me in mind of those relics which one may view only through glass, and must not touch with one's hands." The French language can be made capable of equally noble possibilities. Three hundred years later an obvious image would suggest itself to Du Bellay, no doubt—the image of the vines of Bordeaux, devastated by phylloxera, re-invigorated by skilful graftings from America, producing a healthy grape, nourished by the rich traditional soil and utterly French.

The trumpet-call, we perceive, is to those who pretend to despair of the mother-tongue. The *Deffence* is a nationalist manifesto. The old French cry " *nous favorisons toujours les étrangers* " is on Du Bellay's lips (the last time I heard those exact words they were uttered by a Parisian concierge who had probably never heard

of the Pléïade). Mere translation into French is of little avail
you cannot reproduce original graces. You must invigorate and
enrich the French tongue, and to show how this can be done
Du Bellay, with that charming insouciance Ronsard shares
publishes his Sonnets to Olive, his love, and some *Vers Lyriques*
There is no false modesty about these young eagles.

As for those marks of haste and superficiality modern critics
discern in the *Deffence*, there is a simple and not unamusing
explanation. The literary underworld had run true to form. A
spy from the enemy camp, a henchman of the poet Mellin de St.
Gelais and the Court set, whom we shall meet before long, had
been using his ears, apparently. Those discussions at the Pomme de
Pin, the Closerie des Lilas of the period, or elsewhere, had been
too noisy. " *Taisez-vous, méfiez-vous ! Les oreilles ennemies vous
écoutent !* "—the familiar warning posted in French railway
trains during the war of 1914-18 should be displayed in every café
where literary rebels meet. Nine months before the *Deffence* was
published one Thomas Sébillet rushed out an *Art Poëtique françoys*,
full of adulation of St. Gelais and his master, Clément Marot, and
coolly appropriating at least three of the major Ronsardian dogmas.
A low trick, remarks Professor Gustave Cohen amiably in one of
his Sorbonne lectures ; but Sébillet had not grasped the significance
of Ronsard's ideas, and his attempt to steal a little thunder failed.
At least he succeeded in making Du Bellay hurry his own manifesto,
perhaps to its detriment.

It is clear that Ronsard and his disciples were eminently qualified
for the task, outlined by the *Deffence*, of adjusting the French and
classic cultures. The profundity of Ronsard's own scholarship,
to begin with, is extraordinary. Latin he knew from childhood.
Starting to learn Greek from scratch in his twenties and having
overcome the initial tedium by superhuman grinding, he swiftly
became a passionate philologist, tracking the obscurest Greeks,
including the Alexandrines, to their lairs and wrenching their
treasure from them, as he had from Homer and the great ones.[1]
His fellow-students at Coqueret were Grecians and Latinists to
their finger-tips also, thanks to Dorat's genius. Years of hard work,

[1] Binet says that Ronsard attended lectures at the Collège de France under Turnèbe, in
addition to Dorat's.

lentless as those a great pianist passes in the studios before his
rst recital, equipped these young men adequately for their mission.
    They knew it. No young Parisian group, not even the Symbolists
r the Dadaists, has ever been more conscious of its superiority.
The fanfares from the Brigade greeting Ronsard's first book of
poems in 1550 resemble the fanfares every young literary cenacle
accords its leader when he publishes a masterpiece, to the annoyance
of every rival clique ; but this time the noise was justified. Something was in store for French Poetry—a priesthood, Du Bellay had
said, announcing the new Messiah whose message should culminate
in some great epic. It turned out to be a revolution.

§6

Let us return to the *honorable partie de campagne* lunching on
the grass that merry July day at Arceuil. As the festivity waxes
to its height Pierre de Ronsard, seizing a fresh wineflask, proposes
a toast in the manner of the Ancients.

> *Neuf fois au nom de Cassandre*
> *Je vais prendre*
> *Neuf fois du vin au flacon,*
> *Afin de neuf fois le boire*
> *En mémoire*
> *Des neuf lettres de son nom.*[1]

A noble feat of drinking, hardly less distinguished than that
ritual draught from the great horn of Rory More of Dunvegan,
which every new Laird of M'Leod must empty of claret at one
blow to prove his manhood, without laying it, or falling, down.
Whether Ronsard's companions attached any significance to the
name thus brandished by their leader one cannot judge. It was the
kind of classic name a young man might use to disguise any toast.
Some light-of-love or other, they may have conjectured, cheering
each draught as it descended the poet's throat, and perhaps meditating more splendid challenges. The fashion which was to flower

[1] Nine times to Cassandre's name, nine times I proceed to drink wine from the flagon,
thus to drink nine times in honour of the nine letters of her name.

into such a vogue among the *précieuses* of the next century and o
into the age of Fragonard and Watteau,

> *C'est Tircis et c'est Aminte,*
> *Et c'est l'éternel Clitandre . . .*[1]

had just begun. But Ronsard's " Cassandre " was not a label. The
Cassandre whose name appears thus in his verse for the first time
is a real woman, young, fresh and blooming, and Ronsard is so
desperately in love that she can even draw him from his Greek.
" I am going to read the Iliad through," he will cry shortly to his
servant, going into his study :

> *Je veux lire en trois jours l'Iliade d'Homere,*
> *Et pour ce, Corydon, ferme bien l'huis sur moy :*
> *Si rien me vient troubler, je t'asseure ma foy*
> *Tu sentiras combien pesante est ma colere . . .*[2]

His door is locked and barred to all mankind, with one exception :

> *Mais si quelqu'un venoit de la part de Cassandre,*
> *Ouvre-luy tost la porte . . .*[3]

Athene's rival is a formidable one.

[1] Verlaine: *Mandoline.*
[2] I wish to read Homer's Iliad through in three days : therefore, Corydon, keep the door
well closed on me. If anything disturbs me you shall feel the full weight of my anger, I
give you my word. . . .
[3] But if anyone should come from Cassandre, open the door to him quickly. . . .

III

CASSANDRE

Dedans des *Prés* je vis une Dryade.
(RONSARD TO CASSANDRE.)

§1

ONE OF THE MANY ADVANTAGES ENJOYED BY POETS AND LITERARY men in love over stockbrokers in the same condition is that every step in the progress and decline of a literary love-affair recalls some written precedent. Whatever the joy or anguish, some poet has not only experienced it before but made an issue of it in ode, sonnet, or lyric, to ponder which increases the savour of the emotion a thousandfold. The literary man involved unhappily in love in a higher social *milieu* may wallow deliciously in *Maud*. The bitterness of parting from a fair native of Scotland becomes doubly sweet when Burns's recurring agonies in similar situations are recalled and studied. The happiness of winning some humble rustic heart is intensified, during the earlier stages, by reading *Love in the Valley*. On being spurned in a gondola a poet will recollect vaguely that Byron was also spurned in a gondola, and, although he may shrink from the prospect of wading through Byron's voluminous works to find the incident, which is probably non-existent, the glow of suffering with that great poet will sensibly increase his pleasure.

It is therefore easy to believe that when Pierre de Ronsard, fresh from that intensive study of Petrarch which Jacques Peletier had recommended that day in the bishop's garden at Le Mans, first set eyes on the girl Cassandre Salviati, he realised he had met his Laura. It was an April day of 1546. On an April day in 1327, in the church of St. Clara at Avignon, Petrarch had first seen Laura. Like Laura, Cassandre was young and beautiful; like Laura, she had Italian blood and, apparently, was a blonde, though also described by her poet as a brunette.[1] Ronsard did not, however,

---

[1] Pleasing comment by M. Jusserand : " He describes a blonde and a brunette Cassandre indifferently ; a certain sign that she was a brunette." There was a fashion then of using gold hair-powder, which may explain this or may not.

95

encounter Cassandre in church. She was singing a Burgundian
song to the lute in the Chateau of Blois, where the Court then was.
Her age was about fifteen, early womanhood for a half-Italian
beauty. Her father, the wealthy Florentine banker Bernardo
Salviati, who was allied with the Medici, had financed François I
and married a French wife, and had a fine house at Blois and a
chateau at Talcy, in the neighbourhood.

It is difficult to judge from Cassandre's only existing portrait,
that profile engraving *à l'antique* of 1552 to which I have alluded
in an earlier page, how beautiful she may have been at fifteen.
Her features most emphasised by the anonymous artist are a pair
of ripe breasts and a large, lustrous eye. Her nose is straight
and fine, her mouth well curved, her chin round and dimpled.
Round the laurelled portrait of Ronsard, also *à l'antique*, which
faces hers, is inscribed " ὡς ἐμάνην, ὡς ἴδον ", which he trans-
lates : " I saw her, I went mad." This is hardly an exaggeration
as regards the first phases of this affair, as some of the sonnets
of the Cassandre cycle indicate. For example, this cry to Pierre
Paschal :

> *Je meurs, Paschal, quand je la vois si belle,*
> *Le front si beau, et la bouche et ses yeux,*
> *Yeux le sejour d'Amour victorieux*
> *Qui m'a blessé d'une flesche nouvelle.*
> *Je n'ai ni sang, ni veine, ni moelle*
> *Qui ne se change ; et me semble qu'aux cieux*
> *Je suis ravy, assis entre les Dieux*
> *Quand le bonheur me conduit aupres d'elle . . .*[1]

This is far enough removed from Petrarch's distant contemplation of Laura uplifted in the pure ethereal blue. Nevertheless,
though the 182 sonnets of *Les Amours* vary in emotional content
from loftiest adoration to frankest desire, the vast majority are
purely Petrarchian (Ronsard describes his intention himself as
pétrarquisant), and a few of them are deliberate echoes of the
master, such as the one beginning

[1] I perish, Paschal, when I see her so beautiful, her lovely forehead, her mouth, her eyes—
eyes where victorious Love inhabits, who has wounded me with a new arrow. I have no
blood, or vein, or marrow which does not suffer change, and it seems, when good fortune
brings me near her, as if I am ravished to the skies and seated among the gods.

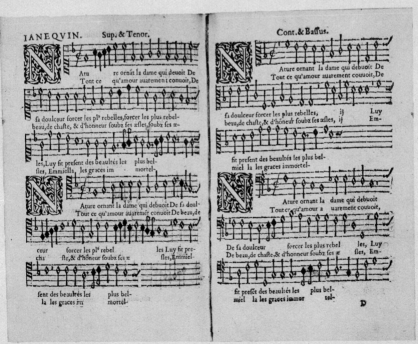

(Above): Ronsard and Cassandre: frontispiece to *Les Amours*, 1552
(Below): Sonnet from *Les Amours*, set for four voices by Clément Janequin

L'an mil cinq cens contant quarante et six
Dans ses cheveux une beauté cruelle
(Ne sais quel plus, las! ou cruelle ou belle)
Lia mon cœur de ses graces épris . . .[1]

Which, as Ronsard's friend the humanist Marc-Antoine de Muret points out in his commentary on *Les Amours*, comes from that of Petrarch beginning:

Mille trecento ventisette a punto
Su l'hora prima il di sesto d'Aprile,
Nel labirinto intrai, ne veggio ond'esca . . .[2]

One hastens to remark that Cassandre did not encourage the more flaming manifestations of her poet's fever. Though no prude, she was eminently virtuous—it was not uncommon even in that age—and, moreover, one year after meeting Ronsard she had been so unresponsive to the lure of the roses and raptures and immortality he offered her as to marry a country gentleman, Jean de Peigné, Seigneur de Pré, or Pray; a solid, equable character in this age of fiery husbands quick on the draw and ever pricked by their honour. Perhaps, like a country gentleman, De Pray never opened a book. Even then he could hardly help knowing, sooner or later, what the most eminent young poet in France was writing to his wife for all the world to read. But aware or not, he could sleep soundly at nights, the honest gentleman. His Cassandre was white as snow, and he himself evidently had not those pre-destined features described nowadays as *une vraie bobine de cocu*. The manor of Pray was some dozen miles from Vendôme, on the road to Blois. Its seigneur seems to have been some remote sort of cousin, removed to a dozen places, of the Ronsard family. Hence, though the poet soon perceived that Cassandre was not for him, he was still able to pay her frequent visits and to play at

[1] In the year one thousand five hundred and forty-six
In her hair a cruel beauty
(Whether more cruel or beautiful, alas, I know not)
Bound my heart, a victim to her graces . . .

[2] In the year one thousand three hundred and twenty-seven,
At the hour of Prime, on the sixth of April,
I entered into the Labyrinth, and how to leave it I cannot tell . . .

barre with her. *Barre* is one of the ancestors, I believe, of lawn-tennis. There is a quaintly Victorian flavour about such scenes as one imagines them ; the lovely Inaccessible lavishing smiles upon her disconsolate adorer, tripping to and fro, gracefully returning the ball, exhibiting with maddening unawareness every visible charm of dimpled cheek and downcast lashes, rounded arm and slender ankle, like one of George du Maurier's damsels torturing a Low Church curate. It is clear that Ronsard's dazzled, enchanted love for Cassandre was, despite a few temperamental lapses, of a very high order ; and when, after her marriage, his Muse ascended with a regretful backward glance or two into the company of the Troubadours and devoted herself to *l'amour courtois*, the transition was neither violent nor difficult. For Ronsard adored Cassandre, almost literally on his knees. The town of Blois is become to him a temple sacred to Love because of her, he says in a beautiful sonnet.

> *Ville de Blois, naissance de ma Dame,*
> *Sejour des Roys et de ma volonté,*
> *Où jeune d'ans d'Amour je fus dompté*
> *Par un œil brun qui m'outreperça l'ame ;*
> *Chez toy je pris ceste première flamme,*
> *Chez toy je vis ceste unique beauté,*
> *Chez toy je vis la doulce cruauté*
> *Dont le beau traict la franchise m'entame.*
> *Habite Amour en ta ville à jamais!*
> *Et son carquoys, ses lampes, et ses traicts*
> *Pendent en toy, le Temple de sa gloire!*
> *Puisse tousjours tes murailles couver*
> *Dessous son aile, et nu toujours laver*
> *Son chef crepu dans les flotz de ton Loire!*[1]

In other moods he is filled in absence with weariness and longing.

[1] Town of Blois, birthplace of my Lady, abode of Kings and of my desire, where in my youth Love conquered me, with a brown eye which transfixed my soul—it was within your walls that I felt this first flame, that I saw this peerless beauty, this sweet cruel one whose fair frankness pierces me. May Love dwell for ever in thy town ; may his quiver, his lamps, his arrows hang in thee, temple of his glory! May thy walls for ever shelter under his wing, may the naked Boy for ever wash his curly head in the waves of thy Loire!

> *Que dites-vous, que faictes-vous, mignonne ?*
> *Que songez-vous ? pensez-vous point en moy ?*
> *Avez-vous poinct soucy de mon émoy*
> *Comme de vous le soucy m'époinçonne ? . . .*[1]

He sees in visions his Cassandre talking, laughing, singing, far away from him and forgetful, and passion suddenly masters him. "I hold you for my own!" he cries—*je vous tiens mienne.* Whether this outburst occurred before or after her marriage I cannot discover. In either case it did not sway Cassandre. She would walk at evening with him over the dewy fields, smiling and magic as ever, to find the fading rose of which he speaks in that fine ode I have set down in an earlier page ; its symbolism she daintily ignored. It would seem that Pierre is admitted on occasion to her dressing-room while her waiting-woman dresses her hair, for he has two sonnets in praise of the glory of her flowing tresses. One of them is mildly notable for the appearance on the waves of a brunette Venus, a pendant to Botticelli's.

> *Quand au matin ma Deësse s'abille*
> *D'un riche or crespe ombrageant ses talons,*
> *Et les filets de ses beaux cheveux blonds*
> *En cent façons enonde et entortille,*
>   *Je l'accompare à l'escumiere Fille*
> *Qui, or' peignant les siens brunement longs,*
> *Or' les frisant en mille crespillons,*
> *Nageoit à bord dedans une coquille . . .*[2]

They walked and rode together and exchanged portraits, and once the river-mists gave Cassandre a chill, and she had to stay at La Possonnière for some days, and Ronsard, also his brother's guest,[3] gave up his bedchamber to her ; which sweet proximity under one roof so inflamed the poet that he became too pressing,

[1] What are you saying, Sweet ? What are you doing ?
What are you thinking of ? Are you thinking at all of me ?
Have you no care for my passion, as the thought of you stabs me? . . .

[2] When my Goddess arrays herself at morning in rich curling gold, covering her to her heels, and the locks of her beautiful fair hair wave and twist in a thousand ways, I compare her to the Daughter of the Foam who, now combing her own brown locks, now frizzing them in a thousand curls, rode the waves in her shell. . . .

[3] The family manor passed to Ronsard's elder brother Claude on their father's death in 1544 ; thence to Ronsard's nephew Loys.

and Cassandre fled. It is clear that although she permitted hi
kisses on occasion, she allowed him no more ; and at least onc
he offended her deeply, and begged forgiveness, in an ode, for hi
horrible faute, cringing like a serf. One must remember, for the
sake of Cassandre's reputation, that a perfervid imagination combines in Ronsard with the richest pillagings from Anacreon
and the erotic neo-Latins to make daydreams like the ode called
" The Kisses of Cassandre " and other incandescent pieces ; they
have no foundation in reality, as Ronsard constantly laments in
waking moments.

> *J'ay pour maistresse une étrange Gorgonne,*
> *Qui va passant les anges en beauté,*
> *C'est un vray Mars en dure cruauté,*
> *En chasteté la fille de Latonne . . .*[1]

If he had an ordinary heart in his breast, he cries, instead of a
salamander nourished in fire, it would long ago have been consumed :

> *Longtems y a qu'il fust reduit en cendre.*

He also describes Cassandre as a *tygresse*.
Hence neither outbursts like

> *Verray-je point qu'en ses bras enlassé*
> *De trop combattre honnestement lassé*
> *Honnestement entre ses bras je meure ?*[2]

nor appeals couched in the metaphysic, like

> *N'estes-vous pas ma seule Entelechie ?*[3]

nor that curious sonnet, built on an image derived from Plato,
in which he tells her of the Black Horse of Desire and the White

---

[1] I have a strange Gorgon for a mistress, surpassing the angels in beauty ; a veritable
Mars in hard cruelty, in chastity the daughter of Latona (Diana). . . .
[2] Shall I never see myself, locked in her arms, decently weary with too much combat,
dying splendidly in her embrace ?
[3] Are you not my sole Perfection ? (*Entelechie* is an Aristotelian word, ἐντελέχεια, with
motive or causative implications.)

Horse of Ideal Love, both running away with him at once—none of these things need give the Seigneur de Pray grounds for unease. The note of the Cassandre sonnet-cycle is resignation and worship, expressed in a hundred graceful, melodious, charming, despairing, allusive, adoring ways by a lover crammed with erudition, luxuriating in his pain and extracting the richest poetic honey from it. Would I were the water that washes your body, he cries in one ode; would I were the perfume that makes you fragrant! In the next stanza following is the cry, almost word for word, of Tennyson to the Miller's daughter:

> *Je voudrois estre le ruban*
> *Qui serre ta belle poitrine;*
> *Je voudrois estre le carquan*
> *Qui orne ta gorge ivoirine.*[1]

One gathers that the intentions of Victoria's Laureate were honourable. This cannot invariably be said for Pierre de Ronsard, though it is often difficult to judge what amount of his outpourings are ungovernable passion and what amount pure virtuosity. Had Cassandre suddenly succumbed, I suspect, Ronsard's joy would have been not unmixed with dismay. He is at his best when kneeling at her feet in the manner of Petrarch, whose transcendentalism is not the same thing as the pale neo-Platonic tomfoolery with which Hélène de Surgères will enrage him in later years.

Half rueful, half smiling, wholly philosophic, Ronsard reviews his case in terms of Jehan de Meung's *Roman de la Rose*, that early medieval epic of which he was so strangely fond, hailing Bel-Accueil and Faux-Danger:

> *Ha! Bel-Accueil, que ta doulce parôle*
> *Vint traistrement ma jeunesse offenser!*[2]

and seeing himself, as it were in a flowered tapestry of that age:

---

[1] I would be the ribbon
That binds your lovely breast,
I would be the necklace
That adorns your ivory throat.

[2] Ah, Kind-Welcome! How thy sweet words have treacherously deceived my youth!

Depuis cinq ans dedans ce verger,
Je vais ballant avecque Faux-Danger,
Tenant le main d'une dame trop caute :
Je ne suis seul par Amour abusé,
A ma jeunesse il faut donner la faute :
En cheveux gris je seray plus rusé.[1]

Eternal optimism of youth! But how gracefully he admits defeat! It is impossible to believe that such adoration in the grand manner did not touch and please, and perhaps awe Cassandre de Pray, however unswerving her fidelity to her marriage-vows. It may also be that at times the goddess wearied of the incense, and a shapely hand covered that red-lipped mouth full of lilies, roses and carnations, *ceste bouche vermeille, pleine de liz, de roses, et d'œilletz,* or strayed somewhat wearily to readjust those lustrous dark locks of gold, porphyry, and ivory——

O cheveulx d'or, O coustaulx plantureux
De liz, d'œilletz, de porphyre, et d'ivoyre!

——about whose tint the poet can never, in later years, be quite certain, unless the gold is that which glows amid the blackest folds of Giorgione's cypresses.

Ronsard's passion for Cassandre will last the next ten years at least, not unalleviated by other loves, but enduring and enthroned ; and when, having at length forgotten, he meets her again at Blois by accident some twenty years hence, middle-aged, buxom, but still enchanting, it will flower again in a St. Martin's summer of deep tenderness, in a poem which may well serve as tailpiece to this chapter.

Meanwhile, thanks in no small degree to her, his fame has soared and burst like a golden rocket, the Court has taken him up, and all France is repeating his songs.

§2

No one who has ever explored the fascinating literary jungle, so full of ambushes and alarms, birdsong and roarings, love-feasts

---

[1] For five years I have gone a-dancing in this orchard with False-Danger, holding a too-artful lady by the hand. I am not abused by Love alone ; my youth is to blame. When my hair is grey I shall be more crafty.

nd massacres, triumphs and panics, will need to be informed that
ne trumpet-chorus attending Pierre de Ronsard, pioneer of the
New Poetry, idol of *les jeunes*, aroused great dissatisfaction in the
ear 1550 among the Old Guard, who found this fuss highly absurd
nd offensive, if not a crime against Letters.

There was indeed every excuse for the Old Guard, led by the
lderly Court poet Mellin de St. Gelais, Reader to the King, and
lready nettled by the *Deffence*. Ronsard's preface to his first volume
of Odes can hardly be called conspicuously modest or conciliatory,
with its royal assumption of the laurel, its slighting references to
courtiers and poetasters and " envious vermin ", its polite exception
of " Heroët, Scève, et Saint-Gelays " from a general dismissal of
the old school (whom it would be a " monstrous error " to imitate),
and its patronage of Clément Marot, their revered master, as " the
only light, in his time, of poetry in the vulgar tongue ". Moreover
the newcomer, saluting Marguerite of Savoy, sister of Henri II
and patroness of the Court poets of whom St. Gelais was chief, as
a second Pallas Athene conquering *le vilain monstre Ignorance*,
went so far as to compare his predecessors, in one poem, to pigs.

> . . . *nos malheureux poëtes*
> *Qui souloient comme pourceaux*
> *Souiller le clair des ruisseaux.*[1]

No literary man likes to suspect he is being called a pig. The
Old Guard twittered with fury. Mellin de St. Gelais, who scorned
to publish for the common herd, lacked none of the vitriol which
flows in literary veins, and took appropriate action. To-day he
would assemble the Old Guard at a series of deafening cocktail-
parties where, after Ronsard's work and character had been torn to
shreds and trampled underfoot, a campaign would be launched by
friendly pens in newspapers and reviews and the logs set amply
rolling. St. Gelais, Reader to the King, knew a simpler way. One
day in May, 1550, he read aloud selected Ronsard odes for the
amusement of the assembled Court, taking exquisite care—one can
hear his drawl and see his eyebrows from here—to mispronounce
here and there, to underline the pedantries, to botch the rhythms,

[1] . . . our unfortunate poets, wont, like pigs, to sully the clarity of streams.

and to make the whole thing as quaint and ridiculous as might be
A genial move, but it failed. The new man was too big to b
laughed (literally) out of Court. Madame Marguerite, who hac
fallen almost instantly under Ronsard's spell, took him up, he:
chancellor, Michel de l'Hospital, became his powerful ally, the
Old Guard and their courtier friends retired to grind their teetl
and meditate reprisals, and Ronsard's conquest of the Court,
despite the cabal, became before long as unquestionable as his
conquest of the Parisian salons, which were already reciting his
odes with delight and singing them to the lute. Within three years
he reigned alone.

An immediate result of his arrival in the great world was two
Court poems, his first essay in the *genre ;* one celebrating Henri
II's recent entry into Paris after coronation, the other a Hymn of
France. Both, loudly acclaimed by the Ronsard clan, seem to me
as unexciting as all Court poetry. Most of his Court odes, except
for their elegance and erudition, do not differ in essence from
similar exercises by Boileau, Molière, Colley Cibber or Tennyson,
and have the deliberate Pindaric base of flattery. Ronsard's kings
and princes are godlike and awe-inspiring in war and peace, his
princesses pearls of grace and beauty, according to the rubrics.
It is a convention, and as we shall presently observe, its rules do
not hinder Ronsard, having awarded the monarch the diadem
and lightnings of Jove, from applying the frankest, freest of criticisms
to him if necessary in due course. Moreover the greater number of
the Odes are addressed not to royalty and the great but to Ronsard's
friends and literary allies, from Dorat and Du Bellay down to
Bertrand Bergier, licensed buffoon of the Brigade ; and the magnificent, hyperbolic, grandiloquent language is the same.

That *autorité dominatrice* in Ronsard which enabled him to
become the natural leader of French poetry and to speak his mind
to kings fails to turn his head, even when, a few years hence,
Elizabeth's ambassador is referring to him in despatches as " Arch-
Poet of France".

Never has poet been so surrounded all his life with such continuous and international praise as Ronsard ; rarely has poet been
so unspoiled by great fame, and so generous to praise the work of
others ; never has poet discarded the laurel with such a splendid

esture at the end. It is a mistake to regard Ronsard's calm assump-
ion of divine right as petty vanity. He is The Poet, the Makar,
he *Vates*, Dispenser of Immortality, one of those consecrated and
et apart,

> . . . movers and shakers
> Of the world for ever, it seems,

he equals and mentors of Royalty. "Only the Poet can say
thou' to (*tutoyer*) kings", declaimed José-Maria de Heredia to
Alexander III in an official ode when that Czar opened the bridge
in Paris bearing his name. The boast sounds faintly absurd in the
mouth of a fine second-rank poet and Academician in frock-coat
and top hat addressing a Czar of All the Russias in the nineteenth
century. It would not sound so absurd made by a Dante, a Shakespeare, a Hugo, a Baudelaire, or by Pierre de Ronsard, who speaks
to young Charles IX in the name of France with such authority
in that long, nobly didactic piece which begins :

> *Sire, ce n'est pas tout que d'estre Roy de France,*
> *Il faut que la vertu honore vostre enfance,*
> *Un Roy sans vertu porte le sceptre en vain . . .*[1]

and later gives his sovereign, in return for a flippant reference to
his poet's greying and thinning hair, a lesson in courtesy :

> *Charles, tel que je suis vous serez quelque jour . . .*[2]

To Henri II Ronsard had spoken with the same authority,
rebuking his military ambitions :

> *Pensez-vous estre Dieu ? l'honneur du monde passe ;*
> *Il faut un jour mourir, quelque chose qu'on fasse,*
> *Et aprez vostre mort, fussiez-vous Empereur,*
> *Vous ne serez non plus qu'un simple laboureur.*[3]

---

[1] Sire, it is not everything to be King of France ; virtue must honour your youth. A
king without virtue wields the sceptre in vain. . . .
[2] Charles, such as I am, so will you be one day. . . .
[3] Do you deem yourself to be God ? The world's honour passes ; one day we must die,
whatever we do ; after your death, even were you Emperor, you will be no more than a
common labourer.

And once more to Charles IX :

> *Punissez-vous vous-mesmes, afin que la justice*
> *De Dieu qui est plus grand, vos fautes ne punisse.*[1]

I cannot think of any other Court laureate who mingles ritu
flattery and plain speech so equably.

A new volume of poems, *Les Amours*, followed soon by *I
Cinquiesme Livre des Odes*, came out in 1552. *Les Amours* contaii
182 sonnets, as we have noted, addressed to Cassandre and strong
influenced by Petrarch.

The British Museum first edition copy—only two others exis
one at Orleans, one in a private collection—is a slim octav
printed by the Veuve Maurice de la Porte, in the Clos-Bruneau
on strong smooth paper in beautiful italic type from, I judge, on
of the Plantin founts ; somewhat close-packed for a modern eye
The title-page is unfortunately missing. A 49-page music-appendi:
contains six sonnets set polyphonically for four voices by Janequin
Muret, Certon, and " the severe and protestant Goudimel ", a:
Pater calls him. Next comes a list of 168 other sonnets from *Le:
Amours* classified for singing according to one or other of these
six models,[2] and at the end of the book comes, oddly, a sequence
of sacred *cantiques*, with music, by Nicolas Denisot, the devout
poet-painter of Le Mans, one of the earliest members of the Ronsard
Group. Thus the purchaser could turn back and fore from Cupid
to Christ, from the Queen of Heaven to the Queen of Cyprus,
with no trouble at all ; a convenience appreciated, doubtless, by
the age.

Among the new Odes the quarrel with the Old Guard is briskly
kept up ; Ronsard respectfully thanks Madame Marguerite for her
favour in the days when his work was being " mellinised " (*mellinisé*)
and compares his enemies to dogs with envenomed fangs baying
the moon. But it seems that Michel de l'Hospital was urging him,
obliquely and diplomatically, to make peace; perhaps at the Royal

---

[1] Punish yourself, so that the justice of God, Who is greater, may not punish your
errors.
[2] Many other pieces of Ronsard's were subsequently set by these and other musicians,
such as Orlando de Lassus, and sung all over Europe.

rder. In the second edition of *Les Amours*, a year later, Ronsard
ddresses Mellin de St. Gelais with a conciliatory smile. He had
he says) been moved by anger, having heard that Mellin had
poken evil of him. Now that Mellin denies it, he offers him
·ternal friendship.

> *Dressant à nostre amitié neuve*
> *Un autel, j'atteste le fleuve*
> *Qui des parjures n'a pitié*
> *Que ni l'oubly, ni le Temps mesme,*
> *Ni la rancoeur, ni la Mort blesme*
> *Ne desnoueront nostre amitié.*[1]

Could anything be more generous (there is nothing little about
Ronsard) ? The Old Guard returns courtesies and rages no more.
Not always are literary tomahawks so swiftly buried, and not always
is a successful poet henceforth so free from attack. Not a dog will
bark at Ronsard's heels in future until the Calvinist chorus begins,
and their enmity is not literary.

§3

Twenty-eight years old, strong, athletic, handsome, charming,
hot-blooded, a neo-Pagan, and the reigning new poet of France—
one would hardly expect Pierre de Ronsard to be without what
the French decorously call " good fortunes " at this time, his
adoration for all time of the goddess Cassandre notwithstanding.
He is not, as we shall find him complaining petulantly to Hélène
de Surgères in due course, the kind of lover who can live on air.

Since he scorns to arrange his love-poems in chronological order
it is not possible to give these pastimes or side-issues any particular
date. I am therefore as likely to be right as anybody in assigning
the Jannes and Macées, Roses and Marguerites to these years of
vigorous early manhood and triumph and careless joy of living.
It is not known who any of these subaltern beloveds were. One or
two of them appear in the anonymously-published *Livret de
Folastries* (1553), which so embarrassed some of Ronsard's friends

---

[1] Erecting an altar to our new amity, I vow by that river which has no pity on perjurers
(the Styx) that neither forgetfulness, nor Time itself, nor rancour, nor pallid Death shall
dissolve our friendship.

with its libertinism—for it was soon discovered to bear the unmis takable Ronsard stamp.[1] The girl Macée moves him to a charming little song, classically derived, fresh and gay.

> *Ma petite nymphe Macée,*
> *Plus blanche qu'ivoyre taillé,*
> *Que la neige aux monts amassée,*
> *Ou sur le jonc le laict caillé . . .*[2]

The rest is the inevitable roses and lilies common to the fabric or tissue of every woman poets admire. The milk metaphor suggests some bucolic idyll, some Galatea, *lasciva puella*, caught and kissed while returning from the dairy; possibly the same maiden, and the same milk, of another incident of this period, full of Arcadian fragrance :

> *Nous estions l'autre jour dans une verte place,*
> *Cueillants, m'amye et moy, les fraiziers savoureux ;*
> *Un pot de cresme estoit au milieu de nous deux,*
> *Et sur le jonc du laict tres luisant comme glace . . .*[3]

He was staying with his brother Claude at La Possonnière between 1554 and 1556, inhaling those deep breaths of his own country without which he could not live ("I died of pleasure", he says somewhere, "to see my trees."), spending his time in country sports of every kind, from boar-hunting to wrestling, and also in gentler diversions :

> *. . . plus je m'exercite,*
> *Plus Amour naist en moy.*[4]

It is evident that Pierre de Ronsard must have enacted, during his escapes from Court to the country, many a scene from Theo critus and Virgil with the laughing wenches of the Bas-Vendômois.

[1] A reprint in 1862 was ordered to be destroyed by the Correctional Tribunal of the Seine. A critical edition was published by Adrien van Bever, in 1919.
[2] My little nymph Macée, whiter than carved ivory, or snow piled on the mountains, or curdled milk on the rushes . . .
[3] The other day we were in a green place, my sweet and I, picking ripe strawberries; a pot of cream was between us, and milk shone on the rushes like ice . . .
[4] The more I exercise, the more Love awakes in me.

ittle those rustic beauties knew what a mass of literature was
acked in every kiss; perhaps, like Goethe, the handsome ardent
entleman was tapping out an experimental new metre with his
ngers on their shapely backs as he embraced them. These passing
oves are of no importance, except that they help a wounded poet
o avenge himself on Woman and regain his masculine self-esteem.
n every age they get in poets' eyes and hair and flit in and out of
heir hearts like fireflies in a tropic summer night, sometimes singly,
ometimes in clusters.

> *Tres morillas me enamoran*
> *en Xaen,*
> *Axa y Fatima y Marien . . .*[1]

Such *amourettes* do not, it is notorious, affect a grand poetic
passion, and they may be brushed away with a single gesture.
Meanwhile they are often as capable of inspiring song as any other
loves. Two at a time hold Ronsard's roving fancy at this period.
I quote the *Folastries*, so far as quotation is seemly:

> *Une jeune pucellette,*
> *Pucellette grasselette,*
> *Qu'eperdument j'ayme mieux*
> *Que mon coeur, ny que mes yeux . . .*[2]

Thus Charmer No. 1. Charmer No. 2 is of different build:

> *Las! une autre pucellette,*
> *Pucellette maigrelette,*
> *Qu'eperdument j'ayme mieux*
> *Que mon coeur, ny que mes yeux . . .*[3]

The refrain is the same, and in weighing their rival attractions,
with which he is intimately acquainted, the poet spares us nothing.
The note of the *Folastries* is erudite hilarity and *gauloiserie* of the

[1] With three dainty Moors I am smitten in Jaen :
  Axa, Fatima, and Marien.
    (Spanish Medieval, anonymous.)
[2] A young little wench, a plump little wench, whom I love madly, more than my heart
or my eyes. . . .
[3] Alas! Another little wench, a thin little wench, whom I love madly, etc., etc.

most Gaulish, in a storm of high spirits which makes it less offensiv
actually, than the smirking and allusive indecency, for exampl
of the Rev. Laurence Sterne. In two of these pieces obscenity
pushed—and how gracefully!—to the limit, and Priapus in persc
rules the garden once again. In another piece there is a gratin
sneering ring, unique in Ronsard's verse, as he describes the ne
devotion of Catin, formerly a procuress but now, with old ag
converted to piety : a harsh piece, the only ugly one he ever wrot
Not content with gibing at the old woman's belated devotions, h
accuses her of influencing a young girl on whom he has designs

> *Ainsi Catin la bonne dame,*
> *(Maintenant miroer de tout bien)*
> *Prescha dernierement si bien*
> *La jeune raison de m'amye*
> *Qu'en bigote l'a convertie.*[1]

This Voltairean piece represents the farthest point reached by
Ronsard in his travels from the baptismal font. It represents a
mood which occurs only this once in all his poetry, and it may be
that he was secretly ashamed of it, along with a few of the other
pieces.[2] On the titlepage of the *Folastries* appears, rather defiantly,
the well-known alibi of Catullus :

> *Nam castum esse decet pium poetam*
> *Ipsum, versiculos nihil necesse est*[3]

The dry reply of his friend Julien Pacate, to whom Ronsard
sent some gay verses at this time demanding, self-defensively, if
it is not better to write about Bacchic orgies than to practise them,
seems to cover sufficiently all the vinous and erotic gambols of the
Folastries :

---

[1] Thus Catin, good lady (now the mirror of all virtue) lately preached so well to the young
understanding of my dear that she has converted her to bigotry.

[2] He was ashamed sufficiently, at all events, to yield to Nicolas Denisot's urgings to
repair his lapse by writing something " more Christian". The *Hercule Chrestien* followed
soon afterwards.

[3] For a worthy poet should himself be chaste ; it is not necessary for his light verses to be.

Cassandre

> *Tu veux avecques ton bel art*
> *Du bon sophiste contrefaire ;*
> *Il ne faudroit, gentil Ronsard,*
> *Ny en ecrire, ny le faire.*[1]

Among this mass of cultured pleasantries is a set of *dityrambes*
celebrating the famous goat episode of Arcueil, in which the poet
goes mad in the approved Bacchic style, leaping with the satyrs
round the wine-god's panther-driven car, crying "*Iach, iach!*"
and "*Evoë!*"; a piece of fine breathless virtuosity. Cheek by
jowl with epigrams from the Greek, finally, is a Rabelaisianly
comic piece depicting the goblin nightmares of the drunkard
Thénot.

> *J'avise un camp de nains armez,*
> *J'en voy qui ne sont point formez,*
> *Tronçez de cuisses et de jambes,*
> *Et si ont les yeux comme flambes*
> *Aux creux de l'estomaq assis ;*
> *J'en voy cinquante, j'en voy six*
> *Qui sont sans ventre, et si ont teste*
> *Efroyable d'une grand'creste . . .*[2]

The unknown artist of the *Songes Drôlatiques de Pantagruel*
might have engraved a dainty plate from this. One wonders
what Cassandre, turning over those sonnets of Petrarchian worship
in her house at Pray, thought of her adorer's latest outbreak.
She had not long to brood over what may have been hurt surprise.
Following another collection of gaieties, almost wholly blameless,
the *Meslanges* of 1554, Ronsard publishes in 1555 the *Continuation
des Amours*, which contains an even greater surprise for Cassandre,
and for his public as well. For now he has formally renounced
Petrarch and petrarchism and turned to simpler, lighter song.
And it is inspired by a grand absorbing passion, and her name is
not Cassandre.

[1] With charming art you are trying to pose as the complete sophist ; but, gentle Ronsard,
you should neither write nor practise such things.
[2] I perceive a camp of armed dwarfs, I see some shapeless ones, without thighs and legs,
their flaming eyes in the pit of their stomachs. I see fifty of them, I see six with no
stomachs, and frightful heads with tall crests. . . .

§4

Before taking leave of the Cassandre cycle, here is a sonnet
echoing one of Petrarch's, which combines a cry of genuine passion
with its mannered airs and graces :

> O traicts fichez jusqu'au fond de mon ame!
>   O folle emprise! O pensers repensez!
> O vainement mes jeunes ans passez!
> O miel, ô fiel dont me repaist ma Dame !
>   O chaud, ô froid qui m'englace et m'enflame !
> O prompts desirs d'esperance cassez !
> O douce erreur ! ô pas en vain trassez !
> O monts, ô rocs que ma douleur entame !
>   O terre, ô mer, Chaos, Destins, et Cieux !
> O nuict ! ô jour ! ô Manes Stygieux !
> O fiere ardeur ! ô passion trop forte !
>   O vous Démons, et vous, divins Espritz !
> Si quelque amour quelquefois vous a pris,
> Voyez, pour Dieu, quelle peine je porte !¹

And here is a plaint addressed to Joachim du Bellay, remembering Du Bellay's love-verses to the unknown Olive and containing one of Ronsard's rare maritime images :

> Divin Bellay, dont les nombreuses lois,
>   Par une ardeur du peuple separée,
> Ont revestu l'enfant de Cytherée
> D'arc, de flambeau, de traicts et de carquois,
>   Si le doux feu dont jeune tu ardois
> Enflame encor ta poitrine sacrée,
> Si ton oreille encore se recrée
> D'ouir les plaintz des amoureuses vois :

¹ O darts, driven into the depths of my soul! O mad endeavour! O broodings perpetual!
O youth, so vainly spent! O honey, O gall fed from my Lady's hand! O heat, O cold
which freezes and enflames me! O quick upsurges of hope, all shattered! O sweet error!
O vainly-traced steps! O hills and rocks, graven by my pain! O earth, O sea, Chaos,
Destiny, and Heavens! O night! O day! O Manes of the Styx! O flaming ardour! O too-
violent passion! O ye Demons, and you, divine Spirits! If any love has ever conquered
you, see, for God's sake, what pain I bear!

Oy ton Ronsard, qui sanglote et lamente,
Pasle, agité des flotʒ de la tourmente,
Croiʒant en vain ses mains devers les Cieux,
*   En fraile nef, et sans voile et sans rame,*
Et loin du bord où pour astre sa Dame
Le conduisoit du phare de ses yeux.[1]

And here is a portrait in oils of the Beloved in the morning of her beauty, as Giorgione might have painted her.

Une beauté de quinʒe ans enfantine,
Un or frisé de maint crespe annelet,
Un front de rose, un teint demoiselet,
Un ris qui l'âme aux astres achemine,
*   Une vertu de telle beauté digne,*
Un col de neige, une gorge de laict,
Un cœur ja mûr en un sein verdelet,
En dame humaine une beauté divine :
*   Un œil puissant de faire jours les nuicts,*
Une main doulce à forcer les ennuys,
Qui tient ma vie en ses doigts enfermée,
*   Avec un chant decoupé doulcement,*
Or' d'un souris, or' d'un gemissement :
De tels sorciers ma raison fust charmée.[2]

Of this his Laura, first of his great passions and noblest of them all save one, since his love is mixed with far less physical desire, it may be said that this primal girlish image never faded completely from Ronsard's mind, for it was connected with youth and spring-time and Italy, and youth's long dreams. Dim and lovely it stands,

[1] Divine Bellay, whose repeated art, fired with an ardour the vulgar know not, has given the little Cytherean god his bow, his torch, his arrows and his quiver back again, if the sweet flame which fired your youth still burns in your sacred breast, if your ear still delights to hear the plaints of lovelorn voices, hear your Ronsard, who weeps and laments, pale, tossed on the waves of pain, stretching his hands in vain to the heavens, in his frail ship, without sail or oar, far from the shore where his lady and his star directed him with the lantern-rays of her eyes!
[2] A childlike beauty of fifteen ; locks of gold, frizzed into a thousand crisp ringlets ; a rosy forehead, a girlish complexion, a laugh which sweeps one's soul to the stars ; a virtue worthy of such loveliness ; a snowy neck, a milky bosom, a heart already ripened in a ripening breast ; divine beauty in a woman of flesh and blood ; an eye whose power turns night into day ; a hand, soft to conjure away pain, which holds my life enclosed in its fingers ; all this sweetly diversified with song, now smiling, now mournful—with such sorceries my reason was ensnared.

a vision never completely exorcised, to revive instantly in all i first freshness, or nearly, at a glimpse of her years afterwards. H had cried to her once :

> *Vous ne devez pourtant, et fussiez-vous Princesse,*
> *Jamais vous repentir d'avoir aimé Ronsard !*[1]

Cassandre was the first woman to whom he said this, thoug by no means the last. It is permissible to believe, since she was no a fool, that she remembered and treasured it as the years proceeded and more and more glory came to the man who had spoken it.

They did not meet again till 1568. Cassandre was thirty-seven and her poet forty-four. Time had spared her looks more tenderly than his. The *Derniers Vers pour Cassandre*, published in 1571, show how deeply Ronsard was moved.

> *L'absence, ny l'oubly, ny la course du jour*
> *N'ont effacé le nom, les graces ny l'amour*
> *Qu'au cœur je m'inprimay dès ma jeunesse tendre,*
> *Fait nouveau serviteur de toy, belle Cassandre !*
> *Qui me fus autrefois plus chere que mes yeux,*
> *Que mon sang, que ma vie, et que seule en tous lieux*
> *Pour sujet eternel ma Muse avoit choisie,*
> *A fin de te chanter par longue poësie . . .*
> *Et si l'âge, qui rompt et murs et forteresses,*
> *En coulant a perdu en peu de nos jeunesses,*
> *Cassandre, c'est tout un ! Car je n'ay pas esgard*
> *A ce qui est present, mais au premier regard,*
> *Au trait qui me navra de ta grace enfantine,*
> *Qu'encores tout sanglant je sens en la poitrine . . .*[2]

---

[1] Why, you could never, even were you a princess,
Repent of having loved Ronsard!

[2] Not absence, nor forgetfulness, nor the run of days
Has effaced that name, those graces, and that love
Imprinted on my heart since my first youth,
Making it your servitor anew, lovely Cassandre!
You who were once more dear to me than my eyes,
My blood, my life, you whom alone, in every place,
For her eternal theme my Muse had chosen,
That it might sing you in a wealth of verse . . .
And if age, which breaks down walls and fortresses,
Has lost us in its course a little of our youth,

It was, as it should have been, another April day. He remarks
it, contemplating the beloved features with emotion, saying to
r that if he were King he would raise a marble column on that
ot to mark the day, so that lovers might make a pilgrimage to
ss it, and remember Pierre and Cassandre. He does not tell us
hat she said to him. Perhaps she had nothing to say.

So they parted, for the last time. Cassandre survived her poet
ore than twenty years, dying at seventy-eight, white, frail, long
nce a widow, worn with troubles and lawsuits. In 1596 we catch
glimpse of her, bedridden, ill, and in financial difficulties, living
a farm on her impoverished estates. But it was decreed for her
hat more than one bright literary nimbus should surround her
ame. Her niece Diane was wooed, unsuccessfully, by Agrippa
'Aubigné, the Calvinist poet. Her daughter Cassandre married
ne Guillaume de Musset, from whom Alfred de Musset directly
lescended.

Cassandre, it matters not! For I have no concern
With the present, but with that first look,
That dart which stabbed me with your childlike grace,
And which I still feel in my bleeding breast . . .

IV

MARIE

Rosa fresca, rosa fresca,
tan garrida y con amor . . .

(OLD SPANISH BALLAD.)

§1

SPRING AND HIGH SUMMER MELTING INTO THE MISTS OF VINTAGE time along the Loire—not even Progress and the internal combustion engine, Caliban's noblest invention, not even the las corruptions and omens of impending doom of the Third Republic could destroy the bloom of this garden of France, as Panurge rightly called it. The soft blissful skies of Touraine; the "quiet kindness of the Angevin air"; the fragrant *noyers grolliers*, Rabelais' walnuts, murmuring on a clear June or September night by his smooth-sliding Vienne; the wide Loire flowing royally past the towers of Tours among pale golden sands; those sumptuous and shining Renaissance sonnets in stone and glass, Amboise, Chenonceaux, Chambord, Langeais, Villandry, Azay-le-Rideau, whose names are like sunlight seen through claret, like the names of all that countryside, Vendôme, Marmoutiers, Chinon, Rochecorbon, Vouvray—all these things remain to-day as when Innocent the pastrycook thumped his dough and Rabelais tippled in the Painted Cellar at Chinon, and the shepherds of Lerné were set "to keep the Vines, and hinder the Starlings from eating up the Grapes", and any old woman met hobbling along by the river at Porthuaux might be the same "old Lourpidon Hag" who dispersed such frigid comfort to Picrochole, world-dictator, after his downfall. When Ronsard rode out, cocking his bonnet and humming an air of De Lassus or Janequin, to meet *la petite Angevine* at St. Cosme-lez-Tours or Bourgueil, that gigantic laughter with which Rabelais had shaken the air of Touraine twenty years before cannot have died away, for it has not quite died away yet. Those sunlit smiling fields and woodlands of the Chinonnais remember the

116

crocholian War, and the Doctor's farmhouse of La Devinière
ill stands a witness on the battlefield, though the Tavern of the
Moon has long since vanished from the plains of Valmy, terrain
f a conflict hardly less memorable.

Strong literary associations attached to scenery can become a
ore, as is well known; the phantasms of fiction often dominate
he living world to a tiresome degree. The distant prospect of
Dorchester Jail is spoiled for many because Tess of the d'Urber-
villes was hanged there. For others the Georgian great world is
banished from the streets of Bath by a titupping procession of
Jane Austen's characters; and there are those who see, to their
annoyance, every time they pass the tall towers of St. Sulpice in
Paris, not the noble apostolic figures of Olier and Bretonvilliers
but a pair of cloaked and muffled spectres, Manon and the Chevalier
des Grieux, eloping in a hackney-coach; puppets of a novelist's
brain, more vivid in the field of vision than all the great Sulpicians
put together. On the other hand Rabelais in person, seated in his
great bronze chair overlooking the glassy Vienne, rules his town of
Chinon absolutely, being especially powerful in the courtyard of the
Boule d'Or. As for Pierre de Ronsard, he needs no statue, in
Vendôme or anywhere else in his countryside.

> The spring's superb adventure calls
> His dust athwart the woods to flame;
> His boundary river's secret falls
> Perpetuate and repeat his name . . .[1]

Certainly the influence of so strong, enduring, perpetually
expressed a love persists. Ronsard is mixed indissolubly with his
fields, and particularly with the *isle verte* in the Loir, which I have
already mentioned. Without any visible apparition, his presence
haunts that place so that the voices of the trees and the water
might be his own.

This cannot be said for the modern village of Bourgueil (Indre-
et-Loire), on the outskirts of which, in the year 1554, lived the
fresh but not reckless Chloë with whom our Daphnis plunged,
forgetting Cassandre, into an idyll of the most Longian kind.

[1] Belloc, *The Four Men.*

§2

Her name was Marie du Pin, or Dupin, and she was a farmer's or innkeeper's daughter—*simple païsante*, says Antoine de Baïf who knew her. Her age, like that of Cassandre and one or two more of Ronsard's loves at first meeting, was fifteen. He himself was now thirty, and, as he had recently complained to the Muses his task-mistresses in a fine dialogue I shall set down in due course, already greying at the temples and noting with dismay the first recession of his hair.

> *Pour avoir trop aimé vostre bande inégale,*
> *Muses, qui defiez (ce dites vous) le Temps,*
> *J'ay les yeux tout battus, la face toute pasle,*
> *Le chef grison et chauve, et je n'ay que trente ans.*[1]

If true, this need not have detracted much from his charm; he was tall and strong, graceful and vigorous. The effect on the rustic Marie of this masterful gentleman can be judged from most of the verse she inspired in him, which is gay, fresh, and tender, admirably suited to a country idyll. At the elbow of every good poet in love walks his Daemon, discreetly suggesting, like a valet, what his Muse should wear that day. A simple confection in *vert champêtre*, one might describe the garb of Ronsard's Muse for this occasion; one of those gowns nevertheless whose simplicity is created by great art. Evidently his flattering attentions and obvious passion sweep little Marie off her feet. She does not know she is assisting the first poet of France in a new artistic experiment, and, did she know, would probably not be interested. Marie has two sisters, Antoinette and Anne. It would have been interesting to overhear her confidences at night, before and after the bedroom candle is blown out, when the attractive but somewhat overpowering seigneur from the Vendômois has said his say and unwillingly retired. One has a suspicion, as with Meredith's rustic charmer in *Love in the Valley*, that a certain amount of giggling goes on. . . .

[1] Having too well loved your assorted company, Muses—you who, you say, defy Time—I find my eyes dulled, my face pale, my head greying and bald; and I am only thirty.

Marie is a dainty, plump, charming little creature as Ronsard
escribes her. Her cheeks are like a May rose, her hair somewhere
etween brown and chestnut, curling cunningly round her pretty
ars; her breasts—he is permitted to salute them, simultaneously
vith her lips—remind him of apples and the first buds of Spring.
'or her sweet sake he hides all his erudition away and sings the
:ind of song a country girl can understand.

> *Ma maistresse est toute angelette*
> *Toute belle fleur nouvellette,*
> *Toute mon gracieux acueil,*
> *Toute ma petite brunette,*
> *Toute ma doulce mignonette,*
> *Toute mon cœur, toute mon oeil . . .*
> *Toute miel, toute reguelyce,*
> *Toute ma petite malice,*
> *Toute ma ioye et ma langueur,*
> *Toute ma petite Angevine,*
> *Ma toute simple et toute fine,*
> *Toute mon âme, et tout mon cœur.*[1]

A posy of wild flowers gathered from the nearest hedgerow,
dewy and delightful. There is, perhaps, one puzzling line as he
repeats it to her:

> *Toute ma grace et ma Charite . . .*

One can see Marie's puzzled frown as she asks her Pierre what
on earth that word means. " Charite." Not " charity?" He bites
his lip, belike. Scholarship has slipped in, past his guard. He must
be careful. It is a Greek word, he probably explains, slightly dashed,
meaning something graceful, lovely. *Greek?* Ah! What a funny
word to use about a girl! Why can't people talk French? Greek
sounds so silly. She likes him to make up nice poetry about her,
though. What was that other one Pierre told her yesterday?

> *Bon jour mon cœur, bon jour ma doulce vie . . .*

Can it be that there are moments, fleeting spasm-like moments,
when Dorat's most brilliant pupil would like to knock this charming

[1] Untranslatable.

rustic head sharply once, twice, against the tree they are sitting
under? No, no. The strange feeling has already gone.

> *Bon jour mon cœur, bon jour ma doulce vie,*
> *Bon jour mon œil, bon jour ma chere amye,*
> *Hé bon jour ma toute belle,*
> *Mes delices, mon amour,*
> *Mon doulx printemps, ma doulce fleur nouvelle,*
> *Mon doulx plaisir, ma doulce colombelle,*
> *Mon passereau, ma gente tourterelle,*
> *Bon jour ma doulce rebelle.*[1]

I think he did not recite these pretty things to Marie, but sang
them; they trip to dainty little tunes in the head as one reads them.
She could not but have been flattered, whether or not she knew
that her poet had already taken his friends into his confidence,
and that all France would read in print, in due course, of his farewell to Cassandre and high Petrarchian worship and his infatuation
for

> *. . . une autre en ce païs d'Anjou*
> *Où maintenant l'Amour me detient sous le jou.*[2]

Some of France will also wonder, perhaps, whether his new
love or his new lyrical experiments were engrossing the poet more
as he proclaimed his decision to adopt for Marie

> *. . . un beau stille bas,*
> *Populaire et plaisant, ainsi qu'a fait Tibulle,*
> *L'ingenieux Ovide et le docte Catulle.*[3]

But I doubt if any echo of this would ever reach the farmer's
daughter of Bourgeuil, who probably never opened any book
but a prayer-book in her life. Meanwhile the course of true love

---

[1] Good day, my heart; good day, my sweet life; good day, apple of my eye; good day,
my sweet love; ha! good day, my most beautiful; my delight, my beloved, my sweet
Spring, my sweet fresh flower, my sweet pleasure, my sweet little dove, my sparrow, my
charming turtle-dove; good day, my sweet rebel!

[2] . . . another fair in this province of Anjou,
Where Love now holds me in his yoke.

[3] . . . a fine simple style, popular and pleasing, such as has been used by Tibullus, and
the ingenious Ovid, and the learned Catullus.

as not running quite so smoothly as it might have done. Ronsard's
tentions, of which he made no secret, are expressed with dis-
ming frankness in a piece in the *Nouvelle Continuation des Amours*
556) in which, turning on his late idol Petrarch, he allows
imself an impatient shrug.

> *Ou bien il jouissoit de sa Laurette, ou bien*
> *Il estoit un grand fat d'aymer sans avoir rien.* [1]

Pierre does not intend thus to be disappointed by Marie; but
he conquest of rustic virtue seems to be not so easy as it appears
rom the text-books. Marie has a temper of her own which resents
ne or two rivals, past and present, whose praises she apparently
has frequently to endure, Cassandre's first and foremost.

> *Marie, à tous les coups vous me venez reprendre*
> *Que je suis trop leger, et me dites tousjours*
> *Quand je vous veus baiser, que j'aille à ma Cassandre,*
> *Et tous jours m'appellez inconstant en amours . . .* [2]

The unknown Janne seems to be in circulation also at this
time ("*Janne me tient aussi dans les liens d'amour*", remarks the
poet casually in passing), and may have supplied matter for a few
more tiffs. Ronsard's dewy little Angevin rose is no ninny. With
all the freedoms she permits, a strong streak of prudence is manifest
in her, from the evidence of Ronsard's own chafings, happy as the
Marie-sequence otherwise is. Whether this was due exclusively
to impregnable virtue drawing a firm ultimate line, one cannot
discover. Over the lovemaking of Ronsard and Marie looms a
perpetual shadow, large, firm, square, and wakeful: the shadow
of Madame Dupin. Only once does Ronsard mention the existence
of this excellent woman; with no enthusiasm, *et pour cause*, as
the columnists say. It is not too much to assume that long before

---

[1] Either he enjoyed his Laurette, or else
He was a great simpleton to love for nothing.

[2] Marie, at every turn you keep accusing me
Of being too fickle, and you keep telling me,
When I want to kiss you, to go to my Cassandre,
And daily you call me inconstant in love . . .

Madame Mère's single hawk-like swoop, her unseen influence h
foiled him ; nor do I shrink from the temptation to listen a mome
to a voice which may often have been raised in the Angevin *pat*
of an evening by the kitchen fire, shrill as Mrs. Poyser's and
unescapable.

" . . . a fine gentleman, I'll be bound! Nearly old enough to
your father, and him a priest into the bargain! "
   " I've told you fifty times already he's not a——"
   " That's what he tells *you*, my girl."

This point cleared up for the fifty-first time, I hear the voic
of Madame Mère proceeding to Theme No. 2.

   " Well, if he isn't one he ought to be, that's all." (Silence.
   " And I suppose if anything happens he'll marry you ? " (Silence.
   " Answer me, miss! "
   " Nothing's *going* to happen."
   " Oh, no! Of course not! You go carrying on this way, my
girl, and before you're much older——"
   " Oh, for heaven's sake, mother! "
   " You mark my words! When I was your age " (etc., etc.)

How often farm-kitchens all over the world have echoed to
dialogues, or monologues, much like this the recording angels
know. Were this not a sober chronicle of reality it would be
amusing to embroider this theme, even summoning up the
conseil de famille, that dread summary tribunal of French family
life, and evoking a glimpse of the Clan Dupin, to its uttermost
aunt-by-marriage-third-removed, disapprovingly engaged in trying
the case of Marie. I am aware that bourgeois respectability was
not quite the fetish in the sixteenth century that it is nowadays,
and Marie seems to have lived under no great maternal discipline.
But on the only occasion, apparently, when Madame Dupin was
present to observe the trend of events for herself, she certainly
took swift and decisive action. If I have unwittingly made her
even for a moment a figure of romance, I ask Madame's pardon.
   From the long narrative poem called *Le Voyage de Tours* it
seems that some time between 1555 and 1560 (Ronsard never

roubles to date these things) a cousin of Marie's was married at
Tours. The wedding-feast was held in the leafy little island of
St. Cosme in the Loire, now joined to the mainland. To this
festivity Ronsard and his friend Antoine de Baïf, whose rustic
love Francine is also to be present, set off joyously one April
morning, carolling like larks; two gay Arcadians, Pierrot and
Thoinet. The feast no doubt resembled those traditional rustic
wedding-feasts common in the remote French provinces even
to-day. One sees the trestle-tables under the apple-trees, the rows
of ruddy, shining, congested faces, the village fiddler sawing
briskly away (to-day he plays the accordion, alas), the serious
eaters, with napkins tucked well into their necks, the bride and
groom giggling together, or stiffly solemn in their finery, the
village funny man proposing some toast full of artless *gauloiserie*.
One hears the guffaws, the modest titters, the noisy applause, the
pop of corks, the clash of cutlery; one sees the rustic heads awag,
the periodical digs in rustic ribs, the uplifted glasses, the flourished
bottles. Late in the afternoon the tables are cleared away, the
fiddler strikes up a *branle* or a *gigue*, and Pierrot and Thoinet leap
for their loves amid the jostling throng.

> *Là Francine dansoit, de Thoinet le soucy,*
> *Là Marion balloit, qui fust le mien aussi . . .*[1]

And when the first dance is over, having haled their sweethearts
to some more secluded spot, the two shepherds begin to ply their
suits alternately, according to the best models of the *bergerie*
recently made fashionable by Jacopo Sannazaro in Italy, and soon
to conquer all Europe and inspire Sidney in England and Monte-
mayor in Spain, among others, to the daintiest kind of pseudo-
bucolics. But hardly has the shepherd Thoinet finished his plaint—
alas! it moves his heartless nymph only to laughter—and the shepherd Pierrot opened his mouth, than the shadow of Madame Dupin
suddenly materialises and swoops. No doubt her eye has rarely
left those two fascinating gentlemen since their arrival. The disconcerting efficiency of Madame is described by Pierrot with
significant brevity:

[1] There Francine danced, the torment of Thoinet; there Marie danced, who was my
own. . .

> *J'ouvrois desja la levre après Thoinet, pour dire*
> *De combien Marion estoit encores pire,*
> *Quand j'avise sa mère en haste gagner l'eau,*
> *Et sa fille emmener avecq elle au basteau.*[1]

Adieu, Arcadia! Pierrot has nothing to do now but strain his
eyes after her vanishing boat as the river breezes swell its sails,
and to pray all the naiads of Loire to give it safe passage to Bourgeuil. A trivial enough incident; indeed, the whole Marie episode
viewed objectively is trivial enough. The simple maid wearies before
long of her impetuous literary lover and his perpetual demands.
A more attractive rival looms on the horizon and Ronsard tears
his thinning hair.

> *Je pleure, je me deulx, je suis plein de martyre,*
> *Je fais mille sonets et me romps le cerveau,*
> *Et si je suis haï; un amoureux nouveau*
> *Gaigne tousjours ma place, et je ne l'ose dire.*[2]

The beggar-maid has rejected King Cophetua. The village
beauty, instead of pining away and dying under the weight of his
magnificence, has sent the Lord of Burleigh packing. A mildly
comic situation, which would not lack banality had the magician
Ronsard not turned all his dross to gold. Having lost his Marie,
his passion becomes purified and sublimated. He idealises her in
memory, she becomes to him the spirit of springtime, of flowers,
of youth, of Anjou; and when, having long since forgotten her,
as he forgot Cassandre, he hears some ten years later that she is
dead, his pain wells up again and he mourns her in that lovely
pagan elegy, *Comme on void sur la branche au mois de May la rose,*
one of the great poems of the world, which I have already set down,
and in a whole sequence of laments.

> *O beaux yeux, qui m'estiez si cruels et si doux!*
> *Je ne me puis lasser de repenser en vous . . .*[3]

[1] I was just opening my mouth after Thoinet, to say how much more cruel Marie was,
when I perceive her mother hurrying down to the river, taking her daughter with her to
the boat.

[2] I weep, I lament, I am full of torments, I make a thousand sonnets and rack my brains,
and yet I am hated; a new lover constantly occupies my place, and I dare say nothing.

[3] O lovely eyes, which were to me so cruel and so kind,
I cannot be weary of remembering you . . .

His dreams are haunted by Death, which has ravished his
~autiful one :

> *Je songeois, sous l'obscur de la nuit endormie,*
> *Qu'un sepulche entr' ouvert s'apparaissoit à moy :*
> *La Mort gisoit dedans, toute pasle d'effroy ;*
> *Dessus estoit ecrit : Le tombeau de Marie.*
> *Espouvanté du songe, en sursaut je m'escrie :*
> *Amour est donc sujet à nostre humaine loy !* . . .[1]

And in a growing ecstasy of emotion and recollection and
~ain, he apotheosises the rustic maid who had turned away from
~im, and places her effigy on a pedestal in a riverside Temple of
~ove.

> *O ma belle Angevine, ô ma douce Marie,*
> *Mon oeil, mon coeur, mon sang, mon esprit, et ma vie* . . .
> *Si j'estois un grand roy, pour eternel exemple*
> *De fidelle amitié, je bastirois un temple*
> *Dessur le bord de Loire, et ce temple auroit nom*
> *Le Temple de Ronsard et de sa Marion :*
> *De marbre parien seroit vostre effigie* . . .[2]

All who have ever read the songs he made for her (he says)
would then hail Marie as a goddess—ah, that Love had joined
them together in the tomb, that every lover's mouth might henceforth sing of them! But whatever Heaven wills, at least his verse
will tell all men a thousand years hence how for six years he loved
her more than his own heart.

[1] I dreamed, as I slept in the dark of night,
That an opened sepulchre appeared to me ;
Death lay therein, all pale with terror,
Above there was written : " The tomb of Marie."
Quaking from this dream I started up crying :
"Is Love, then, subject to our human destiny ? . . . "

[2] O my fair one of Anjou, O my sweet Marie,
Apple of my eye, my heart, my blood, my spirit and my life,
Were I a great king, as an eternal symbol
Of faithful love I would build a temple
On the banks of the Loire, and this temple should be called
The Temple of Ronsard and his Marion ;
Your effigy should be of Parian marble . . .

Ronsard

Or il adveindra ce que le Ciel voudra,
Si est-ce que ce livre aprés mille ans dira
Aux hommes et au temps et à la renommée
Que je vous ay six ans plus que mon coeur aimée ![1]

Thus can a great poet transmute his most hackneyed adventure

Changeons propos, c'est trop chanté d'amours, sings Clémen
Marot, beginning his Vineyard Song; let us change the tune
we've sung enough of love. With a sigh of relief we perceive tha
this rural dalliance has not been the only preoccupation of Pierr
de Ronsard at this time. Love-making undoubtedly stimulated hi
powers (it is the old excuse of literary men), and during these
lovesick years he has written and published (1555) those *Hymne*
in which he triumphs in a new inspiration: the music of th
Spheres, Death, Eternity, the vast cosmic theme handled at lengt
in sonorous alexandrines. It is not claimed by Ronsard's devoutes
modern admirers that the *Hymnes* are an invariable masterpiece
Their rhythms are lofty and sure, their melody noble; but they
are tinged intermittently with a shallow pantheism in the Renaissance taste, the flashing lines are none too frequent, the rhetoric
is often heavy. But such organ-passages as this from the Hymn
to the Stars, dedicated to his one-time enemy Mellin de St. Gelais,
show the familiar power.

Je vous salue, enfans de la premiere Nuict !
Heureux Astres divins, qui par tout se conduit,
Pendant que vous tournez vostre dance ordonnée
Au Ciel, j'accompliray ça-bas la destinée
Qu'il vous pleut me verser, bonne ou mauvaise, alors
Que mon ame immortelle entra dedans mon corps . . .[2]

[1] So, come what Heaven will, at least this book a thousand years hence will witness to
men and to the ages and to your fame, that for six years I loved you more than my own
heart.

[2] Children of the primal Night, I salute you,
   Divine and happy Stars, through whom everything is ordered,
   While you whirl in your appointed dances
   In Heaven, I will fulfil the destiny here below
   That it pleased you to send me, good or evil
   When my immortal soul entered into my body . . .

The astrological whimsy stamps him very much a man of his period, that of Nostradamus and Dee. In the Hymn of the Dæmons there is a macabre little night-piece, later removed, embroidering with imaginative zest another of those goblin superstitions which make the Renaissance age seem nearly as advanced as our own. The poet encounters at midnight a demon hunt, the *wilde Jäger* of German balladry :

> *Un soir vers la minuict, guidé de la jeunesse*
> *Qui commande aux amans, j'allois voir ma maistresse*
> *Tout seul outre le Loir, et passant un destour*
> *Joignant une grand' croix, dedans un carrefour,*
> *J'ouy, ce me sembloit, une aboyante chasse*
> *De chiens qui me suyvoit pas à pas à la trace,*
> *Je vy auprès de moy sur un grand cheval noir*
> *Un homme qui n'avoit que les os, à le voir,*
> *Me tendant une main pour me monter en crope ;*
> *J'avisay tout-au-tour une effroyable trope*
> *De picqueurs, qui couroient un Ombre . . .*[1]

It is the old midnight terror of the woods, related with tales of the *Loup-Garou* on winter nights round blazing farmhouse hearths : the demon huntsmen and their shadow-pack sweeping past in chase of a gibbering shade, the skeleton Master of Hell-hounds blowing his ghostly horn with " Gone away! " and " Forrard on! " Ronsard sees they are hunting a lately-dead usurer of wicked life. His blood freezes, though he bears a heart *qui naturellement n'est sujet à la peur*, and he whips out his sword, like Æneas in the underworld. A peasant without the advantages of a classical education would have made the sign of the Cross. Ronsard hews at the shadowy rout, and it vanishes.[2]

[1] One night, towards midnight, guided by the ardency
Which orders lovers, I went to see my mistress,
Alone, beyond the Loir ; and while passing along a winding way
 Leading to a tall cross, at a cross-roads,
I heard (I thought) the baying of a hunt
Of hounds following my traces, step by step ;
I saw near me, mounted on a great black horse,
A man with nothing but his bones, by the look of him,
Holding out a hand to take me on his crupper ;
I perceived all around me a frightful rout
Of huntsmen, in chase of a Shade . . .

[2] This is the Platonic method. Demons, says Plato, are susceptible to and afraid of blows, cuts, and wounds.

The Hymn to Death, which any Roman Stoic might approve save for its recurringly Christian flavour, is notable for that mighty final salute :

> *Je te salue, heureuse et profitable Mort !*
> *Des extremes douleurs medecin et confort :*
> *Quand mon heure viendra, Deësse, je te prie*
> *Ne me laisse long temps 'languir en maladie,*
> *Tourmenté dans un lict ; mais puis qu'il faut mourir,*
> *Donne moy que soudain je te puisse encourir,*
> *Ou pour l'honneur de Dieu, ou pour servir mon Prince,*
> *Navré d'une grand' playe au bord de ma province.*[1]

These lines powerfully affected Ronsard's contemporaries. The crowd surrounding the Mercat Cross in Edinburgh will shortly hear them read by Messire Pierre de Boscosel de Chastelard as the waiting headsman leans on his axe ; for that imprudent Calvinist and would-be lover of a Queen refused all other consolation. "He held in his hand the Hymns of M. de Ronsard", notes Brantôme, "and for his eternal consolation he read all through the Hymn to Death . . . availing himself of no other spiritual manual, nor of any minister or confessor."[2] This incident may serve as one example of the secure fame which has come to Pierre de Ronsard. He is now acknowledged Prince of Poets, described as "divine" by brother-poets even outside the Brigade, a friend of the King, the lion of such brilliant salons as that of Jean de Morel, Erasmus' disciple, with his three lovely blue-stocking daughters, and the hospitable Jean de Brinon, a Mæcenas who ruined himself (how admirably!) by giving too-lavish entertainment to the children of the Muses ; a literary conqueror of already European reputation in whose face praise is dashed day and night (as Johnson said of Garrick) by the greatest in the land, by foreign notables whose

---

[1] I salute thee, happy and profitable Death,
Healer and comfort of final pain!
When my hour shall come, Goddess, I pray thee
Leave me not long to languish in sickness,
Tormented in my bed ; but since I have to die,
Give me that I may succumb to thee quickly,
Whether for the honour of God, or serving my King,
Stricken with a great wound on the frontier of my province.

[2] *Recueil des Dames : La Reyne d'Escosse.* Chastelard, himself a poet of sorts, had presented Mary, on Ronsard's behalf, with Ronsard's sonnets of regret.

isits to Paris are judged incomplete without a call on the cele-
rated M. de Ronsard, by everybody save, perhaps, a rosy-cheeked
ebellious chit away in Anjou for whom his jealous heart still aches.

And chief among Ronsard's admirers is a Marie of nobler
blood, that Queen who inspired him with a love more pure and
worshipful than any other woman he has glorified.

§3

Ainsi qu'on voit demy-blanche et vermeille
Naistre l'Aurore, et Vesper sur la nuict,
Ainsi sur toute en beauté nompareille
Des Escossois la Princesse reluict.
(Ronsard to Mary, Queen of Scots)

Just as we see, half rosy and half white,
Dawn and the Morning Star dispel the night,
In beauty thus beyond compare impearled
The Queen of Scotland rises on the world.
(Maurice Baring)

Her fair pale face looks out from a convulsed background of
dust and heat, controversy and clamour, rage and venom. In
death as in life she is never secure from hate, from her ex-tutor
Buchanan's vindictiveness to the frigid prejudice of the last don
hired to write in the *Encyclopaedia Britannica* ; nor has she ever
lacked hot and chivalrous lovers.

It is no purpose of mine to essay a fresh solution of her agelong
enigma, even to rally one more sword to this pearl of Scotland.
I shall attempt only to present the girl Mary Stuart whom Pierre
de Ronsard knew and adored, like every other man in France
who came under her spell, and nearly every man in Scotland.
She can certainly be counted among the seven great loves of
Ronsard ; his bedazzled praise of her is no Court formula, nor is
he alone in crying " *O belle et plus que belle !* " " The fynneste she
that ever was ", writes Thomas Randolph, Elizabeth's ambassador,
years later. " We need no lanterns," says Chastelard to Brantôme
on the deck of the Queen's galley returning to Scotland, as night
swoops on the Channel and the sailors busy themselves with
torches, " for the eyes of this Queen suffice to light up the whole

sea with their lovely fire." The last cry of Chastelard as insolence
and imbecility bring him to the axe will be " *Adieu, la plus belle
et la plus cruelle princesse du monde!* " Certainly this gallant and
lovely one was a nonpareil; such a Queen, as stout Samuel
Johnson told the Scots heatedly two hundred years later, as every
man of any gallantry of spirit would have sacrificed his life for;
such a Queen as moved Swinburne a century after Johnson to
cry:

> They never saw your lip's bright bow,
>   Your swordbright eyes,
> The bluest of heavenly things below
>   The skies.

These eyes are strong magic and cannot, apparently, be accurately
described. In the Clouet and the Edinburgh and all other contemporary portraits they are velvet-dark and lustrous. It is said
that when Mary smiled they flashed delicious fires and changed
colour—perhaps with flashes of Swinburne's blue—like opals,
shining mysteriously even when she was grave.

They smiled frequently on Pierre de Ronsard. "Above all,"
says Brantôme, " she delighted in poetry and poets, and most of
all in M. de Ronsard, M. du Bellay, and M. de Maisonfleur,[1] who
have made such fine poems and elegies for her . . . which I have
often seen her read to herself in France and in Scotland, with
tears in her eyes and sighs from her heart." We are fortunate in
having such an observer as Pierre de Bourdeille, Seigneur de
Brantôme; the Gascon knew a phoenix when he met one.

To Ronsard, who had lived in her native land and served in
the household of her mother, blue-eyed Marie de Lorraine, the
admiration of this tall, pale, slender, elegant, gracefully vivacious
royal creature was a perpetual enchantment. The first glimpse of
her was probably vouchsafed him during his first days at Court,
when Mary Stuart was completing her education under the care of
the Guises, her uncles. Her romantic, troubled life from babyhood
enhanced her spell. Everyone at Court knew how, before she
could prattle, England and Scotland were at each other's throats
because of her; how an English invasion had followed her mother's

---

[1] The undistinguished Maisonfleur's surviving poems do not celebrate the Queen of Scots.

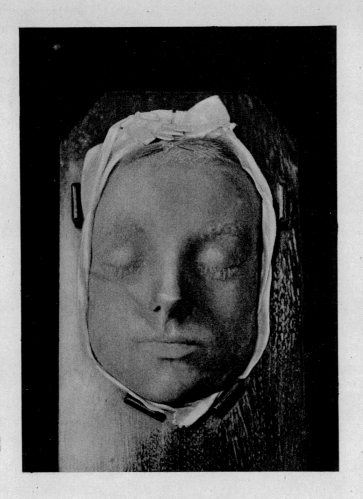

Mary, Queen of Scots
(*from the deathmask at Holyrood Palace*)

fusal of Henry VIII's peremptory offer of his son's hand in
marriage; how a new Franco-Scottish alliance had resulted;
how the child Mary had been hidden away for safety on an island
in Loch Menteith; how, at the age of six, she had been smuggled
oversea to France, just escaping an English fleet sent out to kidnap
her. Now, at the age of fifteen, this slender Scottish beauty, educated
by the nuns of St. Germain-en-Laye (dear little town, so haunted
by Stuart ghosts) could prattle French and a trifle of Italian, so
that it was a pleasure to listen, and could sew, sing, embroider,
touch the lute and virginals with a fairly skilful hand, dance with
grace, ride a good horse, and rhyme in French as prettily as any
high lady of fashion. Brantôme says that at thirteen she recited to
Henri II and the Court a speech in Latin of her own composition,
defending women's rights to a liberal education : there is certainly
a manuscript-book in the Bibliothèque Nationale containing a
number of Latin themes, in her own hand. Her waywardness is
already the talk of the Court. At her wedding to the sickly Dauphin
François (whom she dearly loves : the two young things can
often be seen sitting in secluded corners of the Louvre, whispering
together) at Notre-Dame in 1557 she insists on wearing white, the
official mourning-colour of the Queens of France. She insists also
at intervals, the spirited lass, on speaking the Scottish tongue,
" *qui de soy*," explains Brantôme, careless of the Auld Alliance,
" *est fort rurale, barbare, mal sonnante et scéante* "—" which of itself
is extremely rustic, barbarian, ill-sounding and ungraceful ".
She speaks it so charmingly that it sounds *très-belle et très-agréable*,
though (adds Brantôme) that does not apply to others. Further,
she insists more than once on appearing at Court in the garb of
her native Highlands, " *habillée à la sauvage (comme je l'ay veue)
et à la barbaresque mode des sauvages de son pays* "—" dressed like a
savage (as I have seen her), in the barbarous fashion of the savages
of her country". There is a popular contemporary French wood-
cut called *La Sauvage d'Escosse*, showing a woman wearing this
Highland costume, a voluminous mantle of roughly-dressed
skins (one would have expected a plaid) covering the entire body
except for the ankles and feet, which seem to be bare. Such a
Red Indian masquerade cannot greatly have enchanted the Queen-
Mother Catherine de Médicis, that stout martinet, who already saw

Ronsard

little cause to welcome the ascendancy of this fascinating foreigner
niece of the dangerous Guises. Brantôme hastens to add that even
in this travesty the lovely young *Royne-Dauphine* (she was already
Queen of France in 1559) looked a goddess. He is so much under
her spell, indeed, that he reproduces some of her French verses
which are no better or worse than the other forty-odd sets of verses
of hers which survive.[1]

The tributes laid at Mary Stuart's feet by Ronsard might to a
large extent, borrowing from Gautier, be described as a *symphonie
en blanc majeur.* Her luminous lilial whiteness, *clarté*, is the poet's
perpetual wonder; he compares her constantly to the dawn.

> *O belle et plus que belle et agréable Aurore,*
> *Qui avez delaissé vostre terre Escossoise*
> *Pour venir habiter la region Françoise*
> *Qui de vostre clarté maintenant se decore . . .*[2]

He sees the eighteen-year-old widow, after the death of François
II in 1560, walking alone and disconsolate in the pleached alleys
of Fontainebleau, among swans less white than she.

> *Et vostre main des plus belles la belle*
> *N'a rien sinon sa blancheur naturelle,*
> *Et vos longs doigts, cinq rameaux inegaux,*
> *Ne sont pompeux de bagues ni d'anneaux,*
> *Et la beauté de vostre gorge vive*
> *N'a pour carcan que sa blancheur naive.*
> *Un crespe long, subtil et delié,*
> *Pli contre pli retors et replié*
> *Habit de deuil, vous sert de couverture*
> *Depuis le chef jusques à la ceinture . . .*[3]

[1] The one by which she is chiefly known in anthologies, beginning *Adieu, plaisant pays
de France,* is the work of an eighteenth-century hack.
[2] O fair and more than fair and pleasing Dawn, who have left your Scottish land to inhabit
the land of France, now adorned with your brightness . . .

[3] And your hand, fairest of the fair,
Has naught but its own whiteness,
And your long fingers, five unequal branches,
Bear no pomp of rings or gauds,
And the beauty of your thrilling bosom
Has no necklace but its snowy simplicity:
A long veil, subtly flowing,

He is writing now after her departure from France, gazing at the portrait of herself she gave him, which hangs in his study, next to the portrait of François II. For her doom has already begun. Her boy husband is hardly dead before the Guises are scheming to marry her to Don Carlos, heir to the Spanish Crown, and the Queen-Mother, perturbed and furious, packs her home to Scotland within twelve months.[1] Brantôme's description of the voyage is celebrated. We see Mary Stuart bidding farewell at Calais to the weeping Court company which has travelled with her, and going aboard her galley in tears. The wind rises as they leave port, the oars are shipped, the sails set; the young Queen leans on her elbows on the poop, her eyes fixed on the shore, weeping and saying continually, "Adieu, France! Adieu, France!" As night begins to fall on the Channel her servants ask if she will take some food and repose; her only answer is, "*Adieu donc, ma chère France, je ne vous verray jamais plus!*"—"Adieu then, my dear France, I shall never see you again." She refuses all but a light salad and will not go below, ordering them to make her a bed on the poop and to wake her at dawn, if the French coast is still visible. It is, for the wind drops. Dawn reveals a faint grey line on the horizon of a leaden sea. They wake her, and she rises on her bed, devouring the last of France with hungry eyes. And at last France fades, and she returns to her weeping. "*Adieu, la France! Cela est faict! Adieu, France! Je pense ne vous voir jamais plus!*"

"If she has had good winds," writes Catherine de Médicis to her daughter in Spain a week later, "she should be in Scotland by now."

§4

Ronsard did not forget this Queen, nor she Ronsard. Four years after her departure he will send her his newest volume by the hand of the French Ambassador, with a fine *Bergerie* dedicated to her. Much later, scanning some verses on Bothwell attributed to

---

Fold on fold twisted and wound,
Your mourning wear, serves you for covering
From head to waist . . .

[1] It should be added that envoys from Scotland, Darnley, the Bishop of Ross, and Bothwell among them, had come to her in France, begging her to return. Her own desire at this time was to enter a convent.

her by malicious tongues, he will agree with Brantôme that they are far too *grossiers et mal polis* to be the work of that fair gracious hand. Later yet, in 1578, after Elizabeth has imprisoned her guest he will write a sonnet of indignant chivalry crying shame on the Tudor crone and the indifferent French alike; and calling vainly for a rescue. Ronsard was long since aware, from the eyewitness accounts of Brantôme, that Mary Stuart had stepped into a strange new Scotland drained of joy and colour, swarming with black Genevan fanatics, a Scotland whose lords had abolished the Catholic religion throughout the Lowlands, and even part of the stubborn Highlands, in the year previous, 1560; a Scotland ruled by Knox, her relentless enemy. Full of omen, as Brantôme doubtless remarked, was her arrival in that dark fog which foiled the English squadron sent out to intercept her (nor did Knox himself fail to cry that the Queen had brought with her great Popish clouds of darkness and doom).

A raucous aubade of what the Gascon describes as " vile fiddles and little rebecks " from five or six hundred of the Edinburgh mob and the near-lynching of her chaplain a morning or two later were the next good omens, followed by Knox's violent attempt to forbid her hearing Mass in her chapel at Holyrood ; he would rather have an invasion by 10,000 Frenchmen, he roared. Well can one understand how, in those days, Mary Stuart would often retire to her inner cabinet after a day in which steely pride, irresolution, ice-cold courage, gentleness, craft, obduracy, prudence, rashness, pity and anger had swayed her by turns, and take up M. de Ronsard's sonnets, and read and dissolve in tears, as Brantôme says. She will still read them years later, in prison.

Ronsard has her portrait constantly before his eyes, he tells her. A costly vase engraved " To Ronsard, Apollo of the Muses' Fountain ", and bearing a Pegasus, and, now or later, a buffet worth two thousand crowns[1] were other tokens of her esteem.

He did not need these for a reminder : he evidently adored her, in a way to which even Cassandre had not inspired him. Unlike the passion of the lovesick fool Chastelard, whose mania for hiding under the Queen's bed, in a Holyrood swarming with

[1] M. Laumonier thinks this buffet was sent to him by Mary's secretary, Claude Nau, in her behalf, after his appeal to Elizabeth Tudor.

nox's spies, forced her at length to deliver him to justice,[1]
onsard's love for Mary Stuart is that of a man for a goddess.
ately Queen of France, she was still mistress of Touraine, his
ountryside, which had been given her for an appanage : strange
nat Ronsard never celebrates this. In his laments for her loss there
s a deep personal note one does not find in the laments of the lesser
rench poets courteously bewailing the departure of a comely
guest and one-time Queen; and his language is more beautiful.

> *Comme un beau pré despouillé de ses fleurs,*
> *Comme un tableau privé de ses couleurs,*
> *Comme le Ciel s'il perdoit ses estoiles,*
> *La mer ses eaux, la navire ses voiles,*
> *Un bois sa feuille, un antre son effroy,*
> *Un grand Palais la pompe de son Roy,*
> *Et un anneau sa perle precieuse,*
> *Ainsi perdra la France soucieuse*
> *Ses ornements, perdant la royauté*
> *Qui fust sa fleur, sa couleur, sa beauté . . .*[2]

He again depicts her mourning her sixteen-year-old king, like
a widowed dove weeping disconsolate in the woods. He denounces
cruel Fortune (one wonders how the masterful Queen-Mother, who
so summarily banished her, liked this) for depriving France of those
eyes which shame the stars of Heaven; and he cries aloud to
Scotland, wishing it were the floating isle of Delos, that it might
fly in advance of this queen's ship and never be overtaken.

> *Ha! je voudrois, Escosse, que tu pusses*
> *Errer ainsi que Dele, et que tu n'eusses*
> *Les pieds fermés au profond de la mer !*
> *Ha! je voudrois que tu pusses ramer,*
> *Ainsi que vole une barque poussée*

[1] Lethington's assertion to Mary that Chastelard was suborned by the Colignys to cast a stain on her honour, and thus spoil her marriage prospects, is interesting, and possibly not without foundation. Mary, after her first anger, tried to save his life, but the escape-plan miscarried.

[2] Like a fair meadow despoiled of its flowers, like a painting robbed of its colours, like the sky bereft of stars, the sea of waters, a ship of sails, a wood of its leaves, a cavern of its terror, a great palace without the splendour of its king, a ring without its precious stone—thus will mourning France lose her ornaments, losing that royalty which was her flower, her colour, and her beauty . . .

> *De mainte rame à ses flancs elancée,*
> *Pour t'enfuir longue espace devant*
> *Le tard vaisseau qui t'iroit poursuivant,*
> *Sans décharger jamais à ton rivage*
> *La belle Royne à qui tu dois hommage . . .*[1]

Twenty years later Ronsard will still speak to Mary Stuart in her prison of Fotheringhay, of the day when the winds bore her from a weeping land. Now that those starry eyes, those alabaster brows, that red mouth (a garden of carnations), that ivory bosom, those long, frail, delicate hands, that sweet voice, which could move rocks and woods—now that all this beauty has been reft from France, he cries, how can poets sing? Since her departure the Muses are dumb. And the old haunting theme reappears:

> *Tout ce qui est de beau ne se garde longtemps,*
> *Les roses et les lys ne regnent qu'un printemps . . .*[2]

Now nothing remains to him,

> *Sinon le desplaisir qui me remet sans cesse*
> *Au cœur le souvenir d'une telle Princesse.*[3]

And finally, in his finest sonnet (1578) to this Queen, Ronsard first addresses Mary Stuart herself with all the old thrilled chivalrous worship, as it were kneeling, as ever, at her feet:

> *Encores que la mer de bien loin nous separe,*
> *Si est-ce que l'esclair de vostre beau soleil,*
> *De vostre œil qui n'a point au monde de pareil,*
> *Jamais loin de mon cœur par le temps ne s'egare . . .*[4]

---

[1] Ah! Would, Scotland, that you could wander like Delos, that your roots were not set in the depths of the sea! Ah! would you could speed, like a ship sped by a thousand oars sweeping from its sides, and fly afar before the slow vessel pursuing you, without once receiving on your shore that lovely Queen to whom you owe homage . . .

[2] Everything of beauty lasts not long,
Roses and lilies have but one spring to reign . . .

[3] Only the sorrow which brings back unceasingly to my heart the memory of such a Princess . . .

[4] Though now the sea holds us far apart, the brightness of your lovely sun, of your eye, which has no rival in the world, is never banished from my heart by time . . .

…hen suddenly flaming into indignation, he turns to her gaoler
…izabeth, and then to the one-time chivalry of France :

> *Royne, qui enfermez une Royne si rare,*
> *Adoucissez vostre ire et changez de conseil ;*
> *Le soleil se levant et allant au sommeil*
> *Ne voit point en la terre un acte si barbare.*
>
> *Peuple, vous forlignez, aux armes nonchalant,*
> *De vos ayeux Renauld, Lancelot et Rollant,*
> *Qui prenoient d'un grand cœur pour les dames querelle,*
>
> *Les gardoient, les sauvoient, où vous n'avez, François,*
> *Ny osé regarder ny toucher le harnois*
> *Pour oster de servage une Royne si belle !*[1]

But no knightly French swords flash out at the poet's scorn,
…nd the Queen of Scotland goes at length to her death, one year
…fter Ronsard's lute had been stilled for ever. Brantôme reveals
…hat although English malice refused her a confessor and the last aids
of her religion, for which she undoubtedly died[2]—a revenge since
developed and perfected by the Nazis—this malice failed. She had
with her, devoutly guarded, a consecrated Host, conveyed to her
long since, for just such an emergency, by St. Pius V. So, fortified
by the Last Sacrament, she passed regally to the scaffold, disdaining
the importunate babble of the Anglican Dean of Peterborough, and
three strokes of the axe ended her earthly troubles.

§5

For this interlude I have chosen to begin with two pieces written
in vastly different moods. In the first the poet, secure of fame,

[1] Queen, you who imprison a Queen so rare,
Soften your wrath and change your mind,
The sun from its rising to its sinking to sleep
Views no more barbarous act on this earth!
People, your degenerate lack of will to fight
Shames your forebears, Renauld, Lancelot, and Roland,
Who with glad hearts took up ladies' wrongs
And guarded them, and rescued them—where you, Frenchmen,
Have not dared to look at or to touch your arms,
To save from slavery such a lovely Queen!

[2] A martyr, says Brantôme ; for " it is not the pain but the cause which makes the martyr".
Many have agreed.

girds playfully at the Muses, his sweet tyrants. For some reas
unknown Ronsard banished this charming dialogue from
final collected edition. The final stanza is memorable.

RONSARD

Pour avoir trop aimé vostre bande inégale,
Muses, qui defiez (ce dites vous) le Temps,
J'ay les yeux tout battus, la face toute pasle,
Le chef grison et chauve, et je n'ay que trente ans.

MUSES

Au nocher qui sans cesse erre sur la marine
Le teint noir appartient ; le soldat n'est pas beau
Sans estre tout poudreux ; qui courbe la poitrine
Sur nos livres, est laid s'il n'a pasle le peau.

RONSARD

Mais quelle recompence aurois-je tant suivre
Vos danses nuict et jour, un laurier sur le front ?
Et ce pendant les ans aux quels je deusse vivre
En plaisirs et en jeux comme poudre s'en vont.

MUSES

Vous aurez, en vivant, une fameuse gloire,
Puis, quand vous serez mort, vostre nom fleurira,
L'âge, de siècle en siècle, aura de vous memoire:
Vostre corps seullement au tombeau pourrira.

RONSARD

O le gentil loyer ! Que sert au viel Homère,
Ores qu'il n'est plus rien, sous la tombe, là-bas,
Et qu'il n'a plus ny chef, ny bras, ny jambe entiere,
Si son renom fleurist ou s'il ne fleurist pas !

MUSES

Vous estes abusé. Le corps dessous la lame
Pourry ne sent plus rien, aussy ne luy en chaut,
Mais un tel accident n'arrive point à l'âme,
Qui sans matière vist immortelle là-haut.

Marie

RONSARD

Bien! Je vous suivray donc d'une face plaisante,
Dussé-je trespasser de l'estude vaincu,
Et ne fust-ce qu'à fin que la race suyvante
Ne me reproche point qu' oysif j'aye vescu.

MUSES

Velà saigement dit. Ceux dont la fantaisie
Sera religieuse et devote envers Dieu
Tousjours acheveront quelque grand poësie,
Et dessus leur renom la Parque n'aura lieu.[1]

But in the following piece we see him sunk in despondency, and perhaps in debt, disgusted to death with " the homely shepherd's slighted trade ". It is an ode published in 1554, two years before the preceding piece, and addressed to Jacques de Rubampré. I have compressed it slightly.

Puisque tost je dois reposer
Outre l'infernale rivière,
Hé! que me sert de composer
Autant de vers qu'a faict Homère?

Les vers ne me sauveront pas
Qu'ombre poudreuse je ne sente
Le faix de la tombe là-bas
S'elle est bien legere ou pesante.

[1] Ronsard : Having too well loved your assorted company, Muses—you who, you say, defy Time—I find my eyes dulled, my face pale, my head greying and bald ; and I am only thirty!

Muses : A tanned skin suits the mariner who wanders ceaselessly over the deep ; the soldier is not handsome unless blackened with powder ; he who bends his breast over our books is ill-favoured if his complexion is not pale.

Ronsard : But what should be my recompense for having thus followed your dancing night and day, with laurelled head ? Meanwhile the years I should be spending in pleasure and frolics blow away like powder.

Muses : You will have, in your lifetime, notable glory, and when you are dead your name will flower ; the ages, from century to century, will remember you ; only your flesh will moulder away in the tomb.

Ronsard : Oh! A fine reward ! What does it profit ancient Homer, now that he is no more, in his tomb yonder, having no more head or arms or legs entire, that his fame flourishes or otherwise ?

Muses : You err. The mouldered body under the stone feels no more, nor does it care ; but such an accident does not happen to the soul, which lives above, immortal, free from dross.

Ronsard : Good! I will follow you, then, with a smiling face, even if I perish vanquished by over-study, if only that posterity may not reproach me with having lived an idler.

Muses : That is well said. Those whose imaginings are devout and ordered towards God will always achieve great poetry, and Fate will have no power against their renown.

Ronsard

Suis-je meilleur qu'Anacréon,
Que Stesichore, ou Simonide?
Ou qu'Antimache, ou que Bion,
Que Philète ou que Bacchylide?

Toutesfois, bien qu'ils fussent Grecs,
Que leur servist ce beau langage,
Puisque les ans venus après
Ont mis en poudre leur ouvrage?

Doncque moi qui suis né François,
Faiseur de rimes maternelles,
Hé! dois-je esperer que ma voix
Surmonte des siècles les ailes?

Non, non, il faut mieux, Rubampré,
Son âge en trafiques dépendre,
Ou devant un Sénat pourpre
Pour de l'argent sa langue vendre,

Que de suyvre l'ocieux train
De cette pauvre Calliope,
Qui tousjours faict mourir de faim
Les meilleurs chantres de sa trope.[1]

[1] Since I must soon lie
Beyond the Infernal River,
What does it profit me to write
As many lines as Homer made?

Poetry will not save me
(A dusty shade) from feeling
The burden of my tombstone yonder,
Whether it lie heavy or light.

Am I a better poet than Anacreon?
Or Stesichorus, or Simonides?
Or Antimachus, or Bion,
Philetos or Bacchylides?

And then, though they were Greeks,
What did that lovely language do for them
Since the ages following
Have dispersed their works in dust?

So I, who am but a Frenchman,
A cobbler of rhymes in my maternal tongue—
Eh? Can I hope that my voice
Will rise on the wings of the ages

And here is the poet complaining of his imbecile public in a
nnet, full of tragicomic shrugs and lifted eyebrows and half-
umorous irritation, which Yeats echoed (" Dear Craoibhin
oibhin, look into our case ") during his tussles with the Abbey
heatre public. Ronsard addresses Pontus de Tyard and ends in
better temper than Yeats.

> *Tyard, on me blasmoit a mon commencement*
> *De quoy j'estois obscur au simple populaire ;*
> *Mais on dit aujourd 'huy que je suis au contraire,*
> *Et que je me demens parlant trop bassement.*
>
> *Toy de qui le labeur enfante doctement*
> *Des livres immortels, dis-moy, que dois-je faire ?*
> *Dis-moy (car tu sais tout) comme dois-je complaire*
> *A ce monstre testu, divers en jugement ?*
>
> *Quand je tonne en mes vers, il a peur de me lire :*
> *Quand ma voix se desenfle il ne faict qu'en medire ;*
> *Dis-moy de quel lien, force, tenaille ou clous*
>
> *Tiendray-je ce Prote qui se change a tous coups ?*
> *Tyard, je l'entends bien, il le faut laisser dire,*
> *Et nous rire de luy comme il se rit de nous.*[1]

The old cry of the baffled artist. It brings Ronsard very near
to us moderns to realise that he too was damned as a highbrow
and a lowbrow alternately.

> No, no. It is better, Rubampré,
> To spend one's life in business,
> Or to sell one's tongue for money
> Before a purple Senate,
>
> Than to follow the idle train
> Of poor Calliope,
> Who invariably allows the best singers of her troop
> To die of hunger.

[1] When I began, Tyard, they censured me as being too obscure for the commonalty;
to-day they say I am just the opposite, demeaning myself by using too popular speech. Tell
me, you whose learned labours produce immortal books, what must I do ? Tell me (for
you know it all), how am I to please this obstinate monster of such fickle taste ? When
my verses thunder, it is afraid to read me ; when I lower my voice it does nothing but
complain. Tell me, with what bonds, what forces, what pincers or nails can I hold this
Proteus, changing at every turn ? But I quite understand, Tyard. We must let it have its
say and laugh at it, as it laughs at us.

V

GENÈVRE

I could hardly be perswaded, before I had seen it, that the World could have afforded so marble-hearted and savage minded men, that for the onlie pleasure of murther would commit it.

(JOHN FLORIO, *Montaigne's Essayes.*)

. . . ce réveil de l'esprit juif et l'impur délire biblique que nous appelons ironiquement la Réforme.

(CHARLES MAURRAS, *Anthinéa.*)

§1

THE YEAR IS 1561. PIERRE DE RONSARD HAS JUST PUBLISHEI (December 1560) his first collected edition in four volumes, hi: great reputation is increasing, and the storm clouds are gathering thick and heavy over France.

" Civil war ", M. Jacques Bainville wrote some years ago, " is the vice of the Gauls." Mr. Belloc prefers : " Civil war is a standing function of the Gallic energy." The French Wars of Religion, which have moved addicts of Macaulay's school to romantic poetry and to prose hardly distinguishable ("History is a dramatic poem ", said the cynical Froude) were a conflict, in an age of savage energy, between two masses of Gauls of equal violence, either mass led by nobles of extreme ambition centred furiously on the control of the French Executive ; nor did either side lack the type of Gaul who loves fighting for its own sake.

It is valuable to get this upheaval in proper perspective, and especially to refrain as far as possible from regarding the adherents of the Reform in France as mild and holy psalm-singers wickedly oppressed and chivvied by a brutal Catholic tyranny. The note of the Reform in France from its beginnings is violence ; ostentatious parade, continuous provocation, abuse, threats, challenge, and later, armed menace, alliance with the enemies of France, German and English ; and above all, one must repeat, attempts to lay hands on the Crown. This important aspect of the Reform's

ctivities in France, often glossed over or understated, is the key
o the St. Bartholomew, that fearful business.

The aim of the Calvinist leaders was early demonstrated in the
abortive " Conspiracy of Amboise ", 1560, first of its kind.
The King was to be kidnapped, the Guises put to death. Such
a distant and aloof observer as the Grand Turk, Suleiman the
Magnificent, had been moved previously to an interesting remark
which Brantôme quotes : " Since it [the French Calvinist party]
had rejected many points of the Christian religion, and also the
Pope, he could not like it, the more so because its adherents were
nothing but seditious bunglers (*brouillons séditieux*), never at rest
but forever in commotion."[1] Brantôme adds judiciously that
François I was nevertheless *ung peu rigoureux* to burn a few of them
out of hand.

We find Catherine de Médicis forty years later constantly
straining to reconcile the rival chiefs, and earning unpopularity
with the mass of her subjects by establishing edicts of toleration
and recognition for the Calvinist sect. Normally a violent race
when roused, for good or evil, the French were in no mood for
compromise on either side, and that terrifying spectacle, the Paris
mob rising to slay in a tigerish fury mixed with a strange, quasi-
military discipline—it is so seen again in the Massacres of September,
1792, and during the Commune of 1871—is the logical outcome
of the second Calvinist attempt, made by Coligny, to seize young
Charles IX at Monceaux in 1567 ; also unsuccessful. Guise had
already brought off a *coup* of this kind when he removed the King
from Fontainebleau to Paris ; but Guise had the Queen-Mother's
connivance and the approval of Paris, militantly Catholic, and all
France, barring the strongly Calvinist South. Coligny's attempt,
with the Lutheran Elector Palatine about to reinforce him and
the English about to swoop on Normandy, merely evoked that
rising storm of rage and panic in Paris which swelled to its appalling
crescendo in the St. Bartholomew massacre, sickening every decent
Frenchman on both sides.

It is the present fashion, since modern advanced thought is
not particularly interested in religion, to deplore religious conflict
above any other—to die for South African financiers being nobler,

[1] *Recueil des Dames : Marguerite, Reyne de Navarre.*

apparently, than to die for the eternal verities. (The subtle remark of Manning that all human conflict is ultimately theological being more or less meaningless to the progressive mind, like most of the primal truths, some of its implications would be fascinating to discuss here.) It is essential nevertheless to remember that, the personal ambitions of the Guises and the Condés apart, the foundational religion of the West was threatened in France by powerful enemies, and the majority of Frenchmen were determined that it should not come to harm.

Frontal attacks on the Catholic religion had begun in the reign of François I, some forty years before the civil wars, when France awoke one morning to find printed placards, threatening the King and uttering odious blasphemies against the Blessed Sacrament, posted publicly in several towns, one on the door of the Royal bedchamber at Amboise. The text of one of these placards shows the language habitually employed by the spokesmen of the Reform:

Vostre Christ se laisse manger aux bestes et à vous pareillement, qui estes pire que des bestes en vos badinages lesquels vous faites à l'entour de vostre dieu de paste, de quel vous jouez comme un chat p'un souris.[1]

Others of the placards, which were mainly of Geneva printing, and smuggled over the frontier, describe the Mass as rank sorcery and a juggling-game, and add that there are not faggots and fires enough in the world to mete out to Catholics the fate they deserve. With hardly less savage vehemence the Calvinist pamphleteers will shortly return to the attack, France will be flooded with their productions, prose and verse, and Ronsard, plunging into the fray in defence of throne and altar, will get his fair share of slander, abuse and buffooneries.

It will be unnecessary, thank Heaven, to follow the dreary rhythms of these five wars, except in so far as they affect the fortunes of Pierre de Ronsard; the marchings and counter-marchings of the rival armies, the battles, the sieges, the assassinations by both sides, the intrigues of the leaders, the Calvinist lootings and pro-fanation and destruction of churches and cathedrals and tombs,

[1] Your Christ allows himself to be devoured by beasts and by you equally, who are worse than beasts in the games you play with your god of flour and water, with which you play as a cat does with a mouse.

which they specialised, the bitter Catholic reprisals ; the diastole and systole of a ruthless civil conflict in which there are nevertheless periods of rest and respite. At one time, between May and October, 1562, we find Ronsard himself—" a gentleman of courage, whom poetry had not deprived of the use of his sword", is the tribute of the Calvinist poet Agrippa d'Aubigné—in action. Bands of Calvinist troops were devastating the Vendômois, and the poet, reports the historian De Thou, raised and led a company of country gentlemen in arms. One engagement with the enemy nearly proved fatal, we gather from Ronsard's account to Pierre Paschal :

> *Nagueres le bon Dieu me sauva de leurs mains,*
> *Après m'avoir tiré cinq coups de harquebuse . . .*
> *Je vis encor', Paschal, et ce bien je reçoy*
> *Par un miracle grand que Dieu fist dessur moy.*[1]

That these bullets were intended for him, and were not merely incidental, seems to be implied ; it is not unlikely that so celebrated a Catholic champion should be a marked man. But his pen remains his most powerful weapon. With Ronsard at our elbow we see the misery of the time. He records it like a Major Prophet describing the doom of Israel. Everywhere round him he views the tragic, the ludicrous, the hopeless confusion of France ; on the one hand, the foreign Allies of the Reform already at work, like the Elector Palatine's Lutheran troops, or preparing, like the English, to occupy the Norman ports, Havre, Rouen, Dieppe ;[2] the sack of cities, the trampling of the countryside, massacres, pillagings, arson, rape, and the desecration of the shrines ; on the other hand, the spectacle of duped and cackling sectaries fed with wind and pride and rhetoric, ignorant artisans—even women and children—setting up as interpreters of the most abstruse passages of Holy Writ, an uproar of conflicting tongues and a general orgy of public licence.

---

[1] Not long ago the good God saved me from their hands, after they had fired five arquebus shots at me. I am still alive, Paschal ; I owe this favour to a great miracle God performed for me.

[2] In September 1562 the Vidame de Chartres, on behalf of the French Calvinist party, signed the treaty of Hampton Court. Coligny and Condé bought English help by ceding Havre.

Morte est l'autorité, chacun vit à sa guise,
Au vice desreiglé la licence est permise,
Le desir, l'avarice et l'erreur incensé
Ont san-dessus-dessoubs le monde renversé ;
On a faict des lieux saincts une horrible vœrie,
Un assassinement et une pillerie,
Si bien que Dieu n'est seur en sa propre maison.
Au Ciel est revollée et Justice et Raison,
Et en leur place, hélas ! regne le brigandage,
La force, les cousteaux, le sang et le carnage.[1]

Here and there the gloom is lightened by one of those clea[r]
vivid pictures of the *chose vue* he knows so well how to make
With a sardonic humour he records in his reply to the Geneva[n]
preachers, *Response aux Prédicans de Genève,* how one day he take[s]
a walk down the Faubourg St. Marcel, one of the Parisian quarter[s]
in which the Calvinists were then permitted by law to preach i[n]
public, to hear the great Théodore de Beza holding forth to th[e]
crowd.

Un jour estant pensif, me voulant defascher,
Passant par Saint-Marceau je l'allai voir prescher,
Et là me servit bien la sourdesse benigne,
Car rien en mon cerveau n'entra de sa doctrine ;
Je m'en retournay comme j'estois venu,
Et ne vis seullement que son grand front cornu
Et sa barbe fourchue, et ses mains renversées
Qui promettoient le Ciel aux troupes amassées ;
Il donnoit Paradis au people d'alentour,
Et si pensoit que Dieu luy en dust de retour.[2]

There is another little cameo of De Beza in Ronsard's magnificent *Appel à Théodore de Bèze,* showing the great man, Calvin's

[1] Perished is authority; everyone lives as he pleases, licence is permitted to unruly vice, and lust and avarice and crazy error have turned the world upside down. The holy places are turned into a horrible dunghill with assassination and loot, so that God is no more secure in His own house. Justice and Reason have fled to Heaven, and in their place, alas, reigns brigandry, brute force, knives, blood, and carnage.
[2] One day in heavy mood, desiring recreation, I passed by St. Marcel and went to hear him preach. And there my kindly deafness served me well, for none of his doctrine entered my head, and I returned as I had gone, having perceived nothing but his great horned head and forked beard, and his upturned hands, promising Heaven to the assembled crowds. He handed Paradise to the people round him, and seemed to think God owed him the same in return.

utant and successor, editor of the New Testament, able defender
the burning of Michael Servetus, setting out to preach, his sword
:ded under his long flowing cloak.

> *Un jour en te voyant aller faire ton presche,*
> *Ayant dessous un reistre une épée au côté,*
> *" Mon Dieu, ce dis-je lors, quelle sainte bonté !*
> *O parole de Dieu d'un faux masque trompée,*
> *Puisque les Prédicans preschent à coup d'épée !*
> *Bientost avecq le fer nous serons consumés,*
> *Puisqu'on voit de cousteaux les Ministres armés."*[1]

verhearing which soliloquy, two of De Beza's bodyguards
1 the crowd turn on him with a scowl.

> *" Quoy, parles-tu de luy, qui seul est envoyé*
> *Du Ciel, pour r'enseigner le peuple dévoyé ?*
> *Or tu es un Athée, ou quelque benefice*
> *Te faict ainsi vomir ta rage et ta malice,*
> *Puisque si arrogant tu ne fais pas d'honneur*
> *A ce Prophete sainct envoyé du Seigneur ! "*[2]

The poet's reply is vigorous and embracing, and he leaves his
antagonists grinding their teeth and denouncing him for a servant
of Satan. Ronsard is a man who speaks his mind, no less firmly
when tackling a Calvinist than when contemplating those abuses
of the Church which the Council of Trent is shortly to abolish.
Geneva or Wittenberg itself could not more vigorously invoke
the Apostle in its thunderings.

> *Mais que diroit Sainct Paul, s'il revenoit icy,*
> *De nos jeunes prelatz qui n'ont poinct de soucy*

[1] One day as I saw you going to your preaching,
With a sword at your side under your great cloak,
" My God! " I said, " what holy mildness!
O Word of God, betrayed by a false mask,
Since preachers preach with swords to mark their periods!
Before long we shall be wiped out by steel,
Now we see ministers armed with knives ! "

[2] What! Do you speak of him who alone is sent by Heaven to re-instruct a lost
people ? Why, you are an atheist ! Or else some benefice makes you vomit your rage and
malice thus, since you are too arrogant to pay honour to this holy Prophet sent by the Lord !

De leur pauvre troupeau, dont ils prennent la laine,
Et quelquefois le cuir ; qui tous vivent sans paine,
Sans prescher, sans prier, sans bon exemple d'eux,
Parfumez, decoupez, courtizans, amoureux,
Veneurs et fauconniers, et avecq la paillarde
Perdent les biens de Dieu, dont ils n'ont que la garde ?[1]

He does not spare the Renaissance Popes, " pompously arrayed
in silk and cloth-of-gold " (which means not their sacred vest‑
ments but their everyday luxury), and determinedly he sums up

Il faut donc corriger de nostre sainte Eglise
Cent mille abus commis par l'avare Prétrise.[2]

Like a trumpet of bronze he cries to the whole Catholic world

Las ! des Luthériens la cause est très mauvaise,
Et la deffendent bien ; et par malheur fatal
La nostre est bonne et sainte, et la deffendons mal ![3]

For Ronsard is not one of the new fanatics who would mend
the cracks and wipe out the stains in the fabric of Holy Church by
pulling the whole august divinely-established structure down about
the ears of hapless man. Nor, equally, is he one of those fanatics
of his own side who see every Calvinist equipped with horns and
hoofs. Having fiercely denounced the failings of Catholics, he
agrees readily that there are men on the opposing side who can
set them an example :

[1] But what would Saint Paul say, if he returned to earth,
Of our young prelates who have no care
For their poor flock, whose wool they take,
And sometimes the skin as well ? Who live at their ease,
Without preaching or praying, without setting a good example,
Scented and barbered, courtiers, lovers,
Hunting men, falconers ? Who waste God's gifts
In fornication, having no care of their stewardship ?

[2] We must correct in Holy Church
A hundred thousand abuses committed by a greedy priesthood.

[3] Alas! The Lutherans' cause is extremely bad
And they defend it well ; and by fatal mishap
Ours is good and holy, and we defend it ill !

> *. . . Au reste je ne nie*
> *Qu'on ne puisse trouver dans leur tourbe infinie*
> *Quelque homme juste et droit qui garde bien sa foy. . . .* [1]

And he calls to all Catholics to be worthy of their Faith and to
ally to Mother Church.

> *Ainsi qui voudra bien l'Evangile avancer,*
> *Il faut chasser l'abus et l'Eglise embrasser*
> *Et ne s'en separer, mais fermement la suyvre,*
> *Et dedans son giron tousjours mourir et vivre.* [2]

Within a couple of years the Council of Trent, to which Ronsard
turns to address a resounding plea :

> *O vous doctes Prelatz, poussés du Sainct-Esprit,*
> *Qui estes assemblés au nom de Jesus-Christ,*
> *Et taschez sainctment par une voye utile*
> *De conduire l'Eglise à l'accord d'un Concile,*
> *Vous-mesmes les premiers, Prelatz, reformez-vous,*
> *Et comme vrays pasteurs, faictes la guerre aux loups . . .* [3]

—within a year or two of this the Council will be preparing to
rise from its long labours, having launched that reformation
which, had it come a hundred years earlier, might have spared the
world a Luther and a Calvin, and the conflicts and hatreds and
abysmal misunderstandings they engendered, and still engender.
But it was too late to save Christendom from the rapid multipli-
cation of the new sects, each warring already with the other in a
babel of antagonisms, as Ronsard does not fail to point out to
Théodore de Beza with acid relish.

---

[1] For that matter, I do not deny that one can find, amid their swarming mob, some just
and good man who holds truly to his faith.

> [2] For he who would advance the Gospel's cause
> Must expel abuses and embrace the Church,
> Not separate himself from her, but follow her devoutly,
> Living and dying always in her bosom.

> [3] O you learned Prelates, inspired of the Holy Ghost,
> Assembled in the Name of Jesus Christ,
> Labouring in holiness to conduct the Church
> In the right way, with the accord of a Council,
> Reform yourselves first of all, Prelates,
> And like true shepherds, make war on the wolves . . .

Les Apostres jadis preschoient tous d'un accord,
Entre vous aujourd'huy ne regne que discord :
Les uns sont Zvingliens, les autres Luthéristes,
Œcolampadiens, Quintiens, Anabaptistes,
Les autres de Calvin vont adorant le pas,
L'un est prédestiné et l'autre ne l'est pas,
Et l'autre enrage après l'erreur Mancerienne,
Et bientot s'ouvrira l'escole Bézienne !
Si bien que ce Luther, lequel estoit premier,
Chassé par les nouveaux est presque le dernier,
Et sa secte, qui fut de tant d'hommes garnie,
Est la moindre de neuf qui sont en Germanie.[1]

He would have much more scope to-day.

But it would grossly misrepresent Ronsard to exhibit him at this period simply as a fighter exulting in the fray. The wars of religion and the menace to France have shocked him out of his paganism and his customary pursuit of the lusts and the pride of life. It is a sobered, humble, contrite Christian man who cries to God, in his *Remonstrance au Peuple de France*, the nation's *Confiteor*, in almost the exact words the Byzantine historian Doucas uses in his lament for the fall of Constantinople :

Nous sçavons bien, Seigneur, que nos fautes sont grandes,
Nous sçavons nos péchés ; mais, Seigneur, tu demandes
Pour satisfaction un courage contrit,
Un cœur humilié, un penitent esprit,
Et pour ce, Seigneur Dieu, ne punis en ton ire
Ton peuple repentant qui lamente et soupire,
Qui te demande grace, et par triste méchef
Les fautes de ses Roys ne tourne sur son chef ![2]

[1] The Apostles formerly preached in harmony, but among you to-day reigns nothing but discord. Some are Zwinglians, others Lutherans, Oecolampadians, Quintians, Anabaptists, others go worshipping the footsteps of Calvin, some are predestinate, some are not ; others run amuck after the Mancerian error, and very soon we shall see a Bezian School! In short, Luther, once in the first place, has been chased out of it by new arrivals and is now nearly last, while his sect, once so numerous, is now the least of nine in Germany.

[2] Lord, we know well that our faults are great,
We know our sins ; but, Lord, thou requirest
For satisfaction, a firm contrition,
A humble heart, a penitent spirit,
And for this, Lord God, punish not in Thy wrath
Thy repentant people who weep and sigh
And demand Thy mercy ; and may the faults of their Kings
Not be visited by sad misfortune on their heads!

or the Crown, head of the French family, must bear its responsiility to Almighty God for the miseries France is suffering. Ronsard's passionate sincerity is patent; he has flung away his vinecup and his coronal of roses and shed his antique masquerading ike a cloak. A symbolic painter might depict him at this moment kneeling devoutly before God's altar, smiting his breast with tears, attired in a suit of mourning, grey or black, or, like Pico della Mirandola, in the pied habit of the Dominican Third Order. He will not kneel or weep long; it is not in his nature; a pair of gay bright eyes will soon draw him from the sanctuary to the rosy path again; but Ronsard, who can never be ranked amongst the great religious poets of France, may for this fleeting space of time be accorded a place in their company. Undoubtedly his influence must be counted high among those which saved France from being torn asunder for ever, and secured the Faith.[1] Had he chosen the other side Ronsard would have been as much the hero of the Lodges to-day as Voltaire.

His position in the conflict is not free from embarrassments. Some of his great friends and patrons take the Calvinist side— notably Coligny's brother, the enigmatic Cardinal de Chastillon, Odet de Coligny, to whom Ronsard had, among other tributes, glowingly dedicated the *Hymnes* (1555) in a piece beginning " *Mon Odet, mon prelat, mon seigneur, mon comfort*". This dedication Ronsard removed in 1560, and never celebrated Chastillon again. The struggle between admiring affection for a kind patron and disappointment and disgust at his ostentatious spurning of the Faith was keen, as we perceive from the regrets for the Cardinal which Ronsard preserved henceforth in every edition:

> *Je n'aime son erreur, mais haïr ne puis*
> *Un si digne prelat dont serviteur je suis*
> *Qui bénin m'a servi . . .*[2]

God forgive and protect him, says his sad bedesman:

[1] Binet says Ronsard received an autograph letter of thanks for his services to the Church at this time from Pius V. This letter has not been noted by Vatican archivists so far.

[2] I love not his errors, but I cannot hate such a worthy prelate, whose servitor I am and who has served me so benignly . . .

Dieu preserve son chef de malheur et d'ennui![1]

Another patron on the opposite side is Louis de Bourbon-Condé head of the Calvinist armies, the vivacious, humpbacked, ambitious prideful little man, the great lover of power and women about whom the Parisian populace sang with a wink:

> *Ce petit homme tant joly,*
> *Toujours cause et toujours rit,*
> *Et toujours baise sa mignonne,*
> *Dieu garde d'mal le petit homme!*[2]

Ronsard will conceive it his duty ere long, when Condé prances into the field at the head of the Calvinist nobles and a force of 20,000, to warn this powerful prince to take care, they are turning him into a *roy de tragédie*, a stage-king; a not uncourageous warning, however courteously and respectfully phrased, for Condé had been one of the poet's friends at Court, was a source of benefices, and might yet rule France. And not only some of Ronsard's important friends but some of his closer ones, fellow-poets and protégés honoured in his verse, have also joined the other side, like Louis des Masures and Jacques Grévin and Florent Chrestien. One or two will stab at him before long in vicious anonymous pamphlets, obviously revealing a former intimacy. Ronsard will strike their names, like Chastillon's, from his next edition. For himself there is only one side possible. Fervent nationalism, exalted loyalty to the Monarchy, and traditionalism in religion make him, as I have suggested already, the ideal Action Française leader born four centuries too early. Professor Gustave Cohen compares his religious position to that of Maurice Barrès; I would personally compare it to Léon Daudet's, their temperaments being much more alike. Ronsard himself strikes the traditional note firmly when he declares, speaking of the new sects:

> *De tant de nouveautez je ne suis curieux:*
> *Il me plaist d'imiter le train de mes ayeux,*

---

[1] God preserve his head from misfortune and tribulation!
[2] O this charming little man! always talking, always laughing, always kissing sweethearts true, God keep the little man from rue!

Genèvre

Je croy qu'en Paradis ils vivent à leur aise
Encor qu'ils n'ayent suivy ny Calvin ny Bèze.[1]

It is only fair to the Action Française to remember that its
Catholic thinkers knew more intellectual arguments for defence
of the Faith than this. But Ronsard, though he can state the Creed
and defend it in clear language, is not interested in apologetics.
It seems, from a curious reference in the *Remonstrance* to his early
youth—

J'ay autrefois gousté, quand j'estois jeune d'age
Du miel empoisonné de vostre doux breuvage,
Mais quelque bon Daimon m'ayant ouy crier,
Avant que l'avaller me l'osta du gosier.[2]

—that during his brief visit to Germany with Lazare de Baïf his
ever-keen intellectual curiosity had led him to toy with the new
religions whose professors swarmed in Hagenau, many of them
humanists of the first quality. Even so early the conflicting claims
of Lutheranism and Calvinism, both vocally represented, confused
and bored him. Twenty years later he points to the shortcomings
of the Church as frankly as these sectaries, but he perceives that
their method of cure by breaking up Christendom is damnable.
A formidable antagonist, in this pen-and-ink war which rages
simultaneously with the clash of steel! You cannot score against
him with the disorders of the Church, for he has denounced them
as fiercely as you. You cannot accuse him of being a creature of
the Court, for he has himself apportioned blame to kings and princes
with almost republican verve.

Vous, Princes et vous Roys, la faute avez commise
Pour laquelle aujourd'huy souffre toute l'Église . . .[3]

The Crown and noble patrons, he says, have ignobly trafficked
in benefices and filled the offices of the Church with dolts, rascals,

[1] I am not curious of so many novelties; I prefer to imitate the ways of my ancestors; I
think they live at their ease in Paradise, although they never followed Calvin or Beza.

[2] Formerly I tasted, in my youthful days, some of the poisoned honey of your sweet
brewing; but some kind spirit, having heard my cries, removed it from my throat before
I swallowed it.

[3] You, Princes, and you, Kings, the fault is yours for which the whole Church suffers
to-day.

(*larrons*) and nincompoops. And finally, you can hardly accu
Ronsard of knowing nothing about the Reform. No wonde
therefore, that we find the Calvinist pamphleteers detailed to attac
him, in French and Latin, concentrating on personalities: h
deafness; his tonsure; his atheism (alleged); his venereal diseas
(alleged); his addiction to unnatural vice (alleged); his graspin
after benefices, and so forth.

I propose to glide past and over this slanging-match as grace
fully as may be. Its dust and heat last some time, and, like th
pamphleteering scuffles of Milton's time, it is more violent thar
interesting. Ronsard defends himself with tireless vigour and return:
every stroke. It is not normally an occupation inspiring grea
poetry, and none of the parties concerned is immaculate. If Ronsarc
has had his mistresses, so has Théodore de Beza, who married one.
However, if the perpetual Calvinist yell of "Priest!" and
"Atheist!" at Ronsard's heels is pure silliness, it at least goads
Ronsard into giving the world a picture of his daily way of life
in the country, a valuable bit of autobiography. We see him waking
early, commending himself to God, flinging aside the bedclothes,
dressing, and going into his study to read, to meditate, and to
write for the next four or five hours. After this he hears Mass,
and then spends an hour in idling. A frugal meal follows, and if
the afternoon is pleasant, he strolls in his fields and woods, or to
some neighbouring village; or perhaps he will smell the flowers
or work in his garden, or, lying under a tree in the meadows,
talk with a friend, or drop off to sleep. If the weather is bad he
seeks a few cronies to play at primero, Falstaff's game, or to take
vaulting exercises in his gymnasium, or to devote an hour or
two to wrestling and fencing. His mood is normally merry,
and jokes fly round, for there is no Calvinistic sourness about
him or his friends.

> *Je dis le mot pour rire, et à la verité,*
> *Je ne loge chez moy trop de severité.*[1]

So day wanes into night and at length he seeks his bed again—
he omits the long evening meal and its erudite libations—and

---

[1] I set them laughing, for the fact is I never harbour too much severity.

fter saying his prayers and asking Heaven's pardon for the day's
aults, goes sweetly to sleep. But when the day is a holiday, he
ays, he becomes a pillar of the Church, *une colonne ferme*. Then,
ising before dawn, vesting himself, as his Minor Orders entitle
im, in cassock, surplice, and a cope with golden clasps and fringe,
e loses no moment of the Divine Offices. Taking his seat in choir,
oreviary in hand—he is at this moment an honorary canon of
Le Mans—he recites the offices of Prime, Terce, Sext, and None
with the clergy and cantors and, after the Offertory at High Mass,
censes the officiating prelate, Charles d'Angennes, to whom he
turns aside to pay a classical compliment:

> . . . *mon Prélat des autres l'outrepasse,*
> *Ayant pris d'Agénor son surnom et sa race.*[1]

And so

> *Nous chantons au Seigneur louanges et cantiques,*
> *Et prions Dieu pour vous qui estes heretiques.*[2]

A blameless existence enough, and we need not ponder unduly
on the motives which led Ronsard to suppress, in a later
edition, four lines which originally came just after " *Je ne loge
chez moy* " etc:

> *J'ayme à faire l'amour, j'ayme à parler aux femmes,*
> *A mettre par escrit mes amoureuses flammes,*
> *J'ayme le bal, la dance et les masques aussy,*
> *La musicque et le luth, ennemis du soucy.*[3]

He may later have thought this capable of misinterpretation by
his enemies; or, more likely, one of his friends may have hinted
that these lines might give the impression that the poet was somewhat inclined . . . well, they might give the opposition a wrong

---

[1] . . . my prelate, who surpasses all others, who derives his surname and his race from
Agenor [the Trojan hero].
[2] We sing praises and hymns to the Lord, and pray to God for you heretics.
[3] I enjoy making love, I enjoy talking to women and setting down my love-affairs in
writing; I love balls, dances, and masques, music and the lute, those enemies of Care.

impression. Is it imagining too much to see a blank stare o
Ronsard's face as this is pointed out to him? *Wrong impression*
Oh! Ah! Yes—perhaps so. Yes—one had not thought of tha
The lines had better come out, then, if that is really the impressio
they give. There is a childlike streak in all artists and men of letters
and their surprise at being informed of their most obvious *gaffe*
is perfectly genuine. Actions for damages under our contemporar
British law of libel, that monstrous Chinese enigma, commonly
demonstrate this. Whether Leigh Hunt was astonished when h
was arrested, imprisoned and heavily fined for describing the
Prince Regent in print, quite accurately, as a corpulent libertine
I do not know, but it is quite possible. So, perhaps Ronsard
who, however, did not suffer from the tyranny of libel laws, and
could write what he pleased.

Lovers of the science of invective will find an occasional pleasant
outburst in this offensive-defensive campaign. For example,
Ronsard cries to the Genevan preachers in a body:

> *Sus, Bouffons et Plaisants, que la Lune gouverne !*
> *Allez chercher un asne aux montagnes d'Auvergne,*
> *D'oreilles bien garny, et en mille cordons*
> *Environnez son front de foin et de chardons ;*
> *Troussez-vous jusqu'au coude, escorchez-moy la beste,*
> *Et de ce Prédicant attachez à la teste*
> *Les oreilles, ainsi que les avoit Midas,*
> *Ce lourdaud Phrygien qui grossier ne sut pas*
> *Estimer de Phœbus les chansons et la lyre !*[1]

There is more obvious comic bite, perhaps, in his address some
years later to one of the curled and perfumed *mignons* of Henri
III's Court, who had dared to sneer at his verse. May a thousand
fishwives tear him to shreds with their tongues !

> *Et ce pendant pour bien vivre à ton aise*
> *Je te souhaite une femme punaise,*
> *Je te souhaite un coqu bien cornu . . .*

[1] Up, clowns and jokers, governed by the moon! Go find an ass in the mountains of
Auvergne, well furnished with ears, and decorate his forehead with a thousand festoons of
hay and thistles ; then roll up your sleeves and skin me the animal, and affix his ears to this
preacher, as Midas wore them—that Phrygian lout who was too doltish to appreciate the
songs and the lyre of Apollo!

Puis, ne pouvant au Roy tes comptes rendre,
A Montfaulcon tout sec puisses-tu pendre,
Les yeux mangés de corbeaulx charogneux,
Les pieds tirés de ces mastins hargneux . . .[1]

Apart from this Ronsard has nothing to show in the way of
invective to compare with such classic exhibition-pieces as the
Irish poet's :

May she marry a ghost and bear him a kitten, and may
The High King of Glory permit her to get the mange.[2]

On one point alone the Calvinists get past his guard and
score. He certainly has been seeking benefices ; even a Court
poet must live. At this period (and for long afterwards, one may
recall) literary men depended for existence not on royalties but on
Royalty—or, if they could not aspire thus high, on the munificence
of the noblemen to whom their works were dedicated ; for they got
nothing from their publishers. In Ronsard's time the most usual
douceur from Royalty to a recipient qualified by the tonsure was part
of the revenues of a benefice, generally an abbey. The same acknow-
ledgments were made in varying degree by the great, of which
duty Ronsard reminds them with entire aplomb—and why not ?
Laumonier records that between 1553 and 1557 Ronsard had received
five parish cures from his patrons Cardinal Jean du Bellay, Cardinal
Odet de Coligny, and the Cardinal of Lorraine, his old fellow-
student. But these are very small rewards, and Henri II remains
indifferent to those representations—never ignoble, always proud and
elegant—Ronsard makes once or twice to him at this time. He certainly
seems justified in looking to the Crown. He is again contemplating that vast national epic, the *Franciade*, a new Iliad, a new Aeneid,
which he began to sketch vaguely *sub regno Cassandræ*, and he will
not go on with it until the King grants him one or two of those
favours so lavishly showered on mediocrity. The Crown continues
deaf. For the time Ronsard must be content with his cures and the

[1] Meanwhile, to live at your ease, I wish you a stinking wife and a well-horned cuckoldry
. . . may you, unable to render the King an explanation, be hanged at Montfaucon high
and dry, your eyes eaten by carrion-crows and your feet gnawed by savage mastiffs . . .
[2] James Stephens, *A Glass of Beer* (from the Irish).

salary of 1,200 livres—a livre may be taken as about equal to a fra:
—attached to his office of *ausmonier* or almoner to the King, whic
implies attendance daily for three months in every year in th
Royal bedchamber while the King dresses, the presenting of th
cushion on which his Majesty kneels in his oratory, the distributic
of the Royal alms (*aûmones*) after Mass, and the right to dine :
Court. It will not be until 1565–6 that Ronsard gets his first goo
benefices by the Queen-Mother's favour.

§2

Here is a fresh-enamelled little "period" picture of th
dames of Touraine walking two by two by the Loire in spring
time which is, I think, full of life and charm. It is from :
poem called *Le Satyre*.

> *Hercule un jour passant par Oebalie*
> *Menoit Iole, amoureuse folie,*
> *Comme ils erroient en cheminant tous deux*
> *Par terres, bois, par bocages ombreux . . .*
> *Ses mains estoient de bagues bien chargées,*
> *Riche son col de perles arrangées,*
> *Son chef estoit couvert follastrement*
> *D'un scoffion attifé proprement,*
> *Sa robe estoit de pourpre Méonine,*
> *Perse en couleur, chancrée à la poitrine;*
>   *Ainsy qu'on voit au retour des beaux moys*
> *Se promener ou nos Dames de Blois*
> *Ou d'Orléans, ou de Tours, ou d'Amboise,*
> *Dessus la grève ou Loire se degoise*
> *A flot rompu; elles sur le bord vert*
> *Vont deux à deux au tétin decouvert,*
> *Au collet lasche, et joignant la rivière*
> *Foulent l'émail de l'herbe printanière.*[1]

[1] Hercules, passing one day through Oebalia, took with him Iole, his amorous folly. As they wandered on their way together, through plains and woods and shady groves . . . her hands were richly laden with rings, her neck rich with assorted pearls, her head was covered gaily with a dainty peaked bonnet, her gown was of Meonian purple, dark-bluish in tint, open at the bosom. Thus one sees, when the fine months return, our ladies of Blois or Orleans, or Tours, or Amboise, walking along the banks where Loire sings with her breaking wavelets; on the green banks, pacing two by two, their breasts displayed, their neckwear loosened, they tread the enamelled Spring grass as they follow the river.

And here is a *chanson de Printemps* as deft and gay and
musical and full of flower-scents as any spring song ever sung,
published in 1563.

Je sens en ce moys si beau
Le flambeau
D'Amour qui m'échauffe l'âme,
Y'voyant de tous costés
Les beautés
Qu'il emprunte à ma Dame.
Quand je vois tant de couleurs
Et de fleurs
Qui émaillent au rivage,
Je pense voir le beau teint
Qui est paint
Si vermeil en son visage.
Quand je vois les grands rameaux
Des ormeaux
Qui sont lacés de lierre,
Je pense estre pris ès lacs
De ses bras,
Et que mon col elle serre ;
Quand j'entends la douce voix
Par les bois
Du gai rossignol qui chante,
D'elle je pense jouir
Et ouïr
Sa douce voix qui m'enchante.
Quand Zéphyre mène un bruit
Qui se suit
Au travers d'une ramée,
Des propos il me souvient
Qui me tient
La bouche de mon Aimée.
Quand je vois en quelque endroit
Un pin droit,
Ou quelque arbre qui s'èleve,
Je me laisse decevoir,
Pensant voir
Sa belle taille et sa grève.

Quand je vois dans un jardin
Au matin
S'éclore une fleur nouvelle,
J'accompare le bouton
Au teton
De son beau sein qui pommelle.
Quand le soleil tout riant
D'Orient
Nous montre sa blonde tresse,
Il me semble que je voy
Devant moy
Lever ma belle maistresse.
Quant je sens parmi les prés
Diaprés
Les fleurs dont la terre est pleine,
Lors je fais croire à mes sens
Que je sens
La douceur de son haleine.
Bref, je fais comparaison
Par raison
Du printemps et de m'amye,
Il donne aux fleurs la vigeur,
Et mon cœur
D'elle prend vigeur et vie.[1]

And here is a bacchanal, very Horatian:

Fay refraischir mon vin de sorte
Qu'il passe en froideur un glaçon;

[1] In this sweet month I feel the torch of Love, which inflames my soul, perceiving on all sides the beauties borrowed from my lady. When I see so many tints and flowers enamelling the river-bank, I think I see the lovely colour which stains her cheek so rosily. When I see the great branches of the young elms, laced with ivy, I think I am taken in the snare of her arms, that she enfolds my neck. When I hear in the woods the sweet voice of the gay nightingale in song, I think I enjoy her and hear her sweet enchanting voice. When Zephyr exhales a breath which goes whispering through the thicket, it reminds me of the words my Beloved's mouth speaks to me. When I see somewhere a slim pine, or some other tree rising up, I let myself be deceived, thinking I see her lovely shape, her legs. When I see a new flower open in the garden of a morning, I compare the bud to the nipple of her fair rounded breast. When the laughing sun in the East shows its gold tresses, it seems as though I see my beautiful mistress rising before me. When I smell in the coloured meadows the flowers of which earth is full, I make my senses believe that I smell the sweetness of her breath. In short, I compare in my mind the Spring and my beloved; the one gives the flowers their life, and my heart draws from her life and strength.

Genèvre

Fay venir Janne, qu'elle apporte
Son luth pour dire une chanson ;
Nous ballerons tous trois au son :
Et dy à Barbe qu'elle vienne
Les cheveux tors à la façon
D'une follastre Italienne.

Ne vois-tu que le jour se passe ?
Je ne vy point au lendemain :
Page, reverse dans ma tasse,
Que ce grand verre soit tout plein !
Maudit soit qui languit en vain !
Les Philosophes je n'appreuve ;
Mon cerveau n'est jamais bien sain
Si beaucoup de vin ne l'abreuve.[1]

§3

DUNYASHA : That's a guitar, not a mandoline.
EPIHODOV : To a man mad with love, it's a mandoline.
(Tchehov, *The Cherry Orchard*.)

Public misfortunes (as Dr. Johnson, to quote him yet again, so soundly observed) prevent no man from eating his dinner, and it will not be supposed that the heart of Pierre de Ronsard, wrung however truly by national ills, has been too preoccupied with beating for France to beat for a great new love.[2] She appears, blazing suddenly in his sky, in 1561, as Mary Stuart's sails dwindle on the horizon. She makes the poet happy for a year or more and she inspires an ode and sonnet-sequence which, since she denies him nothing, cannot be ranked with his major verse ; the guitar, so to speak, replaces the lute. It contains nevertheless a fair amount of the Ronsardian grace and fire.

---

[1] Cool my wine, so that it is colder than an icicle ; send for Janne, and let her bring her lute to sing a song ; we will all three dance to the tune. And tell Barbe to come, with her hair twisted in the manner of a madcap Italian. Do you not see that the day is going ? I do not look for to-morrow. Page, pour wine into my cup again, let this great glass be brimful. Accursed be he who languishes in vain ! I do not agree with the Philosophers : my brain is never completely clear unless it is refreshed with plenty of wine.
[2] The Sinope incident, which some authorities place at this period, I propose to transfer to a later date.

Genèvre : only her Christian name is known. She was identifi
tentatively by Guillaume Colletet, many years later, as Genèv
de Vigenère, wife of a Parisian lawyer ; but this is fantasy, f
Ronsard's Genèvre is not a married woman. Still later she w
identified with a woman who kept the Sabot Tavern in the Faubou
St. Marcel, with less likelihood still, though Ronsard's Genèv
certainly lived in this quarter. She was young, blonde, attractiv
eupeptic, and kind, and the poet loved her to distraction, as was h
custom. The story of their meeting as Ronsard tells it affords a
interesting glimpse of Parisian manners at this period.

He was now himself, for the most part of every year, a Parisia
tenant of a small house in the Fossés St. Victor in the Faubour
St. Marcel, now the Rue du Cardinal Lemoine : a pleasant hous
with courtyard and garden, belonging to his friend Antoine d
Baïf, who lived close by. Guillaume Colletet of the Académi
Française, who lived in it fifty years afterwards and was inspire
to a biography, describes *La Maison de Ronsard* in a respectfu
sonnet with that title. Two " superb lions ", presumably of stone
guard the doorway ; the shady, flowery garden is full of bird-song
and its *doubles allées*—doubtless sanded—seem still to bear the
glorious impress of the master's feet. No vestige of this house
remains, and so far as I remember, its site is marked by no
tablet.

The University quarter, Ronsard's spiritual home, had hardly
changed since Villon's day ; its most famous taverns, such as the
Mule in the Rue St. Jacques and the Pomme de Pin in the Rue de
la Juiverie, echoed to the same youthful laughter and song, and
were to do so for a century more at least. The Pomme de Pin is
the Mermaid Tavern of Old Paris. Those dusky panels, huge smoky
beams, thick bottle-glass casements, and uneven oak and b
floors enclosed a repository of more stellar wit, perhaps, than an
tavern in history. Clément Marot and his circle and Rabelais and
his friends following Villon's band, and after Marot, Ronsard and
Dorat and the Brigade, and after them again Molière and La Fontaine
and even the *triste Janséniste* Racine—a notable procession! Would
to Heaven science had discovered some means of rescuing a little
of their table-talk from the ether. Robin Turgis, whose name is
set for ever in Villon's Testaments, is the only one of the Pomme

Fecunde en vin, doulce en ses Citoyens
Fertile en bled, & en maintz esquières lieux.

Tum Priniero

L'aurore grelottante en robe rose et verte
S'avançait lentement sur la Seine déserte,

tirs Ronsard not at all, apparently. The landscape of Paris does
not exist for him as a poet, even the holy academic Hill of St.
Geneviève, which he loved almost as dearly as his native fields.
It may be that he left such things to guttersnipes, like Villon.

On a hot summer evening in 1561 Pierre de Ronsard leaves
his house in the Fossés St. Victor and strolls down to the river
for a swim, all unaware of what awaits him before his hair is dry.
It is towards the end of July in a blazing summer, and Ronsard
takes his swim from one of the creeks beyond the walls habitually
used for bathing by Parisians. One sees him plunging into mid-
stream with that vehemence he displays in everything. Water,
river or fountain, calls to him always imperiously, as to all favourites
of the Muses. Like Spenser's Thames, the Seine ran silver and sail-
dotted in those days. Outside the ramparts, gardens and fields and
pleasant walks fringed either bank.

As Ronsard is enjoying the water and the breeze which has
sprung up—it is latish in the evening, and a crescent moon has
appeared in a clear sky—he sees a slim figure dancing on the bank
and hears a sweet voice singing. It takes little time for this strong
swimmer to swerve and reach the shore. Within a few moments
Ronsard has rushed towards the unknown fair, who has also been
bathing, and is dancing to get warm. Laughing and dripping he
kisses her hand and pays her soft brown eyes a swift compliment
in disparagement of the moon. Then :

> *Puis d'un agile bond je m'elançay dans l'eau,*
> *Pensant qu'elle esteindroit mon premier feu nouveau :*
> *Il advint autrement.*[1]

A riverside idyll which might have happened at Henley in
Shelley's time. Ronsard, plunging madly back into the wave,
has no illusions. Love has once more smitten him in the midriff,
and all the rivers of France cannot quench his flame.

---

[1] Then with an agile leap I flung myself into the water again, thinking it might quench
my first new flame ; but it happened otherwise.

Ronsard

> *. . . car au milieu des ondes*
> *Je me sentis lié de tes deux tresses blondes*
> *Et le feu de tes yeux qui les eaux pénetra.*[1]

When he turns his head again she is gone. He emerges, dresses and goes home in melancholy humour enough, for he does not even know her charming name, nor she his illustrious one.

> *Aussy de ton costé tu ne me connaissois*
> *Pour Ronsard, ornement du langage François . . .*[2]

He tries hard to resist this new enchantment, he says, knowing the inevitable pain it will bring; and moreover he has sworn never to fall in love again. He thinks he has conquered this weakness, but in the Faubourg St. Marcel one evening, quite soon afterwards, he sees his new sweet torment sitting at her door, taking the evening air, after the immemorial habit of Paris concierges—she may even have been of this respectable class—and knows himself for lost.

The siege of Genèvre follows, conducted briefly but according to tactical rules. No more the dancing nymph of the Seine, she replies to his talk of love with deep sighs. She is mourning a lover lately dead, and it is useless anyone's wasting his time, for all her thoughts are henceforth in the grave. Her sighs, her tears, her downcast eyes, her silences at length defeat the ardent new-comer, and he reluctantly takes his leave for ever. But after five days of gnawing his nails at home a fury seizes him. Peste ! This is not the manner in which a seasoned warrior in love's campaigns conducts himself! A truce to this moping! The obvious military metaphor suggests itself:

> *Il ne faut (ce disois-je) ainsi vaincu se rendre,*
> *Tant plus un fort chasteau est difficile à prendre,*
> *Plus aporte d'honneur à celuy qui le prend,*
> *Toute brave vertu sans combat ne se rend.*[3]

[1] . . . for in the midst of the waves
I felt myself bound by your twin gold tresses,
And the fire of your eyes, which clave the water.

[2] On your side, too, you did not know me
For Ronsard, ornament of the French tongue.

[3] One must not (I kept saying) give up like this, conquered ; the more difficult a strong fortress is to take, the more honour to him who takes it. No virtue worthy of the name gives in without a struggle.

Sonnez, clairons ! Chantez, coucous ! See him therefore setting forth in gallant array, like the Cadets of Gascony at Arras, to the assault again. This time the fortress surrenders with hardly a blow. Genèvre is so dazed and breathless, it seems, that only with the flag already hauled down and the citadel keys about to be surrendered does she remember that she does not yet know her masterful new conqueror's name. That superb passage follows which I have already partly quoted.

> *A la fin privément tu t'enquis de mon nom,*
> *Et si j'avois aymé autres femmes ou non.*
> *Je suis, dis-je, Ronsard, et cela te suffise,*
> *Ce Ronsard que la France honore, chante, et prise,*
> *Des Muses le mignon, et de qui les beaux vers*
> *Sont temoins de sa gloire en ce grand Univers.*[1]

And while Genèvre still reels under this revelation he proceeds to tell her of Cassandre, whose beauty he has made famous in the eyes of all the world, and of Marie, whom he loved more than his own life, for whom he made a hundred thousand songs; and he laughingly warns Genèvre of his weathercock nature.

> *Ores j'ayme la noire, ores j'ayme la blonde.*[2]

For he takes his love, now, where he finds it. And when he has finished, not without a certain conquering complacency, it is Genèvre's turn.

She relates at length (one is more than ever somehow certain of her lowly origins) her passion for her young dead lover, the history of the dropsy which attacked him (one may imagine well-relished details which Ronsard omits), of the fatal day when he turned white and cold and began vomiting blood, of his passing away in her arms, of the wild despair with which she tore out her hair and fell in a swoon. As an artist, Ronsard possibly thought the recital over-dramatic and over-long. Its effect is to inspire the brisk declaration that it is madness to mourn a dead love. One

[1] At last, shyly, you asked my name, and if I had loved other women or not. "I am", I said, "Ronsard, and that suffices you; that Ronsard whom France honours, sings, and prizes, Darling of the Muses, whose fine verses are witness to his glory in this great universe."
[2] Sometimes I love them dark, sometimes fair.

must seek solace. A young creature in the bloom of her beauty must enjoy her summertime before the roses... *Air connu.* The familiar Ronsardian gambit. And so another glowing chapter in his amorous chronicle opens.

There is no doubt that Ronsard's passion for Genèvre is formidable. Being separated from her for a time, he will write her from the country a long letter in supple, flowing alexandrines, beginning:

> *Ce me sera plaisir, Genèvre, de t'escrire,*
> *Estant absent de toy, mon amoureux martyre ...* [1]

He tells her how he longs for her, how he wanders perpetually about his fields thinking of her, making passionate love-speeches to himself. How he cannot rest in any place or go to bed. How, exhausted, having tried to compose himself with a book, he at length drops off to sleep in his chair; how his servants shake him, saying it is past midnight and the candles are all burned down; how he stumbles up to his bedchamber and drops again into a chair, bereft of all will-power, while his servants undress him and put him to bed, unconscious of everything. How even then he cannot sleep, tormented by desire and memory and tossing from side to side till the first cocks from neighbouring farms cry day again. A bad attack, even for Ronsard. He flung himself into this affair all the more violently, perhaps, to find respite from the forebodings of the times, from disillusion and depression, from sorrow for the recent death of his much-loved Du Bellay, at the age of thirty-five. For, one perceives from a long frank poem addressed to the Queen-Mother and published in 1563, the glowing fruits of fame have turned sour, the mirage has flickered out, he is for the moment a tired, moody, unrewarded man. Walking " solitary and pensive " by the Seine near Passy, he broods on all his misfortune and blames his stars.

> *La, comme hors de moy, j'accusois la Fortune,*
> *La mère des flatteurs, la marastre importune*

[1] It will give me pleasure, Genèvre, to write and tell you, in this absence from you, of my martyrdom of love . . .

Des hommes vertueux, en vivant condamnés
A souffrir tous malheur des Astres mal tournés,
Je blamois Appollon, les Graces et la Muse,
Et le sage mestier qui ma folie amuse . . .[1]

Thinking of all the mass of poems he has written already, of his grey hairs at thirty-seven, of hope deceiving and just reward eluding him, he hates his life, he says : and he weeps for his dear Du Bellay, another victim of destiny :

Lequel après avoir d'une si docte voix
Tant de fois rechanté les Princes et les Roys
Est mort pauvre, chetif, sans nulle recompence
Sinon du fameux bruit que luy garde la France.[2]

He reminds the Queen-Mother how he has surrounded the Crown of France with loyal praise and glory and how his reward has been to see rascals favoured and the deserving passed over : and he appeals bitterly to Posterity not to judge him by his half-begun *Franciade,* that long-promised rival to the *Iliad,* and dismiss him as a trifler. It is the fault of the ungrateful Crown.

J'avois l'esprit gaillard et le cœur genereux
Pour faire un si grand œuvre en toute hardiesse,
Mais au besoin les Roys m'ont failly de promesse,
Ils ont tranché mon cours au milieu de mes vers . . .[3]

But although the ear of Majesty still continues hard of hearing, a little light appears on the grey horizon. Catherine de Médicis intends to launch during a temporary truce a series of those splendid Court festivities which, as Brantôme shows, were calculated

[1] There, as if beside myself, I accused Fortune,
Mother of flatterers, harsh tormentor
Of men of virtue, living condemned
To suffer, one and all, misfortune from their ill-disposed Stars,
I cursed Apollo, the Graces and the Muses,
And the worthy trade which amuses me in my folly . . .

[2] Who after having, with such a skilful voice,
So many times sung princes and kings,
Has died poor, sick, with no recompense
Beyond the loud fame which France preserves for him.

[3] With a gallant spirit and a generous heart I was ready to undertake such a great work with all my vigour ; but in my need Kings failed of their promise to me, and cut short my zeal in the middle of my work.

propaganda, impressing ambassadors and other observers, hostile
and friendly, with the fact that France was not yet brought to ruin.
She hopes also to bring the rival party chiefs together to
make a solid peace. For this purpose she needs Ronsard, as
James I will later employ Ben Jonson, as pageant-master and maker
of masques. Among the first-fruits of the new employ is a piece
of verse, composed by Ronsard for recital by the French
Ambassador to England during the festivities at Fontainebleau,
in 1564, with a remarkable ring to an English ear.

> *Le monde est le theatre, et les hommes acteurs,*
> *La Fortune qui est maistresse de la scene*
> *Apreste les habitz, et de la vie humaine*
> *Les Cieux et les Destins sont les grans spectateurs ;*
> *En gestes differens, en differens langages,*
> *Roys, Princes, et Bergers jouent leurs personnages*
> *Devant les yeux de tous, sur l'escharfaut commun . . .*[1]

Is it possible that twenty or thirty years later Shakespeare may
have read this piece, written in the year of his birth, and expanded
these opening lines of the celebrated Frenchman—they do not
develop Shakespearianly any further—into Jaques' monologue?
It is unthinkable that the name of Ronsard, with his European
reputation, his influence on the Elizabethan lyricists, and his popu-
larity with Elizabeth herself, should not have cropped up during
those agapes at the Mermaid, and his verse quoted. I have not
traced it in Ben Jonson's works, but I believe the truculent Jonson
somewhere mentions Ronsard with warm praise. There may have
been literary gentlemen on the fringe of the Mermaid Group who,
after the first night of *As You Like It,* flicked over Ronsard's pages
with avenging thumbs, snarling " Plagiarist! " This coincidence
between the two greatest Renaissance poets, though the theme
is fairly obvious, is interesting.

One may pause profitably a moment to reflect that Ronsard's

[1] The world's a theatre, and mankind the players ;
And Fortune, who is mistress of the stage,
Lends costumes, and Heaven and Destiny
Are the great spectators of human life ;
With differing gestures and in different tongues
Kings, princes and shepherds play their parts
Before the eyes of all, on the common boards. . . .

ack of interest in the theatre may have deprived France of a
dramatic poet wielding the alexandrine with the ease of Corneille
and Racine (though lacking their subtlety and godlike restraint),
and more steeped than they in the spirit of Greece and Rome.
Perhaps, like most other human beings, Ronsard had actually tried
his hand at playwriting; perhaps his cabinet-drawers were full,
like most people's, of brilliant first acts. From a couplet of ever-
green truth in one of his poems to Charles IX,

> *Comme un meschant Comique en son theatre faict*
> *Le premier acte bon, le dernier imparfaict,*[1]

I incline to deduce that Ronsard had been once among the
majority and had gracefully learned his lesson. He could hardly
have burdened the revived French stage with anything duller than
the *Eugène* and *Cléopatre* of his friend Jodelle, portents in their day.

Life as masque-provider and producer to the Court of France
cannot have been all roses and nightingales. Persuading princes,
ambassadors, courtiers, Court beauties, and the rich to speak
verse intelligently needs a patience Ronsard did not normally
possess. Coping with three Drury Lane leading ladies at a time
drove Garrick raving mad. Ronsard, preoccupied with problems of
etiquette as well as problems of production, had to choose his
leading ladies from dozens. (Brantôme gives up listing the ladies
of the French Court by name and quality after the first hundred
or so, to save himself a headache, and remarks that even then he
has not got them all in order of precedence; but he mixes up the
generations and is otherwise careless.) Moreover, when the Court
moves, as it does frequently, apart from those pacifying tours of
the energetic and restless Queen-Mother—she reminds one somewhat of the Sahiba in *Kim*—Ronsard must go with it, providing
anything from a baptismal ode for a newborn Royalty to a full-
length masque in verse. He certainly earns whatever new fees
(it is not known what these were) he gets; and he is a happier
man. For one thing, a period of peace has come with the treaty of
Amboise (1563)[2] and he justly praises Catherine for this boon.

---

[1] As a bad playwright in his pieces makes his first act good, his last act weak . . .

[2] By which Condé secured religious freedom for the Calvinist aristocracy, and assisted
in expelling the English from Havre.

Morts sont les mots Papaux et Huguenotz,
Le Prestre vit en tranquille repos,
Le vieil soudart se tient à son mesnage,
L'artizan chante en faisant son ouvrage . . .[1]

With the Court, and enjoying the personal friendship of the
poetry-loving King, young Charles IX, who has taken strongly
to him, Ronsard travels as far south as Bordeaux, if not to Bayonne
where the Queen-Mother is visiting her daughter, Elizabeth of
Spain, wife of the redoubtable Philip II. And at long last he gets
the first of his major benefices, a modest one enough. It is the
priory of St. Cosme-lez-Tours, on the island in the Loire where
ten years ago or less he danced at the cousin's wedding-feast with
his darling Marie. Impossible not to imagine the scent of that old
and passionate love filling his nostrils with remembrance as he
takes formal possession (March, 1565); impossible not to imagine
him revisiting old scenes, hearing vanished voices, torn by old
regrets. But he cannot stay long in St. Cosme. In July of the same
year he is back in Paris and his newest verse-collection, *Elegies,
Mascarades, et Bergerie* is out, the first two portions dedicated to
Elizabeth, Queen of England, whose thirty-two-year-old virgin
hand and black-toothed kisses are now, tentatively, in the market,
so to speak, for bestowal on thirteen-year-old Charles IX; a
pretty match, which Catherine de Médicis seems inclined to favour.
As queens in this age are all mirrors of beauty, it is Ronsard's
duty, glorifying the new *entente*, to laud this hag in a dedicatory
elegy and to flatter Dudley, Earl of Leicester, her fancy man.
With blushes which Ronsard may have shared I quote four lines:

Et lors je dy si cette Royne Angloise
Est en beauté pareille à l'Escossoise,
Comment voit on en lumière pareilz
Dedans un isle ensemble deux soleils . . .[2]

[1] Dead are the words "Papist" and "Huguenot",
The priest lives in tranquil peace,
The old soldier stays at his fireside,
The workman sings at his work . . .

[2] Therefore I say, if this English Queen
Rivals the Scot in beauty
How does one see, equal in brilliance,
Two suns within an isle together. . . .

The divine eyes of Mary Stuart, now the bride of the popinjay
Darnley and beginning to grapple with her major woes, may have
flashed azure scorn at this effort of her darling poet; or rather,
knowing the rules, she may have laughed and pitied him. Perhaps
to show her his true feelings, Ronsard has dedicated the
jewel of this collection, the *Bergerie*, "to the majesty of the
Queen of Scotland", a compliment, as she will understand,
transcending any official flattery of the Tudor crone, whose
delight expressed itself in a fine diamond for the poet and the
Garter for his King.

This volume shows Ronsard in serene possession of the old
sweet elegant magic, though the affectations of the *genre* are not
everybody's taste, including my own. In the *Bergerie*, written
to be recited and sung by the five Royal children in honour of
the stout Chief Shepherdess, twelve noble *bergères* sing in
chorus:

> *Si nous voyons le Siècle d'Or refait*
> *C'est du bienfait*
> *De la Bergère* CATHERINE.[1]

A chorus of noble shepherds answers them in praise of the
shepherd Carlin, Charles IX:

> *J'ay songé sur la minuict*
> *Cette nuict,*
> *Quand le doux sommeil nous lie,*
> *Que deux beaux Cygnes chantoient*
> *Qui sortoient*
> *Du costé de l'Italie;*
> *J'en ay vu d'autres aussy*
> *Tout ainsy*
> *Venir du costé d'Espaigne,*
> *Et d'autres forts et puissants*
> *Blanchissants*
> *Du costé de l'Allemaigne:*
> *Puis en tournant tout en rond*
> *Sur le front*
> *De* CARLIN, *luy faire feste,*

[1] If we see the Age of Gold returned, it is by the benefaction of the shepherdess Catherine.

Ronsard

Et doulcement en chantant
L'eventant,
Luy predire une conqueste . . .[1]

The master—compare the *bergeries* of other Court poets, including those Molière made for Louis XIV—is certainly at the top of his form.

And Genèvre?

That devouring flame has blazed itself out long since, a fire of straw. The lover who could not eat or rest or sleep for madness of longing, whose heart was imprisoned for ever in the blonde silken net of Genèvre's tresses, who evokes in one of his elegies to her the complete fusion into one-ness, the *amour total* of his ideal:

> *Vostre ame estoit dedans la mienne enclose,*
> *La mienne estoit en la vostre, et nos corps*
> *Par sympathie et semblables accords*
> *N'estoient plus qu'un: si bien que vous, ma Dame,*
> *Et moy n'estions qu'un seul corps et qu'une âme . . .*[2]

—the lover who recently, when the Court was at St. Germain-en-Laye, stood tiptoe upon a little hill looking towards Paris, inhaling deep passionate draughts of the beloved's honey-breath, and then, flinging himself on his horse, galloped along the high road, by Rueil and Asnières, and, entering Paris and seeing his Genèvre seated (as ever!) by her door in a sad reverie, trembled from head to foot and turned away, like a Dante, not daring to speak—this tearing Rodomont of lovers, Pierre de Ronsard, has got completely over his fever in little more than twelve months. So, apparently, has Genèvre. It was inevitable. Her adorer has hardly noted with faint surprise that the fires are sinking before the whole thing is over and done. He shrugs and blames nobody but Fate and, perhaps, two wayward temperaments.

[1] I dreamed near midnight, this night, when sweet sleep holds us bound, that two lovely swans were singing, issuing from the direction of Italy; and I saw others also issuing from the direction of Spain; and others, strong, powerful, and gleaming, from the direction of Germany; and then, sweeping round and round over the forehead of Carlin, I saw them honour him, gently fanning him as they sang, and foretelling a conquest for him . . .

[2] Your soul was enclosed in mine, mine in yours, and our bodies with like sympathy and accord were no more but one; so that you and I, my lady, were nothing but one body and one soul.

Fust que le Ciel le commandast ainsi,
Fust vostre faute ou fust la mienne aussi,
Fust par malheur ou par cas d'aventure,
Fust que chacun ensuivant sa nature
Par trop enclin aux nouvelles amours,
Ah! fier Destin, nous rompismes le cours . . .
Si que tous deux faschez de trop de loy
Fusmes contens de rompre nostre foy,
Pour la donner à de moindres, peut-estre . . .[1]

In that flaming epistle to Genèvre from the country he had
already paused to remark (in an aside, so to speak) on a fact which
has puzzled and saddened lovers in every age:

Bref, je ne sais que c'est, mais certes je sais bien
Que j'ayme mieux absent qu'estant prez de mon bien.[2]

Myriads of Romeos must have been disconcerted at realising
suddenly that the appeal of their Juliet is in inverse ratio to her
distance from the point where they happen to be: a tragi-comic
surprise past which other authorities on the art of love have skated
with elaborate unawareness. So far as I remember Stendhal does
not discuss it in *De l'Amour*. Ovid certainly does not. It is a matter,
perhaps, for a Cambridge mathematician.

So the Genèvre affair ends. No hearts are broken, no hard
words fly, there is no recrimination or pining, and *tout finit par des
chansons*. Meditating at her door in the Faubourg St. Marcel on
future summer evenings, Genèvre may have deemed it good
riddance, on the whole, from a too-illustrious, volatile, and over-
bearing lover.

As for Ronsard, he has produced from this affair another volume
of verse, *Les Trois Livres du Recueil des Nouvelles Poësies* (October,
1563), containing finished experiments in yet another new direction,
that of the Nature Idyll and the Bucolic, mingling mythology
with Wordsworthian limpidity and exact observation, and including,

[1] Whether Heaven ordered it thus, whether it was your fault or mine, whether misfortune
or accident, or whether each of us was merely following his character, too prone to new
loves—ah! cruel Destiny, we broke the chain . . . So that both of us, weary of too much
servitude, were content to forswear our troth—to pledge it, perhaps, to less worthy loves . . .
[2] In short, I don't know how it is, but I certainly know I love much better in absence than
when I am close to my dear.

of course, the Genèvre pieces, since every poet worthy of the name exploits Eros as indefatigably as Eros exploits him. From one of four *Hymnes* to the seasons, Autumn, comes that passage remembering his happy childhood and his dream-companions, the nymphs and fauns of the Forest of Gastine and the groves of the Vendômois, which I have quoted in an earlier page. In another piece Ronsard reproduces brook-music so artfully that you hear and see clear water babbling among pebbles and winding thence, more smoothly, among the fields :

> *Du pied naist un ruisseau, dont le bruit delectable*
> *S'enroüe entrecassé des cailloux et du sable,*
> *Puis au travers d'un pré serpentant de maint tour,*
> *Arroüse doucement le lieu de mon sejour . . .*[1]

Robert Louis Stevenson, who devoted so much arduous study to shapes and sounds of vocables, could not better the auditory effect of those recurring " p's " and " b's " and hard " c's " of the first couplet, and the softer " s's " and " c's " of the last line.

So Genèvre, whose passion has helped to stimulate this new poetic triumph, serves her turn, and Ronsard is already in love again, this time with a lady of the Court, to whom his new book is dedicated : a very noble hussy indeed.

[1] From its foot is born a brook whose delectable noise, husky with brawling over pebbles and sand, then flowing in a thousand curves through a meadow, sweetly waters the place of my habitation. . . .

VI

INTERLUDE: CONVERSATION WITH A SHADE

*June night : dusk and open
windows.*

"How thick your roses grow this year! *La Rose embellit toutes hoses*. But I fancy a slightly more vigorous use of the pruning-nife . . . May I enter?"

"Did anyone speak?"

"It is I, *Monsieur mon biographe*. I have been looking at your garden. Your marrows are not very interesting—I speak as a grower. On the other hand I have been following your account of myself with a certain amused attention, I admit."

"I am gratified, *cher Maître*."

"Do you know, *Monsieur mon biographe*, it would oblige me infinitely if you refrained from addressing me as if I were the new laureate of Fouilly-les-Oies?"

"A thousand pardons, Messire de Ronsard. It is a modern trick——"

"You have lived in Paris?"

"Some years."

"Then I discern in that '*cher Maître*' a tinge of irony which is doubly displeasing."

"I beg you to believe no irony could possibly be intended."

"No? No . . . Of course not. (May I take the tall chair? Thank you.) Forgive me. I am rather thin-skinned, as you know. Too prickly, too impetuous . . . I notice you have not made much of *l'affaire* Paschal, that ironic comedy of my youth."[1]

"I did not think it very important."

"Ta, ta, ta! It is diverting, though I did not invariably think so then. Besides, it has didactic value. The splendid conceit of youth! The superb assurance! The joyous ripple of the muscles under the oily bronze as one watches the judges assembling! I

[1] See pp. 52–3, *ante.*

177

am thinking of those Olympian athletes of Pindar's. One is vibra
with life and genius and hungry for glory. *La gloire !* It soun
differently, I believe, on English lips. You islanders are rath
awkwardly self-conscious. Hypocrisy or mere uncouthness
I have never been able to decide. We French have no such—
what's your word nowadays ? "

" Inhibitions ? "

" From *inhibeo*, doubtless. Its present esoteric meaning,
any ? "

" It's just a jargon-word in favour at the moment, chiefly wit.
rich women and their medical advisers."

" Ah, the doctors! *L'argenteuse science*, as my dear Du Bella
so aptly said, or was the epithet my own ? It does not matter
Do your modern . . . inhibitions reward the doctors as the
should ? "

" Satisfactorily, I believe."

" In my time it was ' humours ' . . . What was I saying :
Oh, yes, the Paschal affair. How ardent we were, we of the Brigade
The golden company! And then—*voilà*! Along bustles this
Pierre Paschal with his Italian laurels and his promise of mountains
and marvels. Do you wonder we flattered that bouncing little
Gascon ? "

" Excessively, perhaps ? "

" I know, I know. But consider the bait. Paschal was to enshrine
us, the young paladins of the new French culture, in a temple of
fame, in that choice Ciceronian rhetoric he made his reputation
with in the South. ' Picked Tully every word '—who said that ?
The insufferable Malherbe ? "

" Wasn't it Browning ? "

" Ah, one of yours. . . . Well, mark this Pierre Paschal. A
Gascon, remember, with all the volubility and swagger and tall
talk of his tiresome kind (I except my dear Brantôme). But I
wouldn't call Paschal a charlatan, for all that."

" You called him worse in due course."

" In my ' Invective ' [1] ? Ha, ha. What fun that was! A dainty
little piece of *bon gros latin*, don't you agree ? "

" A model of graceful Latin prose of the Decadence, Messire."

[1] *Petri Paschasii Elogium* (1559).

" I laughed over it then and I laugh now, but dear God! I was
annoyed as well. It was I who made the fellow, after all. When
he first arrived in Paris nobody had ever heard of him! "

" They soon did, certainly."

" Yes, yes. I know. Those odes and dedications. I overdid
it. We all overdid it, perhaps. But don't forget the fellow certainly
had Latin. He was no impostor."

" Merely an exploiter."

" Maybe. Maybe. I should describe him personally as a
character out of the Commedia dell 'Arte. He reminds me strongly
of Brighella—you know Brighella ? The 'one who gets away with
it,' to use your current Anglo-Saxon idiom. You know the rest of
the Paschal epic, of course ? "

" Paschal fooled you neatly, if I may permit myself the word.
In anticipation of favours to come, you and your poets of the
Brigade kept up such a chorus of praise that the very highest quarters
took note of Paschal, and before long the Gascon climbed nimbly
on your shoulders into one of the most enviable literary posts in
France and became Historiographer to the King. Did you hear
any more of his Temple of Fame, in which your statues were to
have stood bathed in golden light, the admiration of all Europe ? "

" Never a word. The little Gascon exploited us, as you say.
I bear him no grudge. I did not need any Paschalian fanfares,
as it turned out."

" You did not, Messire."

" And I got something back with my ' Invective '—without
malice, of course."

" Yes, you took him amusingly to pieces. Even his beard——"

" His nose—do you remember my remarks on his classic nose ?
Naso ad aliquid olfaciendum semper intento. Yes, I think I hit off
Master Pierre Paschal quite satisfactorily."

" We could never do that sort of thing in England to-day, and
now Léon Daudet's gone I can't see who is to do it properly in
France, either."

" Why can't you do it in England ? "

" Your adversary would rush at once to his lawyers and a jury
would award him thumping damages for hurt to his reputation.
The judge would weep."

" Incredible ! So this is what the *blonds nourrissons de la froi*
Angleterre have come to ? Does this obtain equally in Scotland ?

" Even there. You know Scotland, of course."

" I have never forgotten Scotland, its appalling climate, i
adorable Queen, or her blackguard subjects. I am told an Englisl
man has recently written exquisitely about that lovely one.[1] Conve
him my distinguished compliments. There is one other thing
wish to speak to you about, *Monsieur mon biographe*."

" Yes, Messire ? "

" I trust you will continue to reproduce my verse with the mos
anxious exactitude—not merely as to typography, orthography
and arrangement, but as to punctuation, to which I have alway
devoted scrupulous attention. One colon replacing a fullstoj
can ruin an entire sonnet! Whose edition are you using:
Laumonier's, is it not ? "

" Chiefly."

" Laumonier is a fine scholar and a humanist. Some others—
well! Remember that though I was always madly in love I nevei
allowed passion to get the upper hand of poetry."

" That reminds me, Messire de Ronsard. I trust I am correct
in assuming that the lesser and lighter loves celebrated in your
earlier verse were not merely ' literary ', that is to say imaginary ? "

" Good God, were Horace's loves imaginary ? "

" According to the learned Mr. Verrall of Cambridge University,
yes."

" Heavens, *la pudeur britannique !* O virtuous Albion! How
truly charming! How that must enchant Horace, not to speak
of our good Rabelais! "

" You are pleased to laugh heartily, Messire de Ronsard. May
I remind you that quite recently the erudite M. Roger Sorg was of
opinion that Cassandre was your only passion and that all the rest
are either adumbrations of her, or else loves ' to order ' ? "

" I am truly grateful to Monsieur Sorg for clearing that up."

" I may add that there are authorities who even say that
Shakespeare's Dark Lady is a figment of the poetic imagination! "

" Shakesp——? Ah, yes."

" You've heard of him ? He flourished a generation after you."

[1] M. de Ronsard probably meant Mr. Maurice Baring.

"Yes, yes. Were not his somewhat untidy works pruned, revised, and polished a little later by Monsieur Ducis in France, and a Monsieur Garrick in England?"

" That's the man. No doubt——"

But the tall smiling shadow with the noble forehead had already melted into the June darkness. Only a waft of roses, and a late blackbird fluting in the grass.

VII

ISABEAU

Une cour, c'est ridicule, disait la comtesse à la marquise, mais c'est amusant; c'est un jeu qui intéresse, mais dont il faut accepter les règles. Qui s'est jamais avisé de se récrier contre le ridicule des règles du whist?
(STENDHAL, *La Chartreuse de Parme*.)

"A Court is ridiculous", the Contessa would say to the Marchesa, "but amusing; an interesting game, but you must obey the rules. Who ever thought of complaining about the absurdity of the rules of whist?"

§1

LIKE SOME STATELY GALLEON OF THE INDIES RUN, ARMED AND arrayed, riding majestic and enormous with full-bellying sails amid a fleet of skiffs and cockboats, the opulent figure of the Queen-Mother Catherine de Médicis sails through that Court life which so bored Pierre de Ronsard. It is worth while contemplating for a moment this *maîtresse femme* after whom the Calvinists named their biggest piece of artillery; a lewd joke, affording the Queen-Mother unaffected amusement.

She resembled Queen Victoria to a surprising degree, both physically (enlarged some half-dozen times) and in her virtues, which were many. No better mother has ever cherished and brought up a sickly brood of nine. No stricter martinet has ever ruled a Court. At her sharp " *Mon amy!* " the boldest faltered; to her sons " *Maman* " was all that title has ever implied in the French matriarchy. No woman crowned has slaved more dutifully at her task of ruling, or striven harder for national unity and peace, or displayed more patience, prudence, and Machiavellian craft, and occasionally cynicism, in handling affairs and men, or flown into more imperial rages at any affront offered her crown and country. Brantôme saw her once watching the English besieging Rouen, letting fly *toutes les collères du monde* as she ordered her troops to hold fast, daily visiting the forts to examine the situation and to see her batteries at work. " Cannonades and arquebus-

were rained all round her", says Brantôme, "and she cared nothing."

A stout woman in every way, and, despite her half-Italian blood and accent—her father was Lorenzo II dei Medici, her mother Madeleine de la Tour-d'Auvergne, her uncle Pope Clement VII— a Frenchwoman to the marrow, except in her freedom from avarice. It is not recorded that "the shopkeeper's daughter", as some of the French aristocracy called this Medici, was ever frightened or lost her nerve, save once. Her responsibility for the St. Bartholomew nightmare, following this single occasion, is clearly implied, though not directly proved. Brantôme, who with other contemporary historians does not hesitate to award her this blame, attaches it to the Calvinist threats, following the Guises' first attempt at liquidating Coligny, to wipe out the entire Royal family : a reasonable explanation enough.

Catherine travelled frequently up and down France with her suite, on missions of pacification and expostulation, in those coaches she introduced from Italy, and the jolting over rough roads must have ravaged many a fair young spine. Her vast and perpetual correspondence—" I have seen her after dinner", says Brantôme, " write with her own hand twenty pairs of letters, long ones "—and needlework were her chief domestic relaxations. She enjoyed the *lazzi* of the flour-faced Zanies and the leather-masked Harlequins of her native Italian Comedy, their gambols and knockabout humours, as Ronsard records with polite neutrality, looking somewhat down his nose. Her addiction to astrology and artichokes was notable, and she rode a horse as well as most great ladies. Music she loved deeply ; in her chapel a choir of picked *chantres* sang Mass and Vespers (Catherine was devout) daily to the music of the best contemporary French and Italian composers. The Louvre under her immediate supervision was almost as rigid, blameless, and dull as Buckingham Palace in the Victorian Age. Conversation, music, needlework, reading, dancing, and performing at intervals in masques and *bergeries* were the indoor recreations of the Queen-Mother's young ladies, who were selected with care. They dressed in high-necked flowing gowns and slept in dormitories ; and if any of them lapsed from virtue, as one or two did, she was instantly sent packing. " *Un vray paradis du monde et escolle de toute honnesteté* ", is Brantôme's rather

wry summing-up—a true earthly paradise, a school of every
virtue. I am ready to take the word of the Gascon. He mention
elsewhere that this finishing-school atmosphere was mitigate
for some of the Queen's ladies, to some extent, by dinner-partie
given by high nobles, and especially by the Duke of Anjou, late
Henri III. That immoralist owned a silver goblet of immense siz
engraved by a master-silversmith with Raimondi's obscen
illustrations to Aretino's verses. From this goblet it was hi
pleasure to make Court prudes sip wine, noting their embarrassmen
or otherwise, with the interest of a Fabre watching butterflies a
play. A curiously Fourth Form pastime for such a character.[1]

One may gather how the daily routine of the Louvre and
Fontainebleau and the other royal châteaux, varied by the hard
labour of producing Court verses and pageantry, fretted and
wearied the very soul of Pierre de Ronsard, so that we find him
writing a few years hence from the country to Scévole de Sainte-
Marthe : " They say the King is coming to Blois and Tours, on
which account I am flying to Paris, for I hate the Court like death."
But meanwhile he had to live.

It would be difficult, contemplating her portrait, to describe
Mademoiselle Isabeau de la Tour-Limeuil, a very *grande dame*
indeed, a cousin of the Queen-Mother, as a flaming beauty by
modern standards. As I have observed before, the Renaissance
women gaze much less comely from their canvases than the
Renaissance men, though lovers flock round them and poets
tirelessly praise their beauty. It may be that the fashion of dragging the hair back off the brow and frizzing it tightly all round
the head under a gauzy triangular bonnet seems to us now one of
the more unfortunate tricks women so often indulge in, or it may
be that among other charms, including that of the *beau tetin* already
mentioned, they all possessed that swing and sparkle and *chic*
the French still esteem far above prettiness. " *Point jolie, certes*",
says Georges Courteline of a charmer in one of his stories, speaking

[1] The vogue of this famous, or rather infamous, set of drawings, for which Marc-Antonio
Raimondi was imprisoned by Clement VII, was not yet as widespread among the European
raffish as it was in the eighteenth century. Lovers of the most amusing biography in the
English language will remember that Joseph Nollekens, R.A., threw his set in the fire at his
confessor's order and afterwards shed tears. Most surviving copies are now safely locked up.

for his countrymen at large, " *mais à coup sûr bien plus que cela.*"
Certainly Isabeau de Limeuil was noted for a piquant wit and high
spirits and a laughing audacity which, combined with her rank,
could swiftly kindle a man of wit and lower station like Ronsard,
and neutralise the effect of a slightly long nose, a slightly thin mouth,
a slightly tall forehead, and a pair of more than slightly arrogant
eyes. At the age of about fifteen Isabeau is said to have written in
schoolgirlish fun a declaration of love in verse and sent it to Condé,
the Calvinist generalissimo. The sprightly little prince, who loved
women almost as much as he loved power, returned a courteously
formal reply thanking Mademoiselle, regretting that his heart was
reserved for the love of God, and offering her his friendship.
At the time Ronsard falls in love with Isabeau she is about sixteen,
a maid of honour to the Queen-Mother, and already enjoying that
kind of reputation about the Court which men discuss in chuckling
undertones. *Pire que jolie.* The fair Isabeau is what the Regency
buck would call a spanker and the Victorian a slap-up filly. She
has led quite a few would-be lovers to make fools of themselves
and then mocked them, though it would seem that not every
victim has been so unfortunate. But as yet there is no scandal.

The progress of Ronsard's affair with Isabeau de Limeuil, as it
unfolds in his verse, starting in hopeless despair at the social gulf
between him and her and ending in cries of treachery, shows that
this entanglement differs from all his previous ones; not only
because of the lofty rank of the beloved, but because his jealous
heart has to suffer a double torture. Isabeau betrays him twice.
Before that, it is clear that she was to the poet what the Victorian
novelists called " more than kind "; how soon after his siege of
her began it is difficult to judge. In the opening lines of a set of
alexandrines called *A Une Grande Dame* he mingles passion with
humble desperate sighing very skilfully.

> *De vous et de Fortune et de moi je me deuls :*
> *De moi, qui sagement commander ne me peus,*
> *Dès les premier combats dont votre belle vue*
> *Vint assaillir mon cœur, ma raison fust emue . . .* [1]

[1] Of you and of Fortune and of myself is my plaint; of myself, incapable of wise self-
control. Ever since those first engagements in which the sight of your beauty assailed my
heart, my reason is shaken . . .

He goes on to bewail her high station.

> *Et de vous je me pleins, qui tenez si haut lieu*
> *Que pour estre servie il vous faudrait un Dieu . . .*
> *Car pour aymer trop haut et pour n'avoir egale*
> *Ma puissance à la vostre, helas ! je suis Tantale . . .*[1]

Waxing bolder, he assures her that if she will overlook the gulf between them, she will find Pierre de Ronsard no prentice lover, but discreet and expert in the tender arts :

> *J'ai comme aventureux en divers lieux aymé,*
> *Toujours sage et discret des Dames estimé . . .*
> *Je n'y fis jamais faute et ne pourrois le faire*
> *Comme predestiné pour aux Dames complaire. . . .*[2]

But if she spurns him he will have nothing left but to wait for death (poets say these things) ; and when he is dead his shade will await hers in the Happy Fields, where all are equal, and he will take his love's revenge.

> *Tantost je vous verray dessur l'herbe couchée,*
> *Tantost j'auray ma teste en vostre sein penchée,*
> *Tantost je baiseray vostre bouche et vos yeux . . .*[3]

And so on. Such prostration, such promises, and above all, such a self-awarded testimonial could hardly fail to pique the curiosity of any light-minded great lady. Before long Ronsard is pouring out a new triumphant note of joy, like a lark, in that spring-song, most of which I have recently set down (p. 159), which is addressed to Isabeau de Limeuil and begins :

[1] And of you also is my plaint, who are so loftily placed that you need a god to serve you. Setting my love too high and unable to equal my power to yours, I am a Tantalus, alas !

[2] In Love's adventures I have wooed in many places, always prudent, discreet, and esteemed by ladies ; never have I made mistakes, nor could I ever, being as it were predestined to please the fair.

[3] Sometimes I shall see you reclining on the grass ; sometimes I will bend my head over your breast ; sometimes I will kiss your mouth and eyes . . .

Isabeau

Quand ce beau Printemps je voy,
J'apperçoy
Rajeunir la terre et l'onde,
Et me semble que le jour
Et l'amour
Comme enfans naissent au monde . . .[1]

It is very long, and its clear, glad song never falters. He is evidently excited and happy, his Fate has seemingly relented; but his sunshine is soon flecked by shadow. One judges that his lady of quality keeps him dangling for some time in cruel suspense, now according a few favours, now withholding them; and he is, of course, as jealous as the devil of the brilliant high-born crowd in which she moves. Even when Isabeau appears to have signified at length that she is not averse to his prayers, even when the last favours have been granted, he cannot be certain.

J'ay peur que vostre amour par le temps ne s'efface,
Je doute qu'un plus grand ne gaigne vostre grace,
J'ay peur que quelque Dieu ne vous emporte aux cieux,
Je suis jaloux de moy, de mon cœur, de mes yeux,
De mes pas, de mon ombre, et mon ame est eprise
De frayeur, si quelqu'un avecque vous devise . . .[2]

Ronsard had good reason to fear the great. In 1564, a year after he had dedicated the *Recueil des Nouvelles Poësies* to Isabeau, a pretty little scandal broke out. While the Court was at Dijon, beginning that memorable tour of France, lasting two years, which Catherine organised for Charles IX to meet and know his subjects, the Queen-Mother suddenly dismissed Isabeau from her service and sent her in disgrace to a convent at Auxonne. The martinet Catherine had just discovered a secret known to nobody except the Court, half Paris, and the Spanish Ambassador, who mentioned it to Philip II in a despatch of 1563. Isabeau de Limeuil had been for at least a year the mistress of Condé, Duc de Bourbon, who

[1] When I see this lovely Spring, I perceive land and sea in youth renewed, and it seems to me as if Morning and Love are born into the world, like children . . .
[2] I have fears that your love will fade in time; I dread a greater than I who may gain your heart; I have fears that some god may carry you off to the skies; I am jealous of myself, my heart, my eyes, my step, my shadow, and my soul is seized with fright if anyone speaks to you . . .

had returned to Court after the truce of Amboise (March 1563
and she was in what British journalistic delicacy used till recentl
to refer to as " a certain condition".[1] I cannot believe that *l'affair*
Ronsard was still continuing on her side. It had already bee
undermined by recurring attacks of jealousy, not only on hi
part (for we find Isabeau accusing him of paying court and com
posing verses to another lady, which is true. Françoise d'Estrée
is her name, and Ronsard explains that this is quite, quite different
He greatly admires " Astrée ", but it is Isabeau whom he adores).
Plainly Condé, not the sort of man to share an amour,[2] had swep
Isabeau away from Ronsard and everybody else by the year 1563
and the false one seemed infatuated with him ; so infatuated that
when the fiery, high-stomached little man swore to abduct her
from her convent, in the best Don Juanesque manner, her letters
show that she was ready for anything.

Here that Comic Spirit whom Meredith invoked in another
egoist's difficulty prances, genteelly smirking, on the scene. Condé,
though sensitive and raging over the public disgrace of his light-
of-love, is no fool, and second thoughts leave him indisposed to
provoke the Queen-Mother further. He decides to turn to less
dangerous pastimes, leaves Isabeau to languish in her convent, and
a few months later, in the autumn of 1565, being about to marry
Françoise d'Orléans, writes coolly to his ex-mistress asking for his
presents back : the many jewels and books he has given her, and
especially his portrait. It gives one (as it gives Brantôme, who
relates the whole story with relish) a certain pleasure to record that
Condé duly gets his portrait back, embellished on the forehead
with a noble pair of horns, executed in ink by the spirited hand of
Isabeau herself. *Un cocu, c'est toujours comique*, as M. Guitry has
remarked. The suppressed laughter of the Court, the fury of the
Prince de Bourbon-Condé and his bride, and the vengeful glee
of Pierre de Ronsard may easily be imagined.

But if Ronsard, still nursing his jealous pain, thought this business
had advantaged him in any way and that Isabeau de Limeuil would
resume their romance, the poetic fruits of which are less luscious
than usual—perhaps he had suffered for once too genuinely even

[1] A son was born at Lyons, June 1564.
[2] As M. Champion oddly suggests.

write—he was mistaken. A fresh blow awaited him. Sobered
her adventure, Mademoiselle de Limeuil obtained the Queen-
other's permission to leave her convent in the following year,
d a year after that she married the millionaire Italian banker,
ipio Sardini, who owned the lovely chateau of Chaumont on
e Loire. Judging her punished enough, the good-natured
atherine even relented sufficiently, now that the naughty cousin
as decently settled, to take her back into service; so Ronsard
uld feast his bitter eyes once more on her to whom he had
tely cried:

> *Chère maistresse à qui je dois la vie,*
> *Le coeur, le corps et le sang et l'esprit,*
> *Voyant tes yeux l'Amour mesme m'apprit*
> *Toute vertu que depuis j'ay suivie* . . .[1]

Bitterness assails him furiously at the thought that Isabeau
s not only married, but married to a foreigner, to one of those
talians of whom, in a very Gallic wave of xenophobia, he com-
lains at this time to the Queen-Mother, herself half an Italian.
These foreigners who are overrunning France and getting offices
and benefices from the Crown, to the detriment of true Frenchmen
—can nothing be done about them? Evidently Isabeau's marriage
s festering deep in his heart. He was present apparently at the
wedding-ceremony, and saw the crowd, and heard the hautboys,
and contemplated those golden tresses with which he once toyed:

> . . . *cheveux que d'amour fol*
> *J'ay baisez et liez mille fois à mon col.*[2]

Must a foreigner steal these things?

> *Faut-il qu'un estranger me ravisse ma Dame?*
> *Faut-il qu'un autre corps jouysse de mon ame?*[3]

---

[1] Dear Mistress, to whom I owe my being, my heart, body, blood, and spirit, on seeing
your eyes Love himself taught me all the virtues I have since followed . . .
[2] . . . hair that, mad with passion, I kissed and twined a thousand times around my neck.
[3] Must a foreigner ravish my lady from me? Must the body of another take pleasure
with my soul?

He can hardly believe that it is his Isabeau who stands befo
the altar with this Italian ; but so it is.

> *C'est elle, je la voy, je congnoy son visage,*
> *Qui m'a tenu quatre ans en l'amoureux servage . . .*[1]

Despite her portrait Isabeau must have been attractive, f
Brantôme, whom she also moved to verse, not very good, prais
her complexion, her fine eyes, like those of the Cyprian hersel
her sweet voice, her noble forehead. And Ronsard in his jealou
rage calls down maledictions on her husband, the banker Sardin
to whom he accuses her of selling herself, crying to hags an
witches and the Furies to hover round the bridal-bed, prayin
that the banker may be struck with sterility and that perpetu
strife and absence of pleasure may make his married life hideous
a very pretty epithalamion, and a nice pendant to Edmun
Spenser's.

It would seem that her injured lover's reactions did not interes
Madame de Sardini to any extent. Her thoughts were chiefl
centred, as will appear, on the faithless Condé. The ragings of he
late poet probably moved her as little as the discontent of he
husband, whom Brantôme reports as saying to her one day, durin
an exchange of domestic sugarplums : " I have done more for yo
than you have for me ; I abandoned my honour to give you bacl
yours." If the wayward and freespoken Isabeau—she came of a
wayward family ; her elder sister died to the music of *La Defait*
des Suisses, played by her order at her bedside, on the violin—made
a suitable reply, it is unrecorded. She gave Sardini numerous
offspring nevertheless.

Three years after her marriage Isabeau de Sardini, travelling
to her chateau of Chaumont on the day of the battle of Jarnac,
encountered on the road a litter escorted by soldiers. The young
Duke of Anjou, who had just routed the Calvinist forces, rode up
and invited her smilingly to step from her coach and identify the
body. She knelt in the road, uncovered the face, and cried joyously
" *Enfin !* "—" At last ! " It was the corpse of Condé.

---

[1] It is she, I see her, I know that face which has held me four years in the chains of love . . .

§2

Friendship, peculiar boon of Heav'n,
The noble mind's delight and pride . . .
(JOHNSON)

Quia multum amavit should certainly have been chiselled on
the tombstone of Pierre de Ronsard ; nor was this princely heart
so preoccupied with the love of women that it had nothing else
to give. He had indeed a genius for friendship and loved his friends
greatly, and he wrote many pieces in which affection shines with
all those "lambent glories" of which Johnson sang. It is time
perhaps to become aware of this aspect of Ronsard's temperament,
as vigorous as his lovemaking, and I propose to devote this interlude
to one or two of these songs of friendship.

The first dates from just before 1550, in his student days, when
Paris was a sungilt and intoxicating town, the modern Athens,
shrine of the Muses, garden of the Pierides, home of the beloved
master Dorat. He had lately been into Gascony or even further
south—for what purpose is not known ; probably for pleasure—
and had seen the far-off Pyrenees, and now, at home in the
Vendômois again, he waves back to his friends in Paris with a
joyous whoop, for his first book of poems is nearly ready to be
launched on the world and he will soon be rejoining the Brigade.
It is a piece full of youthful exaltation, pride, and happiness.

> *Deux et trois fois heureux ce mien regard*
> *Duquel je voy la Ville où sont infuses*
> *La discipline et la gloire des Muses,*
> *C'est toy, Paris, que Dieu conserve et gard !* . . .

> *Combien je sens ma vie heureuse en elle*
> *En te voyant, au prix de ces monts blancs*
> *Qui ont l'eschine et la teste et les flancs*
> *Chargés de glace et de neige eternelle !*
> *Je vois desja la bande solenelle*
> *Du saint Parnasse en avant s'approcher,*
> *Et me baiser, m'accoler, et toucher,*
> *Me rappelant à son estude belle.*

Ronsard

De l'autre part ma librairie, hélas !
Grecque, latine, espaignole, italique,
En me tanssant d'un front melancolique
Me dit que plus je n'adore Pallas.
Un million d'amis ne seront las
Deux jours entiers de me faire la feste,
Un Peletier qui a dedans la teste
Muses et Dieux, les Nymphes et leurs lacs,
Dorat, reveil de la Science morte,
Et mon Berger, qui s'est fait gouverneur
Non de troupeaux, mais de gloire et d'honneur,
Tiendra mon col lacé d'une main forte . . .

Car si le jour voit mon oeuvre entrepris,
L'Espaigne docte et l'Italie apprise,
Celui qui boit le Rhin et la Tamise
Voudra m'apprendre ainsy que je l'appris,
Et mon labeur aura louange et prix.
Sus, Vendômois, petit pays, sus doncques !
Esjouis-toy, si tu t'esjouis oncques
Je vois ton nom fameux par mes escrits ![1]

The echo of Catullus' homecoming salute to little Sirmio shows
we are far back in Ronsard's first period, and the calm assurance
of fame beyond the frontiers of France is not among the least of
the charms of these early lines.

Here is a gay sonnet to his much-loved Joachim du Bellay in
Rome, announcing a new love we have long since encountered.

---

[1] Twice, thrice happy these eyes with which I see the Town wherein are enshrined the
service and glory of the Muses. It is you, Paris! God save and keep you! How happy I
feel my life at the sight of you, compared with these white mountains whose necks and heads
and flanks are covered with ice and eternal snows! Already I see the noble band of holy
Parnassus coming forward to kiss and embrace and touch me, and recall me to my beloved
studies. On the other hand, alas, my library, the Greeks, the Latins, the Spaniards, the
Italians, scolding me with melancholy brows, tell me I adore Athene no more. But a million
friends will not be weary of greeting me for two whole days—Peletier, in whose head reign
Muses and gods, the Nymphs and their snares, Dorat, awakener of dead Knowledge, and
my Bergier, who has made himself a ruler not of sheep but of glory and honour, will hold
me round the neck with strong hands. . . .

For if the day sees my work begun, then learned Spain and cultured Italy, and those
who drink the waters of Rhine and Thames will wish to know me as I know them, and my
labours will win praise and prize. Ho, there! Vendômois, little countryside, ho there!
Rejoice if ever you rejoiced! I see your name made famous by my writing!

Isabeau

Cependant que tu vois le superbe rivage
De la riviere Tusque et le mont Palatin,
Et que l'air des Latins te fait parler Latin,
Changeant à l'estranger ton naturel langage,

Une fille d'Anjou me destient en servage;
Ores baisant cheveux et ores son tetin,
Et ores ses beaux yeux, astres de mon destin,
Je vis, comme l'on dit, trop plus heureux que sage.

Tu diras à Magny, lisant ces vers icy :
" Et quoy ! Ronsard est donq encores amoureux ! "
Mon Bellay, je le suis et le veux estre aussy,

Et ne veux confesser qu'Amour soit malheureux;
Ou, si c'est un malheur, baste ! je delibere
De vivre malheureux en si belle misere.[1]

To Nicholas de Verdun, one of the Royal secretaries, he writes with equal affection.

Si j'avois un riche tresor,
Ou des vaisseaux engravés d'or
Tableaux ou medailles de cuivre,
Ou ces joyaulx qui font passer
Tant de mers pour les amasser
Où le jour se laisse revivre,

Je t'en ferois un beau present,
Mais quoy ! cela ne t'est plaisant;
Aux richesses tu ne t'amuses
Qui ne font que nous etonner;
C'est pourquoy je te veux donner
Le bien que m'ont donné les Muses.

---

[1] While you contemplate the superb banks of the Tuscan stream and the Palatine Hill, while the Latin air makes you speak the Latin tongue, exchanging your native language for foreign speech, a girl of Anjou holds me in bonds; now kissing her hair, now her breasts, and now her lovely eyes, stars of my destiny, I live, as they say, more happy than wise. You will say to Magny, reading these verses here : " What! Ronsard is in love again, then ? " I am, my Bellay, and I wish to be! Nor will I admit that Love is unhappy—or if it is, what of it ? I am determined to live unhappy in such lovely misery.

Ronsard

> *Dieu veuille benir ta maison*
> *De beaux enfans nés à foison*
> *De ta femme belle et pudique;*
> *La concorde habite en ton lit,*
> *Et bien loin de toy soit le bruit*
> *De toute noise domestique!*

> *Sois gaillard, dispos, et joyeux,*
> *Ni convoiteux, ni soucieux*
> *Des choses qui nous rongent l'âme;*
> *Fuis toutes sortes de douleurs,*
> *Et ne prends soucy des malheurs*
> *Qui sont predicts per Nostredame.*

> *N'aye soucy du lendemain,*
> *Mais, serrant le temps en la main,*
> *Vis joyeusement la journée*
> *Et le jour auquel tu seras:*
> *Et que sais-tu si tu verras*
> *L'autre lumière retournée?*[1]

And finally, a tribute to his last and dearest friend, companion of his latest years, his prop, guardian, nurse and executor, his " second soul ", Jean Galland of Arras, Master of the Collège de Boncourt in Paris, which expresses the very utmost that affectionate and admiring friendship can.

> *Galland, ma seconde ame, Atrebatique race,*
> *Encor que nos ayeux ayent emmuré la place*
> *De nos villes bien loin, la tienne près d'Arras,*
> *La mienne près Vandosme, ou le Loir de ses bras*
> *Accuse doucement nos collines vineuses*
> *Et nos champs fromentiers de vagues limoneuses . . .*

[1] Had I a rich treasury, or vessels graved in gold, pictures or bronze medals, or those jewels to gather which so many seas must be crossed, in which light is born again, I would make you a fine present. But no, that does not please you; you are not amused by the riches which merely dazzle; and that is why I wish to give you the gifts the Muses have given me. May God bless your house with fine children a-plenty, born of your beautiful and virtuous wife; may peace reign in your bed, and may the noise of domestic jars be very far from you! May you be gay, content, and joyous, neither coveting nor envying those things which eat away our souls. May you fly all kind of troubles and take no heed of those misfortunes predicted by Nostradamus! Have no care of the morrow, but, holding to-day close in your grasp, live out the days happily as they come to you, for how do you know if you shall see another sun returning?

Heureux qui peut trouver pour passer l'avanture
De ce monde, ung amy de gentille nature
Comme tu es, Galland, en qui les cieux ont mis
Tout le parfaict requis aux plus parfaicts amis.
Jà mon soir s'embrunit, et desjà ma journée
Fuit vers son Occident à demy retournée.
La Parque ne me veult ny me peut secourir :
Encore ta carrière est bien longue à courir,
Ta vie est en sa course, et d'une forte haleine
Et d'un pied vigoureux tu fais jaillir l'areine
Sous tes pas, aussi fort que quelque bon guerrier
Le sablon Aelian, pour le pris du laurier . . .[1]

Ronsard wrote this shortly before his death—perhaps in that room at the Collège de Boncourt which was his haven of refreshment, happiness and peace in the final years. Had Galland no reputation of his own (and he had a considerable one), to evoke such tenderness from a man like Ronsard would have been high distinction in itself, I think. There are scores of tributes scattered up and down Ronsard's works from which one could make a noble garland of friendship. Perhaps he turned to his friends more constantly, and with more relief, than we know.

§3

Whistler's prose, as every lover of *The Gentle Art of Making Enemies* is aware, is as brilliant and capricious in its virtuosity as his painting. Michaelangelo's sonnets are said by connoisseurs to be nearly comparable to some of his sculpture. Modern painters admire Dante Gabriel Rossetti's poetry almost as much as modern poets admire his pictures. A great deal of Milton's prose is as massy, rhythmic and sonorous as *Paradise Lost;* Chaucer's has almost the same vigour and freshness as the *Canterbury Tales.*

[1] Galland, my other soul, Galland of Atrebatic race, although our forebears traced the walls of our towns very far apart—yours near Arras, mine near Vendôme, where the Loir sweetly enfolds our grape-grown slopes and our wheatfields with its loamy waves. . . . Happy he who can find, to travel this world's adventure, a friend of your sweet nature, Galland, in whom Heaven has stored all the perfect requisites of the most perfect friend! Already my skies are darkening, already my day speeds towards its sunset, half spent, and the Fates neither desire nor are able to help me. Your career has still long to run, your life is in its stride, you spurn the sand under your feet with a vigorous foot and a strong breast, as some strong warrior spurns the Aelian sands and strives towards the laurel. . . .

Artists are often capable of producing work of distinction in widel differing media, though it seems that poets have generally writte far better prose than prose-writers poetry. Voltaire is an out standing example.

These *rengaines* may serve to introduce *L'Abbrégé de l'Ar Poëtique François*, a manual in prose which Pierre de Ronsar published in 1565, while still writhing under the treason of Isabeau de la Tour-Limeuil; the most important of his rare prose-piece and a piece of good writing.

L'Abbrégé is Ronsard's artistic credo, a sequel to the *Deffence* of Du Bellay, a survey of the whole technique of writing poetry by a super-eminent poet and craftsman. Its prose is strong and flexible. Its reigning theme is nobility of inspiration. The Muses, he says, come to stay only with gentle hearts. He says to the pupil-poet, " You must, first of all, have high conceptions, conceptions of beauty ; lofty conceptions, soaring, not trailing on the ground." Then the poet must devote himself diligently to the study of great poetry, and must learn as much of it by heart as possible. The master's directions become more and more interesting, and even surprising. It was no news to contemporaries to read that the poet must perpetually use the pruning-knife and the file ; Ronsard himself had long since been pruning and polishing ruthlessly, as his successive editions showed. But when the intelligentsia came to such commandments as :

" You will converse sweetly and frankly with the poets of your time."

" You will honour the oldest of them as your fathers, your equals as your brothers, the least of them as your children, and you will show them all your writings, for you should never publish (*mettre en lumière*) anything which has not previously been viewed and re-viewed by those of your friends most skilled in this trade (*mestier*),"

I can see not a few uplifted eyebrows, and hear not a few explosions of mirth. The haughty prince of poets was indeed offering counsels of perfection, generous as his own example notoriously was. I am not aware that poets have ever followed these counsels to any extent, except during the eighteenth century and in England, when, as we learn from Boswell, many poets from Goldsmith to Crabbe

submitted their work with admirable humility to Johnson for
"revision", and gratefully allowed the Great Cham to rewrite
what lines he would.

The technicalities of the next section of *L'Abbrégé* may be
swiftly passed over. Ronsard lays down the infallible laws of
rhythm, the alternate employment of " masculine " and " feminine "
rhymes[1] which is so important, the need to make one's verses
adaptable to music, " for poetry without musical instruments,
or without the grace of one or several singing voices is by no
means agreeable". It is his old dogma of the early Pléiade days,
and a sound one, chiming very sweetly with the traditional French
care for *la forme*, and still operative, though I cannot see it serving
modern English poets very far; least of all those scrannel pipers
of the latest school of pettish aridity and exasperation, to whose
verse the rattle of rusty typewriters would go more naturally than
the suave plucking of a lute. Ronsard's further direction that
newly-composed verse must be tested by reading or chanting it
aloud is an equally final test for prose, as Kipling discovered.

Nothing more in the *Abbrégé* need detain us but the section
on the choice and use of a vocabulary, which is admirable. A
prudent selection of Old French words from the old romances,
says Ronsard, blended with vivid modern words of the people
and the language of the crafts (such as the jeweller's, the seaman's,
the blacksmith's, the falconer's), and suitable words from the
dialectes de nostre France, from Norman to Gascon—these will
enrich your poetry and make it vigorous, unlike the skimble-
skamble stuff they speak at Court. The slim book ends with a
discussion on neologisms.

Bloodier problems than those of prosody were at this moment
occupying the Queen-Mother, sitting blankly (as we may imagine
her) before her writing-table in the Louvre, or laying her embroidery
in her ample lap and gazing with knitted brows through tall windows
over the river.

We have seen that in 1560 the Calvinist plot known as the
Conspiracy of Amboise, to kidnap young Charles IX and assassinate

---

[1] " Masculine", having a final accented syllable ; " feminine", having an unaccented
syllable following the last accented one.

the Guises, failed. It was betrayed prematurely to François d
Guise, and forty-five Calvinist noblemen paid with their head:
In March, 1562, while Condé was openly recruiting an army
Guise, following his precedent, removed the King from Fontaine
bleau to Paris for safety, with Catherine's approval. In Decembe
of that year Condé defeated the Catholic forces at Dreux, and on
March 19, 1563, the Edict of Amboise gave religious and politica
equality to the Calvinist nobles and gentry, which were Condé':
terms for assisting to expel the English from Havre.

This peace lasted four years and did not solve any problems.
The Queen-Mother's concessions were highly unpopular. In
February, 1563, on the eve of the peace, François de Guise had
been assassinated at Orleans by a Calvinist emissary, which did not
help matters. Behind the main traffic of hostilities, in some of the
cities, and in Paris especially, a regular symphony of aggression
and retaliation had been proceeding. Mob-battles were frequent
in the capital. Priests were murdered at the altar, as in England
in Mary Tudor's reign. Calvinist throats were cut for interrupting
sermons. No sooner had the Queen-Mother left Paris for the
provinces after signing the treaty of Amboise than trouble flared up
again between, on the one hand, the Cardinal of Lorraine and the
Governor, and Condé and Coligny on the other. Thirteen-year-old
Charles IX, on sound advice, placed Paris out of bounds to them all.

Catherine de Médicis, meanwhile, was posting South to meet
her daughter, the Queen of Spain, at Bayonne. She had a somewhat utopian scheme in mind—a kind of Holy Alliance with
Philip II which would enable her to combat the Calvinist heresy
in France without the use of force, which she abhorred. Condé had
thought fit to enlist foreign assistance in arms ; whether Catherine
had the right to act similarly to avoid force is (one judges from
the average liberal-minded historian) highly dubious, to say the
least. The same point will arise in the English troubles later in
this period. English Protestants in Mary's reign had a right to
intrigue against her with the French ; English Catholics in
Elizabeth's reign were traitors for looking for relief from their
persecutor to Spain. Thus true it is that one man may steal a
squadron of horses, while another may not peep even for an
instant over the tiniest hedge.

Catherine's plan failed, and Coligny himself cut the knot of her perplexities in September, 1567, breaking the truce and committing what MM. Dubech and d'Espezel call his *faute définitive*.[1] His attempt to abduct Charles IX with an armed force at the chateau of Monceaux failed, and the King escaped to Meaux, and thence to Paris. The march on Paris by Condé and Coligny and the siege which followed left no doubt in French minds that a major operation was in progress. Urged by the starving populace the Governor of Paris, Montmorency, took his troops out in November and defeated the Calvinists at Montereau ; Montmorency, separated a moment from his staff, was assassinated. After waiting for the Lutheran Elector Palatine, Johann-Casimir, to send reinforcements, the Calvinist army turned on Paris again, ravaged the countryside, occupied Chartres, and dug themselves in at Jargeau. This time neither side took the initiative, and after two months of inaction the truce of Longjumeau (March 23, 1568) ended this phase.

Pierre de Ronsard, then in Paris, records some of these troubles in his panegyric of Charles IX, his patron and friend :

> *Il vist manger son peuple et voller son argent,*
> *Il vist sa Majesté servir d'une risée,*
> *Il vist de cent brocards sa mère mesprisée,*
> *Il se vist dechassé de ses propres maisons,*
> *Il vist les temples saints, le lieu des oraisons,*
> *Autels et sacrements n'estre qu'une voirie,*
> *La raison renversée et regner la furie . . .*[2]

Twice, Ronsard adds, he was in the young King's company when he was forced to fly from his enemies, *par trahison surpris*. It is plain that his unfitness for military service chafed the poet now more than ever.

The truce of Longjumeau lasted hardly longer—to use a consecrated cliché—than the time the ink of the treaty took in drying. In the same year, 1568, conflict breaks out again. The Calvinists

---

[1] *Histoire de Paris*, Paris, 1926.
[2] He saw his people devoured, his treasure stolen, his kingship treated as a jest, his mother insulted by a hundred taunts ; he saw himself forced to fly from his own houses ; he saw the holy temples, the places of prayer, the altars and the Sacraments turned into a dunghill ; he saw Reason overturned and Madness enthroned. . . .

hold almost the entire South—still the principal stronghold o
French Calvinism, however curious that may seem to those who
believe the Reform to be somehow wrapped up with all the rugged
Northern virtues. In the great port and town of La Rochelle
which smells so strong and chill of Calvin even to-day, the English
forces are assembling. On March 13, 1569, Condé at last gets the
major engagement he has been wanting, sees his army shattered,
and falls. In a hurricane charge at Jarnac on the Charente the
Catholic forces under the eighteen-year-old Duke of Anjou,
younger brother of Charles IX, win that victory which moves
Ronsard to an ode of jubilation in his most masterly manner.

> *Tel qu'un petit Aigle sort,*
>   *Brave et fort,*
> *Dessous l'aile de sa mère,*
> *Et d'ongles tortus et longs*
>   *Aux Dragons*
> *Fait guerre sortant de l'aire,*
>
> *Tel qu'un jeune Lionneau*
>   *Tout nouveau,*
> *Quittant caverne et bocage,*
> *Pour premier combat assaut*
>   *D'un coeur haut*
> *Quelque grand Taureau sauvage,*
>
> *Tel au dépens de vos dos,*
>   *Huguenotz !*
> *Sentistes ce jeune Prince,*
> *Fils de Roy, frère de Roy,*
>   *Dont la foy*
> *Merite une autre province !* . . .
>
> *Ainsy Prince valeureux,*
>   *Bienheureux,*
> *Tu mets fin à nostre guerre,*
> *Qui depuis huit ans passez*
>   *Oppressez,*
> *Nous tenoit les coeurs en serre !*[1]

[1] As a young Eagle sallies, brave and strong, from under his mother's wings, making war
with his long crooked talons on dragons issuing from their lair ; as a young Lion, lately

Another brilliant blow follows Jarnac six months later. At
Moncontour a force commanded by Anjou and Tavannes falls
on the enemy in a surprise attack and routs them, with ten thousand
killed. Truly the Hydra is defeated, sings Ronsard, raising a
classical temple to Anjou and his royal brother; but not, it seems,
yet. There is still Coligny, with his foreign allies. In the next
year Coligny is once more threatening Paris, and the Queen-
Mother buys another precarious period of peace with the treaty of
Saint-Germain (August 8, 1570).

§4

Majora canamus—let us see what fresh engagement has been
fought during this time in the lists of Love by Pierre de Ronsard,
that scarred and seasoned campaigner.

The reign of Isabeau de Limeuil, as we have seen, is now over.
The faithless one has abdicated, amid a storm of invective from
her liege, the throne is vacant, the doves of Venus preen themselves,
the heralds and trumpeters doze, there is an air of expectancy in
the chambers leading to the throne-room, like the interval in a
Spanish arena after the *suerte de muerte*. Almost immediately the
trumpets will sound for a fresh engagement. A somewhat dis-
courteous simile, perhaps.

The enigma of the fair Sinope, which I have deemed more
appropriate to examination at this point than earlier, seems to be
resolved, so far as it can be, by Remy Belleau, who explains that
" Sinope " is derived from " the Greek verb σίνω, signifying
to lose, or spoil, and ὄψ, signifying eyesight ". It would thus,
some authorities think, be a play on " Limeuil " (*lime-œil*), signifying much the same; not a very brilliant conceit, but one typical
of the period. In the same punning way Anne de Acquaviva is
celebrated by Court poets as Calliré or Callirhoë, and Madeleine de

---

whelped, leaves the cavern and the undergrowth with high heart to fling himself on some
huge savage bull—so, to the cost of your backs, Huguenots, you have met this young Prince,
the son and brother of Kings, whose valour merits another province! And thus, most
valorous and happy Prince, you put an end to our war, which for eight years past oppressed
us and gripped our hearts!

Ronsard uses the word " Huguenot " only twice. Its origin is still unknown, unless it
comes from the German-Swiss " Eingenot ", a confederate. " Fifteen false etymologies of
this word are noted by Scheler." (Skeat.)

l'Aubespine as Rhodanthe (Ronsard) and Callianthe (Desportes). What evidence there is that Sinope is possibly Isabeau is afforded by one of the notes supplied to the first edition of the Sinope sonnets (1560) by Belleau, who says the name conceals a lady of high birth whom Ronsard loved with *une affection presque furieuse*. From the sixteen sonnets Ronsard devotes to her we gather further that he met her round about 1560, that she was aged sixteen, haughty, and possessed of the customary magic, and that she drove the poet so mad that at one moment he was almost ready to marry her.

> *Mais je voudrois avoir changé mon bonnet rond,*
> *Et vous avoir chez moi pour ma chère espouse !*[1]

This all fits the beginning of *l'affaire* Limeuil, certainly. I see two objections : one, that so great a lady as Isabeau would never have dreamed of marrying a poet of inferior station, and Ronsard would hardly have cherished such a hope for a moment, even with a dispensation ; and two, that the *cruelle Sinope*, according to Ronsard's own complaint, preferred a younger, richer, and handsome lover, which would hardly apply either to Condé or to Sardini, soberly considered, though it might, of course, to some other lover of Isabeau's, unnamed. Perhaps it is most reasonable to dismiss the marriage-hint as a passing poetic frenzy. One is constantly tempted to accept the vows and cries of poets at their face-value. As Mercury—is it not ?—says in the comedy :

> *Les poètes font à leur guise ;*
> *Ce n'est pas la seule sottise*
> *Qu'on voit faire à ces messieurs-là.*[2]

And it is a fact, as many have noted, that although very many poets have announced their intention of dying immediately for love, the actual total of casualties is infinitesimal.

The cruel Sinope had the instant effect on Ronsard of all the other women he loved :

[1] But would that I had discarded my round bonnet, and that I had you at home for my dear wife!
[2] Poets do as they please ; nor is this the only folly one perceives these gentlemen addicted to.

Isabeau

L'an se rajeunissoit en sa verte jouvence
Quand je m'espris je vous, ma Sinopé cruelle,
Seize ans estoient la fleur de vostre age nouvelle,
Et vostre front sentoit encore son enfance . . .[1]

The ritual development follows; her voice, her step, her hands, her eyes so ravish the poet that he could perish at the thought of her, and so forth and so on; *air archi-connu*. For the edition of 1567 Remy Belleau changed his mind about this lady. Commenting on two lines of a sonnet of the Marie cycle in the second book of *Les Amours* in that year:

Vos yeux estoient blessez d'une humeur enflammée
Qui m'ont gasté les miens d'une semblable humeur[2]

Belleau remarks: " Marie had had trouble with her eyes, and the poet having gazed too closely at them, it affected his own. For this reason he calls Marie ' Sinope ', which signifies ' to lose the sight '." The deduction seems plain, though I have not seen it made before. It is not likely that such a correction was made without Ronsard's knowledge. Evidently, I think, Remy Belleau has been instructed by 1567 to divest the treacherous Isabeau-Sinope of her halo and transfer it to Marie Dupin, already the residuary legatee of a few of the Cassandre sonnets.

It is not a matter of Star Chamber importance, but since she contributed to keep the flame of Ronsard's genius burning, Sinope, like Cowper's hare, must not be omitted from any survey of her poet's life and works. She will probably remain a puzzle to editors, and to-day, in purgatory or Paradise, it matters little to her, I guess.

---

[1] The year was renewing itself in vernal youth when I was smitten by you, my cruel Sinope; sixteen you were, in the flower of your age; your face still remembered childhood. . . .
[2] Your eyes were hurt by an inflamed humour
Which has spoiled my own with a similar one.

VIII

ASTRÉE

There are two very natural propensities which we may distinguish in the most virtuous and liberal dispositions, the love of pleasure and the love of action. If the former be refined by art and learning, improved by the charms of social intercourse, and corrected by a just regard to economy, to health, and to reputation, it is productive of the greatest part of the happiness of private life. The love of action is a principle of a much stronger and more doubtful nature.

(GIBBON, *Decline and Fall of the Roman Empire*.)

§1

A MOST DISTINGUISHED AND GLORIOUS WHORE, *illustrissime et grandissime putain*, says the engaging Brantôme of some great lady of his time. He does not name her. She might well have been any one of the seven beautiful celebrated daughters of Jean Babou, Seigneur de La Bourdaisière, Grand-Master of Artillery to Charles IX, known to their admirers as the Seven Deadly Sins. The eldest daughter but one, Françoise, who married Antoine d'Estrées, Marquis de Cœuvres, in 1559, became the mother of one of the most eminent doxies in History: La Belle Gabrielle, principal mistress of Henri Quatre. One might say a gift for horizontality ran, like art or music, in the Babou family. Yet Françoise d'Estrées, Ronsard's Astrée, must be entered in his amorous accounts as a debit. The poet was not among those she deigned to favour, and he found and left her cold.

Astrée's portrait is more attractive than that of most Renaissance ladies. Though the mouth is hard, the eyes are large and lustrous, and, if they do not quite display, like those of Miss Capes in *Emmanuel Burden*, " a fixed expression of confident affection ", they convey a striking awareness and appraisal, so to speak, of the possibilities of the spectator as a *cavalier servente*. Astrée's reputation at Court is illustrated in an anecdote charming in its glimpse of the manners of the Renaissance great. Soon after her marriage, when she was the mistress of Du Guast, the dashing and cultivated captain

f Guards, one of Brantôme's and Ronsard's intimate friends,
strée happened to go one day into a room in the Louvre where
Marguerite de Valois was talking to the Queen-Mother. "Here
omes the captain's tart (*la garce du capitaine*)," said Marguerite,
who detested her. "I prefer, Madam," said the audacious Astrée,
to be the captain's tart than the general's." To appreciate the
lavour of this insult "the general" must be understood in Hamlet's
ense: "the general populace". Her insolence was to bring
Astrée at length to a violent end.

Pierre de Ronsard apparently saw, and was fascinated by, her
at the Fontainebleau *fêtes* at the beginning of 1564, while he was
still smarting for Isabeau de Limeuil, whose own light jealousy
on this point has been mentioned. Astrée was playing some part
in a masque, in a gown ablaze with jewels and a head-dress of pearls,
and the dazzled poet was instantly struck down. Echoing Tibullus,
he cries that on his tomb must be engraved the distich, with its
untranslatable pun :

> *Ronsard, voulant aux astres s'eslever,*
> *Fut foudroyé par une belle Astrée.* [1]

Naturally his wounds are mortal and he cannot live much longer.
It seems that the goddess smiled kindly on her victim. A little
later, at a Court reception, she picked from the dish and gave him
with her own white hand *mainte dragée et mainte confiture*, many a
sugarplum and many a sweetmeat. He was permitted to celebrate
her beauty, and did so in lines which sparkle like Cartier's windows:

> *De quoy te sert mainte agathe gravée,*
> *Maint beau ruby, maint riche diamant ?*
> *Ta beauté seule est ton seul ornement . . .* [2]

We see Astrée sweeping past (*O dea certe !*) in some stiff, gorgeous
pseudo-antique costume in cloth of gold or silver, intricately
embroidered, bestarred with winking gems, dazzling as an Aztec
idol in the light of a myriad candles ; or girding some knight in

---

[1] Ronsard, trying to raise himself to the stars, was struck down by the lovely Astrée.
[2] What need have you of all these engraved agates, these fine rubies, rich diamonds ?
Your beauty is your ornament, alone . . .

pseudo-Roman armour for a joust and giving him the tradition
kiss, to Ronsard's envy:

> *Heureux cent fois, toy chevalier errant,*
> *Que ma Deësse alloit hier parant . . .*

How far the costumier and the jeweller contributed to Ronsard
bedazement it is difficult to judge. In that age the most ill-favoure
of great ladies could, by artifice and in candle-light, produc
breath-taking effects. In the case of Elizabeth Tudor, it seems
the blaze of a stomacher of solid diamonds could effectivel·
nullify any unpleasing impressions conveyed by black teeth, fou
breath, a hooked nose, a humped back, twitching jaw-muscles
peevish eyes, a blotchy skin, and a voice like a peacock's. Womer
with a certain natural beauty, like Astrée, could by the same device
blossom into goddesses nightly. Astrée certainly deprived Ronsard
of breath, in spite (or because) of her keeping him sedulously a·
arm's length. Occasionally, as we have observed, the goddess
unbends. At one festivity she condescends to wear, in the poet's
honour, a sprig of laurel in her golden hair, ensnaring as Cassandre's
long ago. As then, so now Ronsard is allowed to be present while
Astrée's maid is dressing her tresses. He is not allowed to carry
away a long fine strand of gold he has purloined, but he manages
to steal a comb. And that, except for one single frigid kiss and a
sprig of rosemary, is all Pierre de Ronsard will ever obtain from his
Astrée, for all his cries and groans and implorations. Three months,
and the affair is over. I forget which cynical commentator on the
Astrée idyll argues that Ronsard must in fact have received a great
deal more from the fair, judging by the relatively uninspired nature
of the verse she inspires. His own evidence is sufficient to prove
the contrary. " Good-bye, hair !" he cries.

> *Adieu cheveux, liens ambitieux,*
> *Dont l'or frizé ne retint en service . . .*
> *Comme je vins, je m'en revais, maistresse . . .*[2]

[1] A hundred times happy, wandering knight, whom my goddess was yesterday adorning . . .
[2] Good-bye, hair, fetters of my rash desire, whose frizzed gold holds me a slave no
longer . . . As I come, so I retire, mistress . . .

So he shakes himself free, after a short servitude enough, though
ere is no saying how long it took him to heal of his smarts ; a long
me, I surmise, for the Astrée poems do not appear till 1578, four-
en years later, and even in the edition of 1584 Ronsard is still
membering her, at least in verse. It sounds perhaps unneces-
rily harsh to remark that poets have a considerable advantage
ver the rest of men in being able thus to utilise their most intimate
ys and sorrows to the advantage of their literary reputation ;
et it is so, and if so modest a sorrow as a liver-attack can produce
poem like Baudelaire's *Spleen*, who are the rest of mankind to
omplain ?

So Astrée passes out of Ronsard's life, and well for him, perhaps,
hat she does, for she carried a doom. Shortly after the assassination
f her gay, tough, reckless, charming lover Du Guast by the
Baron de Vitteaux, a noted bravo, in 1575, the young marquis de
Tourzel d'Alègre, whose father had been killed by de Vitteaux
n a duel previously, returned from Italy for vengeance. Having
managed to kill de Vitteaux in the ensuing duel without getting a
scratch, d'Alègre received a visitor one evening soon afterwards.
It was Astrée, Madame d'Estrées, calling to thank the young man
fervently for avenging her on Du Guast's murderer, and offering,
as some slight token of her gratitude, a costly ring, a purse of a
thousand crowns, and if desired, her own fair person. The marquis
gracefully declined the first two gifts and accepted the third, and
this incident blossomed into a love-affair so passionate that Françoise
d'Estrées, aged forty-eight but still a beauty, left her husband and
nine children and retired with d'Alègre to the little town of Issoire
in Auvergne, of which he was Governor. Here she lived with her
lover until 1592, when certain tradesmen of Issoire, rebelling at
length against Astrée's tyranny, and especially her habit of ordering
them to be soundly beaten each time they presented their bills,
conspired with other restive elements and rushed the chateau one
June night. They found the marquis and Astrée asleep, stabbed
them, and threw their bodies out of the window ; two children
sleeping in the same room were spared. " Thus perished the bitch,"
concludes the sprightly gossip Tallemant des Réaux. The moral
theologians of modern retail trade may note with surprise that for
once the customer was not Always Right. The dull little town of

Issoire to-day seems remote from scenes of vengeance, its sho
keepers are placable to a degree, and there is no monument erec
by the tradesmen of France to those grocers and butchers w
solved their economic problem in a way which never occurred
Mill or Ricardo.

Thus unromantically died Ronsard's Astrée, a woman of acti
in Gibbon's sense, in her nightgown, beribboned, frizzed, perfume
and unwept, in a microcosm of the Terror. Her poet had then be
dead seven years, or Astrée would almost undoubtedly have earn
a fine Ronsardian elegy, comparing her with Niobe and Antigon
perhaps, and other tragic heroines, but not with Jezebel, who
she most strongly resembled.

Contemplating once more that routine of Court life which
Ronsard's daily fate at this period (we are now in the late 1560's
that existence "unvaried as the note of the cuckow", as Johnso
said of his brief servitude to Sir Wolstan Dixey, one can under
stand those poems, so frequently written by courtiers, cryin
passionately for refreshment, surcease, and the Arcadian life. It i
likely that there is hardly a courtier among them who would no
have been swiftly dismayed by the discovery that the rural popu
lation does not wave gilt crooks and constantly carve love-sonnet
on trees, that sheep are not washed in bergamot, and that the daily
occupations of Strephon and Chloë are far from decorative and
often revolting. Sannazaro, inventor of Arcadia, was nevertheless
the pioneer of a convention which even to-day makes stockbrokers
spend large sums on urbanising week-end cottages, and held
Renaissance Europe even more firmly in its grip.

> A gown made of the finest wool
> Which from our pretty lambs we pull,
> Fair-linèd slippers for the cold
> With buckles of the purest gold . . .

The rustics of that day would have gaped indeed had they
known what fancies weary fine gentlemen in Town wove round
their hard and frugal existence. But Ronsard, a countryman,
never indulges in Arcadian whimsy, outside his rare Court *bergeries*.
His longings for his Vendômois are those of an exile, and his bore-

m with the Louvre and Fontainebleau goes deeper than the
nui of the glittering courtiers surrounding him. One can imagine
m, after some ball or function in those lofty overheated, over-
rfumed, overcrowded salons, tearing off his stiff gala clothes in
e seclusion of his own room, bathing his aching head with rose-
ater, flinging open his window, taking deep feverish draughts
f cool midnight air, leaning out and staring towards Montmartre, or
ver the Forest of Rouvray outside the St. Honoré Gate—dwindled
o-day to the Bois—thinking of the friendly oaks of Gastine
nd the plash of the Fontaine Bellerie ; and then sitting down,
vith a sigh, to finish the verses he had promised some Court lady,
Mlle de l'Aubespine or Mme de Chateaubrun, or some other of
he myriad fashionables who besieged the Laureate.[1] Perhaps
hat day, prickly as he was, he had suffered a slight from some
powerful fop, or overheard a malicious jest from red enemy lips,
or found Royalty in glum or fractious mood, or been torn by
jealousy or dogged by disappointment and depression. To-morrow
it would all begin again ; the same routine, the same faces, the same
voices, the same endless shining floors, the same gilding and statuary,
the same lutes, the same epigrams, jests, compliments, intrigues,
backbiting, flattery, and yawns. To Mme de Chateaubrun, a good
woman and a loyal friend, Ronsard reveals some of his weariness.

Mais quand Fortune icy m'est adversaire,
Quand je ne puis despescher mon affaire,
Quand quelque ennuy me desrobe l'espoir,
Quand on ne veut ma Muse recevoir,
Quand un fascheux chrysophile rechine
À ma priere, ou me tourne l'eschine,
Ou parle à moy par fraude ou par courroux,
Pour mon support je me retire à vous . . .[2]

Above all, there is the drudgery of his *Franciade*, at which he is
now slogging once more at the Royal order, trying to fascinate

[1] A letter of François de Noailles in 1563 conveys that the *beau monde* was keeping Ronsard busy with its demands.
[2] But when Fortune is my adversary here, when I cannot speed my affairs, when some
trouble banishes my hopes, when my Muse is not welcomed, when some mean money-
grubber baulks at my request, or turns his back on me, or speaks to me in lies or in anger,
then for surcease I fly to you.

himself with his imaginary hero, Francius the Trojan, founder
the Valois line, and those dim, dull, hairy Merovingian king
Pharamond, Clodion, Merovius, Childeric, Chilperic, Dagobe
lumbering through his mind like a drove of oxen, and about
inspiring. Little need some young ambitious poet eating his hea
out in the remote provinces envy the glamorous master as he bit
his pen! Nor, as Ronsard stares out of window and allows h
mind to wander, is there much consolation in the public wea
The skies have palpable thunderclouds massing on the horizo
The air is uneasy. Moreover Ronsard, now verging on middle ag
is not well. In 1568, as we note from a long rhymed epistle, *L
Salade*, published in 1569 and addressed to his poet-secretary an
disciple Amadis Jamyn (charming name, well descriptive of
charming, finicking personality) he has obtained leave of absenc
from Court and is at home, bedridden with that quartan fever, o
ague, so common a scourge at this period. Escaping for a day
from his sickroom, he orders young Jamyn to help him gather a
fresh green salad from the fields, despite his doctor's orders, and
having washed it at the spring, to salt and dress it with vinegar
and olive-oil of Provence.

> *Voila, Jamyn, voila mon souvrain bien,*
> *En attendant que de mes veines part*
> *Cette execrable horrible fiebvre quarte*
> *Qui me consomme et le corps et le cœur* . . .[1]

The vigour of the man! No quartan ague can keep him from
rhyming, impeccably, charmingly, never halting in that easy stride.
He is utterly sick and tired of the Court, longing for repose, a
little self-pitying. Exaggerating, as poets will, he says :

> *Je suis pour suivre à la trace une Cour*
> *Trop maladif, trop paresseux, et sourd,*
> *Et trop craintif; au reste je demande*
> *Un doux repos, et ne veux plus qu'on pende*
> *Comme un poignard les soucys sur mon front.*[2]

[1] Here, Jamyn, here is what does me most good, until this execrable, horrible quartan
fever, which devours my body and my heart, leaves my veins . . .

[2] To follow in the footsteps of a Court I am too sickly, too idle, too deaf, too nervous ;
what I ask for is sweet rest, and no more to have worries hanging over my head like a
dagger.

Reflections follow on the inconstancy of Fortune, the brevity
.d misery of human life, the folly of ambition. He envies the
rene old peasant of the Georgics (" *Coryicium vidisse senem . . .*")
 so many millions of town-weary men have done since Virgil's
ay.

> I chanced an old Corycian Swain to know,
> Lord of few acres, and those barren, too . . .

nd Ronsard cries:

> *Ah! que me plaist ce vers Virgilien*
> *Où le vieillard père Coryicien*
> *Avec sa marre en travaillant cultive*
> *A tour de bras sa terre non oisive!*[1]

And after meditating on the simplicity and happiness of Nature,
nd how mankind has abused it, he pulls himself up with a laugh.

> *C'est trop presché : donne-moy ma salade,*
> *El' ne vaut rien, dis-tu, pour un malade?*
> *Hé quoy! Jamyn, tu fais le medecin!*
> *Laisse-moy vivre au moins jusqu'à la fin*
> *Tout à mon aise . . .*[2]

Mainly from his sick-bed comes *Le Sixiesme et Septiesme Livre
des Poëmes* (1569), from which *La Salade* is taken. The most
interesting piece of verse in this collection, apart from that tender
and lovely farewell to Cassandre, and a few sonnets on the same
theme, is one in which he describes how the Muse constantly drives
him, sick or well, sometimes three days on end, and how, when the
fires of inspiration die down and his verses are written, he is limp,
exhausted, and like one dead.

> *Quand la fureur en moy s'est desbordée*
> *Sans craindre rien, sans raison, ny conseil,*

[1] Ah! how they charm me, those Virgilian lines in which the venerable Corycian sage
with his hoe so industriously cultivates his fruitful soil!
[2] I'm preaching too much—give me my salad. You say it does an invalid no good?
What's this, Jamyn? Are you aping the doctors? Permit me at least to live at my ease
until the end comes . . .

Elle me dure ou le cours d'un soleil,
Quelquefois deux, quelquefois trois, puis morte
Elle languist en moy de telle sorte
Que faict la fleur languissant pour un temps . . .
Je ne suis rien qu'un corps mort et perclus
De qui l'ame est autre part envolée,
Laissant son hoste aussy froid que gelée . . . [1]

In the poem *Hylas* he takes his friend the erudite and ruby-nose
humanist Jean Passerat into his laboratory and shows him th
alembics and crucibles in which he distils poetry gathered, like th
honey of Horace's bee, from all the flowers of life and literature

Mon Passerat, je ressemble à l'abeille
Qui va tantost cueillant la fleur vermeille,
Tantost la jaune : errant de pré en pré
Vole en la part qui plus luy vient à gré,
Contre l'Hyver amassant force vivres.
Ainsy courant et fueilletant mes livres,
J'amasse, trie, et choisis le plus beau,
Qu'en cent couleurs je peints en un tableau,
Tantost en l'autre, et, maistre en ma peinture,
Sans me forcer j'imite la Nature . . . [2]

There is a significant thing, the learned remark, about this volume
of 1569. It contains no alexandrines ; even its sonnets are decasyllabic. The reason Ronsard has temporarily abandoned the
alexandrine, after wielding it so long and masterfully, has been
traced to a visit Charles IX paid him during a brief spell of leave at
his priory of St. Cosme in 1565. The sport-loving fifteen-year-old
King, who had a genuine culture and a genuine admiration and
affection for Pierre de Ronsard,[3] was something of a poetaster

[1] When my poetic fury is at its height, it governs me, without fear or reason or counsel,
the course of a day, sometimes two, sometimes three ; then, dying, it fades within me as a
flower fades, for a space . . . I am nothing but a corpse, dead and stiff, whose soul has
flown elsewhere, leaving its host as cold as frost.

[2] My Passerat, I am like the bee which goes to and fro sucking now the crimson flower,
now the gold, and, flitting from meadow to meadow, flies to the places which please it best,
heaping up much food against the winter. Thus flying and sipping from my books, I gather,
test, and select the beauties which I paint in a hundred colours, sometimes on one canvas,
sometimes another ; and as a master-painter, I imitate Nature without effort.

[3] In 1570 Charles obtained for Ronsard the Order of Christ of Portugal in recognition
(he wrote to the Cardinal-Infante) of Ronsard's " great and signal services to us and the
French Republic " : a curious reward from a King of France.

imself, and, unfortunately, something of a critic. It is at Charles'
suggestion that Ronsard, as he takes up his *Franciade* again, substitutes the decasyllabic line of the Song of Roland and the other
ancient French epics; against his better judgment, as he will
frankly state later in his preface. What the result will be Ronsard
probably well foresees. He bends manfully to his *magnum opus*
nevertheless, and will slave away at it for the next seven years.
And before he has finished his task the brief sunshine of peace over
France departs and the new storm breaks at last.

§2

If the Queen-Mother Catherine thought the treaty of St. Germain
and its concessions, which gave the Calvinist party four fortified
cities, including La Rochelle—key to the Atlantic—and Cognac,
meant the end of the civil war, she was not long under illusion.
It served merely to enable Admiral Coligny, head of the Calvinist
party and ally of the Lutheran German princes, to attend Court
in triumph and take his seat in the Council, not without ostentation,
encouraged by the friendliness of Charles IX, who was at this
time on bad terms with his brother Anjou, the Catholic
generalissimo.

But for the moment it seems that peace is a fact. The Calvinist
Henri of Navarre—later the great Henri Quatre who thought
Paris well worth a Mass—is to marry the King's sister, gay, petite,
plump, charming Marguerite ("Margot") de Valois; a crowning
symbol of that reconciliation for which Catherine has worked so long.
The vivacious little bride-to-be is not ravished by the prospect; she
is in entire sympathy with her brother Anjou, and moreover the
breath of Macaulay's Protestant paladin is, it seems, far from
fragrant; a social handicap not unknown in a period in which
Queen Elizabeth's Welsh astrologer, Dr. John Dee, alleviated the
troubles of the royal teeth by art-magic. But if the Queen-Mother
and her son were pleased with this mixed marriage, the implacable
citizens of Paris were not. Already there had been a minor riot
because Coligny ordered the removal of a pyramid erected over
the site of a demolished house belonging to two Calvinists condemned to death by the Parliament in the late war. For the Navarre-

Valois union the growling Parisians promised *des noces vermeille*
red espousals. The threat came to nothing, but it was observe
during the ceremony at Notre-Dame that when the bride hesitate
before enunciating her assent it was Charles IX who, with a shar
tap on the neck, brought her to reason.

If the Queen-Mother and the King wanted peace, Coligny wante
a propaganda war to assist the Netherlands Calvinists in revo
against Spain ; he was already advocating in Council the annexatio
of Flanders. This policy, with France so weak and Philip II s
strong, was so obviously suicidal that England and even Luthera
Germany, sounded by Coligny, refused him support. The powe
of this man in France is demonstrated by the fact that in his annoy
ance at being unable to drag France into war with Spain he prevailec
on the Council to despatch an expedition into Flanders to help
the Calvinists. After it had been cut to pieces and his action con
demned unanimously, he burst out in a rage in full Council : " The
King refuses to make this war ! God forbid that another one may
happen which he will be unable to evade! " No hint could be
clearer, followed as it was by wholesale Calvinist mobilisation :
twelve thousand arquebusiers, three thousand cavalry. Nor was it
likely that the Guises would ignore such a challenge. As Coligny
left his house in the Rue de Béthisy on August 22, 1572, a man in
Guise pay named Maurevert fired two shots at him, breaking his left
elbow. The consternation of Catherine de Médicis may be imagined.
With the King, she hastily visited Coligny, passing through the
furious ranks of his soldiery, and promised him justice should be
done. But with Coligny vowing vengeance and his Calvinists
loudly promising, among other threats, to overpower the Royal
guards and carry off the Royal family, with the Guises roaring for
action and probably planning another *coup d'état*, with the temper
of Paris at white-heat and a large-scale bloody clash imminent,
the Queen-Mother became distracted. Charles IX likewise lost
his head, raging and irresolute. It is impossible to discover and
disentangle the events and councils of August 22–23. It would
seem that confusion and fear reigned in the Louvre, that the King—
who had previously threatened, abused and dismissed Guise in a
fury on learning that he planned to kill Coligny during a joust
after the Navarre-Valois wedding—changed his mind, urged by

Anjou and the Guises, that the normally courageous Queen-Mother was beside herself for her children and the Crown, and that ultimately the terrible alternative presented itself. Policy had failed. One side or the other must be suppressed, and it was impossible at that time to suppress the Guises, with Paris and most of France solid behind them.

There seems no doubt that the Queen-Mother was finally responsible for the events of Saturday night and Sunday, August 23 and 24, 1572. Brantôme and other contemporaries, Tavannes and Retz among them, have no doubt of it, though they award Catherine the mitigating circumstances I have mentioned. There is likewise no doubt that Catherine realised this frightful responsibility, and that it hag-rode her till her death : for she was, we may recollect, a Christian. There is a passage in Brantôme describing her end in January, 1589, confirming this and pitiless in its brevity. " She died," he says, " at Blois of regret for the massacre which was made." Nor was the haggard old woman, weary with years of trouble and hard work, suffered to die in peace at the age of seventy. The Cardinal de Bourbon, received in her room with some other visitors on a day when she had left her bed, said to her : " Alas, Madam ! You brought us all to the slaughterhouse without meaning it " (or perhaps " without thinking." The exact words are : " *Hélas, Madame, vous nous avez tous menez à la boucherie sans y penser.*"). These words, says Brantôme, and the memory of " the death of those poor people ", so smote Catherine to the heart that she took to her bed again and never left it till her death, shortly after.

On Charles IX the horror rested no less heavily. Some time after the St. Bartholomew his old nurse, a Calvinist, hearing him weeping in the night, approached his bed and drew the curtains. " *Ah ! ma nourrice, ma mie, ma nourrice, que de sang et que de meurtres ! Ah ! que j'ai eu un meschant conseil ! O mon Dieu, pardonnez-moy et me faict misericorde, s'il te plaist ! "*—" Oh, Nurse, my dear ! Nurse ! What bloodshed, what murders ! Oh, what evil counsel I had ! Oh, my God, forgive me and have mercy, if it be Thy will ! " With similar tears and prostration Charles' innocent young Queen, the devout Austrian girl who was wont to spend half the night in prayer, and was before long to enter a convent

for the rest of her life, mourned that terror, which set the bells of
Rome ringing. For Gregory XIII was deceived. He received a
special envoy from Catherine de Médicis and Charles IX announcing
that they had just escaped with their lives from a vast Calvinist
conspiracy, and Salviati, Papal Nuncio in Paris, did not attempt to
enlighten him. Hence that Te Deum at Santa Maria Maggiore for
the safety of the Most Christian King of France which has evoked
bitter rhetoric from the Papacy's enemies in every succeeding
age.[1]

Of the murder of Coligny, which preceded the general massacre,
his principal biographer, Merki, has remarked that the official
account and propaganda drawn up by the Calvinists is based on hear-
say evidence, no eyewitness being available. The Guises personally headed the murder-party which entered Coligny's house at
one o'clock on the Sunday morning, but the story that after Coligny
had been despatched Henri de Guise stamped on the dead man's
face is denied by Brantôme. More appalling than such a murder,
common enough to the time, is the uprising en masse of the tigerish
Paris mob to join the soldiers at their work. Two thousand dead
is the figure accepted by modern historians for Paris; for the
provinces, which followed the capital's lead immediately, various
totals, impossible to check, are given. A well-known story
embellished by the virulent Agrippa d' Aubigné, representing
Charles IX as shooting at fugitives from a balcony of the Louvre,
far out of range, is from Brantôme.

And Ronsard?

There is no mention of the St. Bartholomew in any line of his,
though other poets, notably his old master, Dorat, rallied dutifully
to the occasion and received due reward from the Crown.
Ronsard's silence is significant. Only in a verse on the end
of Coligny, beheaded after his murder and hanged on the
gibbet of Montfaucon, is one permitted to read something of
his disgust and pessimism:

> *Ce guerrier qui tantost*
> *Terre et mer d'un grand ost*
> *Couvroit de tant de voiles,*

[1] Gregory XIII subsequently condemned the massacre.

Astrée

Court de teste et de nom
Pendille à Montfaucon :
Ainsi vous plaist, estoiles ![1]

It was not in Ronsard's nature to celebrate such a butchery, even if it saved the Crown. Moreover, he was correcting the proofs of his *Franciade*. Very faintly the noise of that nightmare must have reached him in his study in the Rue des Fossés-St. Victor on the Hill of St. Geneviève, if indeed any echo of it reached him at all ; for apart from his dullness of hearing, the University quarter was remote and cloistered from the City. Carnage in Paris is often thus localised, like thunderstorms. During the massacres of September 2–5, 1792, when eleven hundred or more prisoners and priests were murdered, life in Paris went on as usual outside the immediate theatres of action ; only in the wineshops round the prisons, or near St. Germain-des-Prés, might the noisy entry towards evening of ruffians splashed with blood, weary with slaughter and roaring for drink, acquaint the stranger that sinister happenings had filled the day. So while the St. Bartholomew raged, Ronsard's detachment may have been absolute. Bending over his proofs and utterly absorbed, he may have been so securely enclosed in his ivory tower that even excited servants' reports of a Paris run mad conveyed nothing to a brain preoccupied with more immediate anxieties : the choice of an epithet, the substitution of a verb, the final polish of a difficult line. A piece of private news reaching Königsberg on a certain day in 1789 so upset the rhythms of Emmanuel Kant that for the first time in living memory the citizens, accustomed to set their watches by him, saw the philosopher issue from his house for his daily walk a full hour earlier than usual, and surmised something world-shaking had happened. It had : the Bastille had fallen. Literary geniuses preoccupied with creation or correction are even less easily put out of their stride than philosophers by the rumblings of the outer world. Pierre de Ronsard may, on coming to the surface, have bitten his lip and inquired sombrely of all his stars why, with his national epic due for publication in September, the end of August should have been chosen for the time to upset France so thoroughly.

[1] This warrior who lately covered land and sea with the canvas of a great host, now dangles, bereft of head and name, on Montfaucon. Such is your pleasure, stars!

Les Quatres Premiers Livres de La Franciade, for which Franc
and cultivated Europe generally had been waiting so long, wit
such high expectations, like the Roman world for the *Aenei*
was published in a quarto volume less than a month afte
the St. Bartholomew. It has been dismissed ever since as a resound
ing failure, even by critics who have read it. Despite his prou
and sensitive championship of his work, dogged perusal suggest
very strongly that the boredom so frequently exhaled from it i
to a large extent that of the poet himself, wrestling with a task s
unwieldy that instead of exhibiting the long procession of the
kings of France from the Trojan Francius, founder of the House
of Valois, down the ages to Henri III, as designed, Ronsard leaves
off with an almost audible grunt of relief at Pépin-le-Bref (died
A.D. 768) and never resumes.

His failure hurt him. In a preface written, just before his death,
to replace two previous prefaces to the poem, he defends himself
against the pragmatists with some hauteur. His actual words are
worth quoting:

> *Fondé et appuyé sur nos vieilles Annales, j'ay basty ma Franciade*
> *sans me soucier si cela est vray ou non, ou si nos Roys sont Troyens*
> *ou Germains, Scythes ou Arabes, si Francius est venu en France ou*
> *non (car il y pouvoit venir), me servant du possible et non de la vérité.*

That is to say, "Basing myself and depending on our ancient
annals, I have built my *Franciade* without caring whether it is
true or not, whether our kings are Trojans or Germans, Scythians
or Arabs, or whether Francius came to France or not (he may have
done); utilising the possible, not the actual". Fair warning enough
to those who took the opening lines for the beginning of an historical
essay:

> *Muse, qui tiens les sommets de Parnasse,*
> *Guide ma langue et me chante la Race*
> *Des Roys Françoys yssuz de Francion,*
> *Enfant d'Hector, Troyen de nation,*
> *Qu'on appelloit en sa jeunesse tendre*
> *Astyanax . . .*[1]

---

[1] Muse, who haunts Parnassus' topmost peaks, guide my song, sing to me the race of
France's kings, issued from Francius, son of Hector, of Trojan birth, who in his tender youth
was called Astyanax. . . .

We need not follow Francius, hero of very ancient French
legend, lately refurbished by the new nationalists, in his adventures,
which are partly Homeric, partly Virgilian, extremely derivative,
and wholly dull. Even as romanticised by Lemaire de Belges
(1512), Ronsard's chief authority, Francius is a major bore and every
now and again we find Ronsard seizing, as it were, the opportunity
to go off at a tangent into dissertations, the happiest of which are
blighted by that prevailing sense of effort. Of the massive whole
two lines, at least, all critics agree, betray the *griffe du maître*.
They describe the French Race :

> *Le peuple rude et fascheux à donter,*
> *Chaud à la guerre et ardant à la proye.*[1]

(*Adsit omen !* lovers of France may well cry, contemplating these
lines in the year 1943.) But we are aeons away from the bronze
fanfares of the Song of Roland, the majestic simplicity of such lines
as

> *Halt sont li pui et li valz tenebros,*
> *Les roches bises, li destreit merveillos.*[2]

which gives you the High Pyrenees in a dozen words, or those
lines in which is heard the echoing thunder of the hoofs of
Charlemagne's *destrier*, and in which is seen the anger of his terrible
eyes :

> *Par grant iror chevalchet Charlemaignes,*
> *Desor sa broigne li gist sa barbe blanche.*[3]

or that line about the lanterns of the ships of the Paynim lighting
up the whole sea like carbuncles. The ships of Francius skip after
each other like infant goats, a curiously infelicitous image :

> *Ainsi qu'on voit la troupe des chevreaux*
> *A petits bonds suivre les pastoureaux*
> *Devers le soir au son de la musette,*

[1] That tough Race, difficult to tame, hot in war and ardent for the prey. . . . .

[2] High are the peaks, and the vales full of gloom.
The rocks grey-brown, the passes marvellous.

[3] In high anger rides Charlemagne;
His white beard flows over his coat of mail. . . .

Ainsi les nefs d'une assez longue traicte
Suivoient la nef de Francus.[1]

It would be unjust to deny vividness and satiric force to Ronsard's picture of the puppet-kings, the later Merovingians :

Ces Roys hideux en longue barbe espesse,
En longs cheveux ornéz presse sur presse,
De chaisnes d'or et de carquans gravéz,
Hauts dans un char en triomphe elevéz,
Une fois l'an feront voir leur visage,
Puis tout le reste ils seront en servage,
Laissant la bride aux Maires du Palais,
Dont ils seront esclaves et valetz,
Masques de roys, idoles animées . . .[2]

But such passages are rare.

So the Great French Epic foundered almost in sight of the slip-ways, and has ever since been submerged fathoms deep in oblivion, as if it were a classic. Visitors to Beauvais Cathedral dizzy with staring up at that stupendous roof may, or might till recently, refresh themselves by contemplating, among the tapestries hung near the Sacristy, two pieces of the sixteenth century representing scenes from the *Franciade*. These, so far as I know, are the only tangible tribute in existence to Ronsard's seven years' toil.

His determination immediately afterwards to have done with Francius and his horde for ever is conveyed in a quatrain first published in 1578, six years later :

Si le Roy Charles eust vescu,
J'eusse achevé ce long ouvrage,
Si tost que la Mort l'eut vaincu
Sa mort me veinquit le courage.[3]

[1] As one sees a flock of kids follow the shepherds in little skips at eventide, to the sound of the pipe, so did the ships, in line of no mean length, follow the ship of Francius.

[2] These hideous kings with their long thick beards, their long hair, elaborately waving curl on curl, their gold chains and their engraved harness, riding high in their triumphal chariots, will show their faces once a year ; for the rest of the time they will be serfs, leaving the reins to the Mayors of the Palace, whose slaves and valets they will be; these masks of royalty, these animated puppets.

[3] Had King Charles lived, I should have finished this long work ; but no sooner had death vanquished him than his passing vanquished my courage.

Two other things may have influenced him as well. Henri III .s the familiar crony of Philippe Desportes, the supple, dainty lianate poet, Ronsard's rival at Court, whose star nevertheless led utterly to outshine Ronsard's; as Henri, to do him justice, mitted. Apart from this discouragement, the new reign was hibiting certain repugnant aspects. With the fashions of Italy, mptuary and poetic, had come in the vices of Italy, or, to be more curate, the vices of the vicious rich of Italy. Among the Corps iplomatique at Henri III's court the presence of the Ambassadors Sodom and Gomorrah and the Envoy-Plenipotentiary of Lesbos ould not have seemed bizarre. The enigmatic King, at whose mplex nature we have already glanced, and his effeminate, brawl- g *mignons* were a target for innumerable satires, lampoons, and rotests from Catholics and Calvinists alike. The Paris mob hurled earty abuse at these fops, the clergy denounced them from the ulpit. The monk Maurice Poncet, curé of St. Pierre-des-Arcis, ade such an issue of this during a course of Lenten sermons at Jotre-Dame, causing his congregations to rock with laughter at is bitter humour, that he was summoned to the Louvre and iolently reprimanded by Henri III in person. "You think fit, hen, Sir," said the Duc d'Espernon sternly when the King had nished, "to preach jesting sermons and make the people laugh?" Sir," replied the monk, "whatever pains I take to that end, I hall never make as many laugh as you make weep." And in 583 Marguerite de Valois and two of her friends were dismissed rom Court, because, as Henri furiously alleged, they were respon- sible for the scandalous gossip circulating in Paris.

Greatly as Ronsard loved the culture of ancient Greece he drew the line, like any other normal man, at its morals, which had now been introduced into the Court of France and were before long to make the court of the slobbering pedant James I of England a European by- word. His refusal to flatter the King's *mignons* in verse, as Desportes and others did, was steadfast, except for an epitaph for Caylus written at the direct Royal order, which could not be gainsaid. Ronsard's position at Court at this period, and until Henri III reformed, cannot have been comfortable. His advice to the new King[1] was

[1] E.g., a long poem recommending a purge of flatterers, sobriety, good counsel, reduction of taxation on the common people, a gentler justice, etc., etc. It has a note of severity, barely concealed.

spurned, and made him unpopular. His contempt for the King'
favourites rings plain enough in the lines addressed to a *mign*
de Cour—in modern idiom it might well be headed "Lines tc
Court Pansy"—whom he depicts to the life : a curled and scent
Adonis who had tittered at him, an *Amour en tableau* sprung fro
a fop effeminate as his mother, a fribble from birth, pampere
greedy, unlettered, impudent, idle, futile, a *petit sot*, a flunkey ar
flatterer in grain. I am not of this kidney, says Ronsard proudly

> *Je ne suis tel, j'aimerois mieux mourir,*
> *Je suis issu de trop gentille race.*[1]

But this is nothing to the attack on the Corydons whic
Ronsard addresses, in a New Year *étrennes*, to Henri III himself :

> *Si quelque dameret se farde ou se deguise,*
> *Attifé, godronné, en collet empesé,*
> *La cape retroussée et le cheveu frisé,*
> *Qu'il craigne ma fureur!*[2]

He wasted no time, remarks Jusserand, in making this piece
public, in his usual manner. The incident once more displays tha
courage Ronsard so amply possessed. No wonder Desportes was
preferred to him, or that in his threnody for Charles IX (to whom
he had addressed, a year before Charles' death, a vigorous warning
on the state of France) he strikes a note of deep personal bereave-
ment. He had certainly lost a friend.

§3

While we have been contemplating the *Franciade*, the Muse of
Comedy has tripped on the stage once more.

The bloody purge of St. Bartholomew brought France no peace,
nor prospect of it, despite the truce of Boulogne in 1573. A new
troublemaker had come to the fore since the tragedy—Catherine
de Médicis' third son, ugly pockmarked popeyed little Alençon,

---

[1] I am not thus ; I had rather be dead : I spring from too decent a stock.
[2] If some sissy youth paints or disguises himself, bedizened and bedecked in a starched
ruff and a short cloak, with frizzed locks—let him fear my fury !

hom Elizabeth Tudor playfully called The Frog. Alençon, ontemplating violence against the hated Guises, and no friend to is brother Anjou, cultivated the Calvinists and was soon heading a iird party, the *Politiques*. But before Henri of Anjou could bring natters to a head by succeeding to the throne, an episode of Ruritanian opéra-bouffe occurred to lighten the general gloom.

In 1573 the Polish Diet surprised Europe and overjoyed Catherine de Médicis, who had royally entertained their ambassadors, by electing Henri of Anjou to the Polish throne. The Poles were attempting a further experiment in that type of government they had long favoured, and which a modern eye will recognise without difficulty as democratic in inspiration. The death in 1572 of Sigismund II, last of the Jagiellon dynasty, which had given Poland a golden age of liberal government (taking the word " liberal " in its nobler sense) enabled Poland, self-styled a republic even under these hereditary kings, to develop the republican theory further by instituting elective chief magistrates. The main terms of the *Pacta Conventa* which Henri of Anjou, their first choice, had to swear to keep are interesting. The King must maintain all the liberties of the Republic and parliamentary government. He has no voice in the election of his successor. His wife is to be chosen for him by the Diet (Henri managed to get this clause temporarily waived on the ground that the sister of Sigismund II was twenty years older than he). He is not to declare war or lead Polish troops over the frontiers without the Diet's consent, and he is to continue that policy of religious tolerance for which Poland, most devoutly Catholic of nations, then as now, was so celebrated that she was called the Heretics' Asylum, *Asilium Hereticorum*, opening her frontiers to exiles of every known sect of the period and allowing them complete liberty, as to the Jews. And if the King fails to carry out these and other conditions, Poland becomes *ipso facto* absolved from allegiance. These were hardly terms of kingship likely to enrapture a wayward egotist like Henri de Valois, Duke of Anjou. We may presume that he accepted them not without sulks and protests, and at his masterful mother's final order.

So, unwillingly—for he was desperately smitten at the moment with the Princesse de Condé, and writing to her in his own royal blood—Henri set out for the uttermost wilds ; not so wild as he and Philippe Desportes, who was among his suite, affected to believe, making gestures with their dainty white hands. Poland had been swept by the Renaissance like the rest of the civilised world. Sigismund I (1506—48) had married a Sforza princess, who brought to Poland many Italian artists and architects, as the restoration of the Castle of Wawel and the Chapel Royal in Wawel Cathedral, a masterpiece of pure Renaissance, testify among other works. In music, the Cracow School of composers and the Chapel Royal of Sigismund I carried on the traditions of the Flemish School, which so long dominated Europe. In science, Copernicus had recently revolutionised astronomical theory. The new scholarship (although Cracow University, one of Europe's oldest, stood out for some time against these innovations with all that mulishness Rabelais gibed at in the Sorbonne) flourished, and the poets Krzycki, Janicki, Dantyszck, and above all Jan Kochanowski could write Latin verse as choice as any in Christendom. Kochanowski, called the Ronsard of Poland and one of Pierre de Ronsard's most fervent admirers, must have eyed the finicking Desportes with little enthusiasm. He was soon to rap those lilywhite knuckles hard, amid the approving laughter of Europe.

Neither Cracow, the capital, nor Warsaw, the political centre, could be truthfully described at this time as a second Paris, and the French dandies found much to raise their eyebrows at. As for the vast Polish plains, aflame with beauty in spring and autumn sunshine but unspeakably desolate in the rains, the Polish marshes, crossed by unmetalled, unditched highroads which at intervals became layers of slippery tree-trunks (such as annoyed Murat's staff in the Russian campaign of 1807, and such as the German military engineers drove across the Pripet in 1916), the huddled log-hut villages, the widely-scattered towns, the dense forests, the half-barbaric aspect of the peasantry, the tall clay stoves, the Jews, the assorted heretics, and the mud, they were a disagreeable shock. Desportes—one can hear his high fluted protests and see his shrugs and grimaces, as of a monkey in an east wind—must have begun quite early to insult the Poles, calling them poverty-stricken barbarians, boasters and babblers, dwellers in stoves, wearers of wolfskins, snorers at table, sleepers on the floor. Henri of Anjou's brooding eyes doubtless conveyed more

an one injunction to the poet to keep his mouth shut and confine
is pleasantries to his notebook. As the French say, the wine was
rawn and must be drunk. Meanwhile Desportes could work
ese impressions into an elegant satiric sonnet-sequence, which
e did.

On the side of the Poles, enthusiasm cooled somewhat soon
fter the arrival of their newly-elected King. Apart from the con-
escending courtesy of Henri and his suite, the Poles did not like
he behaviour they were introducing into a Court which had
varmly encouraged Renaissance culture but was a stranger to
he gambols of Sodom. Moreover the seven-hour sittings of the
Diet and the speeches in a barbaric tongue bored Henri profoundly
and he showed it. It cannot have been long before the Polish
statesmen realised that they had not drawn precisely the best card
from the European pack. The Muse of Comedy, hovering in the
wings, has not long to wait for her cue.

Sleeping heavily and late on a May morning in 1574 after a
ball in the Royal palace at Cracow, where King Henri of Poland
insists on living, because Cracow is nearer Paris than Warsaw,
his Majesty is awakened by an express courier with despatches
from Catherine de Médicis announcing the death of Charles IX.
The heir to the French throne is now Alençon. Henri informs the
Diet, orders Court mourning, and exhibits a massive calm. Towards
midnight on June 14, a week or two later, the watchman at the
garden-gate of the Palace leading to the Faubourg St. Kasimir
sees the King approaching, wrapped in a cloak and wearing riding-
boots. Henri is affable and peremptory. " I have a rendezvous
with a lady in the Faubourg—be so good as to turn the key."
The gate is unlocked, the King strolls past the sentry into the
street, where horses are waiting, vaults nimbly into the saddle,
and spurs with his companions hell-for-leather for the Vistula,
getting directions through the forest from an astonished woodman ; and twelve hours later, as the tocsin is clanging from
all the steeples of Cracow, the King of Poland gallops over
the frontier and heads for Vienna, pursued too late by a
squadron of hussars under Tencynski. He will never be seen
in his Northern realm again. " Good-bye, Poland! " sings
Desportes mockingly,

Ronsard

> *Adieu, Pologne, adieu, plaines desertes,*
> *Tousjours de neige ou de glace couvertes . . .*
> *Ton air, tes moeurs, m'ont si fort sceu desplaire*
> *Qu'il faudra bien que tout me soit contraire*
> *Si jamais plus je retourne en ce lieu.*[1]

A most insulting and ignoble exit, unworthy a Valois an
certainly not typical of Henri of Anjou, who lacked neither grac
nor breeding. The just anger and contempt of the Poles wa
capably transmitted to the world by Jan Kochanowski, whos
ensuing poetic duel with Philippe Desportes leaves him easily th
victor; the Pole's satiric *De Electione, Coronatione, et Fuga Galli*
" Of the Election, Coronation, and Flight of the Frenchman"
leaves little unsaid. In the next year a wiser Diet elected Stefar
Báthory, Prince of Transylvania, who brought Ivan the Terribl
to heel and would have demolished that icy-hearted Muscovite
save for the Pope's intervention.[2] A little later Poland, perpetual
strong-point of Christendom, is to save Europe, under Sobieski,
from the Turk; another three centuries later, under Pilsudski,
from the Bolshevik. *Stabat et stabit.*

Hardly pausing at Vienna, where Maximilian II welcomed him,
Henri of Anjou sped eagerly south by coach to Venice, paradise
of dainty devices, his spiritual home. To greet this guest *de luxe*
the Venetians paraded every bedazzlement of their magic city.
Triumphal arches under a rain of flowers. Regattas, serenades,
masques and ridottos. Canals at midnight bright as noonday with
lanterns and torches, palaces ablaze with waxlights, their façades
draped with festal hangings. State receptions and banquets in the hall
of the Doge's Palace, newly painted by Titian. The lanterns and
masts and streamers, the cloaks and birdmasks of the Piazza,
the lean, dark, cynical, Venetian faces quizzing from every balcony,
and, jostling in the brilliant crowds beneath, all the figures of the
Old Italian Comedy, soon to be glorified by the reed-pen of
Jacques Callot; the Doctor, Leandro, Isabella, red-shanked

[1] Farewell, Poland! Farewell, desert plains, forever covered with snow or ice! Thy air,
thy customs have given me such distaste that things will have to go hard with me
indeed before I return to this place again!
[2] Prince Poniatowski presented the sword of Stefan Báthory to Murat in Warsaw in
1807. The omen was not fulfilled.

antaleone, Arlecchino with his bat, the subtle rascal Brighella, nd the terrible roaring Capitans—Matamoros, Escobombardon, lodomonte, Spavento della Valle Inferna, Sangre y Fuego—twirling heir catlike moustachios and twitching their great sneering ruby oses in the rear. The famous courtesans of Venice swaying past or Henri's inspection, regal, shimmering, jewel-studded, luscious, overpowering, their hair powdered with gold, their opulent snowy osoms dazing the incautious eye. The comely, costly shops of he jewellers and the perfumers, the glassworks of Murano, the Turneresque enchantments of dawn and sunset. On these delights Henri of Anjou gorged himself, visiting the aged Titian and posing for Tintoretto.

Ascension Day was past. The impressive annual ritual of the Wedding of the Adriatic, with the Doge casting his ring into the sea and the traditional "*Desponsamus te, mare, in signum veri perpetuique dominii !*" could not be repeated for Henri's entertainment (it would conceivably have moved him to secret mirth, remembering Du Bellay's gibe about *ces vieux cocus* and the adulterous Turk). To honour him nevertheless the State galley *Bucintoro*, that towering golden fantasy, moved slowly out from the Arsenal amid the roar of cannon to take him and the Doge to a Te Deum at St. Mark's. Flashing fresh-gilded in the sun, beflagged, bestreamered, hung with armorial devices, carrying the notables of Venice in gala array, rowed by the Doge's oarsmen in their purple damask liveries, this extravagant showpiece, built only for pomp, was fortunately not forced on this occasion to lumber humiliatingly to safety before one of those Adriatic storms which so suddenly lash the canals, and must often have seemed a waspish retort from the newly-wedded Bride of the State. One sees Henri standing on the poop of the *Bucintoro*, as Tintoretto sketched him, inhaling all this splendour. He had, as somebody has said, the Venetian poison in his veins.

Too soon the delicious dream ended, and Henri was forced to post back to Paris, where the French Crown awaited him. A difficult brother also awaited him. The Frog's protruding eyes, fixed in no expression of brotherly love, were a rude change from the melting orbs of Titian's beauties, for Henri's second thoughts about Poland had deprived The Frog of a crown. Brotherly resent-

ment expressed itself before long, as the religious war smoked a1
flared up again for the fifth time, in the " Peace of Monsieur
(May, 1576), which Alençon and his Third Party were able to for
on Henri III after an inconclusive Guise victory over the Calvinis
at Dormans. Under this treaty Henri had to yield the Calvinis
all they demanded, namely complete liberty everywhere in Franc
except in Paris (where the citizens would not have it) and seat
in every *parlement*. The Guises' immediate retort was to create
fourth party, the Catholic League, recruited mainly from the soli
middle-class and the lesser nobility.

It will be three years after Ronsard's death before Paris burst
into flame again, and I need not pursue this chronicle of hostilitie
further except to note an unique fact. One of the Parisian clergy
constantly attacking Henri III during these years, the Curé of St.
Sévérin, helped to rouse the citizens against him in 1588, after the
assassination of Guise, by exhibiting a picture representing the
sufferings of the English Catholics, then enduring savage per-
secution under Elizabeth Tudor. This is, I think, the only instance
known to history of English misfortune arousing French indignation.

IX

HÉLÈNE

Age jam meorum
Finis amorum :
Non enim posthac alia calebo
Femina . . .
> (HORACE, IV, 11.)

Come, then, Sweet,
My last of flames,
For never shall another fair
Enslave me . . .
> (CONINGTON.)

§1

BETWEEN 1568 AND 1570, AS WE HAVE NOTED, PIERRE DE RONSARD was at home in the Vendômois, suffering from ague. He divided his leisure now between two country retreats, the priory of St. Cosme-lez-Tours, *S. Cosmas in Insula,* on a little wooded island near the present Pont St. Symphorien, since joined to the mainland, and the priory of Croixval (*Valle Crucis,* like the great Welsh abbey) in the valley of the Cendrine, on the fringes of the forest of Gastine, a dozen miles away. Of the two he preferred St. Cosme, and spent most time there. On his share of the revenues of these and his other benefices, and his meagre Court pension,[1] he was able to live in modest comfort as a country gentleman, delighting, as he often tells us, in all kinds of rural activities and particularly, at St. Cosme, in gardening. In this art, says Claude Binet, Ronsard became skilled. His melons were appreciated by Charles IX, to whom he often sent a basket of fruit, with or without such Chinese compliments as

---

[1] His Court pension was still 1,200 livres a year, payable (but not necessarily paid) quarterly. At this period he drew part of the revenues of five benefices : the two mentioned above, St. Guingalois de Château-du-Loir, Mornant, and St. Gilles-de-Montoire. These last involved him in legal disputes and a certain amount of worry. He also drew 1,000 livres annually from the abbey of La Roë in Mayenne. These were all gifts of Charles IX. The abbey of Bellozane he held only a few months, in 1564.

Vous qui semblez de façons et de gestes
Aux Immortels, imitant les Celestes,
Prenez de moy ces pompons et ces fruicts . . .[1]

As the most illustrious poet in Europe intermittently prunes
and hoes and digs and mops his brow and battles with his gardener
—there is no reason to suppose that a Renaissance gardener looked
any more favourably on his employer's activities or desires than a
modern one—we may discreetly inspect him over the hedge.
Pierre de Ronsard is nearing his fifties. There is, or was, a crayon
half-length of him in the Hermitage Palace at Leningrad, made
about this time. It shows no illuminate, transcendental wraith of
a poet wasted with passion, the flesh consumed by thought, sublimated by dreams. Save for the high splendour of the forehead
and the brooding, heavy-lidded eyes, Ronsard resembles a retired
military man or a solid Court official. One gathers that the waist-
line is comfortable. The head is mainly bald, with close-clipped
grey hair at the back; grey, also, the clipped moustache and
the trim beard. The nose, still nobly aquiline, is a trifle
broader at the wings than that of the engraving of 1552. The
ardent young Apollo has, in fact, become an elderly gentleman, and—eternal tragi-comedy of elderly gentlemen—his heart
remains adolescent. " My September," he will say before long,
half ruefully, " is warm." Due to fall in love more desperately
than ever before, with a girl half his age, he has nothing now to
conquer the beloved with but his genius and a European reputation.
It is his misfortune (and our good fortune, seeing what poetry comes
of it) that his desire is fixed on a *mijaurée* to whom Love itself is
distasteful.

There exists no portrait of Hélène de Surgères, maid of honour
to Catherine de Médicis. Her degree of physical beauty can be
judged therefore only from the tributes of Ronsard, Desportes,
Jamyn, and the other poets who praised her. Ronsard himself,
like most imaginative men, constantly idealises the beloved, and in
Hélène's case he admits it :

---

[1] You who in your acts and gestures recall the Immortals and imitate the Celestial Ones,
accept of me these melons and these fruits. . . .

Hélène

Chascun me dit : Ronsard, ta maistresse n'est telle. . . .[1]

Brantôme remarks playfully : " M. de Ronsard must forgive me,
f he will ; but never did his mistress Hélène, whom he has made
so lovely, possess such looks, nor any other lady he saw or wrote
about in his time—even his fair Cassandre (though I know she
certainly had beauty) or his Marie . . . But poets and painters are
permitted to say and do what they please." There is one more
piece of evidence, quoted by M. Champion, that Hélène was not
quite the dazzling nonpareil her lover makes her. About 1597,
twelve years after Ronsard's death, when yet another edition of
his poems was on the eve of publication, Mlle de Surgères was
still concerned enough for her reputation to beg the acid Du
Perron, who delivered Ronsard's funeral panegyric, to affix a
preface to the Sonnets emphasising that Ronsard's love for her was
wholly spiritual. To which Du Perron, who did not like her,
replied, " Why not your portrait ? " It would be wronging her
to deduce from this tart retort that Hélène had no looks at all.
Few beauties who have driven men mad have the perennial May-
morning magic of Romney's Emma Hamilton; perhaps not even
Nelson's Emma.

Hélène de Surgères, for all her Franco-Spanish blood—she
was descended from the Fonsecas—is a curiously English type,
si j'ose m'exprimer ainsi. One would hardly compare her with a
suburban feather-pate like Fanny Brawne, who so devastated the
heart of Keats, but one of Hélène's principal traits is a similar cool,
lady-like " niceness ". Flattered, as well she might be, by the
passion of the greatest poet in Europe, Hélène is genuinely terrified
at the thought of what " they " will say when they read his outpourings ; how far this fear is attributable proportionately to
Christian modesty, a keen social sense, fear of the Queen-Mother,
egotism, and natural priggishness one can hardly judge. Early
betrothed to young Jacques de la Rivière, a captain in the Guards,
who had fallen in the first civil war, Hélène sedulously wore grey
for his sake all her life, adopting for her device " *Dos ojos non
bastan a llorar tan grave mal* "—" Two eyes are not enough to
weep so heavy a grief". How far this mourning was sincere, how

[1] Everyone says to me, " Ronsard, your love is not like that".

far a sentimental pose, and how far a device for keeping troublesome admirers at a distance from her frigid, dainty person, again
one cannot judge. It was generally accepted by Amadis Jamyn
and other poets who wrote sonnets to her before Ronsard appeared
on the scene that she was that sympathetic figure the inconsolable
dove, weeping for her mate. Jamyn even compared her to Antigone.
She actually belonged to a little clique of neo-Platonic *précieuses*
who were not interested in love ; normal love, that is to say.
Court scandal did not spare her friend Madeleine de Baqueville,
on whose morals Ronsard wrote some frank verses, and the
relations between two more of her clique, Anne d'Acquaviva and
Diane de Cossé-Brissac, " cold as the snows of Savoy " (Desportes),
were more than suspect. Hélène de Surgères herself was never
accused of perversion, I hasten to add ; her coldness, mental
and physical, revealed in her pallor and her fondness for botany,
was absolute. Her conversation often turned on astronomy. Her
fair young body, *nonchalant et revêche*, indifferent and sullen, was
not for any man, her blood was normally chilly. One hot August
day Ronsard finds her, to his amazement, seated before a fire,
pale and aloof in her perpetual grey, reading a book—possibly
the refrigerating manual of Léon Hébrieu on ideal love. It was
humanly impossible to melt such an icicle, and one could wish
Barbey d'Aurevilley had analysed this tragi-comic love-affair, as
worthy the attention of this connoisseur of the bizarre as the affair
between Lauzun and the Grande Mademoiselle.

We first encounter Hélène de Surgères in the Queen-Mother's
service in 1566, as a *fille-damoiselle* at a salary of 200 livres. She
was then about nineteen. Later she becomes a *fille de chambre*,
which does not mean a chambermaid, at 400 livres. Her father
was René de Fonsèque, Baron de Surgères, and her childhood was
spent among the snows of Piedmont, symbolically enough, with
her cousins Jeanne and Diane de Cossé-Brissac, who belonged
later to her group, with Mlles d'Acquaviva and De Baqueville.
The five girls seem to have established themselves at Court towards
1568 as a centre of intellectual *snobisme*, and they were increasingly
admired as they paced the Royal gardens, book in hand, reading
or discoursing on the Platonic Idea of love and kindred topics,
or sitting alone in one of the salons of the Louvre, rapt in maiden

editation. Ronsard gives us a glimpse of Hélène in this latter attitude. It is one of those luminous pictures he knows so well how to summon up in a few simple words:

> *Seule sans compaignie en une grande salle,*
> *Tu logeois l'autre jour, pleine de majesté . . .*[1]

How the scene arises at the magician's wand! The bare, stately room with the Goujon sculptures, the sunshine pouring through tall windows on the vast polished parquet, the pensive young figure as it were enthroned in the middle, the slim pale hands at rest on the lap, the stiff billowy skirts spread round the high carved chair: it is as clear as in a camera-obscura. How often a slight frown furrowed that marble girlish brow at the apparition of M. de Ronsard, ingratiating, devouring her with passionate eyes, eager, humble, reciting to her new verses of the most incomparable kind, inspired by the least transcendental kind of love, M. de Ronsard does not say. He suffered and endured, and came back for more, hopelessly enslaved but not deceived. His clairvoyance detects the basic egotism of the adored one very soon. Sometimes, absorbed in herself, she will not spare him a glance.

> *Toy, comme paresseuse, et pleine de sommeil,*
> *D'un seul petit regard tu ne m'estimas digne.*
> *Tu t'entretenois seule au visage abaissé,*
> *Pensive toute à toy, n'aimant rien que toymesme . . .*
> *J'euz peur de ton silence, et m'en allay tout blesme,*
> *Craignant que mon salut n'eust ton œil offensé.*[2]

And he tiptoes out, so to speak, abashed; a strange posture for the conqueror who had annexed Genèvre with the cry "I am Ronsard!" Under Hélène's cool indifferent gaze his native arrogance withered like a flower in a frosty night, and the poet whose name and fame were known throughout Christendom trembled

---

[1] Alone, without company, in a great room you sat the other day, arrayed in majesty . . .
[2] As if languid, as if full of sleep, you deemed me unworthy of the slightest look; you sat aloof with lowered head, absorbed in self-contemplation, caring for nothing but yourself. . . . Your silence affrighted me and I turned pale and retired, fearing my greeting had offended you. . . .

before this pedantic minx like a schoolboy shaken by his firs
calf-love.

It seems to have been in 1572, on emerging from the dust of the
Franciade, that he became aware of her. The lesser poets about the
Court, and especially Philippe Desportes, had discovered her and
her circle already, and were naming her Minerva. Antoine de
Baïf paid the more obvious compliment:

> *Chantons l'Hélène françoyse,*
> *Digne de plus grand renom*
> *Que cette Hélène Gregeoise*
> *Dont elle porte le nom . . .*[1]

Remy Belleau and Amadis Jamyn had equally charming things
to say, and the ageing Dorat produced a learned posy:

> *Nomen habes Helenes et habes pro nomine formam,*
> *Et nisi casta fores jamquoque rapta fores.*[2]

During Ronsard's absence from Court, in fact, Hélène and her
circle had become the fashion, Hélène herself receiving the majority
of the compliments for her pale beauty, modesty, and learning,
her charming voice and glossy dark hair. Desportes and his
mignardises had become the Court fashion simultaneously, and
although Ronsard had nothing seriously to fear for his reputation,
the discovery cannot have been agreeable. It may have helped
to spur him to those summits of supreme achievement he was
presently to attain in the Hélène cycle.

What summits of beauty and music these are the world has
acknowledged by preserving some half-dozen from this sequence
of 142 sonnets, as it were, in a golden reliquary. There is hardly a
modern French lover of poetry who cannot recite you *Quand vous
serez bien vieille, au soir, à la chandelle* or *Afin qu'à tout jamais de
siècle en siècle vive* at length. They are additionally valuable as
pièces de conviction, documenting the progress of Ronsard's vain
passion for Hélène. How frank he is, how careless of posing!

---

[1] Sing we the Helen of France, worthy of greater renown than that Greek Helen whose
name she bears. . . .

[2] Your name is Helen, and you have the beauty of that name; and were you not chaste,
you would have been ravished from us long ago.

The beloved, when she is in residence at the Louvre—which is not too often, for she is one of the indefatigable Queen-Mother's "flying squad", for ever on duty in those arduous provincial tours—occupies a chamber high up in the palace, and her lover implores her to think of the endless steps he must climb, panting and sweating, only to be rewarded with coldness or disdain:

> *Je ne serois marry, si tu comptois ma peine*
> *De compter les degréʒ recompteʒ tant de fois :*
> *Tu loges au sommet du Palais de nos Roys,*
> *Oylmpe n'avoit pas la cyme si hauteine.*
> *Je pers à chaque marche et le pouls et l'haleine,*
> *J'ay la sueur au front, j'ay l'estomac panthois,*
> *Pour ouyr un nenny, un refus, une voix*
> *De desdain, de froideur et d'orgueil toute pleine . . .*[1]

Few poets, I think, but would have preferred to bequeath to posterity a picture of themselves charging up illimitable staircases with youthful brio and taking the loved one by assault. Can one think of Byron or Shelley, had they lived, exposing themselves to the public eye as stoutish elderly gentlemen wheezing and groaning their way to a sentimental rendezvous? The poet, like the actor, keeps his best side to the audience, and if led by dreams to "thy chamber-window, Sweet", is careful not to arrive there hot, flustered, and gasping. This candour is the more surprising in Ronsard because he still cared sufficiently for appearances, more than ten years later, to issue his final edition with the Apollo-like engraving of 1552 as frontispiece. It is to be deduced that his absorption in Hélène was complete.

Hélène's chamber windows had a view towards Montmartre, with the great Benedictine nunnery crowning its summit, where the Sacré-Cœur Basilica stands to-day. Contemplating this rural and cloistral prospect Hélène is discovered by Ronsard one day, pensive and sighing.

---

[1] I should not care, if you realised the trouble with which I count and recount those stairs so often. You live at the top of the palace of our Kings, and Olympus' peak was not so high; at each step my pulse and my breath betray me, sweat stands on my forehead, my stomach revolts—and all this to hear a "No", a refusal, a voice full of disdain and chill and pride.

Vous me dites, maistresse, estant à la fenestre,
Regardant vers Montmartre et les champs d'alentour,
" La solitaire vie et le desert séjour
Valent mieux que la Cour ; je voudrois bien y estre."[1]

Cold comfort for a lover! It may be that Hélène's daydream at
that moment (she had Spanish blood, we remind ourselves) visualised a life amid whitewashed walls of endless Trappist prayer,
penance, and expiation for the world's sins and her own. Great
ladies in every age have so chosen, queens and princesses have
issued from their cell to dress the sores of lepers. More likely
Hélène merely saw herself, faultlessly coifed and wimpled, gliding
across the glossy parlour-parquet of some aristocratic and less austere
foundation to welcome noble visitors to a choice collation, or to
show off her convent's treasures to polite connoisseurs. Such
exclusive nunneries—the Benedictine house of Santa Maria la Real
de las Huelgas at Burgos for the *señoras doñas*, daughters of the
great families of Spain, was famous—were once found all over
Christendom. The graceful hospitality they dispensed, in an age
of arduous road-travel and dubious inns, sometimes embraced
concerts and amateur theatricals, and has much exercised the
imagination of romancers. It exists no more, which is a pity.

Whatever shape Hélène's fancy for the religious life was taking,
it annoyed Ronsard. He tries to wean her from such fancies by
assuring her in the best manner of the Romantics a couple of
centuries later that convent-walls are no fortress against the assaults
of Love.

Amour dans les deserts comme aux villes s'engendre,
Contre un dieu si puissant, qui les Dieux peut forcer,
Jeunes et oraisons ne se peuvent defendre . . .[2]

Whether this cry, echoed by Pope's Eloisa, banished Hélène's
musings he does not say. A girl with a vocation might very easily
have countered it. Hélène's character and history suggest that her
impulse was a passing whim, like Zuleika Dobson's, born of one

[1] You said to me, mistress, as you stood at your window, looking towards Montmartre
and the fields around, " The retired life and the desert abode are better than the Court ;
well could I wish to be there."

[2] Love burgeons in the desert as in the town, fasting and prayer cannot defeat a god of
such power, who can compel the Gods themselves. . . .

those moments of boredom inseparable from her Court life,
hich was not easy. A week later, bumping in a heavy travelling
oach behind the Queen-Mother over the roads of Anjou or
rovence, she would be looking forward to the next Tuileries
all. Meanwhile she was not averse to allowing her poet a seat in
er coach when she took the air with her cousins or friends
n the countryside round Paris; though even this favour was not
nvariable, as he complains after being left out of a pleasure-trip
o Arcueil, scene of his youthful junketings :

> *Dans ton coche porté je n'eusse fait grand presse,*
> *Car je ne suis plus rien qu'un fantaume sans corps.*[1]

He exaggerates slightly. His figure was no longer slender.
His plaint awakened no glint of tenderness or pity in those eyes
which had deprived him of his peace since the day he had first
gazed on them at Mass in the Queen-Mother's chapel. In a sad,
lovely Shakespearean madrigal he expresses his pain :

> *Si c'est aimer, Madame, et de jour et de nuict,*
> *Resver, songer, penser le moyen de vous plaire,*
> *Oublier toute chose, et ne vouloir rien faire*
> *Qu'adorer et servir la beauté qui me nuit,*
>
> *Si c'est aimer, de suivre un bonheur qui me fuit,*
> *De me perdre moymesme et d'estre solitaire,*
> *Souffrir beaucoup de mal, beaucoup craindre et me taire,*
> *Pleurer, crier mercy, et m'en voir esconduit,*
>
> *Si c'est aimer, de vivre en vous plus qu'en moymesme,*
> *Cacher d'un front joyeux une langueur extresme,*
> *Sentir au fond de l'àme un combat inegal,*
> *Chaud, froid, comme la fievre amoureuse me traitte,*
>
> *Honteux, parlant à vous, de confesser mon mal :*
> *Si cela c'est aimer, furieux je vous aime,*
> *Je vous aime, et sçay bien que mon mal est fatal,*
> *Le cœur le dit assez, mais la langue est muette.*[2]

[1] I should not have taken up much room, riding in your coach; I am no more but a bodiless wraith.

[2] If to love, Madam, is to dream and long and brood by day and night on means of pleasing you, to be forgetful of all else, to wish to do nothing else but adore and serve the beauty that wounds me,

Ronsard

Is it fanciful to hear a far deeper note of suffering in this than all Ronsard's previous outcries of wounded love? The old cliché about writing in one's heart's-blood might for once ring true now. His passion for Hélène is hopeless, and he knows it almost from the first.

Elle a de nos chansons et non de nous souci . . .[1]

He sees himself with pitiless clarity and, although he holds out to Hélène that promise of immortality he has held out to women before, he realises he cannot win her with his golden verse; a young and handsome popinjay would have better luck than the First Poet of France.

Estre beau, jeune, riche, eloquent, agréable,
Non les vers enchantez, sont les sorciers d'Amour.[2]

Yet he goes on, hoping and suffering and pouring out sonnets which, one would think, would make any woman proud and thrilled and humble.

. . . Mon plaisir en ce mois c'est de voir les colombs
S'emboucher bec à bec de baisers doux et longs,
Dès l'aube jusqu'au soir que le soleil se plonge.

O bien-heureux pigeons, vray germe Cyprien,
Vous avez par nature et par effect le bien
Que je n'ose esperer tant seulement en songe.[3]

If to love is to pursue a happiness which flies me, to lose myself in loneliness, to suffer much pain, to fear greatly and to hold my tongue, to weep, to beg for pity, and to see myself sent away.

If to love is to live in you more than in myself, to hide great weariness under a mask of joy, to feel in the depths of my soul the odds against which I fight, to be hot and cold as the fever of love takes me,

To be ashamed, when I speak to you, to confess my pain—if that is to love, then I love you furiously, I love you, knowing full well my pain is deadly. The heart says so often enough; the tongue is silent.

[1] It is our song she cares for; not ourself.

[2] Good looks, youth, wealth, eloquence, charm—these are Love's sorcerers, not the magic of verse.

[3] My pleasure in this month is to see the doves billing beak to beak with long, tender kisses from dawn to the sun's going down at evening.

O happy, happy pigeons, true seed of Cyprus! You enjoy, naturally and by right, the bliss I dare not hope for, even in dreams.

His misfortune is that the only kind of love Hélène de Surgères ill deign to accept, he cannot give her. To expressions of that eo-Platonic, high-thinking niminy-piminy which is the vogue nong her set (and the natural corollary and counter-irritant to ne unbridled lust of the other Renaissance extreme) she will listen,) use a homely folk-phrase, till the cows come home. The principal extbook for students of this affectation was a volume entitled *Dialoghi d' Amore*, by a Spanish Jew known in France as Léon Iébrieu.[1] It consists of discourses between two personages, Philo and Sophia, on transcendental Love, a quasi-metaphysical, oseudo-mystical, cabbalistical, finicking manual which drove Ronsard, who detested such emasculate nimble-wimble, to protest against the vogue of

> *Leon Hebrieu, qui donne aux dames cognoissance*
> *D'un amour fabuleux, la mesme fiction ;*
> *Faux, trompeur, mensonger, plein de fraude et d'astuce . . .*[2]

The conclusion of this sonnet—his one and only outburst of anti-Semitism—is amusing, neat, and, all things considered, unprintable.

Another textbook almost as fashionable among Hélène's group was *La Parfaicte Amye*, by Antoine Héroet of the Lyons School, dealing decasyllabically with the Platonic Idea of love, the bodiless union of affinities, the ultimate bliss, derived from the celestial contemplation of Beauty and Harmony. Shorn of all the *fioriture*, the gospel of this lily-handed school amounts, in practice, if one may be so gross, simply to this, that it is the lover's happiness and duty to pour down the beloved's slim white throat a mixture of as much flattery and deification as her conceit can stand, at the same time looking for no recompense but a touch of the hand in acknowledgment, a distant smile, a glance of acquiescence. That such niffnaffery made a warm-blooded man like Pierre de Ronsard furious is not strange. He was ready enough to flatter Hélène with

---

[1] Léon Hébrieu (Leone Hebreo) fled from Spain to Italy after the Spanish re-conquest of Granada (1492) from the Moors, practised medicine, and is believed to have embraced Christianity. His *Dialoghi* were translated into French by Pontus de Tyard, 1551.

[2] Léon Hébrieu, who teaches ladies a chimerical love, fictitious to a degree, false, deceptive, lying, full of fraud and cunning. . . .

fiery ardour; it was unfortunately not the kind of flattery sh
needed, and she shrank nervously from the flame. He did, indeed
make some effort to control himself, and even summoned th
heroic patience necessary to listen to Mlle de Surgères holding
forth, in her cool, charming voice, on these ethereal themes, and t
assure her that the lecture had done him good:

> *Ma chair, dure à domter, me combatoit à force,*
> *Quand tes sages propos despouillerent l'escorce*
> *De tant opinions que frivoles j'avois . . .*[1]

Ronsard's tongue is well in his cheek, I think. Or perhaps he is
merely grasping desperately at any rope which will save him,
as Maria says in the play, from sailing into the north of his lady's
opinion. Rather than be banned from her presence he will attend
to any intellectual tomfoolery from those red lips, stifling, as one
may well believe, more than one mad impulse to kiss them into
silence. A heavy price to pay for loving a pedant.

§2

In the sweet month of May, as Malory reminds us and poets
innumerable, "every lusty herte begynneth to blossom and to
brynge forth fruyte".

The date of Ronsard's self-dedication for life to the service of
the new goddess is fixed for us in two sonnets, one recording the
ritual day:

> *Ce premier jour de May, Hélène, je vous jure . . .*[2]

and proceeding to swear her perpetual allegiance by Castor and
Pollux, divine twin-brothers of her Trojan namesake. The other
sonnet begins:

> *Je chantois ces Sonetz, amoureux d'une Hélène,*
> *En ce funeste mois que mon Prince mourut . . .*[3]

---

[1] The flesh, hard to conquer, fought me with all its strength, when your wise words
stripped off the covering from so many light imaginings of mine. . . .

[2] This first day of May, Hélène, I vow to you. . . .

[3] I sang these sonnets, lovelorn for a Helen, in that fatal month in which my Prince
died. . . .

" Mon Prince " is Charles IX. It was presumably, therefore, on
ay 1, 1574, that this vow was taken. From another sonnet we
ither that the occasion was discreetly ceremonial. The scene
as the sunny gardens of the Tuileries, near a plashing majolica-
led fountain, and Ronsard made his vow at the table, presumably
f marble, and strewn by him with laurel-leaves, symbol of eternity,
t which Hélène was seated. That Hélène had already made him
ake full cognisance of her perpetually disconsolate state is evident
rom the end of the last sonnet I have quoted, with its superbly
melancholy last line :

> *Je sentis dans le coeur deux diverses douleurs :*
> *La rigueur de ma Dame, et la tristesse enclose*
> *Du Roy que j'adorois pour ses rares valeurs.*
> *La vivante et le mort tout malheur me propose :*
> *L'une aime les regretz, et l'autre aime les pleurs ;*
> *Car l'Amour et la Mort n'est qu'une mesme chose.*[1]

This ceremony over, the poet dogs her footsteps. " I cannot
live two hours without seeing you," he says elsewhere. Hélène,
flattered by his worship though mortally afraid of the gossip of the
Court, seems to have warmed herself sufficiently at Ronsard's flame
at first to exhibit—no, " jealousy " is too fiery a word ; to exercise,
in a refined way, some of the rights of proprietorship over her
slave. Thus, she appears to have insisted on a formal abjuration,
in verse, of the two celebrated major loves before her ; which
order he obeys.

> *Adieu, belle Cassandre, et vous, belle Marie . . .*

What his middle-aged Cassandre thought of this dismissal, published to the world in 1578, it would be pleasing to know. Those
dark, still-lustrous half-Italian eyes may have flashed unwonted
fire, and the Seigneur de Pray on returning from his farms or his

---

[1] I felt in my heart two separate pains,
My lady's rigour, and the grief possessing me
For the King whom I adored for his rare worth ;
The living and the dead move me to all sorrows :
The one demands my sighs, the other my tears,
For Love and Death are but the selfsame thing.

hunting may have noted an unwonted acerbity in Cassandr●
demeanour; the servants may have given it another word. ●
perhaps by now (for she had seen Ronsard for the last time ●
years before) his image had faded sufficiently to make her ca●
less what he said, wrote, or did henceforth. It is always diffic●
for a lover to realise that the old love may have forgotten him wi●
equal ease. Cassandre may by 1578 have become so indifferen●
so wrapped up in her own cares, that if she ever read or was to●
of her dismissal at Hélène's order, she may not have even raise●
an eyebrow; and had any one of her friends expressed curiosit●
concerning that century or so of flaming sonnets of 1552–3, it ●
just possible that Cassandre might quite honestly have been unab●
to recollect where and when she had last seen those slim brow●
volumes, "which must be about somewhere"—one can almo●
hear her saying it. I hope so. It would be unpleasant to thin●
that Ronsard's middle-aged waywardness could still wound hi●
sweet first love.

He himself, intoxicated and tortured simultaneously, is following
Hélène everywhere in the Louvre and the Tuileries, heaping
compliments on her, devouring her with his eyes at Court balls,
watching that pale cheek, cold, smooth, pure, and insensible as
a sea-shell, hoping perpetually to see it flush at a word of love,
enduring perpetual elevated discourse, steeling himself to endless
discussion of neo-Platonic and philosophic subjects, pouring out a
succession of love-plaints on paper surpassing, in their passionate
harmonies and glowing autumnal beauty, everything he has ever
written before, reciting these to her—though not all—giving her
flowers, books, a jewel or two (he was not rich), and gnashing his
teeth in jealousy, as was his nature, when any other man approached
her. With an ironic smile he thanks her, once, for all the improving,
nay, educative conversation she is affording him :

> *J'appris tous les secrets des Latins et des Grecs,*
> *Tu me fis un oracle en m'esveillant apres,*
> *Je devins un demon sçavant en toutes choses . . .*[1]

No doubt Hélène noted the irony (she had considerable brains,

[1] I learned all the secrets of the Romans and the Greeks, you made me an oracle, you opened my eyes, I became a demon of learning in everything.

ad what passes in attractive women for wit). The flowers she
arefully pressed, if of botanical interest, and added to her herbarium.
he lover she continued to keep sedulously at arm's length, so that
ow and again his pain and passion, so rigorously repressed, blaze
uddenly up, and he cries aloud in anger that he is not dangling
fter her to learn astronomy !

> *Je ne vous fais la cour, comme un homme ocieux,*
> *Pour apprendre de vous le mouvement des cieux,*
> *Que peut la grande eclipse, ou que peut la petite . . .*[1]

But his fury is soon spent on such occasions, and he humbly asks
forgiveness.

> *Helas, pardonnez-moy ; j'ay peur de vous fascher,*
> *Comme un serviteur craint de fascher à son maistre . . .*[2]

Perhaps he could have shaken free had she not from time to time
relented and showed signs of something approaching affection ;
a warm fitful Spring wind breathing over the frozen tundras.
Once on a staircase in one of the royal palaces she allowed him to
twine a thread of crimson silk round and round her arm and his
while they talked. Once, in kittenish mood, she powdered his
hair and beard with her own hair-powder, and once she made him
a wreath of laurel. And once, on a thrice-blessed day, she goes so
far as to murmur "*Je vous aime, Ronsard*" ; and though it turns
out to mean little more than " I like you ", it causes the happy
lover's heart to leap, and his ever-sanguine hopes simultaneously.

During her recurring absence in the provinces on duty with the
Queen-Mother, Hélène seems to like him more, and she writes
to him, sometimes, almost tenderly. In August, 1574, Catherine
de Médicis travels to Lyons and proceeds thence to Provence,
whence Hélène sends letters to Pierre, filling him with happiness ;
a gift of oranges and lemons comes from her also. He kisses
them as they were relics. Her letters are not extant ; we can judge
only from the Sonnets what bliss they gave him. In March, 1575,

---

[1] I am not paying you court, like a fop of leisure, to learn from you the secrets of the
skies, and what a major or a minor eclipse can do! . . .
[2] Alas, forgive me. I fear to anger you as a servant fears to anger his master. . . .

Hélène is in Paris, to leave again very soon; and the whole ye
and the next, and the next are full of these distractions. In Hélèn
absences the poet mopes and sighs and bites his nails, and pou
out his longing in verse. When she is in Paris for a brief respir
it is clear that they frequently quarrel. Pierre is losing his sel
control and beginning to demand too much, too hopefully expec
ing his poetry to melt that heart of snow, expecting those lips, fro
which he has heard so much tedious skimble-skamble stuff, t
submit to a rain of kisses. It is illusion. Once more he is hurt an
exasperated and cries aloud:

> *Vous aimez l'intellect, et moins je vous en prise;*
> *Aimer l'esprit, Madame, est aimer la sottise!*[1]

and again:

> *Vous dites que des corps les amours sont pollues:*
> *Tel dire n'est sinon qu'imagination! . . .*
> *Et c'est renouveler la fable d'Ixion*
> *Qui se paissoit de vent et n'aimoit que les nues.*[2]

and he tells himself:

> *Mon ame soies plus fine : il nous faut tout ainsi*
> *Qu'elle nous paist de vent la paistre de fumée . . .*[3]

But Hélène is obdurate.

Less than half a mile from the manor of La Possonnière, within
the liberties of Couture-sur-Loir, stands a farm with the charming
name of La Belle Iris, so evocative that the traveller would half-
expect a chorus of shepherds and nymphs in pastel-tinted silks to
trip from the courtyard, waving gilt crooks and symmetrical
posies and singing, with any amount of nods, becks, smiles, and
minauderies, some rustic trifle of the Grand Siècle.

---

[1] You love intellect, and I esteem you the less for it. To love the intelligence, Madam, is
to love a foolish thing. . . .

[2] You say that the love of the body is pollution. To say such a thing is pure fantasy. . . .
It is to revive the story of Ixion, who fed on the wind and loved only the clouds!

[3] My soul, be subtler; as she feeds us on wind, so we must feed her on smoke. . . .

Ah, gardez bien d'être infidèle
A votre fidèle berger ! . . .

he traveller would be disappointed. Nevertheless there is no farm
. all France and Navarre so steeped in pure lyric poetry. La Belle
is is what Pierre de Ronsard and the Ordnance Survey of his time
new as La Bellerie ; not often is a place-name corrupted so daintily.
ntering the courtyard of this farm, one perceives at the further
nd, dripping from a cleft in the *tuf*, or micaceous chalk of Touraine,
he water of what remains of Ronsard's Fontaine Bellerie, issuing
hence to lose itself in weedy, sluggish, frog-haunted meanderings
n the fields. The fountain, or more accurately, spring, is grievously
hanged since Ronsard glorified it in half a dozen odes. Whether
nother fountain, or spring, in the valley of the Cendrine near
Croixval, some miles away, has suffered equally at the hands of
Time and man I have not discovered. It is likely.

This spring in the Cendrine valley is perhaps the more famous
of the two in the eyes of Ronsardians, It was here, issuing moodily
into the flowery meads from his little priory near by, eating his heart
out for the absent Hélène, contemplating the clear plashing water,
pure, cold, fugitive as the beloved, that Ronsard determined to
consecrate these waters to her. He did so in a poem in which
Laumonier has noted influences of Theocritus, Virgil, Horace,
Propertius, Ovid, Petrarch, Ariosto, and the neo-Latin poets
Andrea Navagero, Flaminio, and Sannazaro. Never was learning
more gracefully dissimulated, or such a wealth of reminiscence
more skilfully blended by a master-craftsman into one crystal
harmony. Of the twenty *Stances de la Fontaine d'Hélène*, to be
recited or sung by two persons alternately, in the pastoral mode,
these sufficiently convey its music.

Vous qui rafraichissez ces belles fleurs vermeilles,
Petits freres ailez, Favones et Zephyres,
Portez de ma Maistresse aux ingrates oreilles,
En volant parmi l'air, quelqu'un de mes soupirs.

Vous, enfants de l'Aurore, allez baiser ma Dame,
Dites-luy que je meurs, contez-luy ma douleur,
Et qu'Amour me transforme en un rocher sans âme,
Non comme il fit Narcisse en une belle fleur.

Ronsard

Fontaine, à tout jamais ta source soit pavée
Non de menus gravois, de mousses ni d'herbis,
Mais bien de mainte Perle à bouillons enlevée,
De Diamants, Saphyrs, Turquoises et Rubys.

Il ne faut plus aller en la forest d'Ardenne
Chercher l'eau dont Renaud estoit tant desireux :
Celuy qui boit à jeun trois fois cette Fontaine
Soit passant ou voisin, il devient amoureux.

Lune, qui as ta robe en rayons estoilée,
Garde cette Fontaine aux jours les plus ardents,
Defends-la pour jamais de chaud et de gelée,
Remplis-la de rosée, et te mire dedans.

Advienne, aprez mille ans, qu'un Pastoureau dégoise
Mes amours, et qu'il conte aux Nymphes d'ici prés
Qu'un Vendômois mourut pour une Saintongeoise,
Et qu'encor son esprit erre entre ces forests.[1]

A third singer, so far silent, takes up at the twentieth stanza
and ends the song with the dedication to the "Saintongeoise"
(Hélène was descended from a Seigneur of Saintonge) :

Fontaine, ce pendant de cette tasse pleine
Reçois ce vin sacré que je verse dans toy ;
Sois dite pour jamais la Fontaine d'Hélène,
Et conserve en tes eaux mes amours et ma foy . . .[2]

[1] You who refresh these lovely rosy flowers, you, little winged brethren, Favonian airs
and Zephyrs, carry to the cruel ear of my mistress, as you fly through the sky, something of
my sighs :
  You, children of the Dawn, go kiss my lady ; tell her I die, tell her of my pain, tell her
Love is changing me into a lifeless rock, not—as it changed Narcissus—into a charming
flower.
  Fountain, may thy source be paved for ever and ever, not with fine gravel, and mosses,
and plants, but with many a pearl born of your bubbles, with diamonds, sapphires, turquoises, and rubies.
  No more need one go to the Forest of Ardennes to seek that water of which Renaud
was so desirous. Who drinks, fasting, three times of this Fountain, whether a passer-
by or a neighbour, becomes a lover.
  Moon, with your gown of starry rays, guard this Fountain on the hottest day ; guard
it for ever from heat and from frost, fill it with dew, and mirror yourself in it.
  Let it be that a thousand years hence some shepherd may prattle of my love, that he may
tell the Nymphs hard by that a Vendômois died for a fair one of Saintonge, and that his
spirit still haunts these forests.
  [2] Fountain, while you receive from this full cup the sacred wine I pour into you, be you
called for ever the Fountain of Hélène, and cherish in your waters my love and my faith.

Mlle de Surgères approved this magnificent compliment—pine tree planted by Ronsard in her honour also glorified the spot—to the extent, it seems, of suggesting, now or later, that the Fountain of Hélène should be framed in marble, to her greater glory.

Meanwhile Ronsard, now in his third year of servitude, continues to make no progress in her affections. She increasingly strikes a chill into his burning veins. "You are my heart, my blood, my life and my light," he cries to her in one sonnet; and a little afterwards: "You keep all the cold, you leave me warm!"

> *Vous retenez le froid et me laissez le chaud.*

And she drives him to raging revolt again with her pallid sophistries and fal-lals:

> *Qu'est-ce parler d'amour, sans point faire l'amour,*
> *Sinon voir le soleil sans aimer sa lumière?*[1]

The younger poets about the Court, Desportes and Amadis Jamyn and their company, won more smiles than he from Hélène, since they continued to minister to her vanity, praising her beauty, her birth, her knowledge, her sweet voice, never worrying her with tiresome cries of passion and absurd demands. She accepted as much incense as these fops chose to burn before her, and this preening complacency hurt still more the jealous elderly Ronsard and aggravated his despair. There came a moment when, during one of their increasingly regular quarrels, she callously gave him leave to carry his heart elsewhere if he pleased; a terrible stab for such a lover. He knew himself to be a fool (and no doubt knew that the Court thought so too, for he can hardly have escaped noticing smiles, or perhaps overhearing a chance titter on occasions). But he is so hopelessly in love that although he threatens Hélène to break away, he knows too well he cannot do it. "She is ice all through," he groans. "Why am I such a slave? Fool! She only wants your songs!"

> *Puisqu'elle est tout hyver, toute la mesme glace,*
> *Toute neige, et son cœur tout armé de glaçons,*

---

[1] What is it to talk of love, and never to make love, but to see the sun and not to love his light?

Ronsard

Qui ne m'aime sinon pour avoir mes chansons,
Pourquoy suis-je si fol que je ne m'en delace?[1]

And once more, threatening but unable to throw off his chains
he implores her to try to love him, and he will love her when her
hair is grey as his.

It is not surprising that before long Ronsard falls into melancholi
and takes to his bed, and a surgeon is called to bleed him, the
universal panacea of the age. "How dark!" is Hélène's only
comment when, discreetly visiting her invalid's chamber after this
operation, her eyes fall on the blood-bowl. She laughs, he says, as
she makes this remark; a curiously inane one for a young woman
of brains. It reveals, perhaps, the depths of her indifference. She is
evidently as sick of being pestered as he is of being kept at arm's
length, and it is permissible to see weariness and even hate in the
eyes of both as conversation drags and stops. Ronsard has suffered
too much. A little later, when he asks her desperately once more
the reason for her continuous refusal to listen to his pleadings, she
raps out "*Puis, je ne le veux pas!*"—"I just don't want to!"
That is final enough. She does not want his love-making or anybody
else's. It bores her. To love is not in her nature. She herself tells
Ronsard this at length quite frankly, we perceive from a sonnet
suppressed by him at the time and published after his death. He
is in a fever of restless love, Hélène calm and cool as usual. In
answer to his plaint she says it is not for any social or religious
scruple that she resists him. It is simply the way she is made.

D'une extreme froideur tout mon corps se compose,
Je n'ayme point Venus, j'abhorre telle chose,
Et les presens d'Amour me sont une poison . . .[2]

And then—one sees the toss of the spoilt head, the lethal coldness
in the eyes, the petulant frown, the imperious tap of the foot:

[1] Since she is all winter, ice all through, and snow, with a heart armed with icicles, since she
likes me only for my songs, why am I such a fool as not to tear myself away from her?

[2] My whole physical being is extremely cold,
I do not care for love, I detest such things,
And Love's gifts are to me poison. . . .

Puis, je ne le veux pas !

oor devil.

The *coup de grâce* administered, Hélène leaves Paris again in
ie Queen-Mother's train. Ronsard has now been in love with
er for five years, as he reminds himself in a shamed and bitter
onnet :

> *J'ay honte de ma honte, il est temps de me taire,*
> *Sans faire l'amoureux en un chef si grison . . .*
> *Voici le cinquiesme an de ma longue prison,*
> *Esclave entre les mains d'une belle corsaire.*[1]

The galley-slave metaphor meant far more to a man of the
Renaissance than it does to us. If he had never toiled and suffered
in the long, wicked, black galleys of the Barbary corsairs, he could
see at any great French port at intervals the shaven-polled long-
term convicts driven below-decks and chained like cattle, each
to his oar, and could hear the overseer's lash, and the oaths and
cries of the *chiourme* as the Royal galleys got under way. Treatment was brutal and conditions appalling (but even as Ronsard
wrote these words there was a little child in Gascony who, himself
to be seized by Mahometan pirates in young manhood and lashed
into slavery, was to become the Apostle of the Galleys and spend
years of his noble life in alleviating existence in this foul underworld. St. Vincent de Paul was just about one year old). When
Ronsard compares Hélène to a corsair and himself to her slave,
therefore, he implies an infinity of hopeless suffering and degrada-
tion. And he is not at the end of his sentence yet. He has nearly
two more years to serve. A smile, however wintry, from the
tormentor on her reappearances in Paris will be sufficient to make
him hug his chains and tug at his oar again, resigned. His state is
pitiable, and he is writing some of the finest sonnets in the world.

§3

Of the 142 sonnets Ronsard addressed to Hélène de Surgères
these six, with one or two already quoted, seem to me the

[1] I am ashamed of my shame, it is time to say no more, to cease to ape the lover with
a head so grey. . . . Here is the fifth year of my long sentence as a slave in the hands of a
lovely corsair.

perfection and quintessence of high love-poetry. Humbe:
Wolfe's rendering follows each.

I

Ma douce Hélène, non, mais bien ma douce haleine,
  Qui froide rafraischis la chaleur de mon cœur,
Je prens de ta vertu cognoissance et vigueur,
Et ton œil, comme il veut, à son plaisir me meine :
  Heureux celuy qui souffre une amoureuse peine
Pour un nom si fatal! heureuse la douleur,
Bienheureux le tourment qui vient pour la valeur
Des yeux, non, pas des yeux, mais de l'astre d'Hélène !
  Nom malheur des Troyens, sujet de mon soucy,
Ma sage Penelope et mon Hélène aussi,
Qui d'un soin amoureux tout le cœur m'envelope :
  Nom qui m'a jusqu'au Ciel de la terre enlevé,
Qui eust jamais pensé que j'eusse retrouvé
  En une mesme Hélène une autre Penelope ?

My golden Helen, nay my gold inhaling,
  that tempers my hot heart with its cool air,
  your eyes at will mislead me everywhere
slave to your virtue noted and prevailing.
Thrice happy he, whose stricken heart is ailing
  for Helen's fatal name, enchanted care,
  exquisite pain for eyelids that outwear
earthlight to shine in heaven a star unveiling.
Anguish of Troy, name! ensign of my grief,
  my wise Penelope, my Helen splendid,
  whose lovely torment holds the heart of me,
name, that enskied a lover beyond belief,
  who could have guessed I'd find when all was ended
  in the same Helen a new Penelope?

II

L'autre jour que j'estois sur le haut d'un degré
  Passant tu m'advisas, et, me tournant la veue,
Tu m'esblouis les yeux, tant j'avois l'ame esmeue
De me voir en sursaut de tes yeux rencontré.

Hélène

Ton regard dans le cœur, dans le sang m'est rentré,
Comme un esclat de foudre alors qu'il fend la nue
J'eus de froid et de chaud la fievre continue
D'un si poignant regard mortellement outré.

Et si ta belle main passant ne m'eust faict signe,
Main blanche qui se vante d'estre celle d'un cygne,
Je fusse mort, Hélène, aux rayons de tes yeux :

Mais ton signe retint l'ame presque ravie,
Ton œil se contenta d'estre victorieux,
Ta main se réjouit de me donner la vie.

Lately as dreaming on a stair I stood
   you passed me by, and, looking on my face,
   blinded my eyes with the immediate grace
of unanticipated neighbourhood.
As lightning splits the clouds, my heart and blood
   split with your beauty, and began to race,
   now ice, now fever, shattered in their place
by that unparalleled beatitude.
And if your hand in passing had not beckoned—
   your whiter hand than is the swan's white daughter,
   Helen, your eyes had wounded me to death.
But your hand saved me in the mortal second,
   and your triumphant eyes the moment after
   revived their captive with an alms of breath.

III

Ma Dame se levoit un beau matin d'esté,
   Quand le Soleil attache à ses chevaux la bride :
Amour estoit present avecq sa trousse vuide,
Venu pour la remplir des traicts de sa clarté.

J'entre-vy dans son sein deux pommes de beauté,
Telles qu'on ne void point au verger Hesperide :
Telles ne porte point la deësse de Cnide,
Ny celle qui a Mars des siennes allaicté.

Telle enflure d'yvoire en sa voute arrondie,
Tel relief de porphyre, ouvrage de Phidie,
Eut Andromede alors que Persée passa,

   Quand il la vid liée à des roches marines,
Et quand la peur de mort tout le corps luy glaça,
Transformant ses tetins en deux boules marbrines.

When the sun yoked his horses of the air
    Helen one summer morning took the breeze,
while Love with empty quiver did repair
    for arrows to his lucid armouries.
I saw the apples of her breast as fair
    as orchard-fruit of the Hesperides,
outshining what the Cnidian laid bare,
    or hers who suckled Mars upon her knees.
The swelling ivories in their rounded arches
    were such as Phidias fashioned in relief
    for his Andromeda, when her young Greek
found her rock-fastened by the sea's cold marches,
    her breasts by mortal terror changed and grief
    into the marbled globe of Verd Antique.

IV

Je ne veux comparer tes beautez à la Lune :
    La Lune est inconstante, et ton vouloir n'est qu'un :
Encor moins au Soleil ; le Soleil est commun,
Commune est sa lumiere, et tu n'est pas commune.
    Tu forces par vertu l'envie et la rancune,
Je ne suis, te louant, un flateur importun ;
Tu sembles à toymesme, et n'as pourtraict aucun,
Tu es toute ton Dieu, ton astre et ta fortune.
    Ceux qui font de leur dame à toy comparaison
Sont ou presomptueux, ou perclus de raison ;
D'esprit et de sçavoir de bien loin tu les passes.
    Ou bien quelque demon de ton corps s'est vestu,
Ou bien tu es pourtraict de la mesme Vertu,
Ou bien tu es Pallas, ou bien l'une des Graces.

Shall I your beauties with the moon compare?
    she's faithless, you a single purpose own.
Or to the general sun, who everywhere
    goes common with his light? You walk alone
And you are such that envy must despair
    of finding in my praise aught to condone,
who have no likeness since there's naught as fair,
    yourself your god, your star, Fate's overtone.
Those mad or rash, who make some other woman

your rival, hurt themselves when they would hurt you
   so far your excellence their dearth outpaces.
Either your body shields some noble demon,
   or mortal you image immortal virtue;
   Or Pallas you or first among the Graces.

V

Vous estes le bouquet de vostre bouquet mesme,
   Et la fleur de sa fleur, sa grace et sa verdeur :
De vostre douce haleine il a pris son odeur,
Il est, comme je suis, de vostre amour tout blesme.
   Madame, voyez donc, puis qu'un bouquet vous aime.
Indigne de juger que peut vostre valeur,
Combien doy-je sentir l'ame de douleur
Qui sers par jugement vostre excellence extresme.
   Mais ainsi qu'un bouquet se flestrit en un jour,
J'ay peur qu'un mesme jour flestrisse vostre amour :
   Toute amitié de femme est soudain effacée.
   Advienne le Destin comme il pourra venir,
Il ne peut de vos yeux m'oster le souvenir :
Il faudroit m'arracher le cœur et la pensée.

You are the scent wherewith your posy's scented,
   bloom of its bloom, the wherefore and the whence
of all its sweet, that with your love acquainted
   suffers, like me, passion's pale decadence.
And if these flowers are by love demented,
   adoring what so far exceeds their sense,
judge if I am divinely discontented
   who know by heart your perfect excellence!
But, as the flower's beauty is diurnal,
   may not, as is the way with woman's kindness,
   a single day bring all your love to naught?
Fate, do your worst. My love will be eternal,
   unless you overwhelm my eyes with blindness,
   and pluck my heart out and uproot all thought.

VI

A fin qu'à tout jamais de siecle en siecle vive
   La parfaicte amitié que Ronsard vous portoit,

Ronsard

Comme vostre beauté la raison luy ostoit,
Comme vous enchaisniez sa liberté captive,
  A fin que d'âge en âge à nos nepveux arrive
Que toute dans mon sang vostre figure estoit,
Et que rien sinon vous mon cœur ne souhaittoit,
Je vous fais un present de ceste sempervive.
    Elle vit longuement en sa jeune verdeur ;
    Long temps aprez la mort je vous feray revivre,
Tant peut le docte soin d'un gentil serviteur,
    Qui veut en vous servant toutes vertus ensuivre.
Vous vivrez, croyez-moy, comme Laure en grandeur,
Au moins tant que vivront les plumes et le livre.

Let all men know reborn from age to age
    the perfect love love-perfect Ronsard bore you,
so that within your beauty, as in a cage,
    his mind's sole liberty was to adore you.
And let these be our children's heritage—
    this evergreen that I have woven for you,
bright with your face, immortal in the page,
    long as the love for which I did implore you.
Nor ever will its verdant youth be withered,
    unless to death your lover must surrender
    his utmost skill through which you live again
    with all your graces in their blossom gathered.
No! but with Laura you shall share love's splendour
    as long as there is life in book and pen.

§4

Melancholy, to see the rocket's far-flung gold and silver fire
fading away against the dark after that brave upward leap and
challenge to the stars, whose continued sparkle in the unconquered
serene seems more than ever cruelly impassive and removed
from the follies of men. Melancholy, to see such a soaring, dazzling
passion as Ronsard's for Hélène de Surgères subside by degrees in
bitterness and end in angry murk. He had no more illusions left
in his seventh year of hopeless pining. He bored her and at long
last he realised it, and took his leave.

Hélène

Adieu, cruelle, adieu ! je te suis ennuyeux ;
*   C'est trop chanté d'Amour sans nulle recompense,*
Te serve qui voudra, je m'en vais, et je pense
Qu'un autre serviteur ne te servira mieux.

*   Amour en quinze mois m'a fait ingenieux,*
Me jettant au cerveau de ces vers la semence :
La raison maintenant me r'appelle et me tanse,
Je ne veux si long temps devenir furieux.

*   Il ne faut plus nourrir cest Enfant qui me ronge,*
Qui les credules prend comme un poisson à l'hain,
Une plaisante farce, une belle mensonge !

*   Un plaisir pour cent maux qui s'envole soudain :*
*   Mais il se faut resoudre et tenir pour certain*
Que l'homme est malheureux qui se repaist d'un songe.

which Humbert Wolfe renders :

Cruel, farewell, since I do but annoy thee,
    and love in song grows tedious unrequited.
I go, and let who will or can enjoy thee,
    though never will he match the love you slighted.
In fifteen months love taught me tricks and fashion,
    planting within my brain the seeds of verse ;
Now reason schools the lunacies of passion,
    and brings me to her side and makes me hers.
Feed not this child, who gnaws upon the heart,
    the angler catching fools upon the string,
the comedy, the perfect liar's art,
    a hundred pains and one joy vanishing.
Nay, let's be sure, however things may seem,
That man is doomed who sups upon a dream.

A few years ago M. de Nolhac discovered an illuminating letter from Ronsard to his friend Scévole de Sainte-Marthe, written from Croixval. The year is unknown, but it belongs obviously to the post-Hélène period :

Monsieur mon ancien amy, c'est (disoit Aristophane), une faix insupportable de servir un maistre qui radoute. Parodiʒant la-dessus,

255

c'est un grand malheur de servir une maistresse qui n'a jugement ni raison en nostre poësie, qui ne sçait pas que les poettes, principalle ment en petits et menus fatras comme elegies, epigrammes et sonetz ne gardent ny ordre ny temps. C'est affaire aux historiographe. qui escrivent tout de fil en eguille. Je vous suplie, Monsieur, ni vouloir croire en cela madamoiselle de Surgères et n'ajouter ny diminuer rien de mes sonnetz, s'il vous plaist ! Si elle ne les trouve bons, qu'elle les laisse, je n'ay [? j'ay] la teste rompue d'autre chose. On dit que le Roy vient à Blois et à Tours, et pour cela je m'enfuy à Paris et y seray en bref, car je hay la Court comme la mort. Si elle veut faire quelque dessaing de marbre sur la fonteine, elle le pourra faire, mais ce sont deliberations de femmes, qui ne durent qu'un jour, qui de la nature sont si avares qu'elles ne voudroyent pas despendre un escu pour un beau fait. Faittes luy voir cette lettre si vous le trouvez bon. Je vous baise les mains de tout affection. De nostre Croixval, ce Vme de juillet.

Vostre humble et ancien amy à vous servir,

RONSARD.

A Monsieur et antien amy, Monsieur de Sainte Marthe, logé au pilier verd, rue de la Harpe, à Paris.

That is to say :

Sir, my old friend : It is (said Aristophanes) an insupportable burden to serve a doting master. To adapt this, it is a sore mis- fortune to serve a mistress who lacks judgment and reasoning as regards one's poetry, and who does not know that poets, especially in small and insignificant bits of trash like elegies, epigrams, and sonnets, take no notice of order or time. This is a matter for historians, who write from point to point. I beg you, Sir, not to listen to Mademoiselle de Surgères in this matter and to add or take away nothing of my sonnets, if you please ! If she does not like them, let her leave them alone ; I have other things to worry about. They say the King is coming to Blois and Tours : on this account I am flying to Paris and shall be there very shortly, for I hate the Court like death. If she wishes to make some marble decoration at the fountain she can do so, but these are women's ideas, which only last a day, their nature being so mean that they would not spend one crown on a worthy deed. Bring this letter to her notice

you think fit. I kiss your hands with all affection. From our
roixval, this 5th of July.
Your humble old friend, to serve you.

RONSARD.

To my old friend M. de Sainte-Marthe, lodging at the Green
illar in the Rue de la Harpe, at Paris.

Savage bitterness, almost misanthropy, one observes. The
fountain of Hélène near Croixval, which he dedicated to her not
o long ago with such tremulous adoring love, can have its marble
al-lals or go hang, he does not care which. She is too mean to
be thinking seriously about this expense, probably. Let her keep
her dainty fingers off the Sonnets ; she doesn't understand such
rifles and he will not have a word changed. And (bitterest hit of all)
M. de Sainte-Marthe may show her these words.

It was not until after Ronsard's death that the reason for Mlle
de Surgère's evident agitation about the Sonnets became clear.
Ronsard had evidently mentioned or even recited to her one or
two sonnets of a vehemently fleshly kind addressed to her, though
not by name. These he kept out of the *Sonets pour Hélène*, published
in 1578, and equally out of the *Amours Diverses* which follow,
mixed with some sonnets to Astrée and others. It seems clear
that Hélène insisted to Claude Binet, Ronsard's youthful first
biographer, that an issue should be made in his book of the purity
of the poet's intentions. " As for Hélène de Surgères," writes
the obliging Binet accordingly, " he made use of her name, her
virtues, and her beauty to embellish his verse . . . having loved her
chastely, and principally for her charming intelligence (*esprit*)
in poetry, and other good things." Binet knew nothing, apparently,
of the bitter letter to Sainte-Marthe, for he blandly continues :
" He consecrated to her a fountain in the Vendômois which bears
her name to-day." And Binet adds, surely from Hélène's dictation,
that Ronsard wrote the Sonnets at the command of the Queen-
Mother, which was quite untrue. One sees the rather hard, intent
eye of Ronsard's love scrutinising Binet's proofs. She even made
a few marginal notes, perhaps. The sonnets of distant, abject
worship and idealisation she fully approved, but not certain others

in the *Amours Diverses*, plainly inspired by her and telling the story
of Ronsard's long siege. These sonnets Ronsard, having omitted
them to please her in 1578, restored in 1584 to their proper place
with the rest of the Hélène cycle. They cannot have pleased Hélène
much, particularly a *chanson* beginning:

> *Plus estroit que la vigne à l'ormeau se marie,*
>   *De bras souplement forts,*
> *Du lien de tes mains, maistresse, je te prie,*
>   *Enlace-moy le corps . . .*[1]

There was an even less pleasing one nestling, like a delayed-
action bomb, among the still-unpublished sonnets. It begins, in
a very frenzy:

> *Maistresse, embrasse-moy, baise-moy, serre-moy,*
>   *Haleine contre haleine, echauffe-moy la vie,*
> *Mille et mille baisers donne-moy, je te prie :*
> *Amour veut tout sans nombre, Amour n'a point de loy.*
>   *Baise et rebaise-moy, belle bouche . . .*[2]

A nice example of what modern jargon calls " wishful thinking ",
and a terrible menace to Hélène's peace of mind. It was first published, with eight other less incandescent pieces, in 1609.

She deserved such an offering as Sonnet XLII of the Second
Book (" *Quand vous serez bien vieille . . .*") less, perhaps, than
Fanny Brawne deserved the sonnet " Bright star, would I
were steadfast as thou art ". However, since this pearl of pearls
among the jewels strewn before her would not have been in existence
to enchant succeeding ages but for that pale cold face, one may
grudgingly admit her some rights in it. Its exquisitely quiet music
can never pall. It is Pierre de Ronsard's swan-song, and it ravishes
perpetually, as that air of Francisco Salinas ravished Fray Luis
de León, so that his soul sailed on a sea of sweetness,

---

[1] More tightly than the vine weds itself to the young elm, with its strong supple limbs, entwine my body, mistress, I pray you, with the bonds of your hands. . . .
[2] Mistress, embrace me, kiss me, hold me close, and breath mixing with breath warm my life; give me a thousand thousand kisses, I beseech you; Love demands all, without count, Love knows no laws; kiss me and kiss again, lovely mouth. . . .

Hélène

*Aqui la alma navega
por un mar de dulzura.*

Before it is read or recited aloud there should, I think, be performed a short piece of stringed music, either by Orlando de
Lassus or some other contemporary master, or perhaps from
Bach: and after that a brief silence before the book is taken up
and the sonnet read, by the light of wax in candlesticks of silver.

*Quand vous serez bien vieille, au soir, à la chandelle,
   Assise auprez du feu, devidant et filant,
Direz, chantant mes vers, en vous esmerveillant :
Ronsard me celebroit du temps que j'estois belle.
   Lors vous n'aurez servante oyant telle nouvelle,
Desja sous le labeur à demy sommeillant,
Qui au bruit de Ronsard ne s'aille resveillant,
Benissant vostre nom de louange immortelle.
   Je seray sous la terre, et fantosme sans os,
Par les ombres myrteux je prendray mon repos ;
Vous serez au fouyer une vieille accroupie,
   Regrettant mon amour et vostre fier desdain.
Vivez, si m'en croyez, n'attendez à demain,
Cueillez dès aujourd'huy les roses de la vie.*

Of the few attempts English poets have made to translate this
untranslatable song, Humbert Wolfe's is nearest.

When you are old, at evening candle-lit,
   beside the fire bending to your wool,
read out my verse and murmur "Ronsard writ
   this praise for me when I was beautiful."
And not a maid but at the sound of it,
   though nodding at the stitch on broidered stool,
will start awake, and bless love's benefit,
   whose long fidelities bring Time to school.
I shall be thin and ghost beneath the earth,
   by myrtle-shade in quiet after pain,
but you, a crone, will crouch beside the hearth,
   mourning my love and all your proud disdain.
And since what comes to-morrow who can say?
Live, pluck the roses of the world to-day.

§5

Having broken his chains at last, Ronsard left Paris for Croixva
There is a defiant elegy of 1578 in which he celebrates his libert
after nearly seven years of torment. Free at last! he cries. Free o
desire, love, and pain, he can sleep now.

> *En pure liberté je passois tout le jour,*
> *Et franc de tout soucy que les ames devore,*
> *Je dormois dès le soir jusqu'au point de l'aurore.*[1]

He welcomes those good old consoling friends he has neglected
so long, who now receive and comfort him again:

> *Aristote ou Platon ou le docte Euripide,*
> *Mes bons hostes muets, qui ne faschent jamais . . .*
> *O douce compaignie, et utile et honneste!*[2]

When he needs other refreshment he walks in his fields again and
looks at the flowers, or wanders in the forest again, or by the riverside. Fishing also, he discovers before Izaak Walton, is a great
sedative and lenitive for sick nerves and battered hearts; and at
night he contemplates the stars and their mystery and drinks great
draughts of calm. But though his pain is eased he is not forgetting
Hélène.

> *Vous vivrez, croyez-moy, comme Laure en grandeur,*
> *Au moins tant que vivront les plumes et le livre.*[3]

This immortality he cries aloud once again:

> *Les autres pour parade ont cinq ou six chansons*
> *Au front de quelque livre, et toy des Iliades!*[4]

[1] In pure liberty I passed all my day, free of all that anguish which devours the soul;
I slept from dark to the first glimmer of dawn. . . .

[2] Aristotle or Plato or sage Euripides, my kind silent guests, who never annoy me. . . .
O sweet company, so helpful, so blameless!

[3] You will live, believe me, like Laura in her greatness, at least as long as pens and books
endure.

[4] Others can boast, at the beginning of a book, some five or six songs; you, whole
Iliads!

As we have seen already, Hélène de Surgères was far more pre-occupied, long after Ronsard's death, with her reputation than her immortality. She was not present, it seems, at his requiem Mass in Paris, or at the afternoon ceremony which followed. She survived Ronsard many years, continued her Court service, and died unmarried, as was her destiny, in what we may reasonably allow ourselves to assume to be a sterile, joyless old age. In a later century she would inevitably have taken up economics or the social sciences and refreshed her natural aridity in these dust-baths of the human spirit; or she might have exuberated into a female politician or lecturer, or joined some inhuman sect, or devoted herself to some society for pampering animals and oppressing the poor. I could also see her signature attached to those indignant international manifestos Anglo-Saxon literary figures used to draw up appealing shrilly to Civilisation and Democracy every time one of the brotherhood was threatened in a foreign country for trying to bilk a taxicab driver. I think Hélène de Surgères in a more progressive age would have done a great deal of advanced public work, mostly harmful. May she rest in peace, for she unwillingly inspired deathless song.

X

"*NUPER IDONEUS . . .*"

Vixi puellis nuper idoneus,
Et militavi non sine gloria;
Nunc arma defunctumque bello
Barbiton hic paries habebit . . .

(HORACE, III, 26.)

For ladies' love I late was fit,
  And good success my warfare blest,
But now my arms, my lyre I quit,
  And hang them up to rust or rest.

(CONINGTON.)

§1

" PETRARCH HAD THE INSOLENCE TO SURVIVE HIS LAURA BY TWENTY
YEARS."

The censure is that of Castello-Branco, the eminent nineteenth-
century Portuguese romantic. Obviously, comments Miguel de
Unamuno, contemplating the ebullient and suicidal Branco with
ironic Spanish eyes, Petrarch should have killed himself forthwith.
Petrarch did not so do? Alas, many a sonneteer has perished of
hunger, but never a one of love.[1]

Hélène de Surgères survived Ronsard, as it happened. There are
still gentle hearts, mayhap, despite the Machine Age, who feel it
indecent in him even then to have gone on living after the final
rupture. Not that Ronsard should have killed himself, God forbid;
but he might—and in the Werther period probably would—have
fallen insensibly into a decline, perishing slowly and in exquisitely
melancholy cadence. To find this amorous Descartes, whose
device could have been *amo ergo sum*, continuing to live for half a
dozen years more in the plenary exercise of his poetic power,
deriving delight and stimulant from the friendship of his own
kind alone, is as faintly disconcerting as the ruddy cheerfulness

---

[1] *Por Tierras de Portugal y de España.*

of those acolytes of the Maison Borniol, whose nice conduct of *pompes funèbres* is a household word throughout Paris.

Perhaps the knowledge that his pain for Hélène had produced some of the world's finest sonnets was a lenitive, even a tonic. The writing of sonnets, remarks Unamuno, is *un gran purgante de las pasiones excesivas*. It is not, I hope, cynical to recall again that though poets suffer more than other lovers at the hands of women, their sufferings are not wasted. The artist's pure joy of creation must conquer. I believe that when Pierre de Ronsard opened, one morning in 1578, the parcel from his bookseller containing the first printed copies—a small format, almost a duodecimo—of the *Sonets pour Hélène*, he felt nothing but unmixed ecstasy as he devoured his lines again, though he was still within a year of shaking free from Hélène's thrall. "My God, what genius!" he may have cried with Swift. Does the musician enjoy this intoxicating compensation? Does the painter? The poet certainly does, turning on malignant Eros in triumph, snatching Love's torch to light his own fireworks.

§2

> *Au milieu de la guerre, en un siecle sans foy,*
> *Entre mille procez, est-ce pas grand' folie*
> *D'escrire de l'amour? . . .*

Thus begins Sonnet XXVI of the Second Book:

> In the midst of war, in a faithless age,
> Amid a thousand lawsuits, is it not the height of madness
> To write about love?

From which we may trace the condition of Ronsard and of France during these years of servitude to Hélène. The civil wars continued to flicker in the provinces. It would seem from Sonnet LXII that once more armed Calvinist bands were abroad in the Vendômois, for Ronsard tells Hélène that his house has been sacked in his absence.

> *Voyant par les soudars ma maison saccagée,*
> *Et tout mon pays estre image de la mort,*

263

Ronsard

Pensant en ta beauté, tu estois mòn support,
Et soudain ma tristesse en joye estoit changée.

The First Poet of France and *Fidei defensor* was a marked man, and
the Calvinists would doubtless ruin his property with peculiar
zest. One sees them smashing up his furniture, looting his treasures,
ransacking his cabinets, burning his papers, perhaps putting an
arquebus-shot or two through that portrait of Mary Queen of
Scots which Ronsard so highly prized. It hung constantly in his
library, as he tells us, and whenever his eyes rested on it, whatever woman he happened to be in love with at the time, we may
presume that his thoughts at least intermittently were with that
rose of Scotland. Actually, which of his houses—Croixval, St.
Cosme, Montoire—was sacked he does not say. La Possonnière,
where his nephew lived, apparently escaped, like the church of
Couture, which was seemingly not worth Calvinist attention and
had no tombs—even in the Ronsard chapel—worthy of desecration.
This visitation must have added considerably to Ronsard's difficulties. The lawsuits he speaks of were part of the ordinary worries
every man of property has to face ; worries over titles, claims,
bounds, repairs, taxes, dues. " *Vous croyez que c'est facile de posséder
quelque chose !* " says the financial wizard Joseph to the rest of
M. Georges Duhamel's delightful Pasquier family. " *C'est un
métier !* "

There is a curiously modern ring about one of Ronsard's business
dossiers, now in the municipal archives at Tours. A certain Fortin
is trying to acquire some land owned by the monks of St. Cosme
to extend his dye-factory, and already polluting the priory's waters.
Ronsard points out to the municipal authorities of Tours [2] that the
said Fortin's chimneys and boilers will do nothing to benefit the
local population and are not a public utility, as claimed, and the
industrialist eventually, if I remember rightly, retires defeated.
This is one of the earliest examples I know of the defence of rural
amenities against Big Business. It is gratifying but not surprising
to find Ronsard on the side of those gallant spirits waging endless

---

[1] Seeing my house sacked by the soldiery, and all my countryside made the image of
death, when I thought of your beauty you were my strength, and my sorrow was suddenly
turned to joy. . . .
[2] In a letter dictated to Amadis Jamyn.

and often fruitless war to-day to save what remains of rural England from defilement. That such things could happen in the Renaissance, and in Touraine, is interesting. On the one hand, all that craftsmanship in fine brick and stone and glass going up everywhere, august and gracious and lovely; on the other, the same kind of yahoo we know so well to-day, who would plant his chimneys in the island-valley of Avilion itself.

Meanwhile, towards the end of the reign of Hélène, Ronsard has appeared before a select public in a new rôle. One of the more innocent of Henri III's pleasures, as I have already indicated, was a love of intellectual dialectic. To enjoy this Henri revived an academy—the first adumbration of the Académie Française—founded in 1570 by Antoine de Baïf in his father's house, under the patronage of Charles IX. Re-established in the Louvre at Henri's orders and named the Académie du Palais, it was formally opened in 1576 with an inaugural speech by Pierre de Ronsard. Its principal members we know already: Dorat, De Baïf, Desportes, Amadis Jamyn, Du Perron, Pontus de Tyard, and Ronsard himself. The Académie du Palais met twice a week, and women of intelligence were not excluded, the learned Madame de Retz, called the Tenth Muse, often attending. For the opening debate Henri III himself set the question: whether the intellectual or the moral virtues are the more excellent and necessary. Ronsard's speech is preserved. It begins with the exordium, then quite new, that the speaker is unaccustomed to public speaking. " My chief trade," explains Ronsard to the King, not without complacency, " has always been poetry "—*mon principal mestier a toujours esté la poësie*. He proceeds to develop, with lucid grace and scholarship, a defence of the moral virtues. Desportes replies for the intellectual virtues (which happen to be Henri's preference) and Amadis Jamyn supports him.

It would be vastly agreeable to step back into Time and be present at this debate. I see Henri III seated, his long melancholy Mephistophelian face supported on one hand, the other toying with a jewelled neck-chain or a gold ear-ring, his burning dark eyes fixed intently on the speakers. The Academy is also seated, I imagine, except for the orator of the moment. During Ronsard's speech one may perceive the fop Desportes'

eyes contemplating the ceiling, when they are not glancing sidelong
for some indication of the Royal reaction. Worn, frail, rugged
old Dorat nurses one knee and stares into space. A faint smile
curves the thin lips of the acid Du Perron as he gazes absently
through the window. De Baïf, eager for his friend, has his eyes
fixed on Ronsard. As the speech ends there is a momentary buzz
before the King nods to Desportes. At the end of the debate Henri
III rises, the Academy rises also and bows low, Henri inclines his
head briefly, murmurs "*Merci*", and goes; after which the
Academy dissolves into informality and, I imagine, a little intimate,
allusive jesting, not unmixed with shrugs. For five of the seven
at least are old friends, and everybody present is perfectly aware
that Henri III has probably gone straight from their lofty sym-
posium to fondle one of his *mignons*. Against these epicene playboys public and private anger and satire are increasing. Scurrilous
pasquinades and mocking sonnets nailed on Parisian house-doors,
recurrent clashes of steel in the streets between the Royal *mignons*
and the bodyguards of the King's enemies—Alençon his brother
and the Guises chiefly—and assassinations in broad daylight are
now recurring incidents behind which the hostile parties may be
discerned preparing for graver action. The Treasury coffers are
nearly empty, taxes are uncollected. The Parisians are grumbling
dangerously, renewed street brawls break out between Catholics
and Calvinists, and the King, who has plunged into one of his
mystical periods of fasting and devotion, is compared freely by
pamphleteers and tavern orators to Heliogabalus, Herod, and
Nero.

Nothing is more baffling than the behaviour of Henri III at this
time. Now taking part in such monstrously extravagant displays
as the celebrations of the wedding of the Duc de Joyeuse, Admiral
of France, costing the country many thousands of crowns, now
living on bread and water and padding on blistered feet to Chartres,
obsessed by the need for an heir to the Crown, he seems mentally
deranged. At thirty-five he is whitehaired, short of teeth, neuras-
thenic, pimply, and impotent. Three of his chief *mignons*—two of
them killed fighting in the Louvre with Guise's men, and the
third removed by an assassin—are buried by him in sumptuous
marble tombs in the church of St. Paul, and Ronsard and

Desportes are ordered to supply epitaphs. One may imagine with
what grindings of the teeth Ronsard executes this order; his
pallid response is sufficient proof. The Catholic League celebrates
Henri's subsequent foundation of the *Chevaliers du Saint-Esprit*
in savage rhyme.

> *Vous, Princes de Sodome, escoutez le Seigneur :*
> *" Qu'ay-je affaire", dist-il, " que me fassiez honneur*
> *Par la pluralité de vos vains sacrifices ?*
> *Je suis saoul, plus qu'assez, de voir vos malefices !"*[1]

This new order of chivalry is an attempt by the unfortunate
King to restore French prestige, rapidly diminishing all over
Christendom. His desperate access of devotion, perfectly sincere,
like other impulses of his curious nature, merges into a rage for
austerity and penance for which the Papal Legate rebukes him,
to his fury. "It is God's will to punish us and we deserve it,"
says a letter of Henri's. He is universally detested. In a poem
addressed to Simon Nicolas, one of the Royal secretaries, Ronsard
pours out bitterness and despair as he did years before, during the
first civil war.

> *Tout est perdu, Nicolas, tout s'empire,*
> *Ce n'est plus rien que du Françoys empire,*
> *Le vice regne et la vertu s'enfuit,*
> *Les grands seigneurs ont pris nouveau desduit,*
> *Farseurs, boufons, courtisans pleins de ruses*
> *Sont maintenant en la place des Muses . . .*
> *Ce n'est plus rien que fard, qu'hypocrisie,*
> *Que brigandage et rien qu'apostasie,*
> *Qu'erreur, que fraude en ce temps obscurcy:*
> *Le Turc vit mieux que l'on ne faict icy.*[2]

And he bursts out :

[1] You, princes of Sodom, hark to the Lord. "What is it to Me", He says, "that you
pay Me honour with your vain repeated sacrifices ? I am more than weary of your evil!"
[2] All is lost, Nicolas, all grows worse, there is nothing left of the pride of France. Vice
is enthroned and virtue flees; our great lords have taken up new pastimes; playboys,
clowns, courtiers full of cunning have now taken the Muses' place . . . There is nothing
now but deceit, hypocrisy, brigandage, apostasy, error, and fraud in this time of darkening. The Turk lives worthier than we do here.

Ronsard

Que je regrette (ô Dieux!) que je regrette
Un si bon temps où la Muse brunette
Avoit en cour tant de lustre et de pris ![1]

Granted that Ronsard is brooding here, perhaps, more over
his own affairs than the affairs of France, the rest of the jeremiad
is sufficiently indicative of his feelings for the public weal. He is
living gloomily enough, full of lassitude, watching the clouds
gather thick and heavy, feeling age coming upon him with the
disasters threatening his country once more. Nevertheless—
characteristically—he remains loyal to his King. In an elegy
published in 1584 he offers Henri his services :

Ne vous arrestez point à la vieille prison
Qui enferme mon corps, ny a mon poil grison,
À mon menton fleuri : mon corps n'est que l'escorce;
Servez vous de l'esprit, mon esprit est ma force.[2]

I cannot help detecting something finely Jacobite in this. The
King is bored with Ronsard's sermonisings. But the King, whatever his vices, is surrounded by powerful and ambitious enemies,
a sick and threatened man. To rally to him thus defiantly is to
invite not only brickbats from the populace but dagger-thrusts
from the bravoes of the Guises, the Calvinists, and the adherents
of Monsieur. Nor does the hyperbole of such a line as

Vostre vertu qui regne au monde sans egale,

make me smile. Ronsard is appealing desperately to a semi-lunatic
in the shoes of the Most Christian King of France to pull himself
together and remember the glory of his office. At its highest, it is
possibly what we nowadays call " suggestion " ; at its lowest,
it is a recognised convention. *Vertu* moreover is not " virtue ", but
the Latin *virtus*, courage, worth ; and courageous Henri III certainly

[1] How I regret—Oh, gods! how I regret—that good time when the nutbrown Muse
enjoyed such lustre and prestige at Court !
[2] Be not deterred by the ancient prison which holds my body, nor my grey hairs, my
bearded chin ; my body is but the outer husk. Avail yourself of the spirit, for my spirit
is my strength.

as. There is nothing of the time-server about Pierre de Ronsard, the least docile Court poet in history, as I have remarked before. A lesser man would be currying favour now with the Guises, who held all the trumps.

It was in 1588, three years after Ronsard's death, that Henri III astonished everyone by waking suddenly from his coma and tackling the Guises once and for all *en grand politique*—the compliment is that of Lucien Dubech, a modern historian. The preliminary manœuvrings involved, military and other, need not concern us. On December 23, Henri struck at the head of the trouble. Henri de Guise and the Cardinal of Lorraine were assassinated, the other leaders of the League arrested. Next day Paris rose in arms for the League. In the April following, Henri, having now only Blois, Tours and Bordeaux to his kingdom, made a masterly political stroke by reconciling himself with Henri of Navarre, who had an army, and marching with him on Paris at the head of thirty thousand men; and on August 1, stabbed in the stomach by a League friar-assassin at the camp of St. Cloud, Henri III died devoutly and courageously, naming Henri of Navarre his rightful successor.

Four years later, at the close of the campaign, Henri of Navarre, having abjured Calvinism at St. Denis amid popular rejoicings, had his excommunication lifted by the Pope and rode into Paris for the Te Deum at Notre Dame. The last of the Valois had responded to Ronsard at last and bequeathed unity to France.

§3

From the balcony of that modest house adjoining the east end of the priory church at St. Cosme-lez-Tours, overlooking the river, Ronsard must have leaned and mused often during these last half-a-dozen years; I think seldom without the ghost of an old tune fiddling in his head, a jigging little country dance-tune, such as is sawed by fiddlers at rustic weddings. It was natural for his idealised youthful love to haunt him in this island, where he had danced with her. Taking refuge in that memory from more recent pain, he had produced in 1578 those sad and lovely and ethereal elegies to Marie I have set down elsewhere.

Pour obseques reçoy mes larmes et mes pleurs,
Ce vase plein de laict, ce panier plein de fleurs,
Afin que vif et mort ton corps ne soit que roses.

Marie was dead. Cassandre was still alive, and not very far
away. He does not seem to have had any thoughts of Cassandre
any more; if he had, he would have been compelled to express
them with his quill, for his Daemon was ever inexorable. Possibly
tempted more than once to see his Cassandre, now grown middle-
aged, a mother, careworn, perhaps stout, perhaps dull, perhaps
no longer remembering his verses or caring to be reminded, he
put the temptation wisely aside. It was better, staring over the
Loire, glittering in sunlight or shrouded in rain, to remember

Une beauté de quinze ans enfantine . . .

and the glory of that golden hair, *frizé de mainte crespe annelet,*
than to shock his heart with the sight of actual wrinkles and grey
lassitude.

His books brought him more solace now than brooding over
the ashes of dead fires—his *bons hostes muets* in calf and pigskin,
sheepskin and parchment. Nor do I think he lacked conversation
in his retirement. The monks, or more accurately friars, of St.
Cosme-lez-Tours belonged to the Augustinian Order, which
educated Luther—" the drunk Augustinian apostate " of one of
Ronsard's polemics—and, to the greater glory of Science three
centuries later, produced Mendel. Their chaplain, seventy-year-old
Jacques Desguez, was a man of Ronsard's own rank and breeding, his
procureur spécial for all business during his absences from Touraine,
and a personal friend; and among the little community, a dozen
friars at most, ruled by a Sub-Prior, there must have been more
than one who could afford Ronsard a pleasant winter evening's
talk. Typical of the Sorbonne is the casual remark of Professor
Gustave Cohen that Ronsard must have "despised the ignorance,
dirt, and simplicity " of the religious nominally in his charge;
it is the stock cliché of the *mangeur de curés.* The professor could
more reasonably apply his remark, from his world's standpoint,
to the Franciscans of Fontenay, from whose convent Rabelais

an away. These were certainly simple peasants, no company for
youthful sceptic bursting with intellectual pride; the type of
persons who esteem sanctity above soap. Then as now the cloister
held every type of man—I like to think incidentally of the Pindaric
Ode Ronsard might have made on that ex-prior of Carmelites who
s at this moment[1] Admiral of the Pacific in the Fighting French
Navy—and the company of the friars of St. Cosme was evidently
good enough for this fastidious scholar. To what order Ronsard's
Croixval community belonged I have not discovered from the
massive folios of *Gallia Christiana*. At St. Cosme he did a great
deal of restoration and rebuilding, says Crichton, and his friars
adored him.

Books and conversation, and an occasional game of trictrac
or primero, that Italian ancestor of poker, were now Ronsard's
only diversions, since his malady deprived him of the field-sports
he loved, and even of that gardening he so delighted in. From
now on his nights are an increasing torment and sleep deserts
him. He had rarely, we gather from allusions scattered up
and down his works, been a sound sleeper. Continuous cerebral
and emotional excitement, and perhaps some arthritic tendency
connected with his early deafness, do not make for restful nights.
And now the fell grip of the gout was slowly and inexorably
tightening on him. Did his master Anacreon, that other devout
singer and worshipper of wine, grimace and wince and groan in
time as a myriad crystal daggers stabbed him? It seems a poor
reward from Bacchus for a lifetime's service. But gout has been
the normal reward of *bons viveurs* from the dawn of the vintage,
and we may surmise that for the most part Ronsard regarded it so
and was resigned.

His twinges were not relieved to any extent by a gift from the
City of Tours in 1576. Every visitor to Tours has admired Michel
Colombe's graceful Fontaine de Beaune in the Place du Grand-
Marché. It was at this fountain in August, 1576, that a nymph in
a fine silk gown was posted to recite a compliment to François,
Duke of Touraine, youngest son of Catherine de Médicis, who
was passing through the city, and who should supply the needful
rhymes but Messire de Ronsard, to whom the Municipality his

[1] 1943.

neighbour sent an envoy begging him respectfully to honour them
with the same? They paid the poet with a consignment of fine
wines, and no *ronsardisant* could ever look at the Fontaine de
Beaune without mixed feelings. A little later, when Mgr. de
Touraine visited Ronsard at St. Cosme, following the family custom
he was received with a present of fruit and a set of verses in which
Ronsard awards himself a modest Horatian laurel for that his little
house thus honoured, though lacking the embellishments of
porphyry and marble and jasper, is yet the home of virtues which
do not flourish at Court. The rich have by our day grown
unaccustomed to these two-edged compliments. Mæcenas and
Mgr. de Touraine alike received them, doubtless, with impassivity,
fingering the jewel at their necks. The rich have no need to
argue.

It is about this time, during a visit to his nephew, possibly, or to
Croixval, that Ronsard is seized with anger on seeing the axe at
work in his beloved forest of Gastine. The woodmen of Henri
de Bourbon, Duke of Vendôme, now King of Navarre, are convert-
ing a few acres of noble timber into a diamond necklace for some
Paris mopsy (or, as Martellière more charitably deduces, into ready
cash to pay some of the creditors of Henri's late extravagant mother,
Jeanne d'Albret, Queen of Navarre. The forest was sold in 1573,
the year after her death). The outrage is sharp and personal to
Ronsard. The tall oaks of Gastine, of which his forebears were so
long wardens, have always been to the poet gentle living friends,
counsellors, comforters, breathing memories of childhood's
happiness, haunted by the kindly nymphs and dryads of Home.
In some of his earliest pieces he had cried his love for their green
murmurous depths:

> *Couché sous tes ombrages verts,*
> *Gastine, je te chante . . ,*[1]

blessing them for inspiration and consolation, commending them
to all the Muses. And now they crash and fall and lie bleeding.
He bursts out indignantly:

[1] Lying under thy green shade, Gastine, I sing thee . . .

272

Escoute, Bucheron! arreste un peu le bras,
Ce ne sont pas des bois que tu jettes à bas!
Ne vois-tu pas le sang lequel degoutte à force
Des Nymphes qui vivoyent dessous la dure escorce?
Sacrilege meurdrier, si on pend un voleur
Pour piller un butin de bien peu de valeur,
Combien de feux, de fers, de morts, et de destresses
Merites-tu, meschant, pour tuer des Deësses? . . . [1]

Perhaps Shelley was remembering this outcry in *The Woodman and the Nightingale*:

And so this man returned with axe and saw
At evening close from killing the tall trees,
The soul of whom by Nature's gentle law
Was each a wood-nymph. . . .

Moreover there is one splendid line of Ronsard's:

Forest, haute maison des oiseaux bocagers,

which seems to flower naturally into Shelley's:

Around the cradles of the birds aloft
They spread themselves into the loveliness
Of fan-like leaves.

Ronsard's anger at the murder of the dryads of Gastine soon declines into melancholy. He realises the futility of it, and he bids farewell to his trees—" Good-bye, oaks! Trees of Jupiter!"— crying shame on the destroyers of " our fathers who nourish us ", *nos pères nourrouciers.* Only a countryman, I think, would use that epithet, being aware that the function of trees is not merely to look beautiful, to give shade in heat, and to provide homes for a myriad birds, but to refresh and invigorate the soil and make it fruitful with the water they collect and secrete ; as many tree-

[1] Hist, woodman! Stay your hand a space! Those are not trees you overthrow! Do you not see the blood of the nymphs who live beneath the hard bark start forth ? Sacrilegious assassin, if a thief is hanged for stealing booty of little worth, how many fires, fetters, deaths, and punishments do you deserve, rascal, for killing goddesses ?

murderers have discovered too late, seeing their land becom
a dustbowl. The conclusion of this arboreal dirge is philosophi
Aware that his own fall cannot be far distant, reminding himse
that all things (as the Oracle of the Holy Bottle reminds Panurge
move towards their end, but that life goes on, Ronsard stops o
a note of pure Lucretianism :

> *La matière demeure, et la forme se perd.*

Matter endures, the form departs.

Mortality was creeping into the air. The Pléïade was breaking up. La Péruse and Des Autels had died long since. On
March 7, 1577, Remy Belleau died at the age of fifty, and Ronsard
journeyed to Paris to be one of the pall-bearers when they buried
this graceful poet, youngest and latest of the Pléïade, in the now
vanished church of the Grands-Augustins. Joachim du Bellay
had taken some portion of Ronsard's youth with him to the grave
eleven years before. Etienne Jodelle had died in 1573, leaving
behind his rhetorical tragedies and three lovely lines of funereal
verse :

> *Tien, reçoy le cypres, l'amaranthe, et la rose,*
> *O Cendre bien heureuse, et mollement repose*
> *Icy jusqu'à la fin.*[1]

Of the joyous inner band four now remain ; Ronsard, Antoine
de Baïf, Pontus de Tyard, now shaping his course towards a distant
bishopric and lost to his fellow-poets, and tough old leathery Dorat,
who, with De Tyard, was to survive them all. The chant of *Dies
Iræ* may have struck heavily on Ronsard's ear that day as he fixed
his sad eyes on Belleau's catafalque.

He returns with relief to his writing-table, for this year he is
completing the fifth edition of his complete poetical works, which
appear in seven volumes in 1578, with some 200 supplementary
pieces, including the splendid elegies for Marie. (I have omitted
to mention the preceding editions, which are chiefly interesting
to technicians by reason of Ronsard's perpetual prunings, deletions,

---

[1] Receive now, O happy, happy dust, the cypress, the amaranth, the rose,
And sleep here sweetly till the end. . . .

hanges in orthography, and other corrections and alterations;
by no means invariably happy.) This return to idealise an old love
and use it for a literary theme seems to show that Ronsard has at
last accepted his destiny and retired from the lists of Venus.

> For ladies' love I late was fit,
>   And good success my warfare blest,
> But now my arms, my lyre I quit,
>   And hang them up to rust or rest. . .

Though hardly his lyre, which was not to drop from this musician's
fingers till they stiffened in death.

In this edition, too, he places the last sonnet to that other adored
one, Mary Stuart. He also takes a formal farewell of Love.

> *Adieu, traicts d'Amour, volez en autre part*
>   *Qu'au cœur de Ronsard !*[1]

And he prepares to face his inevitable visitor.

> *Voicy la Mort qui vient, la vieille rechignée,*
>   *D'une suite de maux tousjours accompagnée . . .*[2]

Now, he says, his only pleasures are those of a man of sixty—
trictrac and cards. He is too ill to attend the Provincial Council at
Angers in August, 1583. In the autumn of that year he has recovered
sufficiently from fever and gout to travel to Paris and stay with
Jean Galland of Arras, Master of the Collège de Boncourt,[3] adjoining the apse of St. Etienne-du-Mont. Here he has lodged, during
his visits to Paris, ever since he gave up his house in the Faubourg
St. Marcel and retired to the country some time ago; here he is
sure of finding old mellow friendships, affectionate attention, and
the admiration of the rising generation.

§4

Jean Galland, an old friend of Ronsard's, we should have met
before; but to number Ronsard's myriad friends, literary and other,

---

[1] Farewell, Love's darts! Speed elsewhere than to the heart of Ronsard!
[2] For here comes Death, the old and surly crone, accompanied ever by a swarm of ills. . . .
[3] Now the staff headquarters of the Ecole Polytechnique.

would lead to endless digression. One of them, Jean Nicot of Nîmes, French Ambassador at Lisbon, to whom Ronsard dedicated an *odelette* in 1554, has a peculiar claim on the attention of the modern world. Nicot presented tobacco-plants from Florida to Catherine de Médicis—as "nicotine" forever recalls—some years before Sir John Hawkins brought tobacco to England. It is not recorded that the French took up smoking and snuffing with the frenzy of the English, who before the end of Elizabeth's reign were desperate addicts, as Dekker satirically records. "Before the meate come smoaking to the board our Gallant must draw out his Tobacco-box. . . . Then let him show his severall Trickes in taking it, as the *Whiffe*, the *Ring*, etc. For these are comple-ments that gaine Gentlemen no mean respect."[1] The French had fewer fogs, mulligrubs, whimsies, and despairs to combat, after all. They did not, however, cut off smokers' noses, as in Russia.

Jean Galland, to resume, was an eminent Hellenist, a member of that inner circle of scholars and intellectuals, with Dorat, Adrien Turnèbe and Denys Lambin of the Collège de France, Ramus, Jean Passerat, Casaubon, Marc-Antoine de Muret, Vatable, the Estiennes, and others to whom Pierre de Ronsard was an intimate and equal. The Collège de Boncourt, which was to educate Voltaire in due course, was founded in the fourteenth century for poor scholars of the diocese of Thérouane, and under Galland's rule was notable for its encouragement of the new drama. After the first performance before the Court, Jodelle had his play *Cléopâtre* produced there, before a large company of wits and *personnages d'honneur*, and Charles IX's Academy had held sessions in its hall. Boncourt's addiction to the theatre does not seem to have stirred the animosity of the rest of the University like the newfangled curriculum of the Jesuits at the Collège de Clermont, in which theatrical performances[2] were as much employed in forming the " complete man "—the goal of Jesuit education then as now—as

---

[1] *The Guls Horn-Booke*, London, 1609.
[2] They were of a didactic nature, given in the vernacular and in Latin. One of the first stage performances of the Don Juan legend was given at the Jesuit college at Ingoldstadt in 1615; in this version Don Juan, corrupted by the doctrines of Machiavelli, denies the immortality of the soul and is carried off by his ghastly guest. At Jesuit prize-givings ballets of the graver kind also formed part of the entertainment.

Ad Tulleum
Primum Præsidem

Lingua Tullee prima Tulliana
Quondam gloria, nunc Catoniana
Idem primus honos seueritatis,
 Hoc est Justitiæ atque sanctitatis;
Cuius gloria summa, per fauorem
Nil cuiquam dare plus minusue Justo:
A Te gratia nunc rogatur ista,
A te sola roganda quæ decenter,
A te sola decenter impetranda :
Ronsardo facias tuo Clienti
In .Causa facili, probata, aperta,
Non prosit fauor ullus vt nocenti,
Sed ne obsit fauor vllus Innocenti :—

                    Ronsardi

Autograph Ode to Christophe de Thou, signed by Ronsard

mathematics and the physical sciences, the Humanities, dancing, and fencing. (Undoubtedly Molière's schooldays at Clermont and the plays he took part in there showed him his vocation.) Is it permissible to think that competition with the Jesuits may have had something to do with Galland's patronage of the drama?

The cloisters of the Collège de Boncourt were spacious, its rooms airy, its courtyard and garden tree-shaded and retired, and it occupied the very centre of Ronsard's Parisian world, close to the hospitable houses of Dorat and De Baïf, adjoining whom Ronsard had lived *sub regno Genevrae*. With what delight Ronsard must have stopped his coach at this friendly threshold, sure of his welcome! Du Perron's funeral panegyric shows us the good Galland hastening out to carry the crippled poet from the gate to his bedchamber. When Ronsard recovers he delights on a fine day to walk and sit in the garden, well furred against chills, surrounded by deferential youth, expounding to them favourite passages of Horace, Virgil, and the Greeks; a pleasant picture of elderly Fame, *le bonhomme Ronsard*, discoursing with smiling authority and charm. Agrippa d'Aubigné, who admired Ronsard despite himself, has preserved one of his *obiter dicta* to the Boncourt students on the love of the French language. " My children, defend your mother from those who would turn a lady of good family into a serving-wench! " he begins, and goes on whimsically to denounce scoundrels who think it elegant to scorn the good old locutions and substitute a half-Latin, half-Italian jargon of their own. Ronsard will occasionally express an opinion on contemporary poets, whom he does not rate very highly, though he never indulges in malice or pomposity. Only once, in his last years, so far as can be discovered, did Ronsard give way to a spasm of irritation against a fellow-craftsman. It was about this time, when the literary salons and Ronsard's enemies were lavishly lauding young Du Bartas, a new and pretentious poet of Calvinist tinge, to the skies and setting him above the First Poet of France, whom Du Bartas himself professed to admire. In a remonstrance to Dorat the old lion, denying any participation in this chorus, seems for once to have forgotten his generosity:

Ils ont menty, Dorat, ceux qui le veulent dire
Que Ronsard, dont la Muse a contenté des Roys,
Soit moins que le Bartas, et qu'il ait par sa voix
Rendu ce temoignage ennemy de sa lyre :
Ils ont menty, Dorat . . .[1]

"I know who I am," says Ronsard haughtily, and he adds curtly that he does not care for *ces vers ampoulez*, this high-flown stuff.

The epithet is just. Du Bartas' verse is a mass of rococo affectations and neologisms, and his temporary vogue was a triumph of bad taste (Goethe admired him, incidentally). The clarity and balance of Ronsard's genius would make him naturally abhor the wilful-precious and the alembicated-obscure, which Gongora was soon to make a European cult. He seems all his life to have carefully avoided any reference—save that slightly supercilious passing mention in the preface to the *Odes* in 1550—to the Platonico-mysticocard School of Lyons, whose leaders were Maurice Scève, Héroet of *La Parfaicte Amye*, Jeanne Gaillarde, and Louise Labé, an advanced type who is said to have fought at the siege of Perpignan, dressed in man's armour, as *le capitaine Loys*. The Lyons poets wallowed in high-thinking obscurity, aided no doubt by the mingled fogs of Rhône and Saône which overhang their great grim city, in due course doomed to be the Manchester of France, except for its superlative cookery. Mlle Labé, apart from her poetry, was hardly the type to appeal to a man who preferred his women feminine.

So Ronsard was seriously annoyed by Du Bartas. But he was now a sick man, we recollect, and a smooth reference by young Du Bartas to "a perpetual dictatorship" (*dictature perpetuelle*) in French poetry had obviously been a shaft directed at him. It is the custom in the literary world, as we noted before, for the young to be supercilious towards their elders—Ronsard had been so himself in his hot youth—and for illustrious Age to take it irritably. Moreover, one or two of Ronsard's own friends were among the Du Bartas *claque*. It is human nature to be annoyed by such things.

---

[1] They have lied, Dorat, who say that Ronsard, whose Muse has been sufficient for Kings, is of less worth than this Bartas, and that he has himself rendered this testimony, derogatory to his own Muse. They have lied, Dorat . . .

I trust these pages have nowhere presented Ronsard as a man
lacking the artist's normal weaknesses. I do not know if I have
likewise made sufficient recognition of that invincible generosity
of his, which more than balances any outbursts of pride. "In
private life," remarks Sainte-Beuve accurately, "he was the kindest
and most modest of men." His encouragement of younger poets
and writers, such as Florent Chrestien, Du Perron, De Thou,
Bertaut, and Pierre de Loyer is sufficiently acknowledged in their
letters and works. "Liberal and magnificent," is the tribute of the
sour d'Aubigné, another protégé. Du Perron in his funeral
oration calls him a father and preceptor. "*Bons Dieux!*" writes
Ronsard to Antoine de Baïf, who had given him a copy of
Scévole de Sainte-Marthe's immense Latin poem *Paedotrophia*,
"what a book you have sent me on behalf of Monsieur de Sainte-
Marthe! It is not a book, it is the Muses themselves! . . . I set it
above all others of this age, even should this offend Bembo and
Navagero and the divine Fracastor!" As for his own work, he
deferred freely and with courtesy, says Binet, to the judgments of
the beaux-esprits and the learned. If the criticisms of the ignorant
and malicious got under his skin—he could not bear, apparently,
the suggestion from anyone that the *Franciade* he had sweated over
so long was inferior to his other works, for such suggestion, in his
view, postulated malice—that is no great marvel. Lacking spite,
he had a temper and could show it, *grand seigneur* as he was normally;
yet I cannot see him threatening, like Browning, to spit in a fellow-
poet's face, or, like Tennyson, driving away a clerical bore with a
stream of foul language.

Ronsard's recorded quarrels are surprisingly few. The duel
with Mellin de St. Gelais, inspired by high-spirited mischief as
much as youthful arrogance, was soon over and never resumed.
A clash with Antoine de Baïf in the Marie period, due apparently
to Ronsard's being charged by de Baïf with artistic insincerity,
lasted just over a year, and they were constant friends again. A
clash with Du Bellay, alleged by Binet to have been prompted by
professional jealousy, has been shown to be a legend. Ronsard's
attack on Pierre Paschal, who had grossly deceived him, was not
unjustifiable, and moreover Ronsard's swingeing Latin diatribe is
full of hidden laughter. The slam-banging of the early Calvinist

wars was mere give-and-take ; Ronsard, himself ignobly assailed
was never outrageous in retort and reconciled himself later with
one of his chief antagonists, his protégé Florent Chrestien. A display
of irritation against André Thevet, who had made fun of his
Franciade, was understandable, like the invective—mainly poetic
and xenophobe—against Sardini, the foreigner who had bereft
him of the false Isabeau. There is less excuse perhaps for Ronsard's
passing animosity, in the 1540's, against the architect Philibert
Delorme, due partly to Ronsard's warm friendship for Delorme's
rival, Pierre Lescot, and much more to the fact that Delorme had
managed to get himself awarded three benefices. With the Du
Bartas outburst, these are all, and I still think Ronsard's dying
belief that he had never wilfully injured any man was well-
founded.

His freedom from the petty backbiting and viciousness common
to the children of the Muses in their scufflings is notable, I repeat.
If Ronsard reigned too long a dictator, as young Du Bartas complained, no literary dictator has been more benevolent. One thinks
of Ben Jonson growling sarcasms at the Devil Tavern, Addison's
sneers amid his little court at Will's, Malherbe's great wig nodding
out sentence from the bench of summary justice, Samuel Johnson
roaring *ex cathedra* that there is no precedence between a flea and
a louse. For a proud super-sensitive, conscious of his superiority,
Ronsard's record in these matters is extremely good. Might one
explain it by recollecting that he was a gentleman—a difficult
thing for any writer to be, as Mr. Somerset Maugham has pensively
remarked ?

§5

Those winter weeks of 1583 at the Collège de Boncourt seem
bathed in mellow afternoon sunshine. Actually, it is recorded,
the weather was vile. But had that winter been of the purest
Côte-d'Azur gold Ronsard's Daemon would not have permitted
lotos-eating and garden-idling amid that congenial company
indefinitely. As Du Perron says, he was preoccupied now with his
last will and testament. We can form a clear picture of him this
stormy winter, slowly ascending the staircase at dusk with the aid
of a student's arm, or leaning on the affectionate Galland, seating

himself in his furred nightgown by his chamber fire in a high-
backed chair, the candles lit on the writing-table, his books and
papers, quills and ink at hand, his curtains shutting out darkness,
wind, and rain, a deep monastic quiet enfolding him. His intention
is magnificent and strenuous. He is determined to revise and
republish the entire *corpus* of his poetic works in one volume,
his final gift to Posterity and one worthy of his fame.

It duly appears, the fruit of the long winter days and nights of
1583; a massy folio published in January, 1584 by Gabriel Buon
at the sign of St. Claude in the Clos-Bruneau, printed in clear,
bold type in double-column like a Bible or an altar-missal; a
startling innovation. On the lintel of this noble volume, in capital
letters, stands Ronsard's last salute to the Muses:

> RONSARD, AFIN QUE LE SIECLE AVENIR
> DE TEMPS EN TEMPS SE PUISSE SOUVENIR
> QUE SA JEUNESSE A L'AMOUR FIST HOMMAGE,
> DE LA MAIN DEXTRE APEND A VOSTRE AUTEL
> L'HUMBLE PRESENT DE SON LIVRE IMMORTEL,
> SON COEUR DE L'AUTRE AUX PIEDS DE CESTE IMAGE.[1]

The frontispiece is that same laurelled engraving of his youth
which appeared in *Les Amours* in 1552, an amiable coquetry in
which modern literary men also largely indulge. The Sonnets to
Hélène are here for the first time collected and, barring six already
noted, complete; a sufficient indication that that damsel's fears
and wishes have no more hold on her late adorer. There are only
some thirty new pieces, which include a significant one called
La Magie, in which Ronsard, remembering his Theocritus, calls
to his page to bring him all the letters, locks of hair, gloves, pictures
and other combustible trinkets he has treasured, that he may
ritually burn them on a pyre and so rid himself by art-magic for
ever of her spell (but he does not mention her by name):

> *Sus, page, verse à mon costé*
> *Le sac que tu as apporté,*

[1] So that ages to come may remember, from time to time, that his youth paid homage
to Love, Ronsard hangs on your altar, on the right hand, the humble gift of his immortal
book; and on the other, at the foot of this image, his heart.

Ronsard

Pour me guarir de ma folie
Brule du soufre et de l'encens . . .[1]

And so, embracingly :

Adieu Amour, adieu tes flames,
Adieu ta douceur, ta rigeur,
Et bref, adieu toutes les dames
Qui m'ont jadis brulé le coeur ![2]

The inclusion in this volume of the outburst against the woodmen of Gastine has moved most of his editors to remark that Ronsard himself has been wielding the axe with far more ruthless skill and vigour than those rustic craftsmen, hewing and hacking remorselessly at some of his finest work, chopping and changing, discarding words, lines, verses, even whole poems, which have since been mournfully gathered together again and if not restored, at least attached as "alternative readings". Few major poets have the courage to slash their life's work like this; but few major poets have cared so passionately for ultimate perfection.

The winter's labour, one perceives, had been severe. Du Perron remarks on the mighty traffic of proofs between poet and printer. It left Ronsard exhausted, but, I think, triumphant. I see him, that January, huddled in his furs in a room overheated by the crackling logs in the fireplace, seated in his high-backed chair by the window watching the driving snow or the lashing rain, or the leafless trees in the garden thrashed by icy winds, utterly worn out, wincing with agony, but with a smile on his lips. *Nunc dimittis!* On the table with his medicine lie the great folio and many letters of congratulation. The tributes of Galland and other loved friends have warmed him repeatedly. But Ronsard grimaces under more savage attacks of gout, and soon has to return to bed, so ill that rumours spread round Paris that he has died, and an enterprising

[1] Quick, page ; empty at my side the bag you bear ; and to heal me of my folly, burn sulphur and incense . . .
[2] Farewell, Love, farewell, thy flames, farewell thy sweetness and thy cruelty ; in short farewell to all the ladies who have ever burned my heart.

hack rushes out the *Last Words, Death and Epitaph of Pierre de Ronsard,* which affords the suffering poet a laugh.

He recovers as the year begins to mend. On the eve of Easter, turning to his religious duties, he summons a confessor, doubtless the College chaplain, and is seen approaching the altar when the bell rings for Communion, dragging himself painfully and devoutly on his poor gouty knees. And before Easter is over impatience seizes him, and he must start back for Croixval at all costs. Perhaps wisely. That hard labour through a stormy Parisian winter has tried him violently.

He does not mention the tedious journey into Touraine. "You may imagine," says Messire du Perron in his funeral oration, " what suffering the bumping and shaking of a coach gave a man in his situation." To the discomforts of a slow, heavy, springless vehicle lumbering over roads of varying quality, mainly bad, one may add the discomforts (at all but the principal stages) of the country inns of the age; adding also to smoke, draughts, noise, smells, and indifferent food, wine, beds, and service, the sick man's fever of impatience, driving him. We do not readily realise what our ancestors endured so patiently on the road, even when in health. A full century and a quarter after this time Prince George of Denmark, travelling in Queen Anne's reign from Godalming in Surrey to Petworth in Sussex, a distance of about fifteen and a half miles, will sit for fourteen hours while his four-horsed coach, bogged axle-deep in mud, is humped along bodily by sturdy Sussex boors, the last nine miles taking six hours.

Four or five months' rest in native air and summer sunshine did so much for Ronsard that in September of this year, 1584, we find him writing gaily to Galland directing him to extract " sixty good crowns " from his bookseller-publisher, Gabriel Buon, " to buy wood to warm myself this winter with my friend Gallandus". It emerges from this letter that Ronsard has never as yet received a penny from his booksellers. We have already noted that this incredible situation was normal in the ages of patronage. However, for once Ronsard is determined to make his latest benefactor disgorge—apparently publishers were a byword for hard dealing and avarice in those far-off days—and Galland is instructed, if Buon proves intractable, to withdraw the *Œuvres* from him and find someone more reasonable. What action Galland took is not recorded; we are therefore deprived, perhaps, of a fascinating interview, full of what the popular Press calls "the Human Touch". Ronsard entrusted his books to five successive publishers in all, namely Guillaume Cavellart, at the sign of the Fat Hen opposite the Collège de Cambrai, the present site of the Collège de France; the Veuve Maurice de la Porte, Buon's predecessor at the sign of St. Claude in the Clos-Bruneau, close by; Gilles Correzet, whose shop was in the Great Hall of the Palais, a booksellers' row soon to yield in importance to the Rue St. Jacques; André Wechel, at the Flying Horse in the Rue St. Jean-de-Beauvais; and Gabriel Buon aforesaid. Ronsard's relations with them we do not know. I conjecture from his temperament that there were times when they thanked God to be rid of him, as long-suffering Mr. Millar did after receiving the final corrected proofs of Dr. Johnson's Dictionary. But they did their work well, setting the charming type of the period with never a blemish; an example of the craftsmanship of the ordinary Renaissance printer. I do not remember that any proof bearing Ronsard's corrections figured in the exhibition at the Bibliothèque Nationale in 1924. It would be deeply interesting to scan one—a mass, I imagine, of cabbalistic marginal and interlinear signs, with every semicolon and comma accounted for; a labour of love. Ronsard would take a poor view of that increasing acknowledgement in modern prefaces to "Mr. So-and-so, who kindly corrected the proofs".

It was necessary to some extent, as it turned out, for Galland to tap a publisher's lifeblood. On December 17, Ronsard writes again from Croixval announcing that as soon as gout gives him respite he will be with his Gallandus more swiftly than the swallow, and enclosing an advance receipt for the last instalment of his Court emoluments. These moneys Galland will collect in person on his behalf from the Royal Treasurer, Pierre Molé; "and if he puts you off and refuses to pay," adds Ronsard with his old gaiety, "say to him as you go out, 'Sir, beware of falling on the point of M. de Ronsard's pen! He is a satirist and your neighbour into the bargain, and he knows perfectly well all that goes on'." And Ronsard ends with a curious request. Galland is to present his humble duty to Mlle de Surgères, whose hands he kisses, and beg her to use her influence with the Treasurer. It would seem, therefore, that not only is Ronsard's salary in arrears, in accordance with Court etiquette through the ages, but he has so far recovered from his old passion that he is able to ask Hélène's assistance in a purely business matter. But has he recovered? Or is this still a hankering, an excuse to reach out and touch that cold beloved hand, however fleetingly, on any pretext? I cannot find the answer. I am not a feminine ornament of the P.E.N. Club.

A few weeks after this letter Ronsard once more begins the long journey—it took a week, perhaps, under winter conditions[1]—from St. Cosme and lodges once more at the Collège de Boncourt, that friendly hearth, whose glow warms his heart long leagues away and beckons him like a tiny ruby beacon along dreary and often dangerous roads to where Galland awaits him with open arms. Happy, cries Ronsard in that affectionate tribute to the Master of Boncourt already quoted, he who can find in the world's rough-and-tumble a perfect friend like you:

> *Heureux qui peut trouver pour passer l'avanture*
> *De ce monde, ung amy de gentille nature*
> *Comme tu es, Galland!*

One would like to see Pierre de Ronsard more clearly on these journeys, hunched drowsily in his wrappings among the cushions, a furred bonnet on his head, his feet on a charcoal *chaufferette*, his hands tucked in his sleeves, or perhaps in a muff, his eyes on the wintry plains rolling slow and endless past, his thoughts a thousand miles, and perhaps two thousand years, away. One would like to see him rouse from a doze towards dusk, as the coach swerves off the high road under an old thick stone archway, flanked by a row of plane-trees rattling in the wind, into the muddy courtyard of an inn, and get painfully out on the cobbles on the arm of his man, while a knot of ostlers and hobbledehoys stare from the stable doors, round which lean fowls are pecking. One would like to see a scolding hostess driving a frowsy chambermaid upstairs to light a fire and air the gentleman's sheets (homespun, coarse, brown,

[1] The principal stages on the highroad from Tours to Paris would be Vendôme, Châteaudun, Chartres, Rambouillet, and Versailles, with good inns at each. But the slow traveller would be frequently dependent on inns along the road, mostly indifferent and often vile.

damp, clean, smelling of marjoram, dried apples, wood-smo[ke] and mildew), and a landlord bowing the way to the wainscot[e] room reserved for the " quality ", unless M. de Ronsard is i[ll] or tired, or in a mood to sup alone upstairs ; to see the compan[y] flourishing its napkins and rising as he lowers himself into a cha[ir] with a stifled grunt and a wincing, courteous smile, and dismisse[s] his man to the kitchen. One would like to see him, a little grey faced in the candlelight, restored somewhat after a spoonful or tw[o] of soup and a sip of wine—well-watered, alas, unless he is floutin[g] doctors' orders—looking round the company and joining th[e] conversation, or still more content to listen, relishing thos[e] savoury provincialisms which enrich the mother-tongue. Th[e] company would be usually dullish, no doubt : a King's officer o[r] two going on furlough or rejoining his regiment, an ecclesiasti[c] and a lawyer or two, a starchy sprinkling of the *petite noblesse* a couple of yawning squires in muddy top-boots fresh from hunting various other travellers of no great distinction in various stages o[f] glumness or volubility, strangers to the Muses. I think it would take very little of M. de Ronsard's conversation to charm such a table into deferent silence, even if he forbore to reveal his identity, which is unlikely.

And after supper one would like to see him rise heavily on his man's arm, with a good-night salute to the company, and go limping up to his chamber, where the candles would be lit and the fire ablaze, or smoking, the sheets turned down, a hot posset or a goblet of medicine waiting on the night-table ; to see his man removing Ronsard's boots, helping him off with travelling-hose and doublet, wrapping him in his furred night-gown, bringing his slippers, drawing up a chair to the fire, trimming the candles, and getting his master a Horace or a Homer out of his baggage before retiring ; to see Ronsard at length, when the doors are banged, locked, and barred and all the house is still, and the clatter of the last departing horseman has died away down the highroad, yawn and stretch and drop his book and prepare himself wearily for bed. And next morning one would like to hear him calling for a draught of Anjou *coupé* and a toast, to see him sitting up, silent and moody after a sleepless night, to be shaved by his man, then laving his hands and face in rosewater, slowly and painfully resuming his

avelling clothes again, hobbling downstairs, paying his bill,
stributing his tips, shivering in his furs on the inn doorstep
the raw morning air, while the ostlers and hangers-on buckle
he last traces ; and then, having been helped into the coach again,
aning back in his cushions with closed eyes as the whip cracks
nd the coach jerks forward and rolls out on to the highroad
gain.

Much of the pleasure and art of Boswell's book is conveyed
n his little pictures of Johnson *en pantoufles*, in bed and at table,
changing his shirt, fondling his cat, buffeting his books, flicking
candlegrease on the carpet. Had Amadis Jamyn or Claude Binet,
who were Ronsard's secretaries and might have been either of them
his Boswell, devoted less time to verse and rhetoric respectively
and more to preserving us intimate glimpses of the master in his
carpet-slippers, they would have enjoyed a brighter fame.

Paris—so much of Paris as penetrated the claustral quiet of
Ronsard's chamber in the Collège de Boncourt—is ominous
enough this winter under its brooding or sunlit skies. At the
Louvre a penitential season has set in. White-haired Henri III
has enforced black velvet for daily wear on his entourage and is
immersed in austerities, wearing a huge rosary at his belt (like the
cynical Cecil in Mary Tudor's reign), making pilgrimages to Chartres,
praying daily in the chapel of the white-habited Hieronymite
monks of the Bois de Vincennes, to whom he has taken a fancy,
for that heir to France his impotence cannot provide. Philippe
Desportes, a titular abbé with some handsome benefices, has taken
to devotion as well. Armed guards surround the King, who fears
the Guises, and rightly. The Guises describe him contemptuously
as a monk, and the Parisian populace calls him *le roi capucin*, since
Henri nowadays has a tendency to wear the Capuchin habit with
a necklace of ivory death's heads, which goes oddly enough with
the Order of the Garter recently brought him by Elizabeth Tudor's
envoy the Earl of Warwick. Henri seems to have abandoned the
government of France entirely to the Queen-Mother, that indefatigable woman. Under and over this reformation of Court morals,
trouble is brewing ; the air is tense, the Guises are hatching some
scheme unknown. And the King has held the first session of his

new order of chivalry, the Chevaliers of the Holy Spirit. All th
news, doubtless, is imparted to Ronsard by Galland on his arriv
at Boncourt in February, 1585.

It would be underestimating the character of this poet, who
we should know fairly well by now, to believe that he has come t
Paris this time solely to enjoy Galland's company and to lister
in his intervals from pain, to the gossip of the day. Once more
soon after his arrival, the college servants carry up books an
paper, extra candles, quills, and ink to Ronsard's chamber, wher
he has had to take straight to bed again; hardly moving, say
Binet, for the next four months, *tourmenté de ses gouttes ordinaires*
His brain is big with new projects: yet another edition of hi
complete works, and, to round it off and increase his fame, ar
essay in a *genre* practically new to him, namely Christian devotiona
verse. It is time to be making his soul, time to signify to the worl
that he has turned his back on the pagan altars he has served sc
long and joyously. He has already returned to the Sacraments;
he desires now to serve God as loyally as he served Venus, Bacchus,
and Apollo.

There was little or no present rivalry in this field. Twenty-five
years earlier France had seen a new spiritual poet arise with every
promise of splendour: a young Dominican nun of Poissy, near
St. Germain-en-Laye, named Anne des Marquets. Her mystical
sonnets I have unfortunately never been able to procure, nor do
they figure in the anthologies. From the flaming eulogies of
authorities like Ronsard and Scévole de Sainte-Marthe, it is clear
that they caused what the newspapers now call a literary sensation.
A hundred times a day, Sainte-Marthe says, he reads Sœur Anne's
exquisite verses, fragrant with the love of God. She is the literary
predecessor of St. Teresa and the Mexican nun Sor Juana
Inéz de la Cruz, some of whose spiritual sonnets and *redondillas*
are in every representative Spanish anthology, with those of the
Portuguese nun Sor Violante de Ceo, her contemporary. Ronsard,
who discovered Sœur Anne's genius while attending that extraordinary assembly known as the Colloque de Poissy (1561),
Catherine de Médicis' well-meaning amateurish attempt to get
Catholic and Calvinist theologians together to establish common
ground—it naturally failed from the first—expressed his admiration

a sonnet which nestles in the massy rich-perfumed rose-garden
of his works like a half-hidden violet.

> *Quelle nouvelle fleur apparait à nos yeux ?*
> *D'où vient cette couleur si plaisante et si belle ?*
> *Et d'où vient cette odeur passant la naturelle,*
> *Qui parfume la terre et va jusques aux Cieux ?*
> *La rose, ni l'oeillet, ni le lys gracieux*
> *D'odeur ni de couleur ne sont rien auprez d'elle :*
> *Aux jardins de Poissy croist cette fleur nouvelle . . .*[1]

He ends :

> *Aussi Dieu pour miracle en ce monde l'a mise,*
> *Son printemps est le Ciel, sa racine est l'Eglise,*
> *Sa foy et oeuvres sont ses feuilles et son fruit.*[2]

Sœur Anne des Marquets apparently wrote no more ; whether
deliberately, or because she died young, I cannot say. Apart from
her sonnets there was no Christian poetry of note in France written
in Ronsard's time except the *cantiques* of Nicolas Denisot of the
Brigade, some pieces by Scévole de Sainte-Marthe, and the religious
verse of Agrippa d'Aubigné.[3] This considerable poet, warped by
bigotry and vindictiveness, is the Reform's major contribution to
French poetry ; the artistic medium in which French Calvinism
has chosen to express itself with the greatest distinction has always
been finance, and the influence in modern France of that small
but powerful body is backed by great wealth. Clément Marot
certainly translated the Latin Psalms into French before Calvin
expelled him from Geneva, and on this account is sometimes claimed
as a Calvinist poet ; but if that charming Pantagruelist and sceptic
ever gave Calvinism more than a nod in passing, it is not apparent
in his life and works.

[1] What new flower appears before our eyes ? Whence this colour, so charming and so
lovely ? And whence this supernatural fragrance which scents the earth and rises to Heaven ?
The rose, the carnation, the graceful lily are as nothing to this for scent and hue ; in the
gardens of Poissy grows this new flower . . .
[2] Thus has God placed her in this world for a portent ; her spring is Heaven, her root
the Church ; her faith and works are her leaves and fruit . . .
[3] Remy Belleau and Desportes each wrote a few devotional pieces, but they are negligible.
Du Bellay has one single powerful poem of this kind, *La Lyre Chrestienne.*

Ronsard therefore had this field practically to himself. It w.
his intention now to excel as a Christian poet, and had death no
intervened he would have carried out a whole sequence of *Hymne*
chrestiennes which he proposed to himself this spring of 158:
flooded with eager inspiration. As it is, he has left us comple-
the *Hercule Chrestien* of 1555, a translation of the Te Deum,
Hymne pour les Saints, with that quaint classic twist we have notice-
already :

> *Les Hymnes sont des Grecqs invention premiere,*
> *Callimaque beaucoup leur donna de lumiere . . .*
> *Ha! les Chrestiens devroient les Gentils imiter*
> *A couvrir de beaux lys et roses leurs testes . . .*

a hymn to SS. Gervase and Protase, patrons of his parish church
of Couture, and a hymn to St. Blaise founded on the response of
the Litany, *Te rogamus, audi nos*, to be sung in procession by the
peasants of Montrouveau, full of warm-hearted simplicity :

> *Garde nos petits vergers*
> *Et nos jardins potagers,*
> *Nos maisons et nos familles,*
> *Enfans, et femmes, et filles,*
> *Et leur donne bons espoux :*
> Je te prie, escoute nous![1]

Of the other religious works he planned at this time only
fragments remain. Among them is part of a gay hymn to Monsieur
St. Roch beginning :

> *Sus serrons-nous les mains, sus marchons en dansant . . .*

Also part of a poem on the Divine Law, dedicated to Henri of
Navarre, formerly suzerain, as Duke of Vendôme, of the Ronsard
family, with an opening summons to Moses :

---

[1] Guard our humble orchards and our vegetable gardens, our houses and families, our
children, wives and daughters ; and give them good wedlock! I pray thee hear us.

Grimpe au sommet du mont et attend que je vienne :
Fait que mon peuple en presse au pied du mont se tienne.[1]

Across the Pyrenees in this same year, 1585, the Carmelite friar
uan de la Cruz, whom St. Teresa playfully called Senequita,
" Little Seneca ", for his grave wisdom and slightness of figure,
dded his *Living Flame of Love* to that achievement in verse and
rose which makes him the greatest of the Christian mystics but
ne :

> *O llama de Amor viva,*
> *que tiernamente hieres*
> *de mi alma en el mas profundo centro ! . . .*[2]

One perceives by comparison Ronsard's limitations. Lacking
spiritual curiosity, experience, ecstasy, suffering, having nothing
mystical in his nature, he could never have ascended to the Empyrean
with Dante or plumbed the Dark Night of the Soul with St. John
of the Cross. Compared with the least aspiration of the company
of major Christian poets, from St. Hilary by way of Villon and
Crashaw, Herbert and Vaughan, Verlaine, Newman, Gerard
Manley Hopkins and Péguy down to Paul Claudel in our own day,
Ronsard's deepest devotional self-expression is gracefully superficial. He could appreciate the mystical intensity of Sœur Anne des
Marquets, but he could not echo it. His version of the Te Deum,
dedicated to the Bishop of Valence, " to be sung in his church "—
a curious direction, for the public singing of French versions of the
Psalms and other hymns of the Liturgy was, and is, the prerogative
and hallmark of Calvinism—is faithful but inadequate, like every
other attempt to translate this mighty hymn :

> *O Seigneur Dieu, nous Te louons,*
> *Et pour Seigneur nous T'avouons :*
> *Toute la terre Te venère*
> *Et Te confesse éternel Père . . .*

---

[1] Climb to the peak and wait until I come ; and let My people gather in a multitude at
the mountain's foot.
[2] O living flame of Love
That dost eternally
Pierce my soul through with such consuming heat. . . .
The *Llama de Amor Viva* is a prose meditation on this celebrated poem, which serves
as preface.

For his intention nevertheless Ronsard has doubtless received hi
reward long since.

Amid these preoccupations he found time to dictate to Claud
Binet, Amadis Jamyn's successor as private secretary, an interesting
piece, which might be described as a manifesto. Its precise
slightly peremptory prose forms the preface to a new editior
of the *Franciade*. It is an essay on the art, essence, and quiddity o
poetry which every modern poet and critic might study to
his benefit, and which, I gather, is unknown to most. Foundec
on the axiom that less and better work is the poet's goal, this
piece of sound and lucid Gallic exposition is full of aphorisms,
such as " Poetry is a naïve and natural thing ". " Every work has
its limits." " The poet is one who can make gods talk to men,
men to gods." " The poet has a maxim very necessary to his art,
namely never to follow after actuality step by step, but to choose
the likely and the possible . . . on which he builds his work, leaving
factual narration to the historian." And, more than once : " Poetry
is of God "—*les vers viennent de Dieu*. Simplicity, restraint, and
precision are the poet's cardinal requirements (Ronsard's succeeding editions, and the final one above all, show how rigorously
he had been applying these principles to his own work). As for
the verse the new modern school—e.g., Desportes and Du Bartas,
unnamed—are pouring out, these versifiers either drag themselves
along the ground, like caterpillars, or puff themselves out to burst-
ing-point, " deeming nothing excellent if it is not extravagant,
empty, and swollen, full of monstrous imaginings and prancing
locutions (*paroles piaffées*) ". Such stuff is nothing but wind.

But chiefly is this treatise interesting, I think, when Ronsard
turns to survey his beloved classics, without the study of which,
he truly says, no poet can hope to enrich his natural talent. Without
bowling over the Latin poets of the Golden Age like ninepins,
as Huysmans' Des Esseintes does in a famous diatribe, Ronsard
is bold enough, in that age of classical fetichism, to declare that
compared with the majestic Virgil, " First Captain of the Muses ",
all the other Latin poets are merely *naquets*, ball-boys at tennis.
Even his lifelong idol Horace, Ronsard admits now, is notable
only for his Odes. Lucretius, whom the pagan Renaissance adored
for his atheism, is less a poet than a philosopher, though certain of

his lines are "not only excellent but divine". (Ronsard is thinking no doubt of the *Suave mari magno* and that line about "the iron titles of the Night".) Catullus has two good pieces, *Athis* and the *Marriage of Peleus*; the rest is not worth the candle. It is to be noted that the Greek poets, whom Ronsard has loved with equal passion, are hardly mentioned in this preface. M. Champion deduces that this omission is deliberate. Greek had as yet made little progress among the mass of the educated French, whom Ronsard is chiefly addressing.

And then, following a digression on the mother-tongue, being variations on a familiar theme : " *Car c'est un crime de lèze-Majesté d'abandonner le langage de son pays, vivant et florissant, pour vouloir deterrer je ne sçay quelle cendre des anciens . . ,*"[1] Ronsard strikes his really startling note—startling, that is, to dons, pedants, and academic troglodytes of his and every other age. For Ronsard, that fine scholar, mocks at the folly of worshipping, in a modern age, the Latin of Cicero. The real Latin (he says) is that which has survived in the traditional hymns of the Catholic Liturgy and the psalms chanted daily and nightly at the lectern, and without this Latin the Roman tongue would have disappeared long ago. A facer for the dons, in truth! It may be that Huysmans and Remy de Gourmont alike derived their iconoclast inspiration from this. The *bon gros latin* of the Church, Ronsard proceeds, is the means by which we make ourselves understood by Germans, Poles and Englishmen (whose native jargon, we must recollect, was regarded by the French, then as now, as barbarous). The one Latin, Ronsard adds, is dead ; the other lives, as it pleases Destiny and God Who orders all things.

When one of the most erudite men the Renaissance produced turns on the Renaissance thus, stabbing it genially in its tenderest part, it is not for such as I to embroider the theme.

In the intervals of enduring his gout, dictating his manifesto, meditating and discussing his new poetic projects, and receiving those visitors whom even the watchdog Galland could not keep away from his bedside—at this time, says Du Perron, Ronsard

[1] For it is a crime of high treason to forsake the language of one's country, living and flowering, for the sake of digging up some ashes or other of the Ancients . . .

was afflicted somewhat by this penalty of fame—he has been steadily dictating more verses to Binet to while away the time: chiefly, apart from those already noted, a Hymn to Mercury. In this invocation (it could have more fitly been addressed, one would think, to his priory's patron, the physician-martyr St. Cosmas) we see Ronsard mirrored in his verse for the first time as a very sick and ageing man :

> *Encore il me restoit entre tant de malheurs*
> *Que la vieillesse apporte, entre tant de douleurs*
> *Dont la goutte m'assault pieds, jambes, at joinctures,*
> *De chanter, jà vieillard, les mestiers de Mercure . . .*[1]

In the violence of his pain—the intensity of which, but for those intervals of relief in which the patient lapses into lassitude and extreme weakness, would wear out human patience, as the eminent Sydenham remarks in his observations on the gout— Ronsard has only one favour to beg of Mercury, the blessed gift of sleep. The winter nights which seemed long enough to the lover of Hélène are now a dragging horror.

> *Donne-moy que je puisse à mon aise dormir*
> *Les longues nuicts d'hyver, et pouvoir affermir*
> *Mes jambes et mes bras debiles par la goutte . . .*[2]

On his night-table, by the candlestick, one may guess, stands a goblet of some soporific. Years before this he had begged Amadis Jamyn in a fine poetic frenzy to crown him with poppies and drop their juice into his wine, that he might sleep and forget the smarts of love. Now he needs opiates in earnest. No doubt Galland is reasonable but firm.

§6

It was close on summer in this year, 1585, before Pierre de Ronsard had sufficiently recovered to think of taking the road to Touraine again, and his decision, announced despite the remon-

---

[1] Still there remained to me, among the so many ills which age brings, so many pains with which the gout assails me, feet, legs, and joints, to sing in my decline the crafts of Mercury. . . .

[2] Grant me that I may sleep at my ease through the long winter nights, and that I may regain the use of arms and legs crippled by the gout. . . .

strances of Galland and other intimates, was not to be gainsaid. He was feverishly convinced now that the air of Paris was not good for him, and his friends had to give way. His bedridden stay at Boncourt this time had been alleviated, apart from Galland's company, by the flattering attentions of a new young poet of promise, subsequently unfulfilled, named Flaminio de Birague, who published early in this year a little volume in which compliments were paid " the divine Ronsard " in imitations of his own style, than which few things could gratify an elderly poet more. Young de Birague subtly heightened the perfume of his bouquet, indeed, by choosing a lady named Marie for the subject of his *Amours*. Moreover, he expressed himself in a manner with which the master could hardly help agreeing :

> *Tu vivras, mon Ronsard, par ce grand univers,*
> *Et ta douce moitié, fameuse par tes vers,*
> *Vivra malgré l'effort des Parques filandières . . .*[1]

It would be preposterous to think of Pierre de Ronsard as purring, but the old lion certainly appreciated these handsome tributes from the new school, even mixed as they were with one or two tributes to Philippe Desportes, who had a following among *les jeunes*. Ronsard's content was undoubtedly disturbed a little by the Du Bartas affair, as we have observed. The old lion growled and struck out blindly. Yet to find such a brilliant disciple as Flaminio de Birague among the young poets was probably balm enough.

So, on June 13, Ronsard orders his coach once more and starts for home, accompanied this time by Galland, " without whom ", says Binet, " he could not live ". One may well imagine that this was Galland's determination as well, arrived at after a myriad vain expostulations, shrugs, and waving of despairing hands. And this time there drew up at the gates of Boncourt a new coach, ordered and paid for by the poet, no doubt with certain recommendations to the maker as to interior padding. And once again one would wish to be transported, like those two sedate English ladies who had

---

[1] You will live, my Ronsard, universal, and your sweet other-half, made famous by your verse, will live, despite the efforts of the spinning Fates . . .

that eerie fascinating adventure at Versailles in the 1900's, into a past age and to accompany the two friends as they cover the slow leagues into Touraine, conversing, dozing, reading, capping classic quotations, meditating, perhaps affectionately quarrelling over the poet's refusal, or inability, to lay down his pen and rest; for during all these last three or four years of sickness Ronsard has been adding indefatigably between pangs to the already monumental mass of his work. It is not his greatest verse (though one piece is fairly near it), but it is, as ever, the verse of a poet of the first rank who can write nothing slovenly, flatulent, or bad. One of the new odes is addressed to Philippe Desportes, who at forty has just published his *Dernières Amours*; for fops grow elderly and less vivacious, their perfumed curls grow thin, like their blood, and their complexions line and wrinkle. To Desportes Ronsard somewhat grimly points out the folly of wasting brain, nerve, and sinew in the pursuit of a fame which can only be apportioned by Posterity, (though God knows Ronsard himself had been deluged with it since his youth!) and the vanity of all things, but especially of a pining for literary immortality.

> *Mais happe le present d'un cœur plein d'allegresse . . .*
> *Le futur est douteux, le present est certain.*[1]

From which variation on his old *carpe diem* love-theme it may be perceived that the pagan leaven remained in Ronsard yet to some extent, and that one cannot at once throw off the habit of thought of a lifetime. On the other hand it may be irony, which the French never expand or explain. I cannot discover whether Desportes, who sedulously ignored his greater rival in verse during his lifetime (though he honoured Ronsard in death), had the grace to reply. He had recently been appointed an honorary Canon of the Sainte-Chapelle, and may have turned, like Ronsard, a new leaf, as a fop may; or even half a leaf. "Because I break one law," said Louis XIV's mistress, Mme de Montespan, when someone at Court expressed malicious surprise at her fasting in Lent, "must I break them all?"

---

[1] But seize the Present with a heart filled with joy; the Future is doubtful, the Present certain . . .

" *Nuper Idoneus . . .* "

A trivial fellow, Desportes; yet among the *mignardises* of his
sonnets, which began to make a name for him among the Court
set, the precious and the dainty, about 1573, there crops up one of
obvious merit, imitated from Sannazaro:

> *Icare est cheut icy, le jeune audacieux,*
> *Qui pour voler au ciel eut assez de courage :*
> *Icy tomba son corps degarny de plumage*
> *Laissant tous braves cœurs de sa cheute envieux.*
>
> *O bien-heureux travail d'un esprit glorieux,*
> *Qui tire un si grand gain d'un si petit dommage !*
> *O bien-heureux malheur, plein de tant d'avantage,*
> *Qu'il rende le vaincu des ans victorieux !*
>
> *Un chemin si nouveau n'estonna sa jeunesse,*
> *Le pouvoir luy faillit, mais non la hardiesse :*
> *Il eut pour le brûler des astres le plus beau ;*
>
> *Il mourut poursuivant une haute aventure ;*
> *Le ciel fust son desir, la mer sa sepulture ;*
> *Est-il plus beau dessein ou plus riche tombeau ?*

Which Maurice Baring finely renders:

> Here fell the daring Icarus in his prime,
> He who was brave enough to scale the skies;
> And here bereft of plume his body lies,
> Leaving the valiant envious of that climb.
>
> O rare performance of a soul sublime,
> That with small loss such great advantage buys!
> Happy mishap! fraught with so rich a prize
> That bids the vanquished triumph over Time.
>
> So new a path his youth did not dismay,
> His wings but not his noble heart said nay;
> He had the glorious sun for funeral fire;

He died upon a high adventure bent;
The sea his grave, his goal the firmament;
Great is the tomb, but greater the desire.

It might serve as epitaph for all that gallant youth which rides the skies to-day and falls in combat.

I have mentioned what I take to be a notable piece among these poems of Ronsard's last phase. It is the sombre ode addressed to his friend Nicolas de Neuville, Seigneur de Villeroy; its note is one of satiety, completion, resignation, and farewell.

Jà du prochain hiver je prevois la tempeste,
Jà cinquante et six ans ont neigé sur ma teste :
Il est temps de laisser les vers et les amours
Et de prendre congé du plus beau de mes jours.
J'ay vecu, Villeroy, si bien que nulle envie
En partant je ne porte aux plaisirs de la vie :
Je les ay tous goutés et me les suis permis
Autant que la raison me les rendoit amis.
Sur l'echafaut mondain jouant mon personnage
D'un habit convenable au temps et à mon age,
J'ay vu lever le jour, j'ay vu coucher le soir,
J'ay vu gresler, tonner, eclairer, et pleuvoir,
J'ay vu peuples et Roys, et depuis vingt années
J'ay vu presque la France au bout de ses journées,
J'ay vu guerres, debats, tantost tresves et paix,
Tantost accords promis, redéfaits et refaits,
Puis défaits et refaits. J'ay vu que sous la Lune
Tout n'estoit que hasard et pendoit de Fortune . . .

Je m'en vais saoul du monde, ainsi qu'un convié
S'en va saoul du banquet de quelque marié,
Ou du festin d'un Roy, sans refrogner sa face
Si un autre apres luy se met dedans sa place.
J'ay couru mon flambeau sans me donner emoy,
Le baillant à quelqu'un s'il recourt après moy ;
Il ne faut s'en fascher : c'est la loi de Nature,
Où s'engage en naissant chacune creature.[1]

[1] Already I foresee the tempests of the coming winter ; already fifty-six years have snowed upon my head ; it is time to forsake verse and loves, to take leave of my happiest days,

" *Nuper Idoneus . . .* "

The substance of this, flushed with a nobler Christian remorse, penitence, faith, and hope, he will repeat to the monks of St. Cosme shortly on his dying bed.

Among the matters Ronsard and Galland discussed as their coach rumbled south were, undoubtedly, Ronsard's future literary projects, his new collected edition, the new series of devotional poems; for Galland was to be his executor. On reaching Croixval, towards the end of June, Ronsard's normal procedure would have been to start work at once; but this time his malady had gained on him so considerably and his pain made him so sleepless and worn that in July we find him moving to St. Cosme, to stay there just over a week, vainly seeking relief, and return then to Croixval, restless, miserable, and alone; for Galland had had to return to Paris and his academic duties. In September Ronsard signs a deed making over to this last and dearest of friends his priory of Croixval and his benefices of Montoire and St. Guingalois. On October 22, he writes to Galland that he has become very thin and weak, *iners terræ pondus*, and is unable to stand upright. It may be that he will fall with the autumn leaves, but God's will be done; and he prays Galland to hasten back.

Once more there is trouble and anxiety to torment Ronsard. Calvinist troops are again on the rampage in Anjou and the Vendômois, and have taken the chateau of Angers. The sick man, longing for rest and surcease, already menaced by *la religion* more than once, moves from Croixval to Montoire, a fortified place, to escape them. Du Perron says Ronsard actually took the road to Paris again; Binet, however, is clear that he travelled no further than Montoire, arriving there on October 28, three days after the

---

I have lived, Villeroy, so fully that as I go I feel no regret for life's pleasures; I have tasted them all, I have indulged them as much as reason allowed. Playing my part on the worldly stage, in a costume suitable to my time and age, I have seen sunrise and sunset, hail, thunder, lightning, and rain; I have seen nations and Kings, and for twenty years I have seen France almost at the end of her days. I have seen wars and debates, truces and peace-treaties, agreements made and broken and made again, and again broken and remade. I have perceived that under the moon there was nothing but chance, and that everything hung on fortune . . .

I go out from the world satiated, as a guest goes satiated from some wedding-feast or from a Royal banquet, not wincing if some other has taken his place after him; I have carried my torch in the race without perturbation, handing it to anyone who runs behind me; for there is nothing to perturb oneself about. It is Nature's law, to which every creature must submit from birth.

Duc de Joyeuse had routed the Calvinists. Meanwhile on the 26th, in great pain with stomach-trouble and increasing weakness, Ronsard had summoned the parish priest of Ternay to Croixval, with a notary, and, having risen and dressed with difficulty, had made his confession, heard Mass, and received the Blessed Sacrament with devotion, retiring to bed afterwards and saying that he was prepared for death whenever it pleased God to send it. The notary he dismissed, saying he felt better and there was no need for haste.

On October 30, Galland, posting to his friend's relief, arrives at Montoire, finding Ronsard so wasted and weak that as he enters the bedchamber the good Galland is overcome and cannot speak, and they both weep. But the mere sight of him does Ronsard good, and he is soon able to resume composition, dictating a piece, among others, which describes his present state:

> *Je n'ay plus que les os, un squelette je semble,*
> *Descharné, denervé, demusclé, depoulpé,*
> *Que le trait de la Mort sans pardon a frappé :*
> *Je n'ose voir mes bras que de peur je ne tremble . . .*[1]

He ends the sonnet (always the sonnet!) :

> *Adieu, chers compaignons, adieu mes chers amis,*
> *Je m'en vay le premier vous preparer la place.*[2]

It smells already of the tomb, one of the elaborate marble tea-caddy tombs of the period, rich in the emblems of mortality. And as the long winter nights waste away in misery he cries to them feebly to drive along more quickly.

> *Meschantes nuicts d'hyver, nuicts filles de Cocyte,*
> *Que la Terre engendra, d'Encelade les sœurs,*

[1] I have nothing left but bones, I seem a skeleton, without flesh, nerves, muscles, and marrow, which Death's dart has ruthlessly smitten ; I dare not look at my arms for fear of trembling in terror . . .
[2] Farewell, dear companions, farewell, dear friends ; I go before you to prepare the place . . .

Serpentes d'Alecton et fureur des Fureurs,
N'approchez de mon lit, ou bien tournez plus vite ![1]

'or the mercy of sleep is denied him, and the peace of Death.

Seize heures pour le moins je meurs, les yeux ouverts,
Me tournant, me virant de droit et de travers,
Sur l'un, sur l'autre flanc je tempeste, je crie,
Inquiet je ne puis en un lieu me tenir,
J'appelle en vain le jour, et la Mort je supplie :
Mais elle faict la sourde, et ne veut pas venir.[2]

The candle flickers on, the weary eyes see the same shadow-pattern on the ceiling, the dawn is at the far-off end of the endless tunnel. During one such night a flash of his old dancing rhythms and love-inspired diminutives returns to Ronsard, and he composes an *odelette* inspired by the Emperor Hadrian's famous dying address to his soul:

Anima vagula blandula,
Hospes comesque corporis,
Quae nunc abibis in loca
Pallidula rigida nudula,
Nec ut soles dabis iocos !

Ronsard murmurs his version next morning for Galland or Binet to write down:

Amelette Ronsardelette,
Mignonnelette, doucelette,
Tres chere hostesse de mon corps,
Tu descens là-bas foiblelette,
Pasle, maigrelette, seulette,
Dans le froid Royaume des morts :

---

[1] Cruel winter nights, daughters of Cocytus, engendered by Earth and sisters of Enceladus, serpents of Alecto and scourges of the Furies, do not approach my bed—or, better, pass more swiftly!
[2] For sixteen hours at least I die, my eyes open, turning, tossing from right to left on one side or the other, raging and crying ; I cannot stay quiet in one place, in vain I call for daylight, in vain I call on Death. She affects to be deaf and will not come . . .

Ronsard

Toutefois simple, sans remors
De meutre, poison, ou rancune,
Meprisant faveurs et tresors
Tant enviez par la commune.

Passant, j'ay dit ; suy ta fortune,
Ne trouble mon repos, je dors.[1]

He desired, he said, to make Hadrian's little poem "more Christian". There is certainly charm, pathos, and resignation in his version if nothing else. Is it as relatively Christian as the version made by his fellow-Catholic Pope, after wandering himself so long among the philosophers :

Vital spark of heavenly flame,
Quit, oh quit this mortal frame . . .?

Perhaps Ronsard felt in the long night-watches that he might have made it a more definite act of faith, for among the very last verses he was able to breathe out while life lasted, is a piece purely and unmistakably Christian :

Quoy! mon ame, dors-tu engourdie en ta masse?
La trompette a sonné, serre bagage, et va
Le chemin deserté que Jésus-Christ trouva,
Quand tout mouillé de sang racheta nostre race . . .[2]

But the end is not yet.

---

[1] Little tiny Ronsardian soul, little sweet one, little soft one, dearest guest of my body, you go weakly down to the depths, pale, meagre, lonely, so small, down to the cold realms of the Dead ; always simple, free from regret for any deed of murder, poison, or hate, despising the favours and riches so longed for by the commonalty.

Passer-by, I have done ; follow your fortune. Do not trouble my rest ; I sleep.

[2] What, my soul! do you sleep there, clogged in heaviness? The trumpet has sounded ; pack up your baggage, take the lonely road Jesus Christ took, when bathed in blood He redeemed our race . . .

§7

As this wreck of a fine athlete lies waiting for death one would like to know what treatment is prescribed for his relief. Did an electuary of Venice Treacle stand in a dish on his night-table? This long-established specific, based on opium and spices, seemed to the celebrated English physician Sydenham in the following century, though he admitted its virtues, susceptible of palliation. Sydenham's prescriptions in cases of gout break down the narcotic force of Venice Treacle with candied angelica, syrup of oranges, Roman wormwood, and other sweet and bitter ingredients. The doctors may have prescribed something of the sort for Ronsard. Quinine, lately introduced into Europe from Peru by the Jesuits, and strict dieting—for example, on milk—would reduce the fevers, syrup of poppies would relieve pain and insomnia; though it did little for Ronsard, in the final phase, as we perceive.

Not always were these lenitives at hand. If, fainting with agony on arriving at a village inn during one of those journeys to and from Paris, he sent for the local Purgon, the best Ronsard could expect was a dose of home-brewed laudanum, a blood-letting, or something yet more homely. His fellow-sufferer the Emperor Charles V, lately dead, had been stubbornly addicted to wearing thick cotton stockings drenched in vinegar and rosewater and bathing his legs in the same tincture: a Flemish old-wives' specific which Dr. Mathys viewed with shrugs, the more despairing because the Emperor refused to give up the spiced and salted Flemish dishes he had been accustomed to all his life. Failing all else Ronsard may well have tried this rustic remedy, though when he reached Paris a man of his international fame and Court standing can surely have not lacked the best medical attention the specialists could provide. I think it not impossible that the great Ambroise Paré, surgeon to the King, then engaged in dulcifying the ferocities of Renaissance surgery, may—though gout was not his province—have lent his revolutionary weight to a consultation. It is pure conjecture. There was no eager Press, eminent doctors could not advertise, and no Boswell, alas, was at hand to note down such trifling particulars for our enlightenment and to show us Ronsard's doctors shaking their great disapproving heads. For Ronsard, we

remember, was of an imperious disposition, and perhaps wave
away more than one well-pondered, elaborate nostrum with
gesture no less fretful and final than Charles V's. We do not know
what dignified sable figures hovered over his bed, pawing their
beards and murmuring smoothly of fluxes and calentures, purgatives
febrifuges, and sudorifics, of the Four Complexions (which are
Sanguine, Phlegmatic, Choleric, and Melancholic, and have each
its corresponding " quality " and " humour ") and of the pure
doctrine of Galen and Hippocrates on these matters, with footnotes and allusions to the School of Salerno ; a discourse diversified,
no doubt, with discreet allusions to the erroneous practice of certain
fashionable sciolists and empirics, and thickly padded with the
customary cabbalistic mumbo-jumbo, *pompeux galimatias et spécieux
babil*, inspiring respect and terror, as to-day. It was a hundred years
before Molière's gibes at the universal panacea—

> *Clysterium donare*
> *Postea seignare,*
> *Ensuitta purgare,*
> *Reseignare, repurgare, et reclysterisare !*

—were to offend the Faculty. Medicine in Ronsard's time, I gather,
based itself equally firmly on the lancet, the clyster, the purge, and
those forgotten sovran herbs—elecampane, calamint, germander,
St. John's wort, and a score more—which were to be gathered
at a favourable time, with or without careful regard to Jupiter, Mars,
Mercury, Saturn, and Venus, their Houses, trines, conjunctions,
sympathies, and antipathies, according to the school of thought.
Harley Street to-day is scornful of such remedies, apart from the
astrology. Only in the cramped and dusty windows of herbalists
up shabby suburban side-streets does the torch of antique Medicine
flicker on, wanly but indomitably. The aroma of these little humble
shops is an authentic waft of the Renaissance, and some disciple
of Des Esseintes with the same sensitive nostrils and imagination
could step back into that age quite comfortably by inhaling this
smell with others of the period, equally obtainable to-day, and
making a bouquet of the odours of incense, rose-water, stables,
old tapestry, pomanders, tarry ropes, beeswax, roast venison,

ndle-smoke, parchments, calfskin folios, and others less pleasing.
ut the doubt persists, as one considers the case of Ronsard, as
o the period of efficacy of those herbs and simples, which seem to
lay eye all too mild to grapple with the malignancy of gout,
owever carefully selected, dried, powdered, combined,
alled into electuaries of nutmeg-size, *secundum artem*, with
larified honey and Canary wine, and swallowed with a herbal
draught.

Musing on what Ronsard must have suffered, I commend
Sydenham's treatise to any who, unfamiliar with the quiddity of
this scourge, connect it vaguely with Hogarthian caricature,
Victorian stage-farce, and old bound volumes of comic intent.
In Sydenham's pages are soberly set down the torpors, chills, sweats,
shivers, and boding heaviness of mind and body which precede
zero hour, before pain leaps suddenly at nightfall on its victim like
a starving wolf, stretching and tearing the ligaments, gnawing and
rending. "The night is passed in torture, sleeplessness, and perpetual change of posture; the tossing about of the body being as
incessant as the pain of the tortured joint, and being worse as the
fit comes on." Note also the cunning with which, in the early
stages, the wild beast withdraws, leaving its victim a brief time for
repose and recovery, to breathe freely and hobble on crippled feet;
and then, spying from afar, springs again and rolls him over with
renewed ferocity. It is plain that the mind of Ronsard was more
than commonly strong and his vitality high. One of the chief
accompanying disasters of gout, says Sydenham, is loss of mental
energy, with vacillation, anxiety, fretfulness, depression, and fear,
the mind suffering with the body. And the great Carolean
physician reflects, in his elegant Latin: "For humble individuals
like myself there is one poor comfort, which is this, that gout,
unlike any other disease, kills more rich men than poor, more
wise men than simple. Great kings, emperors, generals, admirals,
and philosophers have all died of gout. Hereby Nature shows
her impartiality."

§8

Et à l'heure de ma mort soyez le réfuge de mon âme étonnée, et recevez-<i>dans le sein de Votre miséricorde.

(St. Margaret Mary.)

All this Ronsard endured with manly fortitude, sleepless, sipping poppy-juice and chewing the leaves with no avail, meditating dictating, conversing with *belles et graves considerations*, "having his memory and vivacity of spirit," says Binet, "so complete that they seemed unaware of the weakness of his body". He remained at Montoire for the Feast of All Saints, and next day, with Galland, returned to Croixval; and having lain there in misery a fortnight, restlessness drove him again to St. Cosme. Du Perron describes this, the last journey of Ronsard's life, with some eloquence. We see the bent and crippled wreck carried downstairs into his coach, "like a log". The weather is so bad that he has to be carried indoors again, and there he frets three days, refusing to be undressed, more dead than alive. On the third night, unable to endure longer, he orders the coach before daybreak, and insists on setting out. It is a day of furious wind and rain, the roads are thick in mud, the soaked and dreary stubblefields of Touraine stretch away on every side to meet a low leaden sky; and at the end of the first league Galland, or Ronsard himself, stops the coach, for he is fainting and can bear no more. There are six such halts in the twelve or fourteen miles between Croixval and St. Cosme before Ronsard arrives at his house, towards five o'clock on the afternoon of a late November Sunday, as the friars are singing Vespers, and is carried prostrate up to bed.

After three weeks or more of continuous suffering he knows that death is at last on the threshold, and he prepares to receive *la profitable Mort* in a way so admirable, as fitting as an end to a life so full of glory, that I will set his last words and acts down in order.

On Sunday, December 22, Ronsard makes his will, remembering his friends, his servants, and the poor. More than once on this day he asks Jacques Desguez, the chaplain, how much longer, in his opinion, he has to live. His courage is firm and his mind sane

ıd clear, and he has no perturbation, except (says Binet) his
ɔnstant urge to compose more verse.

On Wednesday, Feast of the Incarnation, Ronsard asks the
ub-Prior to confess him and to say the Mass of Christmas in his
edchamber, where he receives Holy Communion with fervent
ɪevotion—" more great ", muses the lawyer Binet, " than one
vould expect from a person nourished on the irreligious debauch-
ries of a Court". Frequently on this happy day Ronsard speaks
ɔf his trust in the infinite mercy of God and the sweetness of the
Divine Love which is helping him to bear his pain, which he so
well merits, and worse. And when, some time later, a friar asks if
he will take some food, he replies, almost gaily :

> *Toute la viande qui entre*
> *Dans le goufre ingrat de ce ventre*
> *Incontinent sans fruict resort :*
> *Mais la belle Science exquise*
> *Que par l'oüye j'ay apprise,*
> *M'accompagne jusqu'à la mort.*[1]

On the day following Ronsard sends for the chaplain and
announces that the end is now close upon him ; whereupon Desguez
asks a necessary question :

" Sir, in what resolution do you die? "

The old fire must flash a moment in those sunken eyes as
Ronsard answers, with a touch of anger :

" In what do you think ? In the religion which was my father's,
and his father's, and his father's fathers' before him! Have I not
sufficiently made known how I wish to die ? "

Gently the aged priest, his friend, replies that he wishes merely
to know Ronsard's last desires and to hear him make of his own
will an affirmation of a Christian end. To which Ronsard answers :

" I desire you and all the brethren to be witnesses of my last
words."

On this Desguez summons the community, and they file in,
headed by their Sub-Prior, and stand round. Whereupon, raising

---

[1] All food which enters the ungrateful maw of this stomach leaves it instantly, without
benefit ; but Learning, exquisite and lovely, which I have absorbed by the ear, accompanies
me till death.

himself on the pillow, Ronsard begins to address them, the wea
voice gaining in strength as he proceeds.

" I have sinned," he begins, " like other men, and perhaps mor
than most. My senses have charmed and led me astray, and I hav
not repressed or restrained them as I should. But none the less
have always held to that Faith which the men of my line have lef
me ; I have always embraced the Creed and the unity of the Catholi
Church. In a word, I laid a sure foundation, though I have buil
on it with wood, and hay, and straw. That foundation, I am
certain, will stand ; as for the light and worthless things I have
built upon it, I trust in the mercy of my Redeemer that they will
all be burned away in the fire of His love."

He pauses, and continues :

" I beg you all now firmly to believe as I have believed, but not
to live as I have lived. You must understand that I have never
plotted against or attempted the life or goods of another, nor against
any man's honour—but after all there is nothing much in this wherewith to glorify oneself before Almighty God."

Here the effort of speech and his strong emotion overcome
Ronsard, and he weeps, and there are few of those present who are
not in tears as well. But after a little while he regains self-command
and proceeds.

" This world is ceaseless turmoil and torment, shipwreck following shipwreck perpetually, a whirlpool of sins, and tears, and pain ;
and to all these misfortunes there is but one port, and that port is
Death. But as for me, I carry with me into this port no desires
and no regrets for life. For I have essayed every one of its pretended
joys, I have left nothing undone which could give me the least
shadow of pleasure and content ; and at the end I have found
everywhere the Oracle of Wisdom, *vanitas vanitatum*."

And so to that great ending[1]:

" Of all these vanities, the loveliest and most praiseworthy is
fame. No one of my time has been so filled with it as I ; I have
lived in it and loved and triumphed in it through my time past,
and now I leave it to my country to garner and possess after I shall
be dead. So do I go away from my own place, as satiated with the
glory of this world as I am hungry and longing for that of God."

[1] Mr. Belloc's translation, from *Avril*.

Having said this he paused again, then humbly offered his sufferings to God and begged forgiveness of any that he had offended, declaring himself free of hatred for any mortal man. And then, having prayed a time in silence, he devoutly received the Last Sacrament. As so often happens, the Viaticum refreshed his spirits and restored his strength somewhat, and he was able soon to beckon an amanuensis to take down his two last sonnets on paper, the one beginning :

Quoy! mon ame, dors tu engourdie en ta masse?

and the last one of all, which begins :

Il faut laisser maisons et vergers et jardins,
Vaisselles et vaisseaux que l'artisan burine,
Et chanter son obseque en la façon du Cygne,
Qui chante son trepas sur les bords Méandrins . . . [1]

Continuing with that last salute to the fame with which God, to whom he was about to render up his account, had glorified him :

C'est fait, j'ay devidé le cours de mes destins,
J'ay vescu, j'ay rendu mon nom asseʒ insigne . . . [2]

and ending with Christian devotion :

Heureux qui ne fut onc, plus heureux qui retourne
En rien comme il estoit, plus heureux qui sejourne
D'homme fait nouvel ange aupreʒ de Jesus-Christ,
Laissant pourrir çà-bas sa despouille de boüe
Dont le sort, la fortune, et le destin se joüe,
Franc des liens du corps pour n'estre qu'un esprit. [3]

---

[1] Now must one forsake houses and orchards and gardens, and all dainty ware carved by the artist's tools, and sing one's obsequies like the dying swan, who sings her death on the shores of Mæander . . .

[2] It is finished ; I have wound the skein of my destiny, I have lived, I have made my name famous enough . . .

[3] Happy who was never thus, most happy who returns to nothing as he began, most happy who, newly changed from man to spirit, abides near Jesus Christ, leaving his remains of clay to rot below—those remains which were the plaything of fate and fortune and destiny—and free from the bonds of flesh, to be no more but spirit.

His feet and legs are already cold by the time he has finishe dictating. He asks, before continuing, to have these verses rea over to him, and finds them faulty, and will dictate no more, bu lies back with closed eyes as the sweats of death come upon hin strongly. Among those around him, kneeling now in tears anc joining in the Prayers for the Dying, are some of the notables of Tours, for news of the great Ronsard's passing has quickly spread. When these prayers are done the dying man says he wishes to be alone. His voice, though weak, is still clear, and none of his faculties has lapsed. The company leaves him; and it is here, I think, that must be placed the brief farewell with Galland. Neither Binet nor Du Perron makes it clear whether Galland had stayed at St. Cosme all this time, or had left for Paris and returned. But he was certainly at Ronsard's bedside in time to embrace and cherish him for the last time, brokenly and with tears, and to commend his friend to God.

And now Ronsard, exhausted, closes his eyes again and lies still. Some time later the Sub-Prior brings him some relics to kiss, and proceeds then with Jacques Desguez to give him Extreme Unction, anointing his principal members in turn with the Holy Oil and begging God's mercy, according to that august last rite of the Church, for sins committed by those eyes which have delighted so long in the beauty of women and the pride of life, those ears which have listened to so much learning, folly, and flattery, those nostrils which have so long and keenly inhaled the most intoxicating perfumes of the world's rose-garden, those lips which have uttered so much passionate love-talk, those fine wasted hands which have wrought so nobly and so lasciviously, those feet which have carried the dying man so often and so eagerly to the banquet of the senses. Drenched in the death-sweat, conscious and calm, Ronsard repeats the last responses and turns his face to the wall.

For an hour or more he dozes, amid the murmur of the Prayers at the Expiry; then rouses, tries to speak, perceives that his speech is failing, beckons to the watcher by his bed—undoubtedly Galland —and speaks his last words on earth. If he begins to ramble (*resver*), he says, faintly, he must be given a push. This last pre-occupation of an artist who can bear nothing slovenly relieved, Ronsard sinks back on his pillow, eyes closed, hands joined with fingers upright, in the hieratic attitude of prayer. Only the quiet fall of his hands on the coverlet some time later announces to those present that the end has come. It is early in the morning of Friday, December 27, 1585, the feast of St. John the Evangelist. Pierre de Ronsard is dead, in his sixty-second year.

§9

If France paid her dead Orpheus elaborate honours, the Austin friars of St. Cosme-lez-Tours buried their honorary Prior as one of themselves.

The tomb dug in the floor of the priory church, on the Gospel side near the high altar, remained covered with austere square brick until, fifteen years later, the then Prior erected a marble monument crowned by that bust of Ronsard preserved to-day at Blois, and illustrated elsewhere in these pages. Attending Vespers at St. Cosme one afternoon in 1589 and contemplating the poet's bare tomb, the historian Etienne Pasquier was moved to a subacid Latin epigram punning on *Cosme* and *cosmos*. Pasquier overlooked the notable ceremonies at the Collège de Boncourt two months after Ronsard's death, organised by *l'ami Galland* and worthy of his friend. The delay is easily explicable. As Ronsard's executor Galland had immediate business in Touraine and Paris alike, apart from legal matters involved in his succession to the three benefices Ronsard had bequeathed him.[1] To allow any other person to arrange the Paris ceremonies would be unthinkable, and the delay need not burden Galland's conscience in any way. We may reasonably assume that Ronsard had not lacked Masses since his death, apart from those offered by his community.

On Monday morning, February 24, 1586, at Galland's invitation, a brilliant throng of intellectuals and noblemen assembled in the College chapel to assist at a *Missa cantata* for the repose of the soul of Messire Pierre de Ronsard, succeeded by as choice a feast of panegyric oratory as any poet has ever inspired. The music of the Mass, polyphonic in five parts, composed expressly for this occasion

---

[1] To hold these Galland, by order of Sixtus V, had to become a priest within twelve months, having been previously a clerk in Minor Orders, like Ronsard. The Council of Trent's reforms in this direction were now operative.

and sung by the *Musique du Roy* from the Chapel Royal, at Henri III's order, was the first important work of Ronsard's rising young friend Jacques Mauduit, a protégé of the Académie du Palais. Those learned in Renaissance music speak highly of Mauduit. His Mass, which has been republished in recent years, was a fitting office for one whose poetry inspired so many musicians all over Europe, and who himself loved music so passionately. As for the ceremony, it is possible, with the aid of a brief letter from the poet Nicolas Rapin, one of the four authors of the *Satyre Ménippée*, to Scévole de Sainte-Marthe, and from Binet's scanty reference, to reconstruct it fairly clearly in the mind.

We see, then, the interior of a tallish Gothic chapel, with Renaissance additions and ornaments; the walls hung in black, with hatchments bearing the Ronsard family arms—azure, three *rosses* (or *rossarts*) argent in fasces.[1] The high Gothic windows are of mixed painted and clear glass. Two wax candles on the altar burn pink and starry in the raw February morning; as the Mass proceeds the chapel will fill with light as tapers are distributed to the assembly and the customary wax torches lighted at the Consecration. A compact blaze comes already from the tall mourning candles round the catafalque at the foot of the choir. Binet's remark that Galland *fit dresser un magnifique appareil en la chapelle* suggests that the catafalque, symbolising the bier of the deceased, was of that lofty elaborate Italian kind the Renaissance favoured, prodigal of sweeping black velvet draperies fringed with silver bullion and spangled with silver tears, hung with the armorial bearings of the dead, covered with the richly-emblazoned College pall. Binet's phrase implies equally, I think, that Galland had ransacked the College sacristy for its most comely Mass-vestments in black damask or velvet, its most ornate altar-vessels, candlesticks, and alms-dishes, its finest altar-linen, the most presentable carpets, tapestries, and other accessories, gifts of past benefactors—Boncourt was not a wealthy college—it might possess. I can even see Galland, horn

---

[1] The *rosse*, a kind of roach, abounds in the Loir. The family name had been sometimes spelled "Rossard". These arms may be seen carved in the Ronsard chapel in the church of Couture-sur-Loir, where Loys de Ronsard and his wife are buried. Another device inspired by the same punning heraldry, *heraldia cantans*, of the Middle Ages may be seen sculptured on the great chimneypiece at La Possonnière, namely an arrangement of briar-roses in flames: *ronce-ard*.

spectacles on nose, examining the incense to be used at the Absolutions and rejecting all but the most translucent male Arabian gums. Nothing could be too fine for such a day.

In the choir-stalls of carved oak are the Master and dons of Boncourt and a few personal guests. The singers of the Chapel Royal (now ending *Requiem aeternam dona eis, Domine*, for the officiating priest has already ascended the altar steps) are presumably in the organ-loft; the waving forefinger we glimpse high up in the shadows is that of Jacques Mauduit conducting the " dying fall " of the Introit. The stone pavement is thronged with notabilities representing the Parlement of Paris, the University, and the arts and liberal professions, suitably cloaked, wrapped, and befurred, for the chapel is icy this February morning and Parisians are notably *frileux*. Seated before the catafalque, the Duc de Joyeuse, Admiral of France, his brother the Cardinal, and other figures of the Court mingle with what Binet calls *la fleur des meilleurs esprits de France*. Dorat, De Baïf, Turnèbe, Passerat, and Ronsard's other intimates among the princes of learning are not mentioned by name. Undoubtedly they were present.

> *Qui Mariam absolvisti,*
> *Et latronem exaudisti,*
> *Mihi quoque spem dedisti . . .*

The tremendous supplications of the *Dies Iræ* rise and fall, the Mass proceeds in its august simplicity and ends, followed by the Absolutions of the Dead; the lights are extinguished, and the chapel of Boncourt slowly empties. What Nicolas Rapin describes as *un disner somptueux aux despens de Monsieur Galland*, a fine collation offered by the College, followed. In the afternoon the crush and confusion in the College hall were so great owing to the flocking of the public that many princes and seigneurs, including the Cardinal de Bourbon, were unable to get in. They missed a notable treat. After the delivery of Latin panegyrics by two Boncourt professors, Jacques Velliard of Chartres and George Crichton the Scotsman—later of the Collège de France, and not to be confused with James (" The Admirable ") Crichton, deceased two years previously—the young, suave, able Messire Davy du Perron,

Reader to the King, ascends the rostrum amid an expectant buzz. Du Perron, not yet in Orders but in due course a Cardinal, is twenty-seven years of age, a sardonic wit, one of the young men of promise whose débuts Ronsard warmly encouraged. His oration, composed after the best models with the encouragement of Philippe Desportes—it will be duly published, with a graceful allusion in the preface to Desportes as Ronsard's only successor—is that long, elegant, dithyrambic, baroque allocution in French from which I have been freely quoting. One bravura passage may suffice for an illustration of Messire du Perron's style. " *O bienheureux sourd, qui a donné des oreilles aux François, pour entendre les oracles et les mystères de la poësie ! O bienheureux eschange de l'ouïe corporelle à l'ouïe spirituelle ! O bienheureux eschange du bruit et du tumulte populaire à l'intelligence de la musique et de l'harmonie des Cieux et à la connoissance des accords et des compositions de l'âme ! C'est ce grand Ronsard qui a le premier chassé la surdité spirituelle des hommes de sa nation !* "[1]

Among Ronsard's women admirers in the audience are the learned Mme de Retz and Mme de Villeroy, *née* Madeleine de L'Aubespine, to whose brains and charm Ronsard dedicated more than one sonnet. The absence of Hélène de Surgères has been commented on. She may have been out of Paris. She need have feared no embarrassments. The verses by her dead lover which Du Perron weaves so skilfully into his rhetoric are chosen with admirable tact. One sees the orator's searching eye rove over the packed assembly with a glint of amusement ; Messire du Perron is not among the admirers of Mlle de Surgères. The recital of a number of elegies and other verse-tributes in three languages follows this oration, when the applause has died away, and a threnody in the pastoral style, composed by Claude Binet, brings the celebrations to an end.

Master Jean Galland could be satisfied with the day. His affection continued to express itself in something like a Ronsard cultus established henceforth at the Collège de Boncourt. Apart from the erection of a marble memorial bust, a requiem Mass for Ronsard

---

[1] "O blessed victim of deafness, who has given the French ears to hear the oracles and mystery of poetry! O blessed exchange of physical for spiritual hearing! O blessed exchange of popular noise and tumult for the comprehension of music and the harmony of the spheres, for the knowledge of the rhythms and melodies of the soul! Our great Ronsard has been the first to abolish the spiritual deafness of his countrymen!"

was celebrated in the chapel every year on the date of his death as
long as Galland was Master (he died in 1612) and probably for some
time afterwards; a literary disputation in Hall by picked undergraduates followed. Why, one cannot help asking oneself, a marble
bust in Paris almost immediately and no monument of piety and
friendship over the tomb at St. Cosme till 1609? From a phrase in
George Crichton's funeral oration it would seem that Ronsard had
ordered a simple tomb: *operosius extructa sepulcra.* Moreover:

> *Je deffen qu'on ne rompe*
> *Le marbre pour la pompe*
> *De vouloir mon tumbeau*
> *Bâtir plus beau . . .*

Perhaps he had lately recalled this youthful order to Galland,
in a mood of proud half-jesting humility. Possibly he had yet
another motive. Might not that bleak brick tomb have been a
delicate rebuke to a king who had erected extravagant marbles over
his dead *mignons* and had sedulously withheld fitting reward from
the greatest poet in his realms? And might not Henri's violent
death, in Galland's estimation, have wiped out the score, so that the
Prior of St. Cosme might proceed? I do not think such conjecture
too fantastic. There is a parallel of a sort in the Royal Library at
Versailles. The books of the Dubarry are bound in the vulgarest
luxury, ablaze with gilding and armorial fal-lals. The books of
Marie-Antoinette are in plain calf with a neat cipher. Nothing could
convey the cut-direct more daintily.

A monument of another kind, *aere perennius*, impressive as any
marble cenotaph, had been swiftly erected to Ronsard in any case.
It was the Renaissance fashion, when a great personage died, for
the poets to combine in an anthology of original funereal and panegyric verse, called a *tombeau*. Ronsard had himself contributed to
more than one of these, notably that of the "Pearl of pearls",
Marguerite de Valois, Queen of Navarre. Her *tombeau* was
promoted in 1551 by Anne, Margaret, and Jane, the bluestocking
daughters of Edward Seymour, Duke of Somerset; their tutor
had been Ronsard's friend Nicolas Denisot, and nine-year-old
Lady Jane's Latin verses, composed for this occasion, are a

tribute to his pedagogy. To the *Tombeau de Ronsard*, promoted by Claude Binet, some twenty-five of the dead poet's most eminent admirers, headed by Jean Dorat, contributed verse-offerings in Greek, Latin, French, and Italian, the only notable French absentee being Philippe Desportes, aloof as ever. The *Tombeau* is an impressive monument, though, as M. de Nolhac observes, some of the sonnets from Italy evidently cost their authors little effort. Italian facility in sonnet-making is proverbial. Readers of Stendhal will recall the fatal ease with which the nobility and gentry of Parma were wont to turn them out in the Napoleonic period to be printed on silk handkerchiefs for ladies' pleasure. Belloc quotes in *Avril* an Italian of the Renaissance who said a man was no poet unless he could rap out a century of sonnets from time to time. It was a national industry.

The other poets of the *Tombeau* took pains. A Greek ode by Dorat proclaims that with Ronsard's death Homer, Virgil, Horace, Pindar, Aeschylus, Sophocles, and Callimachus have quitted the earth anew. The most succinct and satisfying tribute in the collection is the two-line distich of Pontus de Tyard :

Petrus Ronsardus iacet hic : si caetera nescis,
Nescis quid Phoebus, Musa, Minerua, Charis.[1]

Claude Binet was to add the crowning pinnacle to Ronsard's literary memorial. In March, 1586, his *Discours de la Vie de Pierre de Ronsard, Gentilhomme Vandômois*, was published by Gabriel Buon ; a hasty work, attached to the first posthumous edition of the *Oeuvres* and afterwards revised, remodelled, corrected and enlarged. The reputation of this hero-worshipping biography, by a disciple fresh from the master's intimacy, stood unquestioned until nearly the end of the nineteenth century. A few holes have been picked in it by modern critics—Binet is above all careless of chronology—but it retains its essential value and fragrance as a contemporary document, the work of a young man who had sat at Ronsard's bedside and piously collected many memories from his friends. For Binet, a lawyer by trade, was Galland's assistant as Ronsard's literary executor, and took his duties seriously.

[1] See page xi.

" *Nuper Idoneus . . .* "

Thus did the sun of Pierre de Ronsard set in a blaze worthy of
his long and regal passage through the literary firmament, and all
Christendom was aware of the passing of a portent, as when a
voice cried from the Isle of Paxos over the sea to Thamous the
pilot that Pan, the great Pan, was dead.

EPILOGUE

*Il a esté admiré de toutes les nations du monde, dont la pluspart
le lisent publicquement dans leurs escholes françoises.*
(GUILLAUME COLLETET, *Vie de Pierre de Ronsard.*)

For, sparing of his sacred strength, not often
    Among us darkling here the lord of light
    Makes manifest his music and his might
In hearts that open and in lips that soften
    With the soft flame and heat of songs that shine . . .
        (SWINBURNE, *Ave atque Vale.*)

§1

IN THE 1560'S, WHEN ENGLAND DISCOVERED RONSARD, QUEEN
Elizabeth sent the Frenchman a fine diamond and the English
lyric poets from Sidney downwards rushed to imitate his style
with flattering eagerness, as Professor Saintsbury has shown.[1]
In the 1860's, when England discovered Baudelaire, thanks to
Swinburne's fanfares in the *Spectator*, no reputable English poet
from Tennyson down moved a muscle and Queen Victoria
forbore to send the Frenchman even one of those diamond
tiepins she lavished constantly on British stationmasters of
little charm. The difference is piquant. To discuss all the
reasons for it (a fascinating occupation) would fill, perhaps,
another volume.

One may at least suggest that Ronsard's swift conquest of
England—as of Europe, for during his lifetime he was praised
and read and imitated in every civilised country, studied and
commented with owlish attention at Heidelberg, awarded the
admiration of some of the greatest figures of his age, including
Tasso, Montaigne, and Scaliger, and recognised as an international
force in poetry—was materially assisted by the fact that Christendom
was not as yet disrupted, though disruption had set in. The old
Catholic spiritual commonwealth was not yet broken finally. Men
in Finland could still understand the process of thought of men

---

[1] *Elizabethan Literature*, London, 1893.

Spain. The unscalable barriers of chauvinist nationalism, ignorance, prejudice, and hostility set up by the Reformation were building, but not yet in position. To the cultivated Tudor Englishman Ronsard was a poet, not a " foreign " poet. To the cultivated modern Englishman Paul Claudel, to name a great living French poet, is unintelligible, and for the most part hardly a name. The invisible, multitudinous, gossamer bonds joining men who share the same philosophy have been snapped. A kind of wilful walleyedness prevails now, in the arts as in other spheres, so that Racine in England is counted a frigid bore (" *le frisson racinien, à la fois voluptueux, tendre, et triste* ") and in France Shakespeare—a genius Catholic, as G. W. E. Russell said, as the sea is salt—was till a generation or two ago rated at somewhere about the level of Casimir Delavigne. *Air*, once again, *archiconnu*.

It may be reasonably argued, in opposition, that Ronsard conquered Europe chiefly with love-poems, and that the language of eroticism is international at any period. Certainly Ronsard's lyric worship of women's eyes, lips, and hair needs no more exegetic footnotes than the similar exercises of Byron or Pushkin, Goethe or d'Annunzio, and a kiss is a kiss in any language. But here, I think, crops up a vital point for consideration. It is not enough, for those who would extract the ultimate marrow from great poetry, to depend merely on the superficial pleasures of eye and ear. It is necessary for the reader to push further, to penetrate the poet's intimacy, to discover his attitude towards life, to distinguish conviction from those passing moods to which poets are liable ; to share his thought, in a word. The majority of Ronsard's readers were, and are, aware that the vaunted *amour total* was a thing he would discard gladly, like a foolish toy, sooner or later, when the time came to make his soul ; which, indeed, he must have discarded and done penance for every time he approached the Sacraments.

> The flesh is bruckle, the Feynd is slee :
> *Timor mortis conturbat me.*

In this Ronsard differs from all erotic poets not of his faith, however often he fell into fleshly raptures. There is thus an

impassable gulf between him and an equally passionate po[...]
like Swinburne—and having mentioned Swinburne on[...]
thinks naturally of Baudelaire, whose cry from the depth[...]
Ronsard may have echoed more than once after making, [...]
however long intervals, that examination of conscience hi[...]
religion requires.

> *Dans ton île, ô Vénus, je n'ai trouvé debout*
> *Qu'un gibet symbolique où pendait mon image . . .*
> *—Ah! Seigneur, donnez-moi la force et le courage*
> *De contempler mon coeur et mon corps sans dégoûts !*[1]

I have not seen this point raised and examined by any modern
critic setting out to analyse the mind and genius of Ronsard
Those who ignore it ignore a profound thing, a fundamental.
Ronsard would never have attempted seriously, if challenged by
moral authority, to justify his passion to share Cassandre's bed.
What is called the modern mind would, even *in articulo mortis*,
call him a fool not to have shared it from the first if he felt that
way inclined. Hence a lack of contact and continuity between
singer and listener ; a disability and a deprivation. As Mr. Desmond
MacCarthy has remarked in an essay on Milton, "'Put yourself
in his place' is the prime principle of criticism and appreciation—
'also in his times', if the writer is an old one." For it is essential,
Mr. MacCarthy says truly, to master "what a poet aimed at ;
what kind of knowledge, beliefs, and associations he relied upon
his readers sharing with him, and how nicely calculated to achieve
the results were the means he employed". If the cap fits one or two
of Ronsard's foremost British expositors it must resemble the
Tarnhelm in the *Niebelungenlied*, rendering them invisible.

"*Il y a dans votre œuvre, Monsieur,*" said a curiously discerning
Brussels newspaper reporter to Baudelaire, "*quelque chose de
chrétien qu'on n'a pas assez remarqué.*" Victorian Anglo-Saxondom
was shocked by Baudelaire because it had heard he was funda-
mentally diabolic. Modern Anglo-Saxondom is slightly disconcerted
to hear he is not.[2] No diamonds for Baudelaire, at any rate.

---

[1] *Un Voyage à Cythère.*
[2] Cf. Eugène Thébault, *Baudelaire Disciple de Saint Thomas d'Aquin* (Mercure de France,
July 15, 1929).

It is a misfortune for Ronsard and the Pléïade at large that their best-known interpreter to the modern English-speaking world should so far[1] have been a wan, elderly, secluded, rather timorous Oxford don of the daintiest culture, by whose side Ruskin would appear a drunken bargee ; a personage of " exquisite faintness, *une fadeur exquise*, a certain tenuity and caducity . . . one of those who can bear nothing vehement or strong". The words are Walter Pater's ; he is describing not his pallid self, but, comically enough, Pierre de Ronsard. In that twilit hothouse of a book *The Renaissance*, the essay on Du Bellay and the Pléïade flowers into the most risible judgments, from which we may pluck a magistral aside on Rabelais :

" No one can turn over the pages of Rabelais without feeling how much need there was of softening, of castigation."

Tu parles, coco! One can hear that mighty red-nosed shade shaking all Parnassus with his laughter. And on Ronsard :

" To affect this softening is the object of the revolution in poetry which is connected with Ronsard's name . . . This elegance, this manner, this daintiness of execution are consummate, and have an unmistakable aesthetic value . . . These wanton lines have a spirit guiding their caprices. For there is *style* everywhere . . . Ronsard loves, or dreams that he loves, a rare and peculiar type of beauty, *la petite pucelle Angevine*, with golden hair and dark eyes. But he has the ambition not only of being a courtier and a lover, but a great scholar also . . . He is just a little pedantic . . ."

Finally :

" A certain premature agedness . . . the tranquil temperate sweetness appropriate to that, in the school of poetry he founded."

And on the Pléïade :

[1] A recent study by Professor Morris Bishop, of Cornell, has advantaged the United States (*Ronsard, Prince of Poets:* New York, 1940).

" Their loves are only half real, a vain effort to prolong th imaginative loves of the middle age beyond their natural lifetime . . . But they amuse themselves with wonderful elegance . . . *A* certain silvery grace of fancy."

It is only fair to recognise that in a minor work, *Gaston de Latour* Pater does Ronsard a little more justice and even allows him a certain vitality. " Here was a poetry which boldly assumed the dress, the words, the habits, the very trick of contemporary life, and turned them into gold . . . As at the touch of a wizard, something more came into the rose than its own natural blush . . . Here were real people, in their real, delightful attire, and you understood how they moved . . . The juice in the flowers, when Ronsard named them, was like wine or blood." This just clears the eminent Fellow of Brasenose of an accusation any Ronsardian reading *The Renaissance* might be tempted to make, namely that Pater had apparently read no more of Ronsard than the half-dozen favourites of the anthologists; or alternatively, that if he had ventured further, the virility and vehemence of Ronsard's genius had scared that refined spirit and it had shrunk back into its shawls.

For *The Renaissance*, not *Gaston de Latour*, which nobody reads, is the acknowledged and enduring classic, the gospel according to Pater. Re-pondering its exquisite (or, as some think, appalling) rhythms, one is forced to admit Pater's consummate qualifications to appreciate the elegance of Ronsard, and to savour that " sweetness " which is the Paterian *leit-motiv*. As for the old-maiderie which prevents his appreciating Ronsard's stormy vigour, it seems explicable enough when we apply Sainte-Beuve's test. Pater, an agnostic, at this period, of a Low Anglican type, with markedly feminine and introvert characteristics—though I do not for one moment believe the buccaneer Frank Harris's story of that tearful scene with Wilde at Oxford—was one of those products of a repulsively materialist age who, in their hunger for beauty, are hypnotised by the lovely gifts to civilisation of a religion they must perforce despise and spurn. Again and again Pater assures himself in *The Renaissance*, rather anxiously, that the Catholicism which bred the arts he adores is a dead and futile thing. He sweeps it carefully

aside. He will not allow Leonardo da Vinci the benefits of the
Masses ordered in his will (" on no theory of religion could these
hurried offices be of much consequence "). He will not allow a
Botticelli Madonna any ecstasy in her God-appointed mission.
" The pen almost drops from her hand, the high cold words
[of the *Ave* and the *Gaude Maria*] have no meaning for her "—
evidently Botticelli was painting the soul of Mrs. Humphry Ward.[1]
It is no doubt a rooted hereditary contempt for the Catholic religion
—compare his sneer at Winckelmann's conversion—which forces
Pater to ignore Ronsard's swordmanship entirely and to concentrate
on his decorative grace, presenting him as a *petit-maître*, a languid
trifler, a dainty goldsmith and jeweller preoccupied with toys, a
kind of Court craftsman like Fabergé, producing delicious Easter
eggs and musical-boxes and other *colifichets* in rubies and diamonds
and filigree to amuse the great. The strong passion of the *Discours
des Misères de France* and the *Appel à Théodore de Bèze*, like the
aching passion of the *Hélène* cycle, meant nothing, apparently,
to Pater. His ear is a miracle of finesse, perfect and dainty as one
of the shells on the seashore he speaks of in Leonardo's *Saint Anne*,
" that delicate place, where the wind passes like the hand of some
fine etcher over the surface, and the untorn shells are lying thick
on the sand, and the tops of the rocks, to which the waves never
rise, are green with grass, grown fine as hair". He lacks merely
red corpuscles, like the don of Mr. Belloc's celebrated commination :

> Don poor at Bed and worse at Table,
> Don pinched, Don starved, Don miserable,
> Don of the cold and doubtful breath . . .

And he is not the only eminent English critic to write foolishly
of Pierre de Ronsard.

Having been assured by Andrew Lang that Ronsard's Odes are
" almost unreadable ",[2] one finds on reading them—the supreme

---

[1] In justice to Pater, one must remark that Huysmans, most pernickety of Catholic intellectuals, is here on his side. Botticelli (says Huysmans) is one of the few artists of the Italian
Renaissance who frankly acknowledge their Virgins to be Venuses and vice versa ; the phy-
siognomy and the lassitude of both, as Botticelli paints them, being essentially pagan. On
the other hand Huysmans derives no relish from the fact but finds it revolting (*La
Cathédrale, XII.*)

[2] *Ballads and Lyrics of Old France :* London, 1913.

test—that they are nothing of the sort. The Odes are not invariably Ronsard's finest work, but they are eminently readable, full of vigour, variety, charm, gaiety, courtesy, and a graceful pedantry which, boldly faced, grows on one. (To dismiss any written thing as unreadable is, one feels on principle, to invite queries as to the capacity of the reader. Lamb was a tiresome little man in many ways, but he boasted that he found nothing printed unreadable, and he is to be admired for it, I think. A railway time-table can prove fascinating reading, failing all else, and *Punch* is often not without serious interest.) And when Lang says that " we are never allowed to forget that he is the poet who read the *Iliad* through in three days", Lang seems to misjudge again. Ronsard's display of scholarship is no parade, it is a condition normal to him as breathing. Lang is, of course, right about the *Franciade*, " as tedious as other artificial epics "; yet there are moments even in the *Franciade*.

Humbert Wolfe, a more sensitive critic of our own day, has done something recently to pluck away " the tepid wreaths of immortelles that blindness, ignorance, or sheer intellectual cowardice " have heaped on the cenotaph of Pierre de Ronsard. Admirably he defends the poet against the stupid charge of some modern English pundit that Ronsard did not, like Shakespeare, touch the ultimate issues of life and death. " What nonsense all that is! " cries Wolfe. " Ronsard is not, let it be freely admitted, attempting to cover the *pêle-mêle* of Life. Why should he? He happened to be engaged in writing love-poems : he was not making a contribution either to *The Lancet* or to a gardener's handbook. But in so far as he was occupied with love—the strongest passion men and women know—he left untouched no sign, no wonder in all that trembling diapason, and nothing he touched was not richer for the brief neighbourhood of his enchanted fingers."[1] Here, I think, Wolfe in his turn does Ronsard a little less than full justice. Ronsard is by no means exclusively a poet of love. The *Hymnes* and especially that great mass of polemic verse in defence of religion certainly touch on the ultimate issues, and he sweeps the strings constantly with magistral power.

The range of the man, indeed, is fascinating. His extremes

[1] *Ronsard and French Romantic Poetry* : The Zaharoff Lecture for 1934. Oxford, 1935.

of artful simplicity and pedantry-run-mad may be illustrated by two extracts :

(*a*)

Au marché porter il me faut
(Ma mere Janne m'i envoye)
Nostre grand Cochon, et nostre Oye
Qui le matin crioit si haut.[1]

(*b*)

O Cuisse-né Bacchus, Mystiq, Hymenean,
Carpime, Evaste, Agnien, Manique, Linean,
Evöe! Euboulien, Baladin, Solitère,
Vengeur, Satyre, Roy, Germe des Dieux et Père,
Martial, Nomian, Cornu, Vieillard, Enfant,
Paian, Nyctelien : Gange veit trionfant
Ton char enorguilli de ta dextre fameuse.[2]

The first is from a rustic trifle called " The Gifts of Jacquet to Isabeau "—not Isabeau de Limeuil, that high dame, but some rosy dairymaid of the Vendômois—and the second is from a Hymn to Bacchus dedicated to Jean Brinon. This latter, I think, Ronsard must have written in tremendous high spirits, aware that in centuries to come editors would sweat to verify his allusions and curse his playfulness. In two other odes he adds to the name of Bacchus half a dozen other choicely abstruse exotic, esoteric epithets, as if he had just dragged the entire Greek language with a trawling-net. Is this pedantry ? Rather, is it not the merry pastime of a scholar, like the " glorious lyrism, the exquisite virtuosity, the graceful devout skylarking " of the monks who wrote some of those early Latin hymns which so charmed the late Professor Phillimore ?

---

[1] I mun goo to market ('tis my mother Joan dat sends me) with our great pig and our goose, dat made such a hem ornery ole set-out dis marnen (Sussex equivalent).

[2] O Thigh-Born Bacchus, Mystic, Hymenean,
Healer, Joy-Compeller, Pure One, Mad One, Keeper of the Winepress,
Hail! Good Counsellor, Dancer, Solitary,
Avenger, Satyr, King, Germ and Father of Gods,
Warrior, Shepherd, Horned One, Old One, Young One,
Healer, Feaster-By-Night! Ganges sees triumphant
Thy chariot, proud of thy illustrious right hand.

I guess that Ronsard's dancing mood was not invariably uninspired by the gifts of Bacchus, and a half-drained flask of Anjou or Vouvray stood at his elbow, mayhap, as he dashed off these litanies in his second native tongue; hardly a spectacle a Victorian Fellow of Brasenose could approve. The Cambridge tradition is less severe, and I think the great Richard Porson, Regius Professor of Greek a generation earlier than Pater, would have chuckled and whooped delightedly, being himself in liquor more often than not; and as for Byron's tutor at Trinity, who habitually swore in Greek, he would doubtless have shouted " Evoë! " and capered in concert. Porson's own principal vinous inspiration in verse all Cambridge knows :

> I went to Frankfort and got drunk
> With that most learn'd professor, Brunck ;
> I went to Wortz and got more drunken
> With that more learn'd professor, Ruhnken.

The vine brought more gracious madness to Ronsard.

It is this gusto, with wine and without, which bathes so much of Ronsard's work in perpetual sunshine. The dark moods are there, the love-sonnets apart from the Marie sequence are full of aching, but immense tracts of the Ronsard country resemble Touraine in the blue-and-gold of a June morning when the first roses are blowing ; such a morning as reconciled Leonardo da Vinci, walking in old age in his garden outside the walls of Amboise, to exile from Italy.

Ronsard has no corrosive acids in his blood, metaphorically speaking, no Germanic or morbid mullygrubs in his brain. It may be protested that this is precisely due to his lack of philosophic depth ; for the modern spiritual malady, which breeds " philosophic " poets as a dead mule breeds maggots, exalts agnostic pessimism and introspective muddle into a major virtue and esteems *A Shropshire Lad* more highly as poetry of the intellect than " I syng of a Mayden". But what is " depth " ? Ronsard's passing despairs are of the flesh, not the soul, and his mind has an ultimate anchorage which preserves him from any but superficial dabblings in Pantheism and Lucretianism and Epicureanism and all the rest of it. He is as remote from the woolly modern negations as Baudelaire, that Thomist *manqué*. If Ronsard asks few questions of the "circumambient inane", he has no real need to ask any.

§3

That Ronsard should have become a living enchantment again in France seems to me no enigma. In the first place he is essentially a nationalist poet, though to the critics immediately succeeding him the Ronsardian rose-garden, with its massed, tumultuous blooms, so richly profuse, so (apparently) richly diffuse, did not seem a French garden at all. Humbert Wolfe has remarked pleasantly that it was for this crime—non-Gallicity, one might call it—that Ronsard was sentenced to two hundred years' solitary confinement. The French master-poet *par excellence* is, of course, Racine, who " draws restraint upon restraint ", says Wolfe, " closer and closer about him till in his greatest moments he glitters, like a mailed knight, in the shining armour of his superb self-mastery ". Ronsard's genius is not of this kind. Compared with Racine, indeed, he might almost have been an Englishman. Yet his garden, if a Lenôtre has no hand in the planning of it, is no product of that wayward, luxuriant, rather dishevelled licence which damns so much Anglo-Saxon poetry in French eyes. Ronsard has all that French care for *la forme* and *le verbe*, all that highly-civilised discipline, stamp of the French genius, which is seen equally in the vast canvases of Racine and Corneille, in the exquisitely-chiselled miniatures of Gautier's *Emaux et Camées*, and in the free rhythms of Paul Claudel. I think one of the very first reasons for the modern Ronsardian renaissance is that the French have had a bellyful in recent years of the paranoiac excesses of the Cocktail Age—the "Dada" movement and Surrealism, for example—and have turned for refreshment to the pure lyricism, the impeccable technique of a Muse which never pranced to the Voodoo tomtoms under a jungle moon, bedaubed, naked, and grimacing.

And this despite Ronsard's prolixity, so unsuited to the taste of the Tabloid Age. It cannot be denied that his frequent *longueurs* are a defect to a modern eye. They are a mark of his time. The Renaissance artist, when he had something to say, expressed himself, when it so pleased him, at length. He was not afraid of repetition nor perturbed by that highly debatable axiom that brevity is the soul of wit—Ronsard's toying, late in life, with this theme notwithstanding. Renaissance artistic vitality demanded space and was not easily wearied ; nor was the vitality of its educated public. Having more leisure and (by God's mercy) fewer books than we, being unaware of the necessity to rush to and fro at maniac speed in pursuit of the Unattainable, the Renaissance poetry-lover was not heard to complain that an ode of twenty or fifty stanzas was of inordinate length. If it seemed good to the poet to use that amount of words to develop his thought, it provided all the more pleasure to fill a winter's evening,

> *Ces longues nuicts d'hyver, où la Lune ocieuse*
> *Tourne si lentement son char tout à l'entour . . .*

So prolixity and repetition in a poet of Ronsard's stature no more offended or bored the men of his time than repetition and prolixity in a Bach fugue annoys a musician. Their minds, as I have said, were not easily fatigued or fretted. They had not to be kept constantly amused, like children or stockbrokers. They were not fed on spicy scraps by a semi-illiterate popular Press whose sole concern is to entertain ; they sipped their reading slowly and meditatively, as an epicure sips Romanée-Conti. Ronsard lived and sang in a world of mental vigour and endurance whose most jaded moments were brimful of red-hot vitality compared with the numb and nervesick mental exhaustion of our present age. To complain therefore that some of Ronsard's verses are overlong seems to accuse not him but ourselves,

> having used our nerves with bliss and teen,
> And tired upon a thousand schemes our wit.[1]

In Ronsard's violent, fascinating world, as we have noted often before, everything is over lifesize, its splendours, ugliness, crimes, and virtues. When that curious personality who called himself Baron Corvo warned his Edwardian readers in a study of the Borgias that the Renaissance Popes, kings, lovers, men of intellect, and men

[1] Matthew Arnold, *The Scholar Gypsy*.

of war cannot be judged by " the narrow code, the stunted standard
of the journalist and the lodging-house keeper, the plumber and the
haberdasher", he spoke the simple truth (though there exists equally
a standard by which sixteenth-century Popes and twentieth-century
journalists can be judged). The great masters of the Renaissance
exhilarate and dazzle and bewilder our shoddy decline and shame
our machine-made middle-class mediocrity. The spectacle of a herd
of modern trippers shambling through the Chateau of Amboise
is a handy satirical illustration of this truth, needing no embroidery.
Mingling with the perfume of Ronsard's roses is the light and air
and brilliance of his age, and reading his pages we re-enter it with
him in illusion and are enchanted. Here is, I think, one more obvious
reason why Ronsard has returned to the Machine Age. He stands
for so many noble and gracious things now in peril from without
and within : the golden Classic Spirit, the fundamental Culture,
the ancestral Religion which nourishes and supports it all.

If the refreshment Ronsard offers us is pleasant to a weary mind
in London or New York, it is doubly a pleasure in his own country.
Even in modern Paris it is possible to steep oneself still, to some
extent, in his atmosphere. To assist at a High Mass at, for example,
St. Etienne-du-Mont, adjoining what was once the Collège de
Boncourt, is to re-enter Ronsard's world in body and spirit, at its
happiest and most serene. The Mass has not changed since, on some
high feast of obligation, he last heard it there, with a dinner-party
chez Dorat to follow; the fabric and appearance of that great
church is hardly altered. The music (if the *maître de chapelle* has
had the good taste, none too common in Parisian choirmasters of
recent years, as Huysmans complained, to select a Mass by De
Lassus or Palestrina) is the music in which Ronsard passionately
delighted; the prayers he said during the Mass still mingle with
the prayers of the centuries which soak those pillars and arches
with the incense of time immemorial.

Apart from a few churches, it must be admitted, little of Ronsard's
Paris remains. Certainly he belongs nowhere to the modern
University Quarter, of which it might have been said at his death
aquí está encerrada el alma del licenciado. But Blois and Tours
and his native Vendômois and, above all, I have remarked already,
his beloved green islet in the Loir, are impregnated with his

influence. At La Possonnière, that charming house so carefully preserved to-day by pious hands, are the rooms which echoed to his voice and step, the chimneypieces and windowsills he leaned against, the carvings on which his youthful eye so often rested; in the nearby church of Couture are the font at which he was baptised, his family chapel, the tombs of his father and mother. The Loir still runs, the fields he loved and paced so often are there, the remains of Gastine Forest and the wreck of Bellerie. All this countryside, which filled his constant thoughts, holds something palpable of him. So, though much more faintly, like a wisp of a boyish presence half-seen in a dream, very tenuous and elusive, does the vicinity of the Beloved's deathmasks at Holyrood. There is nothing to recall Ronsard in London, except possibly the great mulberry tree which stands in Beaufort Street in what was St. Thomas More's Chelsea garden. It might conceivably have seen the page come up with Lassigny from the river to call on the French Ambassador. But this tree is very old, and only a poet can make an old tree speak; and when it does so it is apt, one gathers from Tennyson's interview with the Talking Oak, to utter sad doggerel.

§4

The world—the Anglo-Saxon world at least—being curiously avid of "messages", hoping doubtless to be handed at last one which will make it comfortable, it may well be asked by pragmatists what Pierre de Ronsard has to offer the modern age.

I hear no especial note of hopefulness in your pragmatist's voice as he demands Ronsard's "message". Poets—unlike politicians, who always have a ringing phrase at hand—are unpredictable fellows, vague, unreliable, wayward in their flight as snipe. Apart from Browning's bustling optimism and Hardy's damp despair no message has issued from an Anglo-Saxon poet for some time on which a plain man can bite, as it were. Unfortunately Ronsard must be rated, I think, unsatisfactory. He speaks with two voices, one agreeable to this age, one otherwise. And Philip sober not only contradicts Philip drunk but gets the upper hand and the last word, and leaves his other self looking like a fool.

It is sufficiently clear from the preceding pages, no doubt, that the voice of Pierre de Ronsard is heard for a great part of his life preaching that popular hedonist gospel which was already old when Horace preached it before him. Enjoy yourself : gather your roses while you may ; drink, kiss and be merry, for Time flies.

> The grave's a fine and private place,
> But none, I think, do there embrace,

as the Puritan Marvell sang, heedless of the New Dispensation or perhaps careless of it, being elect. No message could please the modern world more, and indeed it is being issued, in slightly more pretentious words, by leading minds planning a new world at this moment. The consecrated Jeffersonian formula, prevalent with current after-dinner speakers, " Life, liberty, and the pursuit of happiness ", does not differ essentially from Horace's *carpe diem*. The enormous hidden irony of that " pursuit " has so far appealed to few.

So Ronsard sang the old pagan refrain, defiantly crowning himself with roseleaves, calling for louder music and stronger wine, barring the door with a resolute flourish against commonsense ; though even in the orgiastic years reason can get past his guard now and then.

> *Ceux dont la fantaisie*
> *Sera religieuse et devote envers Dieu*
> *Tousjours acheveront quelque grand poësie,*
> *Et dessus leur renom la Parque n'aura lieu.*

His other voice is speaking now. His eyes, one might say, have a different expression as they survey the festal scene, the flushed vapid faces, the smoky, overheated, over-scented air, the disorderly tables, the intoxicated laughter, the foolish babble, the spilled wine, the guttering waxlights, the trampled roses, the ennui overhanging all the revel and increasing like a cloud. *Vanitas vanitatum. Surgit amari aliquid.* The wisdom of the ages is echoed by his religion. A window has swung open and a bracing breeze of reality is blowing the veils of smoke asunder. But not yet will he fling open every window and door once and for all and cleanse the chambers of his soul, and expel the fantasms and illusions, and breathe a more vital air. Nevertheless :

Ronsard

Nous sçavons bien, Seigneur, que nos fautes sont grandes,
Nous sçavons nos péchés . . .

Ronsard's cry for himself and stricken France in the 1560's
is the cry of one shocked into sanity and facing the eternal verities,
and it is echoing in stricken France at this moment. If any poet's
message were ripe for the present world this is it. It cannot be
recommended as a comfortable or popular one, it does not minister
to thick national complacency and the muddled optimism of fools.
It implies humiliation, confession, penance, reparation; a bitter
and salutary medicine, bark-and-steel for a nation's soul. It is not
to be expected that it will be swallowed in large quantities by
the modern world this year or next.

> They talk of some strict Testing of us—Pish!
> He's a Good Fellow, and 'twill all be well.[1]

To fasten on this aspect of a poet who has endeared himself to
the world as a worshipper of women is probably eccentric, and
even perverse. I observe that no other modern student of Ronsard
has done so, so far as I can perceive. It seems to be agreed that
love of women is his life-work, and the rest of his activities may be
dismissed as of little account. I do not think such a fixed attitude
in the critic bears that scientific stamp which is so desirable; using
the word " scientific " in its primal and ideal sense and disconnecting
it from the brute ignorance common to the modern scientific
mind, outside its own narrow field. In other words, I think that to
concentrate on only half of Ronsard's attitude to life is to fail to
give a true account of him. The instinctive attempt to treat his
religious half as an amiable and unimportant flaw in an otherwise
attractive character is, perhaps, inevitable in any critic who feels
strongly (as most critics do) that such a mood is unworthy of a
thinking modern man. To suggest such a thing to Pierre de Ronsard
in his lifetime was to invite a swashing reply, as his Calvinist
antagonists discovered, for they too tried to prove him irreligious,
though for a different reason. Modern history and biography is
full of eager attempts to smooth away Alpine protuberances in the
lives of certain great figures of the past and to pretend there is

[1] Fitz-Gerald, *Omar Khayyàm.*

nothing really there but the broad easy sweep of the arterial road. That wonderful woman St. Teresa, for example, has been shown to be merely a Freudian case, St. Francis of Assisi a sentimental bird-lover, teetotaller, and humanitarian; and I have read with these round eyes a thesis by a female don of London University, that brabling-shop of strange sophistries, proving that St. Joan of Arc was a pagan, involved in mystic diabolism, who claimed to be Incarnate God. (*Tu autem, Domine, miserere!*)

Ronsard has not yet claimed the attention of any brisk psychic-minded thinker, but when he does it will be obvious to the intelligent that he practised the Black Mass habitually, said the *Pater* backwards, knew the Infamous Kiss, and devoted himself, in the cabbalist symbolism behind that dying speech at St. Cosme, to the Master of Witches. Such entrancing discoveries are accepted at face-value by a public which is easily imposed on by any parade of learning and far too lazy to examine it. For this reason I have brought into sharper light the Catholicism which informed this great Renaissance mind, the fundamentals to which it steadfastly returned. Failing to understand this, one fails to understand Ronsard, as the ineptitudes of Walter Pater demonstrate.

Ronsard's world was bloody and beautiful, ours is bloody and ugly. His world produced masses of great song, ours does not. Amid the miseries of his time Ronsard sang like a nightingale, in the midst of ours the poets are dumb, or, if they attempt to sing, produce nothing but the harsh croaking of spiritual bankruptcy and despair, or tuneless and futile *poncifs*, inspired by a half-hearted woolly optimism full of pathos; being rootless and drifting men afflicted by that malady of the West which, as Comte said, is a continual revolt against human antecedents. The mental health and vigour of Ronsard are tonic. Under his roses and raptures lurk the rooted certitudes. However far into folly the flesh may drive him, the spirit is intact. His dualism, pagan and Christian, resolves, whenever issue is seriously joined, in the triumph of reason, with the plain finality of that monumental line in the Song of Roland which says "Pagans are wrong and Christians are right". That eager wayward sword-keen mind, that vast hungry scholarship, that joyous appetite for life, that lifelong mastery and surfeit of fame bring him to the same conclusion as the strong mind of St. Thomas

More and those other Renaissance humanists who never were beguiled by toys : *sine auctoritate nulla vita.*

Reluctantly I take leave of Pierre de Ronsard, striving to fix one last glimpse of him in my mind. Not that picture, I think, of the handsome athletic youth with the world at his feet ; still less that of the elderly ill-starred lover moping after a shadow. I see him for preference moving slowly on his stick by the side of Jean Galland on a fine winter afternoon in the garden of the Collège de Boncourt, his heart free from vain longings and love-sickness and turbulence, his soul at peace with God, his face lit up with humorous affection. Under the trees in the gathering dusk a group of undergraduates, whom he has lately charmed with the gay brilliance and wisdom of his talk, like some delightful uncle, watch the greatest poet in France drag his gouty legs along, talking constantly, pausing at intervals for breath. From some of the College windows lights already sparkle. From the kitchens, as the door is opened and servants bustle in and out, comes a stream of candlelight and a waft of cooking. The first stars are crackling in a clear frosty sky. The thousand bells of Paris have already rung the evening *Ave,* and the air has a new bite. Ronsard shivers and pulls up the furred collar of his cloak, and turns in his limping walk. It is time for the pleasant evening meal ; after it will follow quiet fruitful hours alone in his chamber, reading, writing, meditating. He catches the arm of Galland in mid-gesture and presses it. " *Mon amy,*" he says with twinkling eyes, " *vous avez étrangement raison.* They are all bandits." But whether he is referring (God forbid) to his five publishers, or to the Court, or the Du Bartas clique, or to certain innkeepers on the road to Tours, or to the Calvinist horde, or the Faculty of Medicine, or even, affectionately, to some friends he has been discussing, I cannot say, for it is already dark, the voices are still, the scene has vanished, as if a curtain had been dropped.

Je m'en vais saoul du monde, ainsi qu'un convié
S'en va saoul du banquet de quelque marié . . .

END

INDEX

Index

Index

etrarch, 74, 95, 96, 97, 106, 111, 112, 121, 245
hilip II, King of Spain, 27, 171, 187, 198, 214
Phillimore, Prof. J. S., 325
Pilsudski, Marshal, 226
Pindar, 75, 76, 104, 178
Pius II, Pope (Aeneas Sylvius Piccolomini), 62
Pius V, St., Pope, 137, 151
Plato, 12, 13, 54
Platonism, Catholic, 13
Platonism, Renaissance, 13, 101, 232, 242
Pléiade, La, 19, 87–8, 274, 321
Poetry, French, Ronsardian laws of, 196–7, 292
—, Latin, Ronsardian view of, 292–3
Poissy, Colloque de, 288
Poland, Renaissance, 223–5
Politiques, Les, 223, 228
Pomme de Pin, La, Tavern of, 92, 162–3
Pope, Alexander, 236, 302
Porson, Richard, 34, 326
Possonnière, La, Manor of, 16, 53, 68, 69, 99, 108, 244, 264, 330
Pray, Cassandre de (*see* Salviati, Cassandre)
—, Jean de, 97, 241
Prose, Latin, Ronsardian view of, 293
Publishers, Ronsard's, 284
Puits-Herbault, Gabriel de, 12

Q

Quevedo, Francisco de, 56

R

Rabelais, 8, 9–11, 18, 35, 55, 71, 85, 116–17, 162, 270–1, 321
Racine, 4, 162, 171, 319, 327
Randolph, Thomas, Ambassador, 129
Rapin, Nicolas, 312, 313
Reformation, The, 17, 18, 142, 200, 319
Reformation, German, the second, 25
Relativity, 12
Religion, French Wars of, 142–5, 151–2, 197–201, 213–17, 228, 263–4, 269, 299–300
Renaissance, The (*see* Ballet)
Retz, Mme de, 265, 314
Rivière, Jacques de la, 31, 231
Romains, Jules, 40
Romeu, Octavio de, 37
Ronsard, Claude de (brother of Pierre), 54, 99, 108
—, Jeanne de (mother of Pierre), 53
—, Loys de (father of Pierre), 15, 16, 53, 54, 57, 69–70, 81
—, Loys de (nephew of Pierre), 99
Rossetti, 195
Rousseau, 9
Rubampré, Jacques de, 139–40
Ruskin, 7, 321

S

St. Bartholomew, massacre of, 143, 183, 215–17
St. Cosme-lez-Tours, Island of, 123, 172
—, Priory of, 172, 229, 264, 269, 271, 285, 299, 306–11, 315
St. Esprit, Chevaliers du, 267, 288
St. Gelais, Mellin de, 92, 103–4, 106–7, 126, 279
St. Germain-en-Laye, 131, 174
Sta. Maria la Real de las Huelgas, 236
Sainte-Beuve, 19, 27, 279, 322
Sainte-Marthe, Scévole de, 255, 279, 288, 289, 312
Saintsbury, Prof. George, 318
Salinas, Francisco, 258
Salviati, Cassandre, 20, 37, 50, 93–4, 95–115, 167, 203, 211, 231, 241–2, 270
Sannazaro, Jacopo, 34, 74, 123, 208, 245, 297
Sappho, 14, 24
Sardini, Scipio, 189, 190, 202, 280
Satanism, 41, 333
Savoy, Marguerite of (*see* Marguerite de Savoie)
Scaliger, 34, 318
Scève, Maurice (*see* Lyons, School of)
Schizophrenia, 25–7
Scotland, Ronsard in, 60–5
Scots College, Paris, 63
Scott, Alexander, 63
Scott, Sir Walter, 61
Sébillet, Thomas, 92
Sects, Protestant, multiplicity of, 150
September, 1792, massacres of, 143
Seymour, Anne, Margaret, Jane, 315
Shakespeare, 11, 29, 43, 164, 170, 180, 319
Shaw, George Bernard, 71
Shelley, 165, 235, 273
Sidney, 123, 318
Sigismund I, II, of Poland (*see* Jagiellon Dynasty)
Simony, Renaissance, 73
" Sinope ", 50, 69, 201–3
Skelton, John, 67
Sobieski, Jan, King of Poland, 226
Socrates, 12, 84
Sorbonne, The, 1, 13, 61, 85, 224, 270
Southwell, Bl. Robert, S. J., 24
Spain, Renaissance, 16–17
Spenser, 18, 88, 165, 190
Stendhal, 15, 175, 318
Stephens, James, 157
Stevenson, Robert Louis, 60, 176
Sterne, 110
Strachey, Lytton, 30
Stuarts (*see* James I; James V; Mary)
Suleiman (" the Magnificent "), Sultan, 143
Summa Theologica, 12
Summers, Rev. Montague, 41
Surgères, Hélène de, 2, 31, 50, 51, 230–61, 284–5, 314
Surrealism, 327

339